$7\frac{50}{T}p$

2-65

CHILD DEVELOPMENT AND ADJUSTMENT

A STUDY OF CHILD PSYCHOLOGY

LESTER D. CROW, PH.D.

Professor of Education, Brooklyn College

ALICE CROW, PH.D.

Formerly Associate Professor of Education, Brooklyn College

A S T U D Y O F

C H I L D

P S Y C H O L O G Y

CHILD

DEVELOPMENT

AND

ADJUSTMENT

THE MACMILLAN COMPANY   NEW YORK

Third Printing, 1965

Library of Congress catalog card number: 62–7031

The Macmillan Company, New York
Collier-Macmillan Canada, Ltd., Toronto, Ontario

Printed in the United States of America

PREFACE

THE SIGNIFICANCE OF childhood years to an individual continues to receive the attention of psychologists, sociologists, educators, and other adults interested in human development and adjustment. The authors' chief concern in this treatment is to present, in uninvolved, readable form, the results of research and objective observation concerning the many aspects of childhood nature. Their purpose is to stimulate the reader toward an intelligent understanding of the life pattern of the developing individual from the prenatal period through the early years of adolescence. The point of view presented is comprehensive, integrated and functional.

Child Development and Adjustment begins with a general consideration of the child's maturational and experiential needs including the historical background of twentieth century concern with wholesome child rearing. Various approaches to child study then are described. The underlying bases of early growth and development and the various phases of the child's personality are discussed in light of environmental influences that may militate for or against growth. Throughout these areas of discussion (Chapters 3 through 17), the child is viewed as an integrated growing individual who is both dynamic and purposeful. Hence each aspect of development is related to every other so that a picture of the whole child emerges.

In Chapter 18, the various problems of adjustment that would be encountered by the child during his maturing years are presented with emphasis on the ways in which he can be helped to resolve his difficulties. The effect of the major influence factors on the child's developing personality that can be found in the home, the school, and the larger community is stressed in Chapters 19 and 20.

The approach throughout the book is positive and constructive. The authors offer suggestions to students, teachers, parents, and other adults who are vitally interested in helping children develop their potentialities for wholesome living. The developmental approach is centered around what can be expected of the normal child, but individual deviations among children also receive attention. The reader is urged to engage in the *Special Project* proposed at the end of each set of "Questions and Topics for Discussion." By continuing this project, chapter by chapter, the reader can compare objectively the behavioral tendencies of his four selected subjects with the personality patterns discussed in the text.

The authors wish to express their gratitude to all who have so graciously given permission for the use of their material in this book.

Lester D. Crow
Alice Crow

CONTENTS

CHILD DEVELOPMENT AND ADJUSTMENT

A STUDY OF CHILD PSYCHOLOGY

I

SIGNIFICANCE
OF CHILDHOOD

CHILDHOOD IS AN intriguing and exciting period. The child is born with fundamental drives. As he interacts with others of his own age and older, the child is developing self-perceptions, in light of his own and others' behavior. He is becoming an individual who is both similar to and different from all the persons who surround him. As he struggles to find a place for himself in his group, the child's behavior may be interpreted variously, sometimes inaccurately, by adults who lack understanding of developing child nature.

CHANGING CONCEPTS OF CHILDHOOD

Uninformed adults tend to classify children according to certain general categories. For example, a well-known rhyme differentiates between the sexes: "What are little girls made of? Sugar and spice and everything nice. What are little boys made of? Frogs and snails and puppy dog tails." Girls are supposed to be gentle and to need adult protection; boys are expected to be noisy and to be able to take care of themselves. The results of psychological studies, however, indicate that, except for obvious sex differences, all children are both alike and different.

We need only to watch a group of children at play to discover differences among them, resulting from (1) their inborn potentialities of growth and maturation, (2) environmental influences on their individual patterns of development, (3) their psychological and social interactions. By way of illustration, during a summer afternoon, four little six-year-olds were playing ball in a park near their homes. Suddenly, Janey said it was time to go home because their mothers had told them to stop playing at five o'clock, and she had heard the church clock strike five times. The other children did not want to stop playing. Fred claimed that he had not heard the clock; Maizie suggested they pretend that they had not heard it. Bobby admitted that the clock did strike, but that his mother wouldn't fuss if he were late. As Janey started for home, Maizie and Bobby called her a "fraidy cat" and "killjoy." Fred, however, took Janey's part, saying that since she had heard the clock, they'd better obey their mothers, although he wished she hadn't heard it!

This simple incident illustrates behavior differences that are present even during early childhood years. These differences are not accidental; they are the resultants of earlier childhood experiences associated with adult attitudes toward child development and child rearing. Although childhood has been glorified in prose and poetry, the child himself has been assigned successively different roles by society.

Differing Attitudes toward the Child   Historically, adult attitudes toward the significance of childhood have taken various forms: (1) ignorance of or almost complete indifference to the importance of the early years of life, (2) extreme rigidity in the treatment of children, (3) much permissiveness in dealing with children's natural impulses. Although each of these adult attitudes toward childhood has had its day, during no historical period, of course, was any one of these concepts held in its entirety by all adults, especially parents.

In any era (including our own) can be found ignorant or indifferent adults, rigid or strict parents or teachers, and almost completely permissive parents and school people. From early times onward adult treatment of children has been affected by economic conditions, social ideals, and religious beliefs. More recently, the results of research in biology, psychology, sociology, and related sciences have exercised tremendous influence on adult understanding of the developing child.

Early Concepts   Among the people of early, simple forms of civilization, mating for the purpose of producing a large family was an accepted practice. In general, parents regarded their offspring as useful assets. In some instances, boys and girls were expected to help with household chores and more strenuous forms of work almost as soon as they were able to toddle. Most adolescents and young adults were called upon to assume responsibility for the material welfare of their aging parents. Because of the high rate of infant mortality, the utilitarian value of those children who survived was greatly increased.

In most primitive societies, children's desires or interests received little attention. They were supposed to submit to the will of their parents. Among some tribal groups, however, young children were given considerable freedom in their play, and were encouraged to develop strong, healthy bodies and to acquire skills needed to assume adult responsibilities. Although many parents were sincerely interested in the welfare of their children, they were ignorant of the particular needs that are characteristic of the childhood years.

Children's needs and interests received some recognition among early national groups, such as the Greeks and Romans. As early as 400 B.C., Plato, a Greek philosopher, suggested that children possessed differing abilities and that these differences should become the bases of training for specialized types of adult service. The views of Plato and of other writers who gave evidence of some appreciation of the significance of childhood received little popular support, however. Childish desires and interests were suppressed to the end that adult self-discipline might be achieved.

During the Middle Ages, children were regarded by many as miniature adults. Their style of dress, manners, attitudes, and interests were supposed to reflect the dress and behavior of adults. It was not until the Renaissance period that earlier philosophic generalizations about childhood received practical consideration.

More Recent Trends   From the seventeenth century to the present, interested philosophers, psychologists, and other research workers have engaged in child study that has developed into the science of child psychology.

Johann Amos Comenius was one of the first educators to be concerned about child development. His writings include *School of Infancy* (1628) and the *Orbis Pictus* or the *World in Pictures* (1654) that was intended to appeal to children's interests. Later in the century, John Locke, in his *Essay Concerning Human Understanding,* expounded the theory that the child's mind is a *tabula rasa* or blank slate on which are imprinted the effects of external experiences. John Locke recognized the fact that children have natural interests. Yet, influenced by the then existing belief in the sinfulness of human nature, Locke asserted that a child's desires and interests should be curbed so that he might become a virtuous, self-disciplined adult.

One of the first proponents of the theory that a child should be permitted to express his interests freely was Jean Jacques Rousseau. In his *Emile* (1762) he presented the thesis that the bases of education should be children's natural impulses and interests rather than adult-imposed criteria. Rousseau's point of view was expanded further by Pestalozzi in his *Leonard and Gertrude* (1792) and *How Gertrude Teaches Her Children* (1801). Both Rousseau and Pestalozzi regarded man as a natural rather than a supernatural being. Moreover, in his elementary schools, Pestalozzi attempted to adapt teaching to each child's individual abilities and interests.

Various studies of child development were published in the 1900's, one of the most significant of which was Friederich Froebel's *Education of Man,* in which he presented his educational ideals, especially in the field of early child training. Two other noteworthy contributions to child study are Darwin's *Sketch of an Infant* (1827) and Preyer's *Die Seele des Kindes (The Mind of the Child),* published in 1882.

In these early observational reports can be found the bases of twentieth-century scientific study of children. To date in this century the studies of Gesell at Yale University, Stoddard at Iowa, Shirley at Minnesota, Bayley and Jones at California, McGraw at Columbia, Shuttleworth and Stuart at Harvard, and of many other investigators have yielded considerable information concerning child growth and development. Childhood now is recognized as an important period of development. Many psychologists believe that during the first six years of life are formed fundamental habits that persist through life.

SURVEY OF CHILDREN'S NEEDS

Psychologists stress the importance for an individual of any age to satisfy certain fundamental wants, urges, or desires that commonly are referred to as his *needs*. So popular has the term "need" become that some people seem to believe that any form of behavior in which a person engages is an expression of a need that should be fulfilled. Psychologically and ethically, this is an erroneous concept of the term.

Human needs probably connote preferences for some situations or forms of activity rather than for others. At any given time, an organism, stimulated either by an inner condition or an external factor of influence, experiences a felt need that demands fulfillment. For example, a hungry man seeks to satisfy his need for food; a woman, caught in a sudden summer shower, runs for shelter; a boy, feeling the need for recognition from his group, engages in daring feats.

General Nature of Children's Needs The possession of certain basic needs is characteristic of all human beings, regardless of their time or place of living. Yet, the way in which these needs are satisfied is dependent not only on inborn nature but also on influencing factors inherent in the physical environment and the culture in which an individual is born and develops. Each era and each culture presents a set of circumstances that molds the child's overt expression of basic needs. The child born and bred in a modern, democratically organized society may experience needs that differ in extent and intensity from those of a child who matures in a different, perhaps more simple, form of culture. Some of a child's needs are physical; others are rooted in the development of the self-concept and of social consciousness. Perhaps one of the most important childhood needs is training toward wholesome and socially approved fulfillment of his many wants, urges, and desires.

The Child's Physical Needs From birth, the child's physical needs include food and drink, oxygen, temperature regulation, elimination of waste matter, activity and sleep, and protection from harmful environmental elements. The experiencing of a physical need is in effect an organic condition of tension or inner imbalance that arouses activity aimed at restoring bodily equilibrium or *homeostasis*. Although physical needs are biologically rooted drives to action or dynamic impulses, the ways in which they are satisfied follow the social patterns of a child's cultural heritage.

The infant may be breast or bottle fed; the number of feedings may vary with custom. The child born in a high altitude adapts to oxygen content in the air which might be harmful for one who had become accustomed to living in a low altitude. The amount and kind of clothing worn by a child depend not only on climatic conditions but also on the fashions of the time. In our own country, for example, little girls who lived in the Middle Atlantic states some sixty years ago wore several petticoats and warm woolen dresses during the winter. Now, in our well-heated houses, their summer and winter clothes are similar, except for heavy snow suits for outdoor wear. Many examples could be cited to show that ways of meeting health-preserving needs differ with time and conditions.

Social Needs   In addition to his physical wants and drives, a child has other needs associated with his developing self-concept and his relationships with other people. Since the child at birth becomes a member of a gradually expanding group, his personal impulses, urges, and desires cannot be divorced from the wants and interests of his fellows. He constantly is interacting with other individuals or groups. He is attempting to achieve personal status and security. He needs affection, a feeling of belonging, and satisfying human relations. He strives to gain recognition and approval; he seeks adventure. He wants to achieve superiority in at least one field of activity. Yet he must learn to adjust to the mores and customs of his society. During the developmental process, the child or the young adolescent continues to set for himself levels of aspiration that will help him achieve his need to be an active, satisfied, and accepted member of his various groups: the family, the school, the community.

Although the baby's needs may seem to be associated primarily with the fulfillment of his physical wants, he is beginning to develop more or less satisfying relationships with family members and their friends. At first, of course, social needs are closely linked to physical wants. The young baby does not need a mother but mothering. The adults around him are accepted by him as ministering to his needs. Generalized feelings of security in the care of an adept adult, fear of the unaccustomed, and rage when desired activity is inhibited are the beginnings of emotionalized reactions that grow out of his needs (see Chapter 10).

The baby's cry for attention is the forerunner of the many modes of behavior he later may learn to utilize for the same purpose. Cooing, gurgling, smiling, and extending his little arms outward are manifestations of the need to give and receive affection that will be evidenced in various other forms throughout his life. Kicking, flailing the arms, and crying or whimpering are early rage signals that through the years may become refined in their overt expression but may not be lessened in intensity. As we consider, in succeeding chapters, the various aspects of child development, we shall discuss further the gradual changes that take place in children's adjustment to their felt needs.

PROBLEMS OF NEED ADJUSTMENT

According to anthropological studies, the degree of intensity of a fundamental need may differ among children. Boys are presumed to be more adventuresome than girls, and less given to seek adult protection. Whether these and other differences between the sexes or among members of the same sex are innate or the resultants of adult expectations is a moot question. It probably is a fact, however, that, as children attempt to satisfy their various needs, they may experience conflicts of adjustment. In Chapter 18 are discussed the dynamics of child behavior. There we consider in detail the effect on the child of frustrating experiences. Here we shall attempt only to call attention to these problems of adjustment that can serve as a background to a better understanding of the significance of childhood.

Conflicting Needs Interpreted broadly, good life adjustment means that an individual is able to satisfy most of his needs or wants in such ways that conflict among his various urges to action, or between his need fulfillment and the behavior motivations of other people, is kept to a minimum within manageable bounds. Maladjustment results when there is a lack of balance in the satisfaction of felt needs.

Maladjusted behavior can be instigated by the pull of two opposing needs. The average child encounters many such situations. A youngster is hungry for candy. He knows where there is some but he has been told by his mother not to eat anything between meals without permission. His mother is not available. He is torn between satisfying his food need or displeasing his mother. What shall he do? If he takes the candy and his act of disobedience is not discovered, either he is encouraged to repeat disapproved acts or his feeling of guilt interferes with his enjoyment of the candy.

As a member of a family, school, or community group, the child craves the loving attention of his associates. He soon discovers, however, that in order to gain their affection he must meet their standards of appropriate conduct. Conflicts may arise between what he wants to do and what he believes he is expected to do. A little girl was walking down a street with her mother when she observed a beloved woman coming toward them. She had been taught that little ladies do not skip or run except in play, but she wanted to let her friend know how glad she was to see her by running to her and embracing her. What should she do? It would be unladylike to run but the woman might be hurt if she continued to walk sedately by her mother's side.

To an adult, incidents such as these may seem trivial matters; to a child they often constitute serious problems of adjustment. He is motivated to adapt his behavior in light of the stronger or more persistent of two or more conflicting needs. He learns to use certain attention-getting devices with one person and other forms of behavior with another. He plays parent against parent; he engages in one mode of behavior in school and another in the home. In most instances, the child does not deliberately set out to play different roles in different situations. More or less unconsciously, he is giving expression to his personal and social needs in ways which seem to offer satisfying fulfillment of them as he becomes aware of differing adult attitudes toward his developing self-concept.

Adult Attitude and Child Adjustment Our attitudes toward children tend to be colored by memories of our own childhood and by our experiences with and relations to children. A child may be regarded variously by his parents as a little angel, a perpetual question box, a nuisance, or the potential fulfiller of their own frustrated ambitions. One childless woman attempts to "mother" all children who seem to need her loving care; another, perhaps because of her childless state, regards children (especially boys) as little monsters whose one aim in life is to annoy or harass her.

According to an adult's mood and a child's behavior at any one time, the youngster may seem to be any one of the kinds of individual listed. Yet no one characterization is completely valid. Adults sometimes forget that a child has a meager background of experience compared with their own. He is not yet able to recognize the possible harm to himself or to others of impulsive, disturbing behavior. He is struggling toward social integration but is not yet ready to appreciate fully the consequences of some of his acts, as he strives to satisfy his desire to gain attention, demonstrate his superiority to other children, or retaliate if he believes, rightly or wrongly, that he has been treated unfairly. As adults, we often are motivated by urges similar to those of the child, but experience has taught us that a subtle rather than an impulsive approach to our problem will net us greater profit.

ADULT NEED TO UNDERSTAND CHILDREN [1]

Twentieth-century psychologists have emphasized the importance of recognizing differences as well as likenesses among human beings. Probably at no age period are individual differences so marked as they are during childhood and early adolescence. The impact of differing cultural influences on differing biologically inherited potentialities is extremely

[1] Much of the material in this unit adapted by permission from *Adolescent Development and Adjustment*, by Lester D. Crow and Alice Crow. Copyright, 1956. McGraw-Hill Book Company, Inc. New York, pp. 39–42.

strong during these years. Hence variations in rate of growth and maturation, combined with differences in attitude and behavior, require that adult treatment of, and attitudes toward, growing children reflect an appreciation of (1) behavior characteristics common to children, (2) individual differences among children of the same age, and (3) the continuous changes that occur in the development pattern of a single child.

Parental Concern for the Child Parents become concerned when or if their younger children exhibit behavior different from that which had been displayed by their older sons or daughters during the developmental years. Some fathers and mothers are unable to reconcile themselves to the fact that their children seem to lack certain qualities that are characteristic of parental personality. Many of the problems of home and family adjustment could be avoided if parents and other relatives possessed a greater understanding of child nature.

Regardless of their ability to comprehend the whole of the child problem, parents as well as teachers need to realize that this "whole" is larger than many adults realize. In fact, it involves an understanding not only of the children of one's acquaintance, but also an understanding concerning ways in which all children are alike and ways in which they deviate from a general pattern. It involves knowing the problems that beset the child, when he should be helped, and when he should be left alone. It involves knowing what happy, well-adjusted childhood really means and knowing what can be done for children during their growing years. Also, if one understands child psychology, he may be able to give delicate and subtle assistance which will enable the child to develop adequately.

The implications in the above are clear. They embody an ideal state of understanding, the attainment of which requires much extensive and intensive study of children and their problems. That there is an existing need for the application of such study is evidenced by many examples of handling of child problems by parents and school people. Adults must learn to understand children and recognize and fulfill their responsibilities toward them. For example, a teacher who forbids a stutterer to participate in class discussion because, according to the teacher, the child's struggles to express his thoughts "make me nervous" is failing to recognize the child's need for teacher understanding and help.

To this point, our discussion has placed major emphasis on adult obligation to children. It is equally necessary for children to understand themselves, their problems, and their own share of responsibility for the kinds of changes that are taking place during their growth. Unfortunately, one of the results of child study has been the development among some adults of a sentimental compulsion to condone or minimize preadolescent participation in asocial or delinquent behavior. To understand the causes of such behavior does not mean that it is excused. Children probably can be served best by studying them, and then providing stress-and-strain-free opportunities through which they will be able to achieve (1) independence from adult control, (2) self-determination, and (3) self-realization.

Areas of Special Interest   There is general agreement that an individual's personality represents the whole complex, interrelated organism that functions constantly as responses are made to inner and outer stimulating forces according to developed reaction habits and the strength of natural drives, urges, and acquired interests and ambitions. To accept the concept of "wholeness" of personality implies that the most effective approach to the study of children might be to limit the study to a consideration of all the various phases of the personality of a single child.

There also is value in studying each of the various behavior traits, provided that attention is given to the possible effect upon the particular personality phase of the interaction that may be taking place between it and other personality considerations. A behavior trait can be described as a single, persistent mode of response to a stimulus situation that tends to evoke it. A trait does not function in isolation, however. Hence it is not enough to discover that one child appears to be more industrious, cheerful, cooperative, alert, aggressive, timid, or courteous than another. Since a behavior trait is a learned reaction and is an expression of an acquired attitude, the source of its acquisition also must be understood, as well as its interrelation with other segments of the individual's whole personality pattern.

A child's physical characteristics, for example, have a significant effect upon the kinds of personal and social attitudes and so-called trait responses that he may develop. During childhood the personality-patterning process that is taking place within a maturing individual is affected by the physical and psychological changes which he is experiencing, by the expansion of his intellectual powers and his increasing skills and broadening knowledge, by his developing urge to achieve satisfactory group relations, and by his growing concern about life values.

Child personality development is a two-way process. Environmental conditions and situations set the stage for the kinds of experiences through participation in which the boy or girl is helped or hindered in his development and adjustment. In addition, the attitudes, behavior habits, degree of emotional control and self-understanding, and kind of personal-social relationships that are carried over from early childhood through the adolescent period determine in great part the extent to which child experiences result in the development of well-adjusted or maladjusted life patterns.

Children tend to live in the present; immediate settlement of adjustment problems rather than long-range solutions are their goal. A playmate appropriates a young child's favorite toy; he fights for it, trying to wrest it from the other child, regardless of whether the toy may be broken in the struggle. An older child wants to feel superior to his classmates, but his school achievement is mediocre; he attempts to gain their attention by recounting imaginary tales of adventure in which he has participated or reports of his family's great achievements. So strong is his urge to find a place for himself in his peer group that he may come to believe the stories he tells. When his associates discover the truth about him, he may become very much discouraged, retreat into himself, or develop antisocial attitudes.

Parents and teachers are gaining increased understanding of children's developing needs and their adjustment problems. There are adults, however, who seem unable to give the supportive kindness that will enable children to satisfy their normal urges and interests through wholesome, socially approved behavior. Some parents still seem to believe that children's impulses are by nature sinful and that through rigid disciplining the display of adult-disapproved conduct can be inhibited; other parents, having a mistaken concept of the term "freedom of behavior," hesitate to curb in any way their child's actions or expressed attitudes, even though the ultimate results may be harmful. The rigidly reared child is a frustrated child; the permissively brought-up child often is an unhappy child who resents the undue license he experiences.

Understanding and well-intentioned parents and teachers who attempt to follow a middle course between harsh rigidity and extreme permissiveness sometimes find it difficult to know how to handle the child who himself seems unable to choose between innate, conflicting urges and wants. For example, the parents may be financially unable to provide for their child all of the many things that most children want and his schoolmates have: attractive clothes, plenty of spending money, intriguing toys, opportunities to join clubs or to take interesting trips. The fact that a child recognizes his parents' inability to satisfy his normal wants does not in itself solve his problem. Ingenious, sympathetic parents and teachers can help him find other ways of fulfilling his need to be accepted by his schoolmates, such as achieving success in his school work, evidencing an attitude of cooperation in and out of class, being a good sport, and placing emphasis on spiritual rather than material values.

Teachers encounter children in their classes who lack the personal and background advantages enjoyed by their classmates: the physically unattractive child, the slow learner, the child of indifferent or neglectful parents, the spoiled or overprotected child. These children, each in his own way, can be experiencing serious adjustment problems, which busy teachers may fail to recognize unless they are alert to behavioral symptoms of maladjustment. Many schools include in their staff at least one trained counselor to whom teachers can refer these children for special help in meeting their problems as they seek a satisfying adjustment of their fundamental needs to ever-changing patterns of external stimulation.

In this chapter we have attempted to show that childhood is a significant period of life and that the child has many needs, not the least of these being the need for (1) intelligent discipline, (2) respect for authority, and (3) association with understanding and emotionally mature adults. The newborn infant is neither bad nor good; he is a living organism having physical and social needs and potentialities of growth and development into the kind of mature adult who can become an asset or a menace to society, according to the direction in which he is stimulated to develop. The child is not putty that can be molded by more or less expert adults; he is not a miniature adult or a well-constructed or faulty machine. He is a dynamic living being, struggling to achieve a way of life that will be personally satisfying but that may or may not be socially acceptable.

Group influences affect the child from early infancy. During his formative years he is stimulated by many factors, some constructive and others destructive: favorable or unfavorable adult attitudes, a rich or a meager cultural heritage, personally satisfying or annoying experiences. The baby responds in a general, over-all fashion to environmental stimulations. With increasing age he develops individuality within the framework of social purposes and expectations.

The remainder of this book is devoted to the tracing of patterns of development and adjustment experienced by the child as his innate potentialities are realized through experiences with physical, social, and cultural factors of influence. To facilitate presentation, the various aspects of physical, motor, emotional, and social development are treated separately. This approach enables the reader to focus on each and to achieve a clear perspective of the functional relationships between and among them, as attempts are made to relate one phase of development with every other. The purpose is to help the reader appreciate the integrated nature of the flesh and blood child's many phases of personality development.

QUESTIONS AND TOPICS FOR DISCUSSION

1. Ask five or six adults with whom you are acquainted what their opinion is of children: their likes, their dislikes, their criticisms and their praise. Have them differentiate between boys and girls.
2. What was Rousseau's attitude toward the education of girls?
3. Recall any habits which you developed as a small child and which still persist.
4. List some of the needs of the modern child that may have been less recognized in the nineteenth century.
5. In what areas of activity may a child need training? Why?
6. Explain what is meant by homeostasis. In what ways are your homeostatic needs met?
7. What are some of the factors responsible for change in physical needs?
8. Compare the experiences of a rural and an urban child in the fulfillment of his social needs.
9. Give examples of conflicting needs of children.
10. List at least three differences that you find among four children known to you.
11. What are some of the aspects of child rearing that teachers of young children should know?
12. *Special Project:* If possible, select four children whom you know well. Distribute them as follows: (1) a boy and a girl between the ages of two and five; (2) a boy and a girl between the ages of six and ten. As you continue your study of child psychology, observe them in light of each area of development you study during the semester. Keep a running record of your findings, noting the extent to which and the ways in which these children differ from developmental trends reported in this book.

TEXTBOOKS IN CHILD PSYCHOLOGY AND SOURCE BOOKS

Almy, Millie, *Child Development.* New York: Henry Holt and Company, 1955.

Ausubel, D. P., *Theory and Problems of Child Development.* New York: Grune and Stratton, Inc., 1958.

Baldwin, Alfred L., *Behavior and Development in Childhood.* New York: Henry Holt and Company, 1955.

Breckenridge, Marian E., and Vincent, E. Lee, *Child Development,* 4th ed. Philadelphia: W. B. Saunders Company, 1960.

Carmichael, Leonard (ed.), *Manual of Child Psychology.* New York: John Wiley and Sons, Inc., 1954. (Source book.)

Crow, Lester D., and Crow, Alice, *Readings in Child and Adolescent Psychology.* Longmans, Green & Co., Inc., 1961. (Source book.)

English, Horace B., *Dynamics of Child Development.* New York: Holt, Rinehart and Winston, Inc., 1961.

Garrison, Karl C., *Growth and Development.* New York: Longmans, Green and Company, 1959.

Hurlock, Elizabeth B., *Child Growth and Development,* 2nd ed. New York: McGraw-Hill Book Company, Inc., 1956.

Hutt, Max L., and Gibby, Robert G., *The Child: Development and Adjustment.* Boston: Allyn and Bacon, Inc., 1959.

Jersild, Arthur T., *Child Psychology,* 5th ed. Englewood Cliffs, N.J.: Prentice-Hall, Inc., 1960.

Landreth, Catherine, *The Psychology of Early Childhood.* New York: Alfred A. Knopf, 1958.

Lee, J. Murray, and Lee, Morris M., *The Child and His Development.* New York: Appleton-Century-Crofts, Inc., 1958.

Martin, William E., and Stendler, Celia B., *Child Behavior and Development.* New York: Harcourt, Brace and Company, 1959.

Merry, Frieda, and Merry, Ralph, *The First Two Decades of Life.* New York: Harper and Brothers, 1958.

Millard, C. V., *Child Growth and Development in the Elementary School Years.* rev. ed. Boston: D. C. Heath and Company, 1958.

Mussen, P. H., and Conger, J. J., *Child Development and Personality.* New York: Harper and Brothers, 1956.

Olson, Willard C., *Child Development,* 2nd ed. Boston: D. C. Heath and Company, 1959.

Peck, L., *Child Psychology.* Boston: D. C. Heath and Company, 1953.

Rand, Winifred, Sweeney, Mary E., and Vincent, E. Lee, *Growth and Development of the Young Child,* 5th ed. Philadelphia: W. B. Saunders Company, 1953.

Seidman, J. E., *The Child: A Book of Readings.* New York: Holt, Rinehart and Winston, 1958. (Source book.)

Stone, L. J., and Church, Joseph, *Childhood and Adolescence.* New York: Random House, 1957.

Strang, Ruth, *An Introduction to Child Study,* 4th ed. New York: The Macmillan Company, 1959.

Stuart, Harold C., and Prugh, Dave G. (eds.), *The Healthy Child.* Cambridge, Mass.: Harvard University Press, 1960.

Thompson, G. G., *Child Psychology.* Boston: Houghton Mifflin Company, 1952.

Thorpe, Louis P., *Child Psychology and Development,* 2nd ed. New York: The Ronald Press Company, 1955.

Watson, Robert I., *Psychology of the Child.* New York: John Wiley and Sons, 1959.

2

CHILD STUDY
APPROACHES†

CONSIDERABLE RESEARCH HAS been undertaken in the field of child study. There is available for utilization by parents, teachers, and other persons interested in the welfare of children a large body of information concerning child growth and development. For the most part, data obtained concerning young child development have scientific validity and practical value. The significance in the life of an individual of his childhood experiences is recognized by psychologists and educators. A growing awareness of the problems experienced by children has stimulated among psychologists a vital interest in the factors of child adjustment. Important gains already have been made in the study of growth, behavior, and personality during childhood.‡

BASIC CONSIDERATIONS IN CHILD STUDY

Great interest in child development is shown by the fact that psychologists have devoted much time and energy to the study of child be-

† Some material in this chapter identified by a ‡ and an * adapted by permission from *Adolescent Development and Adjustment,* by Lester D. Crow and Alice Crow. Copyright, 1956. McGraw-Hill Book Company, Inc., New York, ‡ p. 38; * pp. 42–55.

havior during the developmental period. These studies continue in spite of the handicaps that are present and have to be dealt with. The very young child, for example, cannot communicate his own thinking and feelings to the observer. The one-way screen and the observation dome, however, have helped to objectify the study of child behavior. Studies such as Gesell's and Thompson's evaluation of co-twin control (1929) and Shirley's study of motor development (1933) show that growth and development are continuous processes that run along relatively smoothly from early beginnings to the attainment of maturity. There still exists controversy among psychologists concerning the amount and kind of stressful experience that is general among children and preadolescents.

Child studies vary in purpose. Some investigations focus upon obtaining greater understanding of growth progress; others attempt to discover the interests, attitudes, ambitions, beliefs, opinions, and habitual behavior patterns of children at progressive stages of their development. To be valuable, any study of child behavior and personality must give consideration to such factors of influence as (1) the changes that are taking place during early childhood in physical structure and physiological functioning and in personal and social urges and interests, (2) environmental stimulations and opportunities for development, and (3) early background of development and training. The findings that result from studies can then be utilized by others to help children develop personality qualities that will enable them to become competent and well-adjusted human beings.

Difficulties Involved in Child Study *   Various obstacles are encountered by psychologists, educators, and other evaluators when they attempt to study all phases of child life and adjustment. Some of these difficulties are alike in all study projects that involve the analyses of various aspects of human behavior. To isolate one phase or segment of the total personality for scientific study purposes is almost impossible. Also, the subtle interrelationships that usually exist among and between individuals and their environment are elements that interfere with any effort to discover actual cause-effect relationships as associated with child behavior.

Other factors of difficulty in the collecting and interpreting of data include a lack of clear understanding of the purpose of the study, the predispositions of the subjects, and the accuracy with which the measuring instruments have been administered. In addition, a study has value to the extent that the findings are valid and reliable and applied con-

structively and realistically. Unfortunately, there still are too many instances of child study projects that are completed with great care and
the results published, but then become buried because they seem to have
little if any practical implications.

Attempts to study children are presented with certain specific, difficult problems which need to be resolved. Among these problems can be
mentioned the limitations of verbal response on the part of very young
children and resentment that may be exhibited by the older child. These
can be formidable hurdles to surmount. Then, too, older children are
sensitive to possible criticism of their attitudes, beliefs, or behavior. For
example, a child may recognize that he is not achieving up to maximum,
but he is not likely to welcome suggestions from his elders to the effect
that he should give more attention to his grooming, manners, expressed
attitudes, or achievement than he has in the recent past.

Parents, teachers, and other adults are not always helpful in their
suggestions and displayed attitudes toward study approaches. Parents who
are invited to cooperate in a study of child behavior sometimes fear that
questions presented to them concerning their children carry implications
of poor approaches in child rearing. Also, in the evaluation of their
child's strengths and weaknesses, parents often find it difficult to be completely objective. Moreover, if a child is known to err, the parents tend
to place the blame for the mistakes on conditions outside the home. Other
people are blamed for inability to understand the child.

It sometimes is difficult to conduct studies of child behavior in
schools. Administrators and teachers are reluctant to participate in such
projects with the pupils under their supervision. School people believe
that any information possessed by them concerning children and their
families should be held in confidence unless the individual pupil and his
family are willing to release it. This barrier is being eliminated or reduced
in many enlightened school systems. Nevertheless, teachers are reluctant
to waste time on an investigation which they believe may not have immediate educational value.

Although some of the difficulties of studying children still exist, there
is an increasing recognition of the value of the results of such studies. With
the removal of many of these obstacles and a greater understanding of
the application of improved study techniques will come increased interest
in these activities. As we consider the various techniques and approaches
to child study, an attempt will be made to indicate ways through which
better use can be made of the findings.

GENERAL CHILD-STUDY APPROACHES

Although there are many approaches to the study and evaluation of child behavior, the layman's evaluation is conducted informally and reflects his own attitudes and values. A child study, however, to be valid must follow scientific procedures and represent an objective approach. The person engaging in the evaluation of child behavior makes careful preparation for the study. In order that his conclusions are valuable he also observes carefully, measures accurately, classifies obtained data objectively and completely, and verifies his conclusions. There are two general study approaches: the cross-sectional approach and the longitudinal approach, both of which have some bearing on normative studies.

Normative Studies * The type of study approach to be used depends on the particular purpose of the investigation. Parents, teachers, social workers, or any other adults who are working with children of the same age group, for example, allowing for individual differences, need to be informed concerning what is considered to be relatively normal in one or another phase of development or behavior. They must discover to what extent specific members of the group deviate from established norms based on accurate measurement or evaluation of many individuals. These large-group investigations generally are referred to as *normative studies.*

Normative studies of respective developmental stages have provided a wealth of information concerning the probable general rate and kind of changes that can be expected to take place during childhood. On the basis of obtained findings it is possible to determine the existing status of individuals and to predict their progress in one or another area of development. The correctness of evaluation of any one child in comparison with the norm of his peer-age group, however, is dependent upon two factors; the reliability of the established norm and the effect upon him of various environmental influences that are peculiar to his particular experiences but not common among the great majority of the group with which he is being compared. Hence it is necessary for comparisons to be made in terms of conclusions that are based on data resulting from wide, representative, cross-sectional investigations.

The Individual Study Approach The individual study, discussed more fully later, yields significant data concerning the child who is studied, and may give insight into the nature of other similar children. In order to arrive at valid conclusions concerning general trends of child development, however, there are needed many individual studies that parallel one another both horizontally and vertically and that represent adequate sampling. Many such studies have been completed and a vast array of them are under way. The great need is to establish valid and reliable conclusions from obtained data.

The Cross-sectional Approach (Horizontal Study)   In the cross-sectional approach different children are studied at different ages. This is conservative of time, since a large number of children, at any given age, can be studied at the same time. Then, too, there is no need to wait for time to pass before retesting can be done. The cross-sectional approach has been used extensively in the obtaining of much data now available concerning children. The cross-sectional approach refers to that type of study in which specific characteristics of a large group of same age or same status subjects are investigated to discover the average or general trends of specific characteristics for the group. When averages (norms) have been ascertained, comparisons can be made between the individual's characteristics studied and the norms for the group.

General growth and development trends of children have been discovered through the utilization of cross-sectional approaches. Height and weight charts, for example, have been produced from studies which were conducted at various age levels, respectively. Information pertaining to mental growth also has been obtained in many instances from making comparisons among many children of any one age at any one time. These results have been accepted as representative of norms of individuals. The cross-sectional approach is valuable in that it is a convenient technique that can be used to evaluate the status of a young person at any stage of his development.

There are weaknesses in the use of the cross-sectional or horizontal approach to gather data on child behavior. Although the results of a cross-sectional study usually represent a sampling of the whole population at a given stage of growth and development, there is difficulty in the obtaining of an adequate sampling. In this case the norms may not be reliable for wide application. Hence something needs to be known about the sampling in order to make intelligent application of the norms.

An important characteristic of child growth that is not accounted for in the use of the cross-sectional approach is differences in rate of growth among individuals. It is not advisable, for example, for one to assume that all children who have the same chronological age, say, one, two, eight, or ten years, respectively, have reached the same maturational stage of development. Yet all or most of them reach maturity beginning in the middle teen years up through the middle twenties. The factor of rate of growth is particularly significant during the early years of childhood. The fact that an eight-year-old group of children may yield a greater range of differences than is found in older age groups of children is another weakness of the cross-sectional approach.

We now illustrate the cross-sectional approach by presenting several examples of such studies. Young [1] analyzed certain variables in a developmental study of language. His data are based on twenty-eight periods of ten minutes each distributed over four different types of situations in the nursery school. He made a comparison of language responses of privileged nursery school children and relief cases. The study data were organized according to socio-economic status.

Honzik and Jones [2] studied the relationship of height to intelligence in a group of 200 children of Berkeley, California. The children ranged in age from twenty-one months to seven years. Low correlations were found at each age.

Dayton [3] studied the correlation between physical defects and intelligence of 14,000 retarded school children in Massachusetts. The correlations between intelligence quotients and physical defects were $-29 + .01$ for boys and $-25 + .01$ for girls. This means that the relationship between intelligence and physical handicaps is relatively low in Massachusetts.

The Longitudinal Approach (Vertical Study) *   In spite of their weaknesses, cross-sectional studies have great value as a means of providing information concerning the maturational and developmental processes. Parents, teachers, and other adults usually are interested in the general psychological principles of evaluation only to the extent that they apply to specific boys and girls. Parents want to know about the developmental progress of their children. The teacher, at any level, needs to understand each of his pupils: his developmental history, his present status, and his probable future progress. The child also should learn of his own personal strengths and weaknesses.

Complete data about children can be obtained only by means of a continuous study of individuals from the prenatal period through maturity. The study of the *same* children at *different* ages is known as the longi-

[1] Young, F. M., "An Analysis of Certain Variables in a Developmental Study of Language," *Genetic Psychological Monographs*, 23: 3–141, 1941.

[2] Honzik, M. P., and Jones, H. E., "Mental-Physical Relationships during the Pre-school Period," *Journal of Experimental Education*, 6: 139–146, 1937.

[3] Dayton, A., "The Relationships between Physical Defects and Intelligence," *Journal of Psycho-asthenics*, 34: 112–129, 1928–29.

tudinal approach. Such longitudinal or vertical studies may be time-consuming, costly, and difficult to complete. Longitudinal studies are extremely valuable, but usable and reliable conclusions must wait for the passing of the required time before they are available.

The longitudinal approach has the weakness (1) of selecting samples that can be available for study for an extended period of time, or (2) of availability of the researcher for the same length of time. Nevertheless, the longitudinal approach is preferred in scientific developmental research. This approach, which usually involves individuals or small groups of individuals, also can be used to establish averages or indicate trends for traits studied. It therefore has some of the advantages of the cross-sectional approach. The most reliable method that can be used to measure accurately individual growth is the longitudinal method.

Many longitudinal studies of child development and behavior have been made during the past thirty years. Included among these are the well-known studies made by Shuttleworth in the Center for Research in Child Health and Development at Harvard University, the studies made by Jones and Bayley at the Institute of Child Welfare of the University of California, and the Gesell studies at the Yale Clinic. A few of the less well-known studies are presented here to illustrate longitudinal approaches; others are presented as supportive data throughout the book.

Bridges [4] studied the development of primary drives of seventy-two children over a period of four months in a foundling home, by means of timed observations. Among other things she found that infants exhibit a drive for survival from birth onward.

Burlingham [5] studied the relationship of three sets of twins admitted to a nursery school in infancy for a period ranging from two to four years by means of general observations with diaries and detailed sleep and developmental charts. Among other findings she noted that imitation started at the age of twelve months, although it is usually normal at the age of nine months.

Despert [6] studied the anxiety, phobias, and fears of seventy-eight nursery school children (thirty-five anxious and forty-three nonanxious) over a period of three years by means of pediatric examinations, observations in the home, records of play, and records of specific fears and phobias.

[4] Bridges, K. M. B., "The Development of Primary Drives in Infancy," *Child Development,* 7: 40–56, 1936.

[5] Burlingham, D. T., "The Relationship of Twins to Each Other," in *Psychoanalytic Study of the Child* (Vol. III). New York: International Press, 1949.

[6] Despert, J. L., "Anxiety, Phobias, and Fears in Young Children," *Nervous Child,* 5: 8–24, 1946.

She found that an important factor in the genesis of anxiety feelings in young children stems back to unfavorable birth conditions.

Paulsen [7] studied personality development in the middle years of thirty children. This ten-year study was made by means of Rorschach ink-blot tests and social histories, school records, and interviews with children and guidance personnel. The tests were started in the first grade and repeated every two years. One finding was to the effect that the greatest intellectual development takes place in the interval between the ages of six and eight.

Hildreth [8] studied four boys (three gifted, one average) over a period of seven years by means of observations and tests which included such measuring instruments as the Stanford-Binet Intelligence Scale, the Goodenough "Draw-a-Man" Test, the Vineland Social Maturity Scale, manual dexterity tests, the Hildreth Personality and Interest Inventory, science achievement tests, and character sketches. She reported that the three gifted children were superior on the Vineland Social Maturity Scale and manual dexterity tests, had many interests, and read many books. The IQ's of the gifted tended to remain constant.

The value of any study approach depends on the personnel involved and the care with which it is conducted. Both extensive facilities and continuity of personnel are needed for a systematic and thorough use of either the cross-sectional or longitudinal approach. Both approaches have enabled researchers to obtain much information on the developmental processes and to establish norms with which the performances of other children can be compared.

SOURCES OF MATERIAL FOR CHILD STUDY

During children's developing years information can be gathered about them from a variety of sources. The more important sources include (1) present verbal and nonverbal behavior of the child, (2) past records of the child that have been compiled and preserved, (3) available material that the child has produced in the past, (4) memories of the child concerning his past interests, activities and behavior, or his introspections, (5) memories of parents or other adults concerning the child's behavior,

[7] Paulsen, A. A., "Personality Development in the Middle Years of Childhood; a Ten-Year Longitudinal Study of Thirty Public School Children by Means of Rorschach Tests and Social Histories," *American Journal of Orthopsychiatry*, 24: 336–350, 1954.

[8] Hildreth, G., "Three Gifted Children; a Developmental Study," *Journal of Genetic Psychology*, 85: 239–262, 1954.

and (6) records of evaluations or measurements made of the child in one or another situation.

Reliable data are valuable in the study of child behavior. Introspective material may reflect biases or be affected by facts that are important, yet may not be recalled at the moment. Records of behavior or products of the child's achievement are excellent sources, since they are objective and can be evaluated by more than one person. Also, comparative evaluations sometimes can be made between children of different generations providing records have been kept of children of the earlier generation.

TECHNIQUES OF EVALUATION IN CHILD STUDY

An understanding of child development and adjustment is more complete and accurate when various techniques and instruments of evaluation are used to provide the data. The procedures or instruments used in the evaluation of child behavior usually include (1) observation, (2) the interview, (3) questionnaires, (4) standardized testing instruments, (5) projective techniques, (6) experimentation, and (7) the case study or case history. We shall present a brief description of each of these child study approaches.

Observation An individual's displayed behavior is constantly being observed by others. Roughly, this method can be classified as (1) observation of behavior that takes place among associates daily in an informal manner, (2) planned observation that is conducted by a trained person, or (3) observation of behavior without the subject's being aware of the fact, such as through a one-way vision screen or by motion pictures of displayed behavior. Methods used in observation may be *open* or *closed*. The former include *diary* and *specimen description;* the latter *time, event,* or *trait sampling.*

Informal observation may introduce such factors as the personal bias of the observer or his emphasizing of certain aspects of behavior and disregarding of others. Formal or planned observation is controlled in terms of the specific purposes of the study and is relatively free from personal prejudice. This type of observation often is used by the teacher in the classroom. The utilization of the one-way screen or motion picture gives the observer an opportunity to study reactions in a more natural setting. Arnold Gesell's detailed studies of the behavior patterns of young children testify to the value of this mode of observation. It is generally known that he made use of the glass dome. Many institutions of teacher education are employing one-way vision screens and sound-amplifying equipment in providing first-hand experiences in the study of children's behavior for their trainees.

Planned observations of children are needed to discover and record behavior under various conditions. When a child is the subject of planned observation, the situation should be made as informal as possible and notes should not be taken during the observational period, but entries should be made as soon as the child or the observer has withdrawn from the situation. Similarly, the child who is being observed through a one-way screen should not know or suspect that he is being observed unless it is a daily routine affair for him, or unless the project calls for his co-operation with the knowledge that he is being observed.

The Interview *   The interview is a valuable technique for study-ing personal characteristics of individuals. It is helpful in the gaining of better understanding of an individual's attitudes, interests, beliefs, and thought patterns. The face-to-face relationship between interviewer and interviewee affords opportunities for interaction between the two, with the interviewer pursuing a definite purpose to gain additional insight about the interviewee. The success of the interview technique is directly propor-tional to the skill of the interviewer and the displayed attitudes of the interviewer and the interviewee.

The form and purpose of the interview range from the simple, brief giving or receiving of information to the intensive and protracted inter-view between a psychiatrist and an emotionally disturbed patient. The interview is used mainly to study the interviewee's personal characteristics, his interests and ambitions, and his personal problems for solution of which he may need help. The interview can be used to advantage by a teacher, since this face-to-face relationship gives rise to the display of characteristics and modes of thinking that are not always revealed in group situations.

Older children tend to be secretive about their affairs and tend to respond to the interview situation with suspicion. It becomes a challenge to the interviewer to establish rapport between the two so that the inter-viewee will have confidence in the former. The older child resents note-taking during an interview unless he is permitted to see what is being written. Once he is convinced that the interviewer is sincerely interested in his welfare, he usually is very cooperative, and reports honestly details concerning his feelings, attitudes, and interests. Through tactful question-

ing and listening the skilled interviewer can often discover personal qualities that heretofore have not been observed by him or by others with
whom the child worked.

Basic principles and procedures of a good interview include the following considerations:

1. The interview should be held in a place with as much privacy as
   possible.
2. When possible, the interviewer should be supplied with available
   information about the interviewee.
3. An interview should be held in an atmosphere permeated by
   friendly attitudes.
4. Good rapport and confidence should be established for free expression of beliefs or ideas.
5. The interviewer should stimulate responses rather than talk excessively.
6. The interviewee should be assured that what he says is in complete confidence.
7. The interviewee should develop the feeling that he has gained
   from the time spent in the interview.
8. The interview should not be extended beyond the reasonable time
   required to accomplish its purpose or to make satisfactory progress.
9. If another interview seems necessary, the way should be made easy
   for it.

Utilization of Questionnaires *   One of the oldest study approaches used in the study of the traits of older children and adolescents is
that of the questionnaire. It also has been used to assemble data about
children before they are able to read by having them filled out by older
children or even adults retrospectively. Much valuable data can be obtained, however, from preadolescents through the use of this method. The
questionnaire can serve many useful purposes. Information supplied by
children on a questionnaire can be valuable to anyone preparing for an
interview with a child who has submitted answers to the items in the
questionnaire. Thus the interviewer's time can be saved and he can conduct a more intelligent interview.

Some questionnaires are devised to discover the emotional, attitudinal
or other personal attributes of children. These need to be used sparingly.
It sometimes is difficult to get children to respond truthfully to questionnaires that have personal implications. Thus, self-administered personality questionnaires are to be used with caution and the results

interpreted in light of other displayed personality traits known to the evaluator. Too often the results of questionnaires stimulate invalid and unreliable conclusions.

Standardized Testing Instruments * Standardized intelligence tests, achievement tests, and interest inventories are being used to accumulate data concerning maturational and experiential progress of children. Self-evaluating and personality rating scales, though less well standardized, also provide the psychologist with helpful material in child study. The value of these instruments depends in part upon the care taken in their construction, in part upon the way they are administered, in part on the accuracy of the children's responses, and in part on the interpretations made of the data collected.

Rating scales that are devised for the evaluation by others of a child's attitudes, behavior, or other personality characteristics have value to the extent that the raters are sufficiently acquainted with the child rated to give adequate opinions concerning him. Raters also must be able to give an unbiased opinion in their evaluative judgments. Great care must be exercised that prejudice does not motivate the decision concerning the traits involved.

Projective Techniques The utilization of certain techniques enables the child to express freely, either verbally or in action, his feelings, attitudes, and thinking. These techniques in which the individual is encouraged to project himself into the situation *(projective techniques)* are used to attempt to evaluate his total personality pattern rather than to discover the degree of possession of isolated traits. In the administration of any of these personality measuring instruments, the administrator must be certain that the individual understands what he is to do and that any resistance to participation in the project has been overcome. Only a trained specialist should attempt to administer or interpret the results of these tests.

Various types of projective approaches now are in use. Included among them are finger or easel painting, therapeutic play activity, the Draw-a-Man Test, the Rorschach Ink-blot Test, the Thematic Apperception Test (TAT), the Children's Apperception Test (CAT), and modifications of these. The Children's Apperception Test (see Figure 1) substitutes animals for human beings but portrayed in human situations.

FINGER AND EASEL PAINTING Children usually like to participate in various activities, such as finger painting and working at the easel. These techniques are used especially with young children. Through the use of prepared mud children produce more or less meaningful represen-

Figure 1. Children's Apperception Test, Card No. 4.

Published and copyright 1949 and 1958 by the C.P.S. Company, Box No. 83,
Larchmont, New York.

tations as they paint (smear) the material with their fingers. They also
may make use of crayon or water color to achieve similar results. These
unstructured forms of activity can be used to reveal to the trained observer
valuable information about the child. It gives the child an outlet for his
emotionalized attitudes, and the observer insight into the child's behavior.

THERAPEUTIC PLAY ACTIVITY   Therapeutic play activity serves the
purpose of aiding in the evaluation of a child's reactions to various play
materials available in a well-equipped playroom. As the adult observes
the child's responses to play materials, such as a doll family, he can discover much about his attitudes and displayed behavior. The child may
wander around the room and play freely, since no restrictions are placed
on him. Thus the trained observer can record activities and behavior
and interpret them, taking care that the child's behavior which seems to
deviate from recognized norms is not misinterpreted as representing abnormally hostile, rejecting, or disturbed feelings.

DIARIES   Children exchange confidences with their peers concerning their interests, their likes and dislikes, and their developing philosophy
of life. They hesitate, however, to share their thoughts, aspirations, and

emotional reactions with an adult. Some give written expression to their feelings and interests in the form of a diary. Many girls and some boys keep diaries for a short period of time. In this most secret archive, they enter daily or weekly reports of their activities, interests, and attitudes. Many of them are emotionally charged. To this extent the diary does not represent an accurate account of preadolescent experiences. Moreover, children who engage in this activity go to great lengths to keep the diary from falling into the hands of parents, or brothers or sisters. In fact, most children who have kept diaries are unwilling, even after they are in their late teens or early twenties, to release them for scrutiny. Recently, several diaries have been made available to the authors. Several items are presented here from the diary of a thirteen-year-old girl.

"I just don't know what I'm going to do. All I have in common with my parents is fights. I wish we could be pals."

"I have had many arguments with my friend, Sharon. She must think that without her I'm lost. But she should think again. Of course, I'll continue to be friends, but I'm sure she senses the wall between us. If I wanted to I could insult her."

"I spoke to and got the autographs of Robert Wagner and Terry Moore. I hope that in future years my family will be healthy and happy. I pray that peace on earth will come soon."

"Jerry and I acted the same as usual toward each other today, like friendly enemies."

"My father thinks that I should cultivate new friends. My parents don't ever try to understand me."

"Jeffry will be at Linda's party. I've just decided that he is disgusting. The only nice thing about him is his drums. I love drums and he plays them well."

"My parents do not want me to see boys so much (much, ha!) and that I should not stay with Sharon because she has a bad influence. Little do my parents know that Sharon and I have different ideas on lots of things and that she does things that are queer. My parents say that when I get older, I will think of them."

AUTOBIOGRAPHICAL SKETCHES Other informal study approaches to child adjustment involve objective adult appraisal of various forms of written expression that are submitted by children in connection with their schoolwork. Autobiographical sketches can be helpful in the gaining of insight into the thinking and attitudes of children. These are usually accepted as confidences, and if betrayed by the adult the children become exceedingly resentful, and exhibit attitudes of suspicion and scorn toward the adult. From these, alert, experienced teachers can gain valuable information concerning pupil characteristics. The value of this is increased when the teacher establishes good rapport with the children themselves and also with their parents.

RORSCHACH INK-BLOT TEST   One of the best-known types of projective techniques is the Rorschach Ink-blot Test. It consists of a series of ten cards on each of which is an ink blot of irregular shape. The subject is asked to respond to it, indicating what it looks like. As the subject gives his interpretation of it, the examiner notes the kind and number of responses given, the quality and completeness of the responses, and the like. The subject is permitted to turn the card in any position. After the ten cards have been examined and described, the subject goes through them again, indicating the areas on the respective ink blots that represented what he had described. Figure 2 illustrates the nature of ink blots but is not one of those in the Rorschach Test.

THEMATIC APPERCEPTION TEST (TAT) AND CHILDREN'S APPERCEPTION TEST (CAT)   Either of these tests is relatively unstructured. The TAT consists of twenty cards on which pictures, in black and white, appear on nineteen; one card is blank. The subject is asked to tell a story about the picture, indicating what happened before, what is happening now, and how it will end. The blank card is used to give the subject freedom of imagination as he relates a story. The TAT is better adapted to the older child, adolescent, or adult. It should not be used for children under the age of seven.

The Children's Apperception Test (CAT), which contains ten cards with pictures of animals, has been constructed for use with younger children. (See Figure 1 and Chapter 14 for its application.) As the child responds to the animal pictures of which the test is composed he reveals something about his personality. His stories about the pictures disclose his emotional reactions to parent-child and parent-parent relationships or other experiences he has had in his immediate environment.

The Experimental Approach *   Basically, the experimental method of study in child development is a form of directed observation of an isolated factor under carefully controlled conditions. It has been most valuable in discovering basic knowledge concerning child behavior. The knowledge gained by Shirley in her study of motor development, by McGraw in her study of developmental phases in the assumption of an erect position, by Bridges in her study of early emotional reactions, by Dennis in his study of maturation through isolation, or by Gesell and his associates in his numerous studies in child development has helped to

Figure 2. Ink-Blot Sample Similar to Those Used in the Rorschach Test.

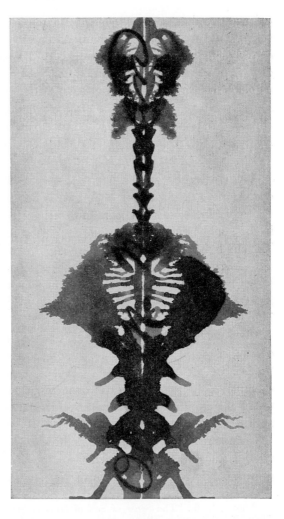

place child psychology on a sound scientific footing. As the instruments and methods of experimentation are refined, the discovery of more precise knowledge in child development can be expected. However, experimental investigations of human characteristics are difficult to organize and conduct satisfactorily in any area of behavior except those concerned with simple reaction patterns.

Numerous experiments have been completed to determine the importance of maturation in human learning. The methods used for this experimentation include (1) *isolation* or *single group,* in which the individual child or a group of children is separated from other children for the duration of the experiment; (2) *co-twin control,* in which identical twins are used as subjects by giving practice in certain maturational, developmental, or learning functions to one twin, while at the same time denying similar training opportunities to the other; (3) *matched groups or parallel groups,* in which an effort is made to use two similar groups, matched in traits except for the one directly related to the behavior to be studied; and (4) *genetic study of large groups,* in which large groups of children are used to discover whether a pattern of development appears, regardless of differences in environment.

Examples of each type of study follow:

ISOLATION OR SINGLE GROUP METHOD   The study made by Ames [9] concerning a *sense of self* of nursery school children as manifested by their verbal behavior by means of observations through a one-way screen in the Child Development Clinic at Yale is an example of this method. The children ranged in age between eighteen months and four years.

MATCHED GROUP OR PARALLEL GROUP METHOD   This method is illustrated by a study made by Bayley [10] in which she studied the crying of infants. In this study Bayley recorded the crying behavior of sixty-one infants (thirty-one boys and thirty girls) over a period of a year.

CO-TWIN CONTROL METHOD   The co-twin control represents a special approach in which a comparison is made between two individuals. Studies by Gesell,[11] Burlingham,[12] Dennis,[13] and McGraw [14] are excellent examples of this approach. Control of conditions becomes important in the use of this approach. The study by McGraw combined the single child approach with the co-twin control.

GENETIC STUDY OF LARGE GROUPS   An excellent example of this type of study method is the extensive research on physical and mental growth conducted by Shuttleworth [15] at Harvard.

[9] Ames, L. B., "The Sense of Self of Nursery School Children as Manifested by Their Verbal Behavior," *Pedagogical Seminary and Journal of Genetic Psychology,* 81: 193–232, 1952.

[10] Bayley, Nancy, "A Study of the Crying of Infants during Mental and Physical Tests," *Pedagogical Seminary and Journal of Genetic Psychology,* 40: 306–329, 1932.

[11] Gesell, A. I., "The Method of Co-twin Control," *Science,* 95: 448, 1942.

[12] Burlingham, D. T., *A Study of Three Pairs of Identical Twins.* New York: International Universities Press, 1952.

[13] Dennis, Wayne, "The Effect of Restricted Practice upon the Reaching, Sitting, and Standing of Two Infants" (female twins), *Pedogogical Seminary and Journal of Genetic Psychology,* 47: 17–32, 1935.

[14] McGraw, M. B., *A Study of Johnny and Jimmy.* New York: Appleton-Century-Crofts, 1935.

[15] Shuttleworth, F. K., "The Physical and Mental Growth of Girls and Boys Aged Six to Nineteen in Relation to Age at Maximum Growth," *Monogr. of the Soc. Res. in Child Development,* 4: No. 3, iv–291, 1939.

The Case-Study Approach * The case study represents an accumulation by a trained person of data concerning an individual. It includes the total history and is the most comprehensive method of studying the child. Its greatest use is in connection with the maladjusted child or the delinquent. A complete case history contains correct and adequate information about the child's family, prenatal history, birth history, developmental history, personal and social history, and educational history. Thus is a record compiled concerning his physical, physiological, mental, and emotional development from birth to the time of the study. The child's home conditions, his educational, vocational, and social experiences, as well as any other factors of influence become a part of the case study. Many other study approaches are utilized to obtain the data for the complete case history.

Data once gathered need to be organized and interpreted. This usually is done by the person making the investigation. The case-study approach is employed by the staffs of psychological clinics in their study and treatment of children referred to them for the resolution of an existing personal problem. It also is combined with a genetic study of developmental changes in the attitudes and in the behavior patterns of children.

STUDY APPROACHES USED IN THE CLASSROOM

It is almost axiomatic to mention that a teacher's degree of success in motivating his pupils depends largely on his recognition of learner needs, abilities, interests, ambitions, and attitudes toward the school, himself as the teacher, and the value of the educational offerings. The teacher's understanding of his pupils is especially needed in the nursery school, the kindergarten, and the elementary school. In spite of crowded school conditions, the interested teacher has many opportunities to study his pupils and thereby gain insight into their adjustment problems. Data contributed by classroom teachers are extremely helpful as aids in investigations of child development.

Anectodal Records and Reports * Compared with the controlled observational techniques that were described earlier, a teacher's observation of child behavior is relatively informal and may be affected by the teacher's prejudice or lack of insight. Yet, there is value in the day-by-day observations made by teachers of the fact that a certain child displays a particular behavior pattern in his relationships with his classmates and his teacher. The value of teacher observations is increased if and when several teachers agree in their interpretation of a child's personality characteristics, either during the same school year or during much or all of his stay in the school.

In an increasing number of schools it is becoming customary to encourage teachers to submit written reports concerning their pupils to the appropriate administrative authority. These anecdotal records usually consist of brief descriptions of classroom incidents involving the display by one or another child of significantly atypical behavior that either is superior to the accepted or would seem to need readjustment. From an accumulation of such teacher reports concerning a large number of children can be achieved an understanding of behavior trends that is extremely valuable to the student of child psychology, as well as to the guidance personnel of the school.

Themes and Other Written Material * The teacher is in an excellent position to gain insight into child interests and attitudes as these are displayed by his pupils in their written compositions or themes. Children often divulge special things about themselves in their writings. Hence many teachers have their pupils write autobiographies, or discuss in written form their interests or ambitions, their unusual experiences, or the problematic situations which they have encountered. Interesting bits of information concerning children can be gathered through the utilization of this study approach.

Too much credence, however, should not be given to what children write about themselves. Some are honest and frank in their accounts about themselves, their background history, and their experiences; they feel secure in their relationships with their peer and adult associates, and are achieving successfully in their various areas of activity. There also are many children who are uncertain of their group status. They are sensitive to the economic, social, and personal ability differences that they believe exist between themselves and their peers. Hence in their written accounts of themselves they tend to misrepresent or to exaggerate personal experiences or conditions. If a child's report about himself can be checked against other valid data, any inconsistencies between them yield valuable information about individual attitudes. Regardless of the accuracy of his autobiographical material, however, a child is given an opportunity through participation in self-describing projects to evaluate himself and his experiences more objectively than he otherwise might do.

Other Classroom Techniques Some teachers use the question period as a means of studying children's reactions. One period a week (usually about an hour in length) is set aside by the teacher for answering children's questions about anything of current interest to them. As one child poses a question, the teacher encourages his classmates to try to answer it; he himself fills in gaps or sends children to source materials. This procedure gives the teacher a good opportunity to observe the interests of his pupils and their behavior interactions.

The teacher also can observe his pupils' behavior in committee projects, in other classroom activities, or in their free play. He is thereby enabled to discover the more or less popular children in the class. Another approach to determining peer relationships among the members of the class is by the utilization of the sociometric technique. According to this approach, the social status of particular children is discovered by having each child write on a piece of paper the names of from one to three other pupils who are his best friends, whom he would like to have sit next to him, or with whom he would like to work on a project. The results are arranged in the form of the sociogram which indicates the degree of popularity of each child. See Chapter 11 for a further discussion and illustration of the sociogram.

QUESTIONS AND TOPICS FOR DISCUSSION

1. Discuss the importance of careful research in the study of child behavior.
2. Enumerate ten major child adjustment problems that warrant evaluation by means of scientific procedures.
3. Differentiate between the cross-sectional and the longitudinal approaches in the study of child development. Give examples.
4. List several limitations of observation as a technique of evalution of child behavior.
5. Discuss the value of the interview to the child; to the teacher or the counselor.
6. Illustrate some of the weaknesses of the use of a questionnaire in the evaluation of child behavior.
7. Ask a student who has written a diary to read excerpts from it if he is willing to do so. What emotional overtones are still present?
8. Enumerate difficulties associated with the experimental approach in the study of child development and behavior.
9. Construct a sociogram based on the choice of members of your class with whom each would like to work on a committee assignment.
10. Organize the class into committees of four students each. Ask each committee to plan a research study in child psychology and to prepare a research design to be used to complete the study.

11. *Special Project:* Observe the behavior of your subjects for four periods of one hour each. Write an anecdotal record of each of your observations. What did you learn about each child? How objective were you in your reports? If possible, obtain the results of standardized tests administered to the subjects. Make note of their performance in these tests and refer to them as you continue your study of the children for the remainder of the semester.

SELECTED REFERENCES

Ames, Louis B., Learned, J., Metraux, R. W., and Walker, R. N., *Child Rorschach Responses: Developmental Trends from Two to Ten Years.* New York: Paul B. Hoeber, Inc., 1952.

Anderson, John E., "Methods of Child Psychology," in L. Carmichael (ed.), *Manual of Child Psychology,* 2nd ed. New York: John Wiley and Sons, 1954.

Bayer, Leona M., and Bayley, Nancy, *Growth Diagnosis: Selected Methods for Interpreting and Predicting Physical Development from One Year to Maturity.* Chicago: University of Chicago Press, 1959.

Bell, R. O., "Convergence: An Accelerated Longitudinal Approach," *Child Development,* 24: 145–152, 1953.

Cohen, Dorothy H., and Stern, Virginia, *Observing and Recording the Behavior of Young Children.* New York: Bureau of Publications, Teachers College, Columbia University, 1958.

Harrower, Molly, *Personality Change and Development: As Measured by the Projective Technique.* New York: Grune and Stratton, Inc., 1958.

Maier, Norman R. F., *The Appraisal Interview: Objectives, Methods and Skills.* New York: John Wiley and Sons, 1958.

Mussen, Paul H. (ed.), *Handbook of Research Methods in Child Development.* New York: John Wiley and Sons, Inc., 1960.

Stone, A. A., and Onque, G. C., *Longitudinal Studies of Child Personality.* Cambridge, Mass.: Harvard University Press, 1959.

Suchman, J. Richard, *Observation and Analysis in Child Development: A Laboratory Manual.* New York: Harcourt, Brace and Company, 1959.

3

BIOLOGICAL AND CULTURAL FACTORS OF CHILD DEVELOPMENT

THE IMPORTANCE OF growth and development becomes more meaningful as the forces and factors of influence are better understood. An understanding of these factors enables adults to provide optimal development opportunities for the growing child. Among the various influences that affect growth are both those which are found within the individual himself and those which operate through his environment. We therefore shall consider both biological factors and cultural influences as they affect growth and development of human beings.

PRINCIPLES OF GROWTH AND DEVELOPMENT

The patterns of growth and development vary among individuals. Although each individual possesses definite combinations of traits and characteristics that develop into a unique personality, it does not follow that all individuals follow a common pattern of development. A careful

study of patterns of individual growth enables us to understand the likenesses and differences that exist among the various general and specific
patterns of growth and development.

Meaning of Growth and Development   The terms "growth" and
"development" are used to represent the results of rather definite influences in the emerging life of the organism, the child. Growth is limited
largely to structural and physiological changes within the physical constitution of the individual from the moment of conception through the
prenatal and postnatal periods to adulthood. Development is concerned
with both growth and those innate potentialities of behavior that are
sensitive to environmental stimulation. Because of their interlocking nature, however, it is not easy to differentiate completely between the
meaning of these terms. As a child grows in height and weight and his
body organs increase in size they also increase in power to function and
are influenced more and more by environmental factors that may help
or hinder their progress. During the child's developmental process numerous factors of influence affect the direction of his development.

Special Aspects of Growth and Development   The processes of
growth and development, although not interchangeable, are inseparable.
The processes of maturation and learning indicate that growth has general aspects of *quantity* and *quality*. The body organs of a child grow in
size until they have reached their full growth, and increase in function
during this growth. Thus the maturing child passes through many phases
of development which are the result of the interaction of learning and
maturation. Eventually he reaches the end of these successive stages of
growth and development and comes to full maturity in all areas. Some
aspects of maturity come relatively early; others come much later; and
a few seem to be delayed far beyond normal periods of expectancy.

The fact that maturation accompanies growth in size can be illustrated in many ways. The baby's heart cannot function properly until it
has grown to proper size; the digestive tract not only grows in size but
changes in structure as well. Thus, after birth, the baby can digest nothing
but his mother's milk or similarly prepared food; later he is able to
digest more complex food and widen his taste for various kinds of nutri-
tious food. Not only does the functional efficiency of the digestive tract
increase with the growth of its structure but the individual is enabled
thereby to gain satisfying physical well-being as well. As the structure of
each vital organ matures, its functional efficiency is potentially increased.

SIGNIFICANCE OF BIOLOGICAL INHERITANCE

The moment of conception is a most important moment in the life of a child. At the time of the union of the parent cells, the biological pattern is set for the individual. His potential for growth and development is determined thereby. The extent to which his full potential of growth and development is to be realized depends on the environment that exerts an influence on him from the time of conception through birth and throughout his entire life span. The attainment of his full potential may be interferred with by such factors as congenital disease, birth injury, physical injury, or disease during his developing years. This illustrates the fact that hereditary and environmental influences are not separate entities, but complement and supplement each other in an interlocking manner as the child grows into maturity.

Principles of Heredity Human beings from generation to generation have displayed common characteristics, thus making certain principles of biological inheritance seem almost self-evident. Biological inheritance progresses according to certain definite principles, as traits or characteristics are transmitted from one generation to the next. In the process of heredity the germ cells, not the somatic or body cells, are the bases of transmission of specific characteristics from parents to child.

The general principles of heredity include the following points:

LIKE PRODUCES LIKE Human beings tend to be alike from generation to generation. Potentialities of development, not acquired skills, knowledge, and attitudes, are handed down from parents to their offspring.

NOT ALL TRAITS ARE INHERITABLE Only certain human traits are believed to be inherited. Although it is known that certain traits are transmissible through heredity, it is not easy to determine the extent to which others are inherited. The impact of the environment on certain traits is significant.

EQUAL PROPORTIONS ARE TRANSMITTED BY EACH PARENTAL LINE Fifty per cent of a child's characteristics probably are inherited from his mother's line and the other 50 per cent from the father's. In brief, one-half of a child's native traits are inherited from his parents, one-fourth from his grandparents, one-eighth from his great-grandparents, and lesser percentages from more remote ancestors.

ABSOLUTE PREDICTIONS ARE IMPOSSIBLE   Chance plays an important role relative to the kind of genes that will be present in a new life.

TRAITS MAY BE EITHER DOMINANT OR RECESSIVE   Some traits are dominant over others, and thus seem to upset the general principle that "like produces like." The stronger genes are referred to as *dominant* because their traits are more likely to appear in successive generations than are traits produced by the weaker or *recessive* genes. Traits containing dominant and recessive genes are inherited according to a theory of inheritance propounded by Gregory Mendel upon his experiments in the crossing of peas. His theory of heredity (sometimes referred to as the theory of the genes) is generally accepted. The way it works is illustrated in Figure 3.

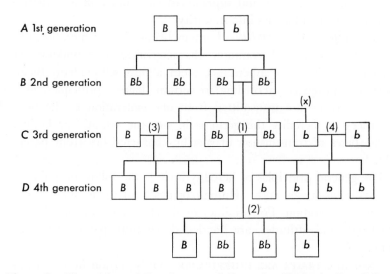

Figure 3. Illustration of Dominant and Recessive Traits in Eye Color.

B in the first generation is a pure brown-eyed parent (his parents were both brown-eyed) and *b* is a pure blue-eyed parent (his parents both had blue eyes). In the second generation all children have brown eyes but carry a recessive blue trait. In the third generation the three to one ratio appears. There are three times as many children having brown eyes as blue, although only one of these is pure. The other two carry a blue recessive trait which if paired with another of the same characteristic (1) will again give, in the fourth generation, the three to one ratio (2). If a pure brown-eyed individual mates with another pure brown-eyed individual, all offspring will have brown eyes with no recessive trait of blueness (3). The same is true for matings of pure blue-eyed parents (4).

From Drake, Raleigh M., "Heredity and Early Development" in Skinner, C. E., and Harriman, P. L. (eds.), *Child Psychology,* p. 26. New York: The Macmillan Company, 1941.

The Process of Heredity   A new life begins when the sperm of the father fertilizes the ovum of the mother. Thus is a new individual started on his way in life, the first stage of which is a *zygote*. (See Figures 4 and 5.)

During the first twenty-four hours the fertilized egg divides into two cells; after forty-eight hours into four cells. This growth and division con-

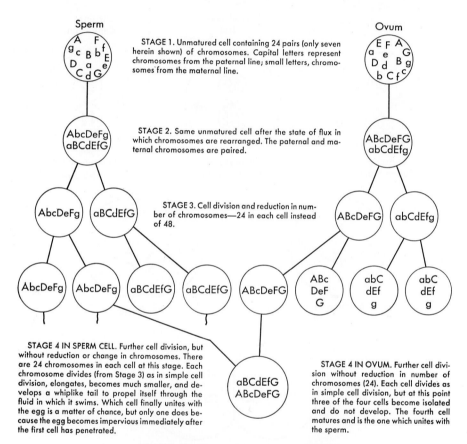

Sperm

STAGE 1. Unmatured cell containing 24 pairs (only seven herein shown) of chromosomes. Capital letters represent chromosomes from the paternal line; small letters, chromosomes from the maternal line.

Ovum

STAGE 2. Same unmatured cell after the state of flux in which chromosomes are rearranged. The paternal and maternal chromosomes are paired.

STAGE 3. Cell division and reduction in number of chromosomes—24 in each cell instead of 48.

STAGE 4 IN SPERM CELL. Further cell division, but without reduction or change in chromosomes. There are 24 chromosomes in each cell at this stage. Each chromosome divides (from Stage 3) as in simple cell division, elongates, becomes much smaller, and develops a whiplike tail to propel itself through the fluid in which it swims. Which cell finally unites with the egg is a matter of chance, but only one does because the egg becomes impervious immediately after the first cell has penetrated.

STAGE 4 IN OVUM. Further cell division without reduction in number of chromosomes (24). Each cell divides as in simple cell division, but at this point three of the four cells become isolated and do not develop. The fourth cell matures and is the one which unites with the sperm.

STAGE 5. The sperm and ovum, each containing 24 chromosomes, unite to form a new cell, containing 48 chromosomes, which develops into a new life. This new individual then carries a new set of chromosomes, one line coming from the paternal and the other from the maternal line. The life cycle is now ready to begin all over in another generation.

Figure 4.   Diagram Showing the Process of Heredity.*

(Note: Perhaps 23 rather than 24 pairs of chromosomes)

* Ibid., p. 24.

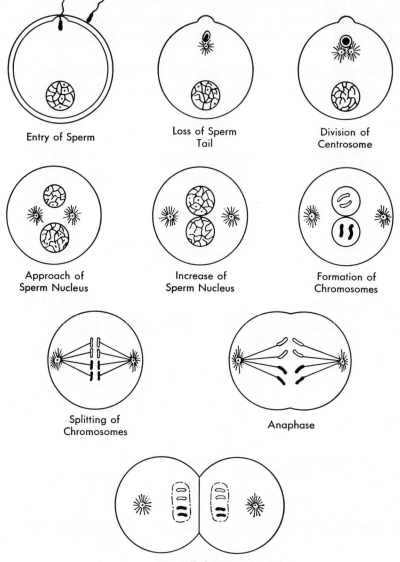

Figure 5. The Process of Fertilization.

Paternal chromosomes are represented as black; maternal chromosomes as white. Miss Dorothy C. Walter had this figure examined in 1961 by someone in the Department of Biology at Brown University and reported that "nothing pictured is outmoded."

From Walter, Herbert Eugene, *Genetics,* p. 186. New York: copyright 1938 by The Macmillan Company. Reprinted by permission of Dorothy C. Walter.

tinue until, after nine days, a hollow ball is formed of these divided cells. These cells continue dividing and, in about thirteen days, three layers of specialized cells are formed. The three layers of specialized cells become the ectoderm, mesoderm, and endoderm. As they continue their division, the cells differentiate in such a way as to form the skin, muscles and digestive system, and other organs. (See Figure 6.)

Chromosomes In the human, each unmatured sperm and each unmatured ovum has twenty-three pairs of chromosomes or forty-six chromosomes.[1] These threadlike particles are found in the nucleus of each germ cell. When the sperm enters the ovum and a new zygote is formed, the full number of forty-six chromosomes are present. Inherited potential is found in this zygote, especially in the chromosomes which it contains. More specifically, the genes contained in the chromosomes are the carriers of the special potential. Not only do the chromosomes contain the inherited potential in ability and structure but they also determine the sex of the new organism.

DETERMINATION OF SEX The unmatured germ cell contains twenty-three pairs of chromosomes. However, through the process of meiosis the number of chromosomes is reduced to twenty-three. As a result, the mature ovum contains twenty-three chromosomes, one of which is an X chromosome. The mature sperm contains twenty-three chromosomes, one of which is either an X chromosome or a Y chromosome. If, during fertilization, the Y chromosome of the sperm unites with the X chromosome of the ovum, the zygote will develop into a boy; if the X chromosome of the sperm unites with the X chromosome of the ovum, the zygote will develop into a girl. Hence, the factor that determines the sex of the offspring is the X or the Y chromosome received from the father. (See Figure 7.)

PRENATAL GROWTH AND DEVELOPMENT

The fundamentals of growth are better understood when we gain insight into the processes that take place before as well as after birth. The structures developed by the living organism while it still is in its mother's uterus lay the foundation on which later growth and development build. Also, the functioning of the organs during the prenatal period enables them later to serve the developing individual. The child's

[1] Stern, C., "The Chromosomes of Man," in Symposium of *Genetics in Medical Research. J. Med. Educ.,* 34: 310–314, 1959.

FERTILIZATION

Time zero: The sperm penetrates the egg

CELL DIVISION

About 24 hours: The fertilized egg divides in two

About 48 hours: Each new cell divides in two

About 9 days: A hollow ball of cells is formed

DIFFERENTIATION

About 13 days: Inside the ball are three layers of specialized cells

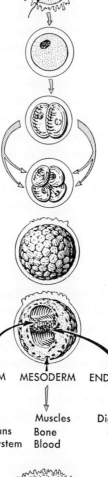

As the new individual grows inside its mother, these layers become:

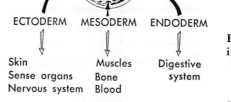

ECTODERM	MESODERM	ENDODERM
Skin	Muscles	Digestive
Sense organs	Bone	system
Nervous system	Blood	

EMBRYO

2 to 8 weeks

FETUS

Third to ninth month

Figure 6. Early Steps in Human Development.

By permission from *Introduction to Psychology,* by T.C. Morgan, p. 28. New York: copyright 1956 by McGraw-Hill Book Company, Inc.

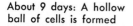

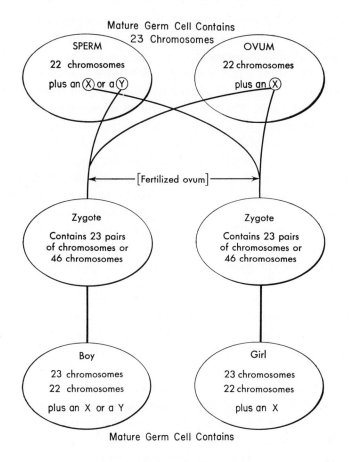

Figure 7. Determination of Sex.

The chance union of the X or the Y chromosome of the sperm with the X chromosome of the ovum determines the sex of the new human life.

behavior after birth is a continuation of that which was started during the prenatal period.

Although embryologists have been hampered and limited in the gaining of direct information concerning the exact processes of growth in human beings during the period immediately following conception, they have made some satisfactory progress for the later (fetus) stage of development. They have been successful in making observations during this period. The fetus, both within the uterus and, in some instances, after it has been removed has been studied. It has been studied in the latter condition only when surgery was necessary to protect the mother. This approach to gain information concerning the developmental process has not proven to be very satisfactory, since the fetus usually does not live long in an artificial environment.

Germinal Stage   It is not easy to determine exactly when conception occurs; often the time of the last menstrual period before pregnancy serves as a good guide. The period of growth during the first two weeks (period of the ovum) is called the *germinal* stage. During this stage the new life bears no resemblance to a human being and receives little or no nourishment from the mother, since it is not yet attached to the uterus wall. Yet, important changes are taking place in this free-floating mass which already has started the production of new cells. The fertilized ovum becomes the zygote and continues its journey down the Fallopian tube toward the uterus. The time required for this journey is about three days. During this time and later, cell division continues at a rapid pace. All the while, the chromosomes within each cell split lengthwise in such a way that each cell contains a set of all the original genes. (See Figure 5.) Cell differentiation also begins during this stage.

The Embryonic Stage   During the next six weeks or by the end of eight weeks after conception, the new life is passing through the *embryonic* stage. During this stage the embryo attaches itself to the uterus and is fed through a special structure that is formed to provide it with adequate nourishment and protection. At the point of implantation, membrane tissues (called the placenta) develop outside the embryo but within the mother's uterus and are joined to the embryo by means of the umbilical cord. (See Figure 8.)

Since there is no direct blood connection between the mother and child, nourishment is transmitted from the mother to the developing child by a process resembling osmosis. Thus the new life is able to get oxygen, water, and nutrition from the mother's blood. The placenta also functions in the removal of waste products from the embryo. It should be kept in mind that the two circulatory systems—that of the mother and that of the new life—are entirely separated. The mother's blood does not feed the developing embryo or fetus directly by circulating through it. The separation is also as complete for the developing nervous system.

Other structures for the protection of the new life also are developed early. There is a kind of water jacket, called the *amniotic sac,* that surrounds the embryo and is filled with amniotic fluid. Through its functioning the embryo is protected from severe blows and jolts during pregnancy. The fluid is discharged shortly before the baby is born, while the placenta and the umbilical cord are discharged as afterbirth.

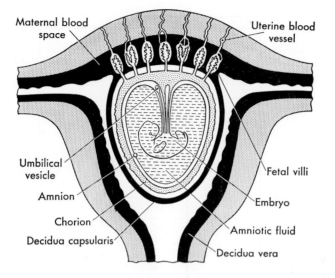

Maternal blood space — Uterine blood vessel — Umbilical vesicle — Amnion — Chorion — Decidua capsularis — Fetal villi — Embryo — Amniotic fluid — Decidua vera

Figure 8.   Relation of Uterus, Membranes, and Embyro during Early Pregnancy.

From Carmichael, L., "Origin and Prenatal Growth of Behavior", in Murchisen, C., (ed.). *A Handbook of Child Psychology,* 2nd ed. Worcester: Clark University Press, 1933. By permission of the publisher.

The heart structure begins to appear in about eighteen days and, at the end of the third week, starts to function. The fundamentals of the nervous system are being set at this time also. First the neural tube is developed in the outer embryonic layer. The brain and the upper end of the spinal cord eventually develop from the lower part of this tube. During this period all bodily organs as well as sense organs are making their appearance. The patterns of the face, head, ear, brain, hand, and foot as they are developing in the embryo are illustrated in Figure 9.

The Fetal Stage   The period of development beginning with about the ninth week and extending until birth is known as the period of the *fetus*. During this time (about twenty-eight weeks) certain basic structures and functions continue their maturation as the new life is being prepared for an existence which will be independent of the mother.

During the fetal period the rhythm of the new life's heart-beat is twice as fast as that of the mother's. As the circulatory changes take place, the chest movements appear to supplement the action of the fetal heart. Movement also begins in the digestive organs as a result of internal stimulation. The semicircular canals, which are a part of the equipment for walking, are believed to begin their functioning during the seventh

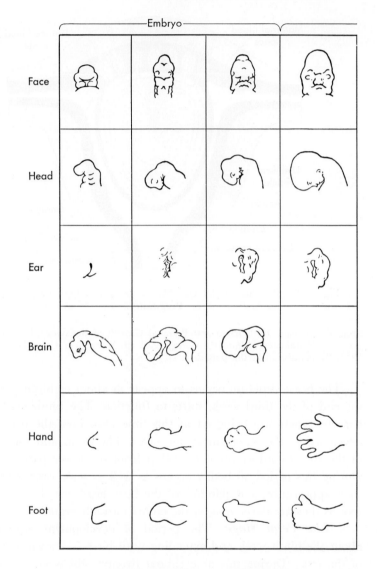

Figure 9.   Patterns of Development.

After *The Miracle of Growth,* 1950, University of Illinois Press,
Urbana. By permission of the University of Illinois Press.

week and attain their adult size by the time of birth. The approximate
life sizes of the developing embryo and fetus are illustrated in Figure 10.

The maturation of nerve and muscle tissue enables the fetus to begin
generalized movements in response to external stimuli. Such movements
as flexion of the head and shoulders, bending of the trunk, and rotation

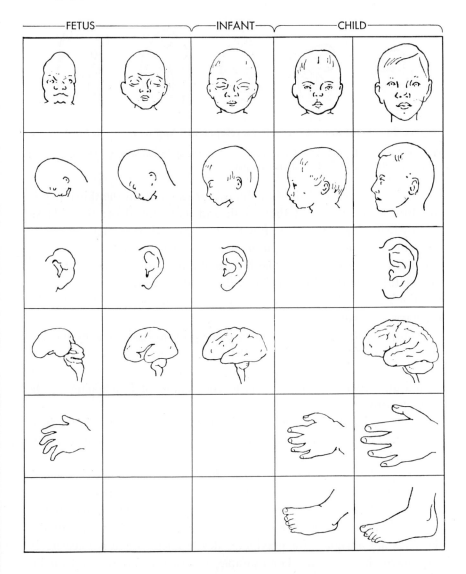

of the rump are made possible by stimulating the area around the mouth and nose. The maturation of the tonic-neck reflex is taking place. This reflex persists for many weeks after birth. The early movements of the head and shoulders are basic to the later development of manipulation and posture. Many of these and other spontaneous movements are too weak to be perceived by the mother. Even though some of these movements are vigorous, the mother ordinarily is not aware of them until about the fifth month.

Various structural changes continue as the fetal stage moves toward

Figure 10.   Fetal and Embryonic Development (Approximate Natural Size).

From Skinner, C.E., and Harriman, P.L., (eds.), *Child Psychology,* p. 34. New York: copyright 1941 by The Macmillan Company.

its termination at the birth of the baby. For example, in the third month, structure in the region of the mouth and nose is evident; the kidneys, already being formed, start to function; by the end of the fourth month, the fetus becomes six to eight inches in length, or approaches about one-half its length at birth. The hair, nails, and skin are developed during the fifth month. Also sufficiently developed at this time to begin their functioning are the glands of internal secretion, such as the thyroid, pituitary, and pancreas.

Some sensory development takes place prior to birth. The eyelids can be moved during the sixth month; eyes respond to light during the seventh month, and hearing may be possible by this time; if proper stimuli are provided, smell and taste are capable of functioning by the time of birth.

After an incubation period of about 280 days the baby is ready to be born. The successive stages of the development are illustrated in Figure 11.

Prenatal Influences on Growth   The prenatal environment is important to the full growth and development of the human organism. During its development, the fetus is entirely dependent on the mother for nourishment; unless her diet and the other conditions surrounding the fetus are adequate for maximum development, there is likely to be an unfavorable outcome. For example, in order to insure good quality of teeth and bones, the mother's diet should contain sufficient calcium. In fact, the expectant mother needs to be careful not only of her diet but of her health in general.

It is known that the organism responds to stimulation during the prenatal period. There is little evidence, however, to credit certain common beliefs that a pregnant woman can "mark" her unborn child as a result of unusual experiences, such as the arousal of intense emotions during her pregnancy. Since there is no neural connection between the

Figure 11. Stages in Prenatal Development According to the Dickinson-Belskie Models.

(Reproduced by permission of the Cleveland Health Museum, Cleveland, Ohio.)

mother and the fetus it becomes difficult for the mother to exert any influence over the fetus through neural channels. Conditions may prevail during the pregnancy, however, that can influence the developing organism. Such influences, resulting from environmental conditions rather than from native inheritance, are called *congenital influences*. We present some congenital influences as listed by Schwesinger:

1. *Malnutrition.* Excessive malnutrition of the mother's organism during the intra-uterine period may deprive the growing child of essential nutritive elements. Such deprivation may hamper the child's physical development.

2. *Disease.* Mothers suffering from such wasting diseases as diabetes, cancer, tuberculosis, and pellagra are likely to affect their unborn offspring adversely. Physical effects similar to those noted in malnutrition may be produced.

3. *Infection.* Infectious diseases, particularly syphilis, frequently attack the nervous system and may result in congenital weakness or instability. An apparently healthy mother may house germs that prey on her unborn child.

4. *Toxins.* The developing child may be affected by toxic poisons that seep through blood vesel walls into the umbilical cord. It was formerly believed that alcohol could affect sex cells before conception, but this belief has been largely discredited.

5. *Endocrine imbalance.* A deficiency or excess of endocrine secretion in the mother may seriously hamper the physical and mental development of an offspring. It is well known that cretinism, a disorder marked by general retardation and emotional and mental subnormality, may be caused by a deficiency of the thyroid hormone.

6. *Birth injuries.* Injuries resulting from the use of obstetrical instruments and pressure on the soft skull of a fetus during labor and delivery may result in arrested development, feeble-mindedness, cerebral palsy, or other abnormal tendencies. Various defects are sometimes erroneously assigned to this cause, but parents naturally prefer to avoid admissions of germinal weakness.

7. *Emotional shock.* It is possible that severe emotional shock may force an excess of the powerful adrenalin hormone into the blood stream going to the fetus (by osmosis). Whether such a process affects adversely the mentality and nervous stability of the developing child is a moot question. Little of a certain nature is known about this problem and it is thus best to suspend judgment regarding it.[2]

During pregnancy well-informed mothers give careful attention to their diet and do their best to avoid contracting any contagious disease. They plan a well-balanced diet both prior to and during pregnancy, since the physical development of the child is likely to be affected by the mother's nutrition. Experimental evidence indicates that optimum diets of mothers before and during pregnancy tend to reduce the number of stillbirths, premature babies, and congenital abnormalities, and to favor healthier babies and better teeth.[3] A well-balanced diet includes plenty of milk and vegetables and other food that supply the necessary vitamins, especially vitamins E and A. The mother's nutrition during pregnancy may affect the size of the infant at birth, and alleviate or reduce unusual headache, untimely nausea, blurring of vision, abdominal pain, and the like.

[2] Schwesinger, G. C., *Heredity and Environment,* pp. 331–332. New York: copyright 1933 by The Macmillan Company.

[3] Peckos, Penelope, "Nutrition during Growth and Development," *Child Development,* 28: 273–285, September, 1957.

It is unfortunate for a mother to deprive the prenatal individual of optimum conditions for development by failing to have proper rest, by wearing tight foundation garments, by ignoring sensible rules of physical or mental health, or by attempting to use abortive measures. One or more of these conditions is bound to be detrimental to the developing life, varying in degree according to the extent, duration, and time of the violation. Wanted babies usually are provided with a favorable environment by the prospective parents, during both prenatal and postnatal development. Frequently, the woman who becomes greatly disturbed when she discovers that she is pregnant becomes a somewhat neurotic or uninterested mother after the baby's arrival.

As continued study and experimentation yield more definite data concerning the effect of prenatal influences on the organism from the moment of fertilization to birth, we may become better able to differentiate between what the newborn baby has inherited by way of the genes and what modifications of original nature have taken place as a result of his uterine existence. The mother who understands the significance of her own attitude and behavior during pregnancy can do much to eliminate many prenatal maladjustive factors. Teachers who have a knowledge of the importance of prenatal environmental influences also may be better able to guide the developing child in his after-birth journey through life.

Diseases contracted during the prenatal development of the child may have an adverse effect on the fetus before birth and the later development of the child. Syphilis, for example, may cause stillbirth, miscarriage, blindness or deafness and, possibly, congenital mental deficiency. Although gonorrhea has caused much blindness, this type of blindness can be prevented by placing drops of a solution of silver nitrate in each eye of the child at birth.

Other contagious diseases such as measles, mumps, whooping cough, and the influenza viruses may have serious effects on the offspring if contracted by the mother during certain periods of gestation. For example, if German measles are contracted during the first four months of pregnancy, the child may possess such defects as deafness, defective teeth, mental deficiency, heart abnormality, or combinations of such defects.

The effects of the Rh blood factor and of radiation on the embryo or fetus, although significant, are not fully understood. The Rh blood factor has been known to cause abortions, stillbirth, and mental deficiency. X-ray treatment or atomic radiation apparently increases the likelihood of stillbirths and malformations. Mongolism occurs more frequently if the mother is over forty years of age than if the mother is under twenty-five.

An adequate supply of oxygen also is needed for proper development and mental functioning. There is experimental evidence that oxygen deprivation (anoxia) ten days before birth impairs the ability of rats to learn. Prenatal anoxia in cats tends to reduce the ability at maturity to perform in a maze. Also, oxygen deprivation of cats after birth decreases the rapidity of response. There is a tendency to stereotype rather than to discriminate.[4] This suggests the importance of an adequate supply of oxygen to the human fetus.

ENVIRONMENTAL AND CULTURAL INFLUENCES

In the foregoing discussion we attempted to show that at any stage of development an individual's characteristics result from the interaction that constantly is taking place between his inherited potential and the many factors of the environment by which he is stimulated. Every human being has the inherent ability to respond to stimulation in such ways as to effect changes in his behavior and attitudes. The nature and extent of these changes depend upon the child's stage of maturation and his readiness to learn.

Environmental Influences and the Developing Child The first six years of a child's life are very important. Hence the environment in which he lives during those years is equally significant. The ways in which the young child's needs and wants are satisfied, the material in the home by which he is stimulated, the language spoken in the home, the attitudes displayed toward him by his parents and other members in his family, and the interrelationships among the respective members of the family represent some of the factors of influence that exert a continuous impact on him.

During this period certain habit patterns are being developed, often without the child's awareness of them. His parents and later his teachers guide his developing habit patterns. In his restricted environment he learns that some of his behavior responses are approved and others are not. He participates in numerous trial-and-error responses. When these

---

[4] Meier, G. W., Bunch, M. E., Nolan, C. Y., and Scheidler, C. H., "Anoxia, Behavioral Development and Learning Ability: A Comparative Experimental Approach," *Psychological Monographs*, 488, 1960.

responses become trial successes, his learning is facilitated. As he develops his attitude patterns, he may acquire one attitude toward his father and another toward his mother. He learns in some instances that he can, to his advantage, play one against the other.

A three-year-old child wants to turn on the radio and his mother forbids this behavior. He turns to a friend with whom he is visiting with a request for approval of his behavior. When permission is given, he gleefully turns the knob of the radio. Although it is the first time he has seen this particular radio, he discovers that after it is turned on it is too loud and that he needs to turn the knob to the left to reduce the loudness of the sound. This he does. However, when he turns another knob that tunes in a different station, he is unable to cope with the new problem. In any event, his attitude toward his mother is affected by her denial of his behavior. He displays an unpleasant attitude toward her, while showing a more accepting attitude toward the person who approved his behavior with the radio. Experiences of this kind make it very difficult for parents who are trying to train a child not to touch the property of other people.

By the time the child enters nursery school, kindergarten, or the first grade, his behavior patterns reflect the attitudes that he has developed through whatever guidance he has been given to that time. These environmental influences tend either to help or hinder his further personal and social development.

At this age many children exhibit satisfactory independence of action and ease in the presence of adults and peers. They display an attitude of cooperation and self-control. Other five- or six-year-olds give overt evidence of dependence on their mother or other adult who has cared for their needs. Still others may be shy in the presence of strangers, demanding in their relations with their peers, and unable to handle their own affairs. Some of this difference can be credited to rate of maturation; to an even greater extent it is likely to be rooted in the kind of home and neighborhood in which the children are reared.

The child is born into an environment which for the first five or six years of his life is largely a one-way street concerning the strength of its impact on him. There is interaction at all times, but the developing child is at the mercy of the influences of the environment in which he finds himself. His attitudes are formed in his immediate environment; his ideas emanate from it; and, in general, the environment sets his social patterns. Fortunately, as he grows and develops, he is enabled to interact more and more with the forces of the environment and eventually comes to the point where he can give direction to his own behavior and exert his own influence over the environment in which he finds himself. The factors of influence found in a child's environment are illustrated in Figure 12.

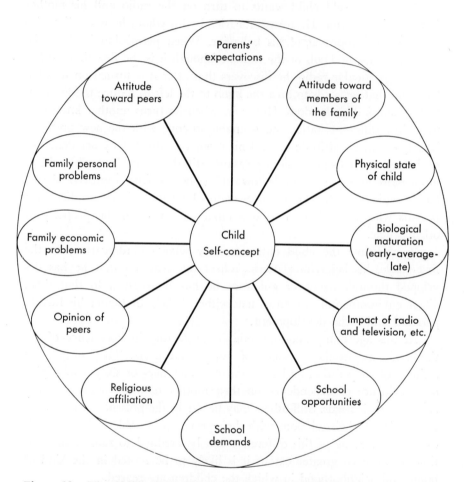

Figure 12. The Child's Behavior and Self-Concept Resulting from the Impact and Interaction of Environmental Influences.

Cultural Patterns and the Developing Child The various elements of a child's environment that stimulate his development into a social person combine to give him his *social heritage*. This social heritage is as important to the developing child as is his biological heredity. It is through the continued stimulation of his native potential that he is molded into the social being that he becomes. It is clear, therefore, that

Figure 13. Children in Lebanon with Their Pet Lamb.

the culture in which a child is reared is valuable to him since it plays an important role in shaping his personality.

The culture in which a child grows and develops comprises the physical and material elements of the environment in which he is reared as well as the factors of influence that are inherent in the traditions, mores, beliefs, attitudes, and behavior patterns of his community group. The ease of transition from childish to adult understanding of personal and group rights and responsibilities depends in part on the nature and consistency of the culture in which he lives. There are many complex interrelations of the various facets of culture in any society. These include a variety of classifications and groupings of both personal and social attitudes and activities.

CULTURAL FORCES A culture makes its impact upon the child in a variety of ways. These cultural or subcultural forces include the family, the church, the school, the press, the radio and television, the movies, and organized and informal groups with which he is associated during his period of development. Social heritage is transmitted in some instances by specific instruction toward stated objectives; in others through the use of punishment and rewards; in still others through informal unstructured means. Some types of behavior are obligatory for the best interests of the individual and of society. Definite steps are thus taken either by an individual or society to exact a high degree of conformity of conduct. The approach may be as informal as a frown or as formal as a court sentence to pressure the individual to conform to acceptable conduct.

Certain modes of behavior are prescribed by the group within which the child grows. Included among these customs are grooming, eating, forms of conversation, attitudes toward people and religion, and driving on the right-hand or left-hand side of the road. In many aspects of behavior, however, the developing individual is given considerable freedom of choice. Within reasonable limits he has the privilege of choosing what books he will read, selecting his recreational activities, picking a playmate for a game, and making a vocational choice.

There are many forces in a child's culture which influence his daily behavior and in which he neither exercises a choice nor does society do more than give supervisory direction to the agencies supplying the stimuli. Thus do advertisements, newspapers, movies, and radio and television programs influence attitudes, and in countless subtle ways motivate his behavior with or without an awareness that he is being so affected.

United Press International Photo

Figure 14. Children Playing in Sand, Paris, France.

GENERAL ASPECTS OF CULTURE   The maturing individual is inducted into his particular life pattern in many diverse ways. Some aspects of his culture appear to be absorbed almost unconsciously and assimilated more or less profitably. Other patterns are learned by way of relatively formal educational experiences. To a greater or lesser extent, all growing individuals experience the effects on their developing personality characteristics of their national culture as well as that of the people of other lands. These characteristics include (1) rapidly evolving technological changes in media of intercommunication, modes of travel, labor-saving devices, medical research, forms of recreational activities, and the like, and (2) social changes, including attitudes toward parent-child relations, educational aims and objectives, rights and responsibilities, as well as personal and group appreciation of spiritual, political, and socio-economic life values.

IMPACT OF CULTURE   Comparisons between relatively primitive cultures and some more sophisticated modern ones, as they affect child development, have yielded interesting results. There is general agreement among anthropologists, sociologists, and psychologists that children, wherever they are found, are relatively similar in their growth or maturational patterning. Thus, many differences that exist among the types of behavior of children reared in different cultures would seem to result from the cultures themselves rather than from the inherited traits of the individuals. For example, in her study of children in New Guinea, Margaret Mead [5] found that they were gentle and noncompetitive as compared to the children of modern Western cultures. Competition and aggressiveness among children are believed to represent cultural components and reflect the behavior of the individuals exposed to a particular kind of stimulation.

Improved methods of communication and transportation are leading to greater intermingling of different peoples, with resulting changes in traditions and cultures in certain national groups. In many places in the world parental attempts to foster traditional attitudes and modes of behavior are coming into conflict with youthful struggles to achieve different styles of dress, hair-do, and democratic status in the home as well as in government.

Language also is a part of culture. Although language patterns differ among national groups, many people are realizing that the culture of a country is better understood when one has mastered the language used by its citizens. Culture will always exert an impact on people but, within limits, the best interest of all may be served by sharing common beliefs, attitudes, and modes of behavior.

Biological Inheritance versus Social Heritage   Psychologists differ in the emphasis they place on what a child receives from the germ

[5] Mead, Margaret (ed.), *Cooperation and Competition Among Primitive Peoples.* New York: McGraw-Hill Book Company, Inc., 1937.

cells in the way of potential development and the effect upon him of
environmental and cultural influences. Although some earlier writers
claimed that biological inheritance and social heritage represented a fifty-
fifty relationship, few modern psychologists adhere to this rigid differentiation. It is recognized that either basis of development may play a
greater part in the life of the young person than the other.

Various studies in this area tend to stress the relative importance of
the potentialities which the child possesses as a result of being born in
a particular family and the extent to which inherited capacities can be
encouraged or discouraged by the environment in which he is reared.
The significance of biological inheritance as this is influenced by cultural
factors can be illustrated by an account of a family of seven children,
four boys and three girls, born of untrained parents, reared on a midwestern farm, and attending the same rural school as their parents before
them. (See accompanying picture.)

Figure 15. A Family Picture Taken in August, 1910.

The mother of these children was a gentle woman greatly concerned
about the welfare of her children. She had continued her education
through the eight years of the elementary school. The father had continued his formal education into high school. Numbered among the

antecedent relatives of both the father and the mother were lawyers, doctors, and other community leaders. For financial reasons, however, the father was compelled to forego his desire to go to college and turn to earning a living for his growing family through farming, an occupation in which he was little interested and only moderately successful. Hence the growing family encountered many privations. Yet, in spite of early monetary struggles, the seven children, now ranging in age from about sixty-five to fifty-three, have gained for themselves places of distinction in the world of affairs, in spite of much struggling to achieve their goals.

At this writing, the oldest, a boy, is a well-known hybrid seed corn grower and cattle rancher. Recently, his company successfully bred the *first multi-eared* corn. The next in line, also a boy, is a professor in an eastern college and an author. His next younger brother is the director of adult education in a large midwestern school system and has held presidencies of various important civic and professional organizations. The oldest girl taught in midwestern schools and now is the wife of an executive of a leading rubber company. The youngest brother began his career as a lawyer and then turned to the building business. The second youngest girl teaches in a Western college. The youngest girl is a teacher-librarian in a midwestern school system and is the wife of a member of the faculty of a local university. The children of these seven brothers and sisters also are carving out good futures for themselves in the professional, business, and sports worlds.

The experiences of this family are more noteworthy when they are compared to the activities of other young people who were born and reared in the vicinity of the old homestead. Many of the neighbors' children who attended the same rural school as the seven children remained on the farm where they are eking out a hard-earned existence. A few of them migrated to neighboring towns and cities where they are engaging in factory or small business activities.

The success story of this family probably had its origin in the germ cells inherited from both parents which made it possible for them to develop inherent potentialities for the good of others as well as for their own well-being and contentment. The achievements were made in spite of the fact that neither parent had received much formal schooling. It might be noted also that none of these seven men and women has retired from participation in worthwhile activities in spite of the fact that some are financially able to do so.

It must be admitted, however, that the younger generation is profiting by both inherited and environmentally induced advantages. These children, now as parents and grandparents, are providing cultural media that are encouraging their young people to serve society in light of their special interests and abilities.

QUESTIONS AND TOPICS FOR DISCUSSION

1. List some of the environmental factors that influence a child's development.
2. To what extent and in what ways do you seem to "favor" your mother's and your father's family?
3. How far have the various parts of the human body and their functioning developed by the time of birth? Be as specific as you can.
4. To what extent and how can a mother influence her unborn child?
5. Describe the home and neighborhood conditions of your four selected children.
6. What is your attitude toward outsiders who interfere with parents' attempts to rear their children? Justify your answers.
7. List and describe briefly the subcultures that exist in your community.
8. Which of your customary habits of behaving can you ascribe to the influence of the culture group in which you live?
9. In what ways has the study of a language other than your own helped you to gain greater understanding of cultural differences?
10. *Special Project:* Note and compare the observable characteristics that seem to be inherited qualities of each of the four children you are studying.

SELECTED REFERENCES

Gesell, Arnold, *Infant Development: The Embryology of Early Human Behavior.* New York: Harper and Brothers, 1952.

Ginsberg, Eli (ed.), *Golden Anniversary White House Conference on Children and Youth* (Vol. 1). New York: Columbia University Press, 1960.

Goldschmidt, R. B., *Understanding Heredity.* New York: John Wiley and Sons, Inc., 1952.

Harris, Dale (ed.), *The Concept of Development.* Minneapolis: University of Minnesota Press, 1957.

Harrison, R. J., *The Child Unborn.* New York: The Macmillan Company, 1951.

Hebb, D. O., "Heredity and Environment in Behavior," in Dulany, D. E., Jr., *et al.* (eds.), *Contributions to Modern Psychology.* New York: Oxford University Press, 1958.

Hurlock, Elizabeth B., *Child Development,* Chapter 2. New York: McGraw-Hill Book Company, Inc., 1956.

Kollman, F. J., *Heredity in Health and Mental Disorder.* New York: W. W. Norton and Company, 1953.

Mead, Margaret, *Coming of Age in Samoa.* New York: W. W. Morrow, 1953.

Miracle of Growth, The. Urbana, Ill.: University of Illinois Press, 1950.

Munn, Norman L., *The Evolution of Growth and Development,* Chapters 1 and 2. Boston: Houghton Mifflin Company, 1955.

Murphy, Gardner, *Human Potentialities.* New York: Basic Books, Inc., 1958.

Olson, W. C., *Child Development,* 2nd ed. Boston: D. C. Heath and Company, 1959.

Scheinfeld, Amran, *The New You and Heredity.* Philadelphia: J. B. Lippincott, 1950.

Snyder, L. H., *The Principles of Heredity.* Boston: D. C. Heath and Co., 1951.

Stuart, Harold C., and Prugh, Dane G. (eds.), *The Healthy Child: His Physical, Psychological, and Social Development.* Cambridge, Mass.: Harvard University Press, 1960.

Tyler, L. E., *The Psychology of Human Differences,* 2nd ed. New York: Appleton-Century-Crofts, Inc., 1956.

4

POSTNATAL GROWTH
AND DEVELOPMENT

ATTENTION HAS BEEN called to the types of development that occur before birth and to the difficulty of accurate observation of growth and behavior prior to birth. During the prenatal period, the new life has been developing from a sort of massive, chaotic behavior toward a more precise, differentiated reaction potential. At birth, however, a baby already has had different past experiences both within the mother's uterus and during the birth processes.

THE DEVELOPMENTAL SEQUENCE

Various factors affect the direction that will be taken by the growth pattern. It is known that in general (1) growth is from the head downward or in a cephalocaudal direction, and (2) body growth and function proceed from the center to the periphery of the body or in a proximodistal direction. The early responses of the child to stimulation are head movements, followed by those of sitting up and moving his body. Later, the ability to stand and to walk are developed. Young children attain a stage of maturation that enables them to pick up small objects with their fingers. Much can be said, however, in favor of providing the young child with manipulative materials that will enable him to develop control of mass movements, and later, as the child matures, of changing to materials that will enable him to achieve finer coordinations.

Continuity in Growth   The infant, through a process of maturation and interaction, develops a sensitivity to the relationships that exist between himself and his physical and social environment. Both biological maturation and cultural influences make their relative impact on the child's growth progress. Sequential patterns of growth in motor control can be traced with some degree of accuracy, although it is difficult to chart developmental sequences in the more complex phases of the child's behavioral responses.

Keith Feels Secure in His
Mother's Arms.

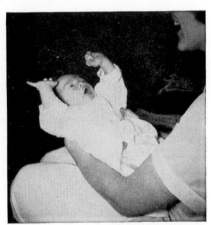

Terry Shows Head Control and
Arm Movement.

Figure 16.   Different Behavior Displayed by Children at an Early Age.

Growth is continuous until maturity. The product of a child's inheritance as it interacts with environment is propelled by a strong impulse supplied from deep inner sources. What happens at any one stage of growth and development has its impact on ensuing periods. The developmental pattern of a child becomes a significant predisposing influence in meeting the hazards of middle age and later. Thus the experiences in early life are extremely important to the individual as well as to those who are entrusted with his education.

The milestones of growth and development appear in an orderly sequence. There is a developmental sequence in learning to stand, to walk, to talk, to draw, to write, to tell the truth, to be altruistic, and to achieve independence. Although these sequences take similar form in the development of their patterning, they do not move along in time at a similar steady pace. There are periods of accelerated and of decelerated growth. During the first five years growth is marked, yet the rate of growth takes place at a decreasing rate.

Maturation   There appears to be within each individual a strong urge to grow. Each child's developmental pattern is definite and specific, but differences exist among the growth patterns of individuals. This internal growth process of body organs and functions is called *maturation*. It means that specific body organs are "ready" to function at certain times and are not able to function until a minimum growth (maturation) has taken place. For example, the walking of a child must await the development (maturation) of his legs and other parts that coordinate walking movements; toilet training is not possible until he has developed an awareness of a fullness of the bladder and the rectum through the maturation of the nerves that connect with these parts; learning to read is not achieved until the child develops his nervous system for language capacity, eye control, ability to concentrate, and the like.

After conception, the developing organism is affected by both nurture and maturation. These processes proceed in an interlocking fashion as the growth and development of the individual continues. Neither nurture nor maturation exerts a continuous and separate impact at any one time. Nature has provided for certain body organs and functions to undergo the maturation process at appropriate times during the growth journey from conception through birth to maturity.

Maturation is concerned with those changes over which the individual has little or no control, such as the anatomical, physiological, and chemical changes that occur during growth and development. Growth takes place in an environment in which nurture enables maturation to become full-blown, and in which maturation is required as the individual moves gradually toward maturity. Not only are mass responses developing into differentiated behavior but the process of integration is also taking place.

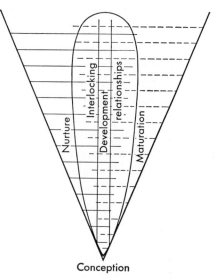

Figure 17. The Interlocking Effect of Nurture and Maturation on Growth and Development.

We have attempted to illustrate this interlocking and interacting process in Figure 17.

Just as special body parts are unable to function until there is sufficient maturation or "readiness," so is learning delayed until both the nervous system and personal interest have become "ready." Studies in this area of investigation give evidence that until a child has developed some readiness to learn, it is useless to spend time in training in any activities associated with such body parts that, as yet, have not undergone maturation. Extended effort in specific training at this time not only may prove a fruitless venture but may establish negative feelings toward the training and have an adverse effect on later learning. A display of interest in an activity usually is a good index of readiness. Specific instruction in appropriate activities at this point can be of great benefit to the child. In fact, he is likely to become so interested in the learning situation that he will continue it until it takes on skill proportions.

THE NEWBORN—THE NEONATE

It must be remembered that the prenatal organism grows from a single cell in about nine months to attain a weight of about seven pounds. The actual time of gestation varies from a low of 24 weeks through the full-term period of 280 days to a high of 52 weeks or 360 days. Since great growth and development take place during the prenatal period, a graph of human growth would take the form of a curve showing negative acceleration.

The birth experience is important to the newborn. A natural, easy birth may have a favorable effect on the newborn's growth and development, but such factors as length of labor, type of presentation, nature and extent of help needed from the attending doctor, the use of anesthesia, and the like make for differences in birth experiences and sometimes alter the direction of development. The newborn early exhibits a vast amount of diffuse and apparently uncoordinated movements in his activity.

Meaning of "Neonate"   The period from birth to the time when the newborn makes a stable adjustment to his new environment in which he finds himself is generally referred to as the *neonatal period*. This period extends from birth until the end of about two or three weeks. Authorities differ as to its length. Some suggest to the end of the first postnatal week; others as long as four weeks. The developmental process during this period includes the perfection of the vegetative process.

Immediately after birth, the newborn experiences the start of breathing by either the spontaneous or provoked birth cry, and he is ready to become an independent, nonparasitic human being. At birth, the neonate has all of his structure and is a complete human being. He has a layer or film which protects his skin at birth, but this dries in a short time. The newborn, on the average, weighs about seven pounds and is about twenty inches in length, boys being slightly heavier and longer than girls. Although his organs are developed and ready to function, he needs the help and protection of his mother in many ways. He needs to be fed and protected against changes in temperature and conditions that may prove harmful to him.

Neonates not only are different in their size, weight, and experiences, they "feel" different. At first glance, all babies seem to look alike, yet there are significant differences among them in their appearance. Their body proportions are different during this period from what they will be in later years. For example, the neonate's head is about one-fourth of his total length as compared with a one-eighth to one-tenth proportion to his total length in adulthood.

The newborn is seldom awake. He sleeps for unbroken periods of about three hours, unless awakened by stimulation of hunger pangs, intense noise, or light. Sleep consumes about twenty of the twenty-four hours of the day.[1]

Response to Sensory Stimulation The sense organs, both external and internal, have been fully developed by this time. These include the *exteroceptors,* nerve endings in the eye, nose, and ear; the *interoceptors,* nerve endings in the internal membranes of the stomach and the like; the *proprioceptors,* nerve endings in the muscles, tendons, and joints. The internal sense organs are ready to function at birth. Thus the neonate is able to have an awareness of a variety of experiences from either external or internal stimuli. Internal stimuli produce rhythmic or periodic responses that, on the whole, are of long duration.

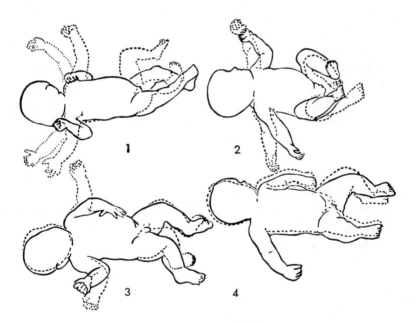

Figure 18. The Moro Reflex.

1. Characteristic bowing posture of the newborn. **2.** Reduction in activity, extension and abduction of upper extremities, bowing eliminated. **3.** Greater reduction in the degree of action. **4.** Characteristic response of quick body-jerk.

From McGraw, Myrtle B., *Growth: A Study of Johnny and Jimmy,* p. 48. New York: Appleton-Century-Crofts, Inc., 1935.

[1] *See* Pratt, K. C., *et al.,* "The Behavior of the Newborn Infant," Ohio State University, *Stud. Contr. Psychology,* No. 10, 1930.

The neonate's behavior responses give evidence of his maturational limits at this age. Most of his bodily movements, except for the reflexes that are present, are diffuse and in mass. The *pupillary reflex* occurs early, as does the *Babinski reflex* (the extension of the toe when the sole of the foot is stroked gently), and the *Moro-embrace reflex* (the jerking of the body and the throwing out of the arms to a sound, or the striking of a blow on the neonate's mattress). (See Figure 18.) It is characteristic behavior for the neonate to lie on his back with his head averted, one arm extended and the other arm flexed toward the head-chest region. This general position, the rudiments of which were started during the fetal period, is known as the *tonic-neck reflex.*

Beginning at birth and during the first few months of life, the infant may be able to support his weight by grasping a rod extended to him. This grasp suspension reflex is called the *palmar* or *Darwinian reflex.* Other unlearned responses, appearing at birth or soon thereafter, include crying, hiccoughing, yawning, sneezing, sucking, smiling, and swimming. The *swimming reflex* is the name given to the arm and leg movements made by an infant when placed in water. (See Figure 19.) An infant, however, is likely to demonstrate these movements if placed prone on his stomach on a flat dry surface. Reflexes such as the Moro, Babinski, and Darwinian are believed to disappear by about the fourth month. They are believed by some to serve as the bases for later development of more complex behavior patterns.

RESPONSES TO SIGHT STIMULI   That the newborn is able to see is not doubted, but the extent of his sight still is questionable. The fact that he is able to fix his eyes on an object and follow it as it moves or is moved through space leads one to infer that he is seeing or receiving impressions of one sort or another. For some children these eye movements, however, are not coordinated. Differences in their ability to fix their eyes on an object are apparent to a careful observer. It usually takes several weeks after birth before the eyes develop sufficient coordination for them to fix moving objects in their field of vision.

If a small spot of color is placed within a larger field of another color with equivalent illumination, the neonate will pursue movements for all hues included, but will not pursue a colorless field of a different illumination.[2] The *visuopalpebral reflex* (a closing of the eyes or, if the eyes are

[2] See Chase, W. P., "Color Vision in Infants," *Journal of Experimental Psychology,* 20: 203–222, 1937.

Figure 19. Three Phases in the Development of Aquatic Behavior of the Human Infant.

A. Reflex swimming movements; **B.** Disorganized behavior; **C.** Voluntary or deliberate movements.

From McGraw, Myrtle B., *The Neuromuscular Maturation of the Human Infant*, p. 34. New York: Columbia University Press, 1943.

already closed, a tightening of the eyelids) was believed by Kroner [3] to appear during this period. Preyer, however, believed that this was innate blinking and wished to distinguish it from the protective wink reflex to an approaching object which appeared much later. The *ocular-neck reflex* (a bending backward of the head to a sudden light stimulus) depends upon the intensity of the visual stimulus.

RESPONSES TO HEARING STIMULI   As was stated in the previous chapter, the fetus can respond to physical vibrations that produce sound. This does not help us determine just what the newborn hears at the time of or shortly after birth. Although some investigators believe that the neonate is deaf at birth, it is believed by others that the newborn responds in some way to sound within the first few days of life.

Auditory stimulation caused by musical tones may have some effect upon other body organs, such as a reduction in respiration and pulse rate. Auditory stimuli, if of short duration, and sufficiently intense, may elicit such responses as lip reflexes, circulatory and respiratory changes, and gross muscular reactions. With successive repetitions of the auditory stimulations, gross muscular responses decline. If the stimuli are of long duration, the effect is to lessen the activity as the intensity of the stimulus is increased.

RESPONSES TO TASTE STIMULI   The newborn is responsive to certain taste stimulations, although it is uncertain whether he can differentiate all four taste qualities. As he engages in his sucking response, some solutions such as salt, sour, or bitter tend to interrupt this response, whereas sweet solutions tend to provoke and maintain it. With increase in age go an increase in sucking response to sugar solutions and an increase of facial responses to quinine when taken internally.

RESPONSES TO SMELL STIMULI   Powerful odors such as ammonia and acetic acid evoke reactions in newborn infants, while apparently milder odors do not. It is not known, however, whether these reactions are to be credited to the sense of smell or perhaps to pain. Some stimuli, believed to be smell-producing, lead to movements of avoidance; others produce either sucking or licking responses.

RESPONSES TO TEMPERATURE STIMULI   The neonate reacts to temperatures that are hotter or colder than the temperature of his body. He appears to respond less to extremes of heat than to extremes of cold. Although the response involves more than the part stimulated, the greatest

[3] Kroner, T., *Ueber die Sinnesempfindungen der Neugeborenen.* Breslau: Grass, Barth, 1881. (Abstracted in Peterson and Rainey, 1910; Preyer, 1882; and Peiper, 1928.)

reaction occurs in the stimulated segment. Stimuli deviating farthest from the thresholds produce the most vigorous movements of the parts stimulated. The sucking response and the respiratory and circulatory movements are affected by these deviating stimuli.

RESPONSES TO PRESSURE STIMULI   Pressure or contact also stimulates the newborn. He displays a variety of reactions in his body positions as he is stimulated by pressure or pain stimuli. There are differences in sensitivity from one body area to another and in the extent to which the various neonates are sensitive to pressure or pain. Further study is needed before the differential sensitivity of the cutaneous areas of the body can be reported accurately. They seem, however, to have positive utility. There is lack of agreement relative to the nature and extent of pressure and pain stimuli on the just-born as compared with later periods. Also discernible are responses stimulated by the sensitized movements of the body as a whole, the *static-kinesthetic* response.

Duct Glands   Most of the duct glands are ready to function at birth. Their secretions may be limited in amount and occur only in the presence of specific stimuli; they can, however, be stimulated by substitute stimuli. Salivary, gastric, sweat, and tear glands secrete during the neonatal period. Tears, however, are not accompanied by crying. Mammary secretion is found in most neonates regardless of sex.

Feeding and Other Responses   The feeding response helps to orient the head of the newborn to the nipple of the mother's breast so that ingestion of milk can take place, and is fundamental to continued life. Several reflexes are involved in these responses, such as the *search reflex,* the *rooting reflex,* the *lip reflexes,* and the *sucking* and *swallowing* movements.

Figure 20.
A Nine-Month-Old Child
Reaches for Food.

The *plantar reflex* responses (extensor and flexor) appear to be protective responses: the former through a withdrawal of the toes and the latter through attack. The location of the stimulus becomes important to determine whether the protective response is associated with withdrawal or aggressive behavior.

The response of the fingers in the *palmar reflex* is somewhat analogous to the response of the toes in the plantar reflex. The exception is in the variability between extension and flexion of the latter. The palmar reflex responds both to light pressure on the palm, giving the closure response, and to pull on the finger tendons, giving the gripping or clinging response. Halverson [4] found that the right hand of infants can support more weight than the left, and that when they use both hands they can support more than 70 per cent of their weight when lifted or suspended.

Effect of Experience on Ability   The extent to which the experiences of the newborn affect his psychic states continues to be explored. Certain inferences concerning the impact of experience on ability have been made from responses to the stimulations of such sensitivities as the auditory, olfactory, gustatory, tactual, and the like. Although individual differences are known to exist between neonates in the nature and extent of their responses, whether we can speak of their intelligence depends upon how we define it. Norval [5] found that for two newborn babies having the same weight, a baby who is one inch longer than the other at birth will walk twenty-two days earlier than the shorter child. To some psychologists, the zero point of intelligence is at birth. This does not imply that maturation of the nervous system is sufficiently complete for the infant to synchronize his activities or acquire symbolic processes. There is little evidence of a general integrating factor which pervades all his activities. Irwin contends that intelligence is not present in the neonate, since the criteria which he sets for intelligent behavior are not met. These include "(1) the evolution and presence of the cerebral cortex; (2) the evolution and presence of distance receptor organs; (3) the achievement of upright posture; and (4) the use of substitutive or symbolic behavior." [6]

[4] Halverson, H. M., "Studies of the Grasping Responses of Early Infancy," I, II, III, *J. Genetic Psychology,* 51: 371–449, 1937.

[5] Norval, M. A., "Relationship of Weight and Length of Infants at Birth to the Age at which They Begin to Walk Alone," *J. Pediatrics,* 30: 676–678, 1947.

[6] Irwin, O. C., "Can Infants have IQ's?" *Psychological Review,* 49: 69, 1942.

GROWTH DURING INFANCY

The period of infancy begins at the end of the neonatal period and extends to the time when the child uses his first meaningful words. Although authorities do not agree upon the time nor the characteristic behavior that terminates this period, it usually extends for about one and one-half to two years.

Basic Changes The infant undergoes prodigious growth and considerable learning. The rapid growth of physical structures and functions which is taking place during this period is basic to the personality patterns that are being formed. The infant learns to stand erect; his earlier mass movements become differentiated and coordinated as maturation occurs. For example, at one month of age the average infant, if lying down, can lift his face; at four months he is able to sit on his mother's lap if support is given to his back; at seven months (earlier in some instances) he can sit alone. A nine-month-old child can reach for his food, as observed in Figure 20; at ten months he starts to creep, and so on. Thus physical development, with understandable exceptions, follows a rather definite time schedule. As each child enters upon each new level of development, his earlier patterns of response, such as creeping on the floor, cease to function or are not used by him.

Developmental Behavior during the First Year The child inherits specific ability in such functions as motor development, language usage, adaptive behavior, personal-social behavior, and reflex action. His experiences during the first year of life give direction to each of the behavior patterns that are formed or are forming. Same-age children perform somewhat differently in these behavior areas. Sufficient individuals have been studied to establish norms of behavior for these developing traits during the first twelve months of postnatal life. These behavior traits have been collected, organized, and classified by many researchers in the field. Some of these results have been organized in chart form by Drake and are presented in Table 1.[7]

Although they are presented here in summary form, each is discussed in appropriate chapters later. It may be observed at this point that, although these behaviors reflect strong hereditary influences, they require a satisfactory environment for full expression.

[7] Drake, R. M., "Developmental Norms for the First Year," in Skinner, C. E., and Harriman, P. L. (eds.), *Child Psychology*, pp. 48–50. New York: The Macmillan Company, 1941.

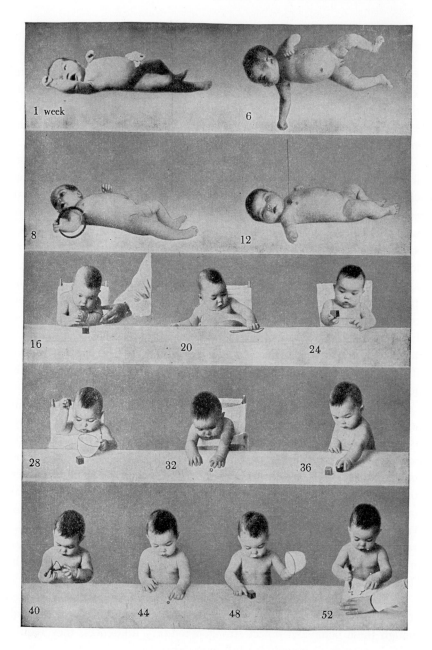

Figure 21. The Growth of Infant Behavior Delineated in Weeks at Fourteen Age Levels.

From Gesel, Arnold, *The Guidance of Mental Growth in Infant and Child,* as used in *Child Psychology* edited by Skinner, C. E., and Harriman, P. L. New York: copyright 1941 by The Macmillan Company.

TABLE 1

Developmental Norms for the First Year *

(From Gesell, Goodenough, Blanton, Shirley, and Strang)

	Motor development	Language	Adaptative behavior	Personal-social behavior	Reflexes
At birth	Can move hands and legs in random fashion; spreads and closes hands; turns head when lying face down.				Plantar (Babinski). Moro knee, pupillary wink, sneezing, hiccoughing, yawning, grasping.
1 month	Can hold chin up; make crawling movements.	Heeds sound; cries differentially for pain, hunger, discomfort.	Stares at massive or moving objects; holds on to objects placed in hand.	Selects face as object of regard.	
2 months	Can hold chest up, or head erect for a moment; reaches.	Listens to speaking voice; makes all vowel sounds.	Prolonged regard; eyes follow moving person.	Is quieted by touching; turns head to hear speaking voice; makes pushing movements with legs when upheld.	
3 months	Reaches for objects but misses; can hold head erect short time if held to shoulder; can move from side to side.	Vocalizes moods of pleasure.	Eyes follow small object; turns head freely to look; looks for source of sound.	Quieted by voice or music; cries when adult leaves him; shows anticipation.	Moro reflex disappears.
4 months	Holds head steady; sits up with aid; carries object to mouth.	Responds vocally when socially stimulated; makes all consonant sounds.	Looks about in new situation; regards cube on table; closes in with both hands on dangling ring; turns head to follow a vanishing object; looks for lost toy.	Plays with rattle; inspects own hand; splashes in bath water; makes adjustments in anticipation of being lifted.	Grasping reflex disappears; replaced by voluntary clasping.

* Drake, Raleigh M., "Heredity and Early Development," in Skinner, C. E., and Harriman, P. L. (eds.), *Child Psychology*, pp. 48–50. New York: The Macmillan Company, 1941.

TABLE 1

Developmental Norms for the First Year—*Continued*

	Motor development	Language	Adaptative behavior	Personal-social behavior	Reflexes
5 months	Grasps voluntarily; turns over; can pick up a cube from table; holds bottle.	Vocalizes pleasure and displeasure.	Eyes cooperate in prehension and manipulation; plays actively with rattle.	Is quieted by caress; disturbed by sight of people; smiles at another child.	
6 months	Can grasp dangling object; sits without support for few moments; holds two cubes, one in each hand; plays with toes.	Speaks several well-defined syllables; expresses recognition of familiar things; vocalizes pleasure; imitates sounds.	Expectation in response to the repetition of a stimulus; recognizes own name; shows fear, disgust, distress, excitement, delight.	Distinguishes between friendly and angry talking; holds up arms to be taken up; recognizes familiar people.	
7 months	Can sit alone; rotates wrist freely; picks up pellet with partial finger prehension; reaches persistently for remote cube; stands firmly with help.	Vocalizes satisfaction in attaining an object.	Sustained interest in play.	Reacts to image in mirror by manipulation or approach.	
8 months	Stands with help; can raise self to sitting position.	Vocalizes in interjectional manner.	Definitely looks for fallen spoon; uses handle in lifting cup; shows interest in details of a bell; deliberate choice of a toy; reaches for toy outside of crib.	Pats or smiles at own image in mirror; shows interest in frolics of others.	

TABLE 1

Developmental Norms for the First Year—*Continued*

	Motor development	Language	Adaptative behavior	Personal-social behavior	Reflexes
9 months	Starts to creep; opposes thumb to forefinger in picking up objects.	Says da-da or equivalent; listens with selective interest to familiar words.	Uses string to pull ring; gives attention to scribbling demonstration; shows curiosity for hidden objects; rubs self with soap and towel; points with index finger.	Cries if other child receives attention.	Babinski reflex disappears.
10 months	Creeping is well developed; pulls self up to standing position; picks up pellet with precise pincer movement.	Imitates sounds; makes adjustments to some words.	Explores form board holes; imitates ringing of a bell.	Imitates movement of another child; opposes toys being taken away.	
11 months	Walks when led; lowers self from standing to sitting position; holds crayon to make stroke.	Says two "words"; adjusts to simple verbal suggestions; imitates sounds or words.	Imitates scribble; uses string to pull objects; secures cube wrapped in paper; holds cup to drink from.	Strives for attention of another child; repeats performance when laughed at.	
12 months	Pulls self up to stand alone; walks with help.	Uses four words.	Builds tower with two blocks; taps a bell; removes paper cup from head; uses spoon.	Cooperates in dressing.	

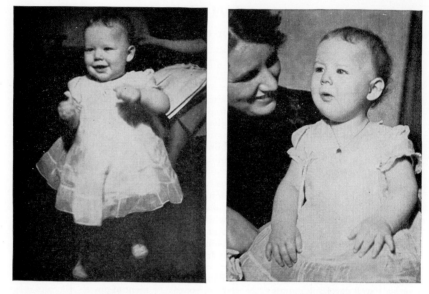

A (Girl)   *B* (Boy)

Figure 22.   Picture Taken on the First Birthday of Each Child.

A   *B*

Figure 23.   Picture Taken on the Second Birthday of Each Child in Figure 22.

ANATOMICAL GROWTH

Growth in height and weight usually is thought of when mention is made of anatomical growth; yet, other structural changes, such as eruption of teeth, body build and contours, and growth of skeleton also are significant. We shall consider each of these areas of growth.

Growth in Height and Weight   Numerous cross-sectional studies have been made of the height and weight of growing individuals. Some studies also have taken on the character of a longitudinal approach. One study conducted by Stow and reported by Charles [8] is illustrated in Figures 24 and 25. These studies were conducted over a ten-year period, and

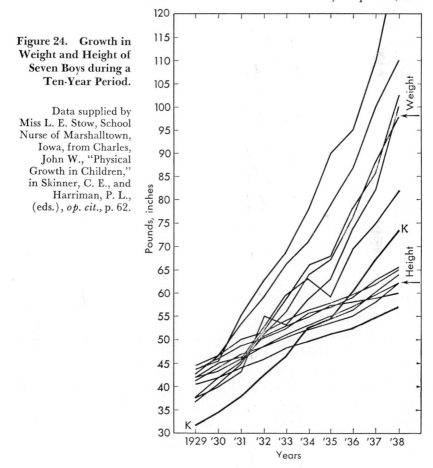

Figure 24.   Growth in Weight and Height of Seven Boys during a Ten-Year Period.

Data supplied by Miss L. E. Stow, School Nurse of Marshalltown, Iowa, from Charles, John W., "Physical Growth in Children," in Skinner, C. E., and Harriman, P. L., (eds.), *op. cit.*, p. 62.

[8] Charles, J. W., "Physical Growth in Children," in Skinner, C. E., and Harriman, P. L. (eds.), *Child Psychology,* pp. 62–63. New York: The Macmillan Company, 1941.

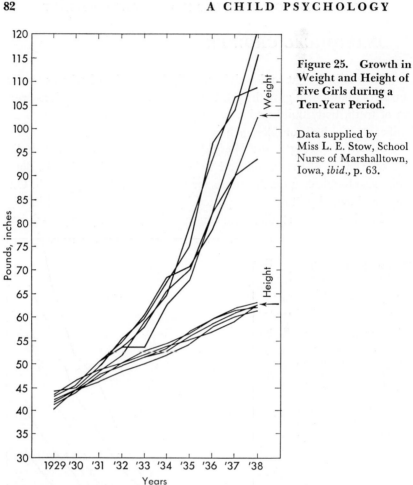

Figure 25. Growth in Weight and Height of Five Girls during a Ten-Year Period.

Data supplied by Miss L. E. Stow, School Nurse of Marshalltown, Iowa, *ibid.*, p. 63.

involved the weight and height of seven boys and five girls. It is interesting to note that for these individuals, the differences in weight were much greater than the differences in height.

The height of the average child during the first year after birth increases by about eight to ten inches, and by about four inches during the second year. By the age of four years, boys and girls have attained about 60 and 57 per cent of their total height, respectively. (See Figure 26.) The increase becomes more equal between the ages of six and twelve when there is a spurt of growth in height on the part of girls. This is associated with the fact that they mature earlier sexually. There are important individual differences among girls in growth that seem to depend upon the time at which the girl reaches her menarche. The close relationship between anatomical and physiological aspects of development is shown by the fact that tall girls often reach puberty earlier than do short girls. There are, of course, exceptions to these generalizations. (See Figure 27.)

The weight of the average child during the first year is doubled by the end of the fifth month, reaching about fourteen to sixteen pounds. Thereafter, the average gain is relatively smaller, about one pound a month by the end of the first year. This actually represents a decrease in weight growth which continues into the second year, decreasing relatively less to a weight growth of approximately one-half pound per month.

Reed and Stuart meaured the height and weight of 134 individuals (67 boys and 67 girls) from birth to 18 years of age. The averages for each sex at each age level are given in Table 2.

It should be kept in mind that the data in these figures represent averages and should not serve as specific guides for either parents or teachers. Unfortunately, some parents have taken these averages too seriously and have attempted so to feed their children that their height and weight would conform to these standards. In some instances, there was overfeeding; in others, underfeeding which led to undernourishment. These data have definite value when they are used to understand the relationship that should exist between a child's growth status and his age as compared with other children in his group. In using the data of these figures, parents and teachers should avoid interpreting the averages too

Figure 26.   Girl (Fig. 23) at the Age of Five Years and Two Months, and Boy at the Age of Three Years and Seven Months.

TABLE 2

Means of Height and Weight According to Age and Sex *
(67 boys and 67 girls) †

Age	Height ‡ (cm)		Weight (kg)	
	Boys	Girls	Boys	Girls
1	75.4	73.9	10.2	9.6
2	87.8	86.2	12.6	12.1
3	96.4	95.4	14.5	14.3
4	103.7	103.3	16.4	16.4
5	110.3	110.2	18.3	18.6
6	116.7	116.6	20.3	20.8
7	121.5	121.3	22.8	23.2
8	127.4	127.1	25.4	26.0
9	133.0	132.7	28.3	28.9
10	138.1	138.4	31.6	32.5
11	143.2	144.7	35.3	36.6
12	148.9	151.2	39.4	42.0
13	155.7	156.8	44.8	47.2
14	162.7	160.3	50.8	51.3
15	168.9	162.0	56.1	53.7
16	172.8	162.7	60.5	54.6
17	175.1	163.1	63.4	54.9
18	176.3	163.5	65.8	55.6

† Each of the 134 children is represented in the data for every age.
‡ Supine length to age 6, standing height from 6 to 18 years.
* Adapted from Reed, R. B., and Stuart, H. C., "Patterns of Growth in Height and Weight from Birth to Eighteen Years of Age." *Supplement to Pediatrics*, Charles C. Thomas, Publisher, Springfield, Ill., Nov., 1959, p. 905. By permission of publisher and American Academy of Pediatrics.

strictly. Each child is to be considered as a distinct individual, having his own particular growth pattern.

Body Type Although the skeletal structure of a neonate is composed mostly of cartilage, during childhood a process of ossification takes place. The skeletal structure, for example, by pubescence consists of about 350 bones, which number is reduced to 206 by adulthood. Some of this ossification depends on nutritional factors, but it continues during the adolescent years. Young people in their early adolescence often are accident-prone because their youthful energy impels them to participate in activities for which their skeletal maturation is not yet complete.

Although there is relatively little difference in the body contour of the male and the female child, by adolescence these body proportions or contours become characteristic of the physical growth of either the boy or the girl. The adolescent boy's form usually is characterized by straight leg lines, slender hips, and broad shoulders. On the average, the girl's body lines become curved and her hips become wider, while her shoulders tend to remain narrow.

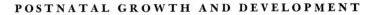

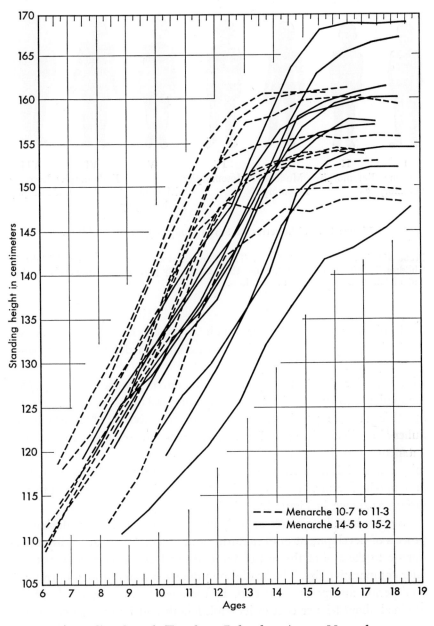

Figure 27. Growth Trends as Related to Age at Menarche.

Courtesy of Shuttleworth, F.K., "Physical and Mental Growth of Boys and Girls Aged Six through Nineteen in Relation to Age at Maximum Growth," *Monographs of the Society for Research in Child Development*, Vol. 4, No. 3, pp. 248–249, 1939.

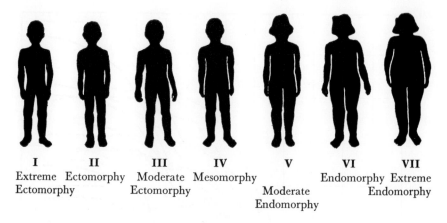

I   II   III   IV   V   VI   VII
Extreme Ectomorphy Moderate Mesomorphy   Endomorphy Extreme
Ectomorphy   Ectomorphy   Moderate   Endomorphy
                                          Endomorphy

Figure 28. Silhouettes of Seven Body Types in Children.

From Massler, Maury, and Suher, Theodore, "Calculation of 'Normal' Weight in Children," *Child Development,* June, 1951, 22:80. By permission of the senior author and of Child Development Publications.

In his attempt to explain personality, Sheldon classified individuals on the basis of physical characteristics as falling into definite body types— somatotypes. These general types are *endomorphic* (body soft and round, with behavior dominated by massive digestive viscera); *mesomorphic* (muscular and bony, with heavy physique and thick skin); and *ecto-morphic* (fragile physique and sensitive to exposure).[9] Massler and Suher [10] applied this method to children who are relatively free of sub-cutaneous fat. They made extensive anthropometric measurements on midwestern children between the ages of five and one-half and seventeen and one-half years. They classified their subjects into seven different groups as shown in Figure 28.

Studies have been made of body proportions and contours during the process of development until maturity is attained. The head is dispropor-tionate to the size of the rest of the body at birth as compared with its later comparative size. The head shows the most rapid growth during the fetal period and postnatal period. By the age of five years the head has attained about 91 per cent of its adult length and by the age of ten has

[9] Sheldon, W. H., *et al., The Varieties of Human Physique.* New York: Harper and Brothers, 1940.

[10] Massler, M., and Suher, T., "Calculation of 'Normal Weight' in Children," *Child Development,* 22: 75–94, 1951.

attained about 95 per cent of its full growth. These changes, as well as other body proportions, are shown in Figure 29.

Eruption of Teeth   Two sets of teeth erupt in the growth of every normal individual. The arrival of the child's first tooth is a time for rejoicing for the parents; the shedding of the first tooth of the temporary set is a time of great anxiety for both the parents and the child. The entire problem of teething gives parents and others much concern.

The sockets for the temporary teeth are formed in the third month of the fetal period and, by the time of birth, have developed to the extent that all are present in the baby's gums. Although an occasional child has been born with a tooth, as a rule teeth do not erupt until the baby is about six months of age. The twenty temporary teeth normally erupt, tooth by tooth, within a period of twenty-four to thirty-two months, or slightly over two years. The permanent set begins to appear shortly before the age of six, earlier for girls than for boys. The closeness of the erupted teeth by numbers in Figure 30 reveals certain spurts of dental development during certain years. It is evident from the scale that girls are more advanced than boys at each age level in tooth erup-

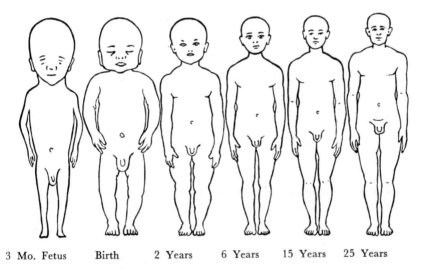

| 3 Mo. Fetus | Birth | 2 Years | 6 Years | 15 Years | 25 Years |

Figure 29. Changes in Body Proportion, Fetus to Maturity.

From Stuart, H. C., Healthy Childhood, p. 55. Copyright, 1933, by D. Appleton-Century Company, Inc. By permission of Appleton-Century-Crofts, Inc. (From drawings by Scammon, Calkins, and Stratz.)

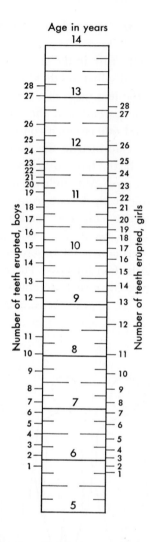

Figure 30. Dental Age Scale.

Courtesy of Cattell, Psyche, *Dentition as a Measure of Maturity*. Cambridge, Mass.: copyright Harvard University Press, 1928.

tion. The data for this scale is based on the examination of about 12,000 children of north European stock, at different age levels.

PHYSIOLOGICAL ASPECTS OF GROWTH

There are numerous aspects of growth that are largely physiological in nature and that occur along with those anatomical aspects which we have been discussing. In fact, there is much overlapping between the two; in many instances, one depends on the other. For ease of treatment, however, we are presenting them separately. The difficulties associated with any study of physiological development and functioning have reduced the number of studies dealing with them. Available, however, are substantial data relative to growth changes during the years when the individual progresses toward maturity.

The Circulatory System   The heart, as the chief organ of the circulatory system, undergoes significant changes as it develops. The child's heart increases in weight rapidly. At the age of about six, it weighs nearly five times as much as it did at birth. By the age of twelve, it is about seven times heavier and when fully developed about twelve times its weight at birth.

Not only does the heart increase in size but it does this at different rates at different times. For example, the growth rate is reduced somewhat between the ages of six and ten. During the early adolescent years there usually is a rapid spurt of heart growth. Cardiac difficulties that sometimes appear during adolescence may result from the fact that the aorta artery does not increase in size proportionately with the increase in size of the heart. Thus the heart does not always adjust to the new conditions without developing some cardiac problems. It is important to give individual attention to wide differences in heart development in order to deal adequately with problems associated with cardiac conditions.

When respiration starts after birth, the heart starts to beat more strongly but more slowly than it did during the prenatal period. As the heart grows in size, however, there is greater steadiness of heartbeat as well as an increase in blood pressure in the arteries. From a possible rate of 140 beats during the first month of life, the rate decreases to about 106 at the end of two years, and to about 90 at the end of four years. The pulse rate for girls is slightly higher than for boys during the first two years, then falls below that of boys and remains so with a possible exception at the age of about eighteen. The normal pulse rate for adults is approximately 65 to 72 beats per minute for men, and 70 to 80 for women.

Although for the most part there is little difference in blood pressure between boys and girls during early childhood, girls tend to exceed boys between the ages of ten and fourteen, after which the rise is rapid in boys, who maintain the advantage thereafter. The reduction in activity in girls may be caused, in part, by lowered blood pressure during this period. The effect of exercise on blood pressure has been studied and charted. According to the findings of the California Adolescent Growth

Study, exercise affects blood pressure and pulse rate. *Systolic* blood pressure (maximum pressure attained at each heartbeat) is increased, and *diastolic* pressure (pressure maintained in arteries as the heart dilates and fills) is decreased.

Differences in Rates of Growth Progress   Growth of each body part or each function does not continue at the same rate during the same period of time. Some of these different rates can be detected easily, such as spurts in physical growth followed by periods of little difference, or by apparent language development followed by a slowing down of the ability to use words. Studies have been made which show that some parts of the body grow in size at different rates at any given time.

Growth progress studies of the various organs of the body, for example, reveal interesting data concerning the manner in which individual organs develop in relationship with each other. A study concerned with the respective rate of growth of four basic types of body tissue (lymphoid, neural, general, and genital) reveals significant differences existing among them. This is clearly shown in Figure 31.

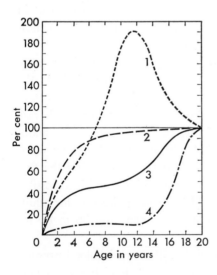

Lymphoid Type 1.
   Thymus Lymph nodes
   Intestinal lymphoid masses

Neural Type 2.
   Brain and its parts. Dura
   Spinal cord. Optic apparatus
   Many head dimensions

General Type 3.
   Body as a whole. External dimensions
   (with exception of head and neck).
   Respiratory and digestive organs.
   Kidneys, Aorta and pulmonary trunks.
   Spleen. Musculature as a whole.
   Skeleton as a whole. Blood volume.

Genital Type 4.
   Testes. Ovary Epodidymus.
   Uterine tube. Prostate. Prostate urethra.
   Seminal vescicles.

Figure 31.   The Development of the Four Types of Tissue and Different Parts and Organs of the Body during the First 20 Years of Life.

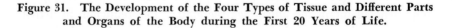

From Scammon, R.F., "The Growth of the Body in Childhood," in Harris, J. A., *et al.* The Measurement of Man, p. 193. Minneapolis: copyright by University of Minnesota Press, 1930.

The findings of this and other studies indicate that the growth of some internal organs is similar in many respects to height and weight growth patterns. An examination of Figure 31 will reveal that there are significant changes in rate of growth of various body parts during the period of development from birth onward.

ENDOCRINE GLANDS IN RELATION TO GROWTH

The endocrine system and the nervous system are intimately inter-related. The endocrine or ductless glands are potent factors of influence on growth, both directly and indirectly. The endocrine glands and the nervous system normally cooperate in the regulation of bodily functions and the integration of behavior. According to Hoskins, "The evidence is now conclusive that what we are—physically, sexually, and emotionally —depends in no small measure upon the functions of our endocrine glands." [11]

The endocrine glands, located in various parts of the body (see Figure 32), consist of glandular masses which deliver their secretions directly into the blood by osmosis. These substances, or hormones, as they are distributed to the various parts of the body, function to maintain chemical balance and physiological integration. The influence of hormones affecting both organic and physiological processes begins long before birth. Hormones influence differentiation of tissue, nutrition, physical growth, sexual activity, brain development, and mentality. The secretion of these internal glands can modify the behavior of the child or his personality, either directly or indirectly.

Reference has been made to the fact that these endocrine glands begin to develop and to function during the prenatal period. The enlargement of the pituitary gland in women during pregnancy indicates the need of increased hormone production in the development of the fetus. The endocrine glands, thyroid, pituitary (hypophysis), suprarenals (adrenal), thymus, and pineal together with their growth trends and maturational patterns are illustrated in Figure 33.

The Pituitary Gland The pituitary gland which secretes a number of powerful hormones consists of an anterior lobe, an intermediate or middle lobe, and a posterior lobe. Each lobe secretes one or

[11] Hoskins, R. G., *Endocrinology*, p. 16. New York: W. W. Norton and Company, copyright 1941.

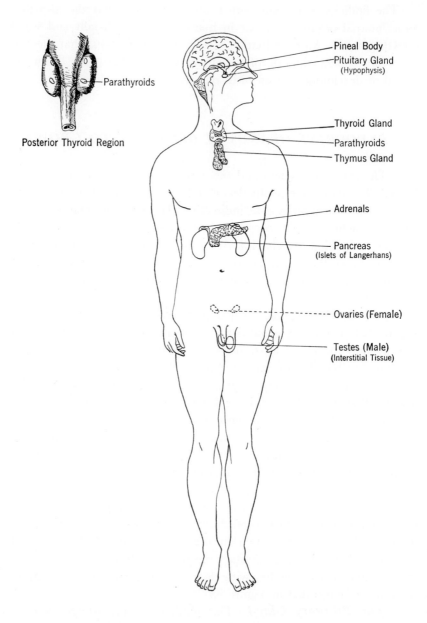

Figure 32.   Diagram Showing Location of the Endocrine Glands.

From Crow, L.D., and Crow, A., *Understanding Interrelations in Nursing*, p. 148.
New York: copyright 1961 by The Macmillan Company.

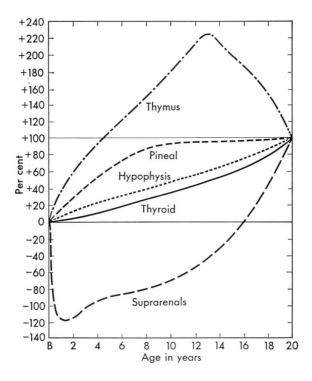

Figure 33. A Diagrammatic Graph Showing the Modes of Postnatal Growth Followed by a Number of the Organs Usually Described as Ductless or Endo-secretory Glands.

From Harris, Arthur, *et al., op. cit.,* p. 200.

more hormones. Although the exact nature and function of all these hormones have not been discovered, it is known that the anterior lobe secretes both growth and gonadotrophic hormones. The growth hormone seems to promote growth, particularly of the skeletal structure. A deficiency of the growth hormone during childhood results in a type of dwarfism. If there is hyperactivity of the anterior lobe before puberty, the result may be gigantism, with elongated skeleton and proportionately large bones in the extremities.

Other hormones produced by the anterior lobe of the pituitary gland exercise a controlling influence over other glands: the master sex hormone over the gonads, the thyrotrophic hormone over the thyroid, and the adrenotrophic over the cortex of the adrenals. There is a marked increase in the number of hormones secreted by the anterior lobe during the prepubertal period; they remain active throughout the reproductive period of life.

The posterior lobe of the pituitary secretes two known hormones and possibly several others. Some of these affect the activity of smooth muscle tissue in a way somewhat similar to adrenaline. Thus the tonus of smooth muscles is controlled by the posterior lobe.

Hypoactivity of both the anterior and posterior lobes seems to result in an immaturity of the sex organs or sexual infantilism; hyperactivity seems to be a cause of sexual precocity. Pituitary insufficiency may affect such psychological conditions as drowsiness, forgetfulness, lack of coordination, and a neurasthenic state. Irritability, distrustfulness, and psychasthenic symptoms may be contributed to by pituitary excesses. See Chapter 18 for a discussion of neurasthenic and psychasthenic states.

The Thyroid Gland   The thyroid gland secretes a complex organic hormone known as *thyroxin*. This endocrine gland, which is partly under the control of the anterior lobe of the pituitary, aids in the control of metabolism and the normal development and functioning of the body. In normal amounts this secretion promotes physical growth, brain cell development, and mental activity. An overactive thyroid (hyperthyroidism) gives rise to behavior that is characterized by excitability, emotional outbursts, crying spells, insomnia, increased sensitivity, anxiety, and the like. Thyroid enlargement resulting from cell increase in young adolescents is a common cause of emotional instability.

When a deficiency in thyroid secretion (hypothyroidism) exists from birth or infancy, stunted physical development or deformity results. This condition, known as cretinism, may be improved somewhat by the use of thyroid extract. Children with mild cases of hypothyroidism usually are dull, sluggish, and apathetic. These children move about slowly; seem sleepy; have low sensitivity of sense organs, a phlegmatic emotional tone and arrested intelligence, and learn slowly. Symptoms of hypothyroidism include such behavior as motor restlessness, carelessness and destructiveness, and speech disturbances.

The Parathyroid Glands   The parathyroid glands (four in number) are located in the neck region but slightly lower than the thyroid gland. The hormone secreted by them acts as a regulator of the calcium metabolism of the body. When there is an insufficiency of parathyroid secretion the individual may exhibit behavior spasms, emotional upset, and even uncontrollable impulses. Fortunately, extreme calcium deficiency seldom occurs; when it does, treatment with parathyroid extract and a proper diet often bring relief. The importance to life of these glands is realized when it is known that death follows extirpation in a few days.

The Adrenals (Suprarenals) There are two adrenal glands, each having equal structure and function. One of the two is situated over each kidney. Both are composed of two parts: *adrenal cortex* (the outer layer) and the *medulla* (the inner core). The hormones secreted by each part of the adrenal glands have specific but different functions. The medulla secretes a hormone called *adrenaline,* which helps to energize and activate the body when sudden demands are placed upon the body. It has a close functional relationship with the sympathetic branch of the autonomic nervous system.

The cortex of the adrenal gland produces a hormone called *cortin.* This hormone is vital to life and appears to have some relationship to sexual development. An insufficiency of the cortin hormone sometimes occurs during or following an acute infection, resulting in excessive fatigue, lowered resistance to disease, low blood pressure, weak heart action, and diminished sex interest. The injection of adequate amounts of cortin may help to restore normal functioning. Excessive secretion of cortin, on the other hand, may result in premature puberty.

The Gonads The gonads are sex glands and exert a great influence on growth. The *interstitial* cells of the testes secrete hormones in the male that are different from the hormones secreted by the *corpus luteum* of the ovaries of the female. The primary function of the testes is to produce sperm cells, of the ovaries to produce ova or egg cells. Since these functions take place through ducts and are directly connected with reproduction they do not strictly represent an endocrine function. The hormones secreted by the interstitial cells of the male and by the corpus luteum cells of the female account for the secondary sex characteristics. *Theelin* is one of the sex hormones in the gonads which stimulates the breasts and reproductive organs, and remains active until the menopause.

The testicles of the male and the ovaries of the female develop within the abdominal cavity before birth. The ovaries are retained in this abdominal cavity throughout life; during the seventh prenatal month the testicles may descend into the scrotal sac, but are more likely to be delayed until some time after birth. The gonads show a slight rise in growth in infancy, thereafter slowing down until about the tenth year, after which a sharp rise occurs which continues throughout puberty. On the average, the testes are about 10 per cent of adult size at the age of fourteen, and are relatively mature at twenty. Likewise the ovaries are about fully de-

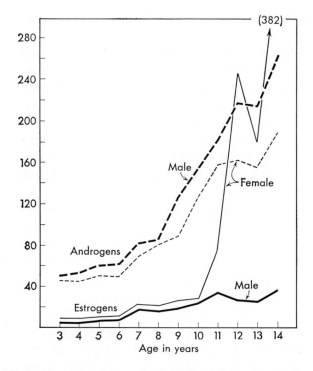

Figure 34. Age Changes in Excretion of Sex Hormones.

The female sex hormone, produced by the ovary, is the chief estrogenic hormone.

After Nathanson, I.T., Towne, L.E., and Aub, J.C., "Normal Excretion of Sex Hormones in Childhood," *Endocrinology,* Vol. 28. p. 861, 1941.

veloped at twenty. Certain hormones, the androgens and the estrogens, are secreted at an early age and show a rapid rise at puberty. (See Figure 34.)

The estrogenic and androgenic hormones are secreted by both boys and girls into the urine at a relatively early age. The amount of the secretion is rather small and not significantly different for either sex during the early years. At the beginning of puberty, however, the male excretes estrogens at about the same rate as earlier, but the female excretes them at a much increased rate. The latter may have some relationship with the menarche. There is rate change also in the excretion of androgens, although this rate difference is not so great as with the estrogens.

The importance of the gonads in normal sexual development is great. If they are diseased or removed there is a lessening of normal sex interest to the extent of sexual infantilism. Male aggressiveness is reduced and the secondary sex characteristics do not appear. Puberty does not appear in either sex if these glands are removed or damaged prior to that period.

The Pancreas   The insulin hormone is produced in the pancreas (islets of Langerhans). This hormone is concerned with sugar metabolism. It plays an important role in the control, utilization, and storage of sugar by the liver. Malfunctioning of this organ is accompanied by alterations in mood, increase in irritability, and decrease in mental activity.

The Thymus Gland   The thymus consists of two lateral lobes and is located in the neck region below the thyroid and parathyroid glands. The hormone secreted by the thymus appears to influence the gonads in such a way as to check the development of the reproductive organs in the young child. It consists largely of lymphoid tissue and grows in size until about the age of thirteen, after which it decreases; at one time it was believed to atrophy in adulthood. Blood formation, nutrition, and growth seem to be influenced by this gland.

The Pineal Body   The pineal gland is a small cone-shaped structure about the size of a pea, located at the base of the brain, behind and above the pituitary gland. Although the exact function of this gland is not known, it is believed that it also has some effect upon the holding back of sexual development in the young. This gland seems to serve no definite function in adulthood.

Important Considerations   Endocrine glands exert both a direct and an indirect influence on growth and development. Each ductless gland has a growth rate that is peculiar to itself and different from that of the others. Each gland also affects different phases of growth at significant times in the course of development. The regulation of metabolism, the absorption and utilization of calcium, the regulation of skeletal growth and sexual stimulation, and the reinforcement during emotional stress illustrate how these endocrine glands function in an interlocking manner as they influence growth and development, both directly and indirectly.

QUESTIONS AND TOPICS FOR DISCUSSION

1. What is meant by the cephalocaudal trend? What is its significance?
2. In what ways does the developmental pattern of a child become a significant predisposing influence in meeting the hazards of middle age? Be specific.
3. Select three areas of child activity. Show the effect of maturation on the development of these activities.
4. What is meant by the vegetative process of the neonate?
5. If possible, observe a group of newborn babies in a hospital and report on differences in their appearance and behavior.
6. Describe the tonic-neck reflex.
7. Trace the sensory development of the young baby.
8. Summarize the progress of developmental behavior during the first year of life.
9. If you have brothers and/or sisters, compare your growth pattern during childhood with theirs. What likenesses or differences do you find?
10. Discuss the effect of the endocrine glands on growth.
11. Give the functions of each of the endocrine glands. Which seems the most important to you?
12. *Special Project:* By consulting their mothers, trace the early growth and development patterns of your four selected children.

SELECTED REFERENCES

Bayley, Nancy, "Individual Patterns of Development," *Child Development,* 27: 45–74, 1956.

Burlingham, D., *Twins: A Study of Three Pairs of Identical Twins.* New York: International University Press, 1952.

Carmichael, L., "The Onset and Early Development of Behavior," in L. Carmichael (ed.), *Manual of Child Psychology,* 2nd ed., pp. 60–185. New York: John Wiley and Sons, Inc., 1954.

Carlson, A. J., and Johnson, V., *The Machinery of the Body,* 4th ed. Chicago: University of Chicago Press, 1953.

Geldard, F. A., *The Human Senses.* New York: John Wiley and Sons, Inc., 1953.

Gesell, Arnold, *Studies in Child Development.* New York: Harper and Brothers, 1948.

Gesell, Arnold, and Thompson, H., *The Psychology of Early Growth.* New York: The Macmillan Company, 1938.

Ginsberg, Eli (ed.), *Golden Anniversary White House Conference on Children and Youth,* Vol. 2. New York: Columbia University Press, 1960.

Lerner, I. M., *Genetic Homeostasis.* New York: John Wiley and Sons, Inc., 1958.

Pratt, K. C., "The Neonate," in L. Carmichael (ed.), *Manual of Child Development,* 2nd ed., pp. 215–291. New York: John Wiley and Sons, Inc., 1954.

Thompson, H., "Physical Growth," in L. Carmichael (ed.), *Manual of Child Development,* 2nd ed., pp. 292–334. New York: John Wiley and Sons, Inc., 1954.

Turner, C. D., *General Endocrinology,* 2nd ed. Philadelphia: W. B. Saunders Company, 1955.

Watson, E. H., and Lowrey, G. H., *Growth and Development of Children,* 3rd ed. Chicago: Year Book Publishers, Inc., 1958.

5

MOTOR GROWTH
AND DEVELOPMENT

CERTAIN MOTOR BEHAVIOR is practiced prenatally. The infant and the young child begin early to develop motor control of the body in order to carry on the life processes. The satisfaction of the organic needs (food, water, and elimination) and the avoidance of harmful stimuli require motor control. Although they must await their maturational level before they can function effectively, motor activities such as head and eye movement, manipulation of objects, sitting, standing, crawling, walking, running, jumping, vocalization, and handwriting are important to the child in his growth and development. Each of these complex movements needs to be mastered if it is to serve the individual all through his life. The nature and extent of the motor skill he acquires in various areas determine the degree to which he will succeed in social, educational, and vocational areas. We are concerned here with a consideration of the nature of motor growth and its importance to the developing child.

MOTOR DEVELOPMENT DURING PRENATAL AND NEONATAL PERIODS

We present a brief statement of the movements that occur during the prenatal and neonatal periods of life.

Prenatal Movements   The new life begins to stir before the end of the ninth week. Although his movements are feeble during his early prenatal life, the fetus gives evidence of movements during the third month. The new life represented by the fetus can rotate its rump, move its arms, and extend its legs somewhat. At first these movements are general; later they become more specific in character and apply to special parts of the body. Head movements, for example, are performed independently of trunk movements. The various body parts become active with little or no apparent association among such parts as the head, hands, and feet. Nevertheless, this behavior represents a definite growth plan that works for the unification of the motor responses of the developing individual.

From about the sixteenth week, the movements of the fetus, which are slight at first and later more vigorous, can be recognized by the mother. There also may be movements of the eyeball, blinking, protruding movements of the lips, and grasping movements of the hands. Other movements that are recognizable by the mother include jerks and turning movements.

The movements begin in the neck region and the course of development is away from this region toward the extremities. Hence movement continues in an integrated pattern down the body and outward through the four limbs. The rear part of the shoulder region is the location for the first neurally induced activity and is a mass reaction which takes place simultaneously with independent reflexes. Thus, both reflexes and the developing locomotor pattern are being readied to function.

The ontogenetic trends and sequences of behavior growth (stages similar to those through which the whole race has developed) are illustrated and summarized in Figure 35. Prenatally, the new life experiences trunk flexion at the end of eight weeks, and trunk extension by ten weeks; the swallow, sneeze, and Babinsky reflexes appear by fourteen weeks; hand closure and grip by eighteen weeks, and the tonic-neck-reflex appears by the twentieth week. The trunk movements are in all directions, beginning with sidewise bending of the trunk. Rotation movements, swimming reaction, posture, and four-limb locomotion grow out of the trunk movements. In general, by the sixth month there is an increased tendency toward independence of response, and by the seventh month responses involve a working together of various muscle groups. Prenatal movements are fundamental to later motor development.

Neonatal Motor Development   Adequate motor growth during the prenatal period enables the newborn to make many diffuse movements essential to his start in life. Thus, the neonate is in a state of great

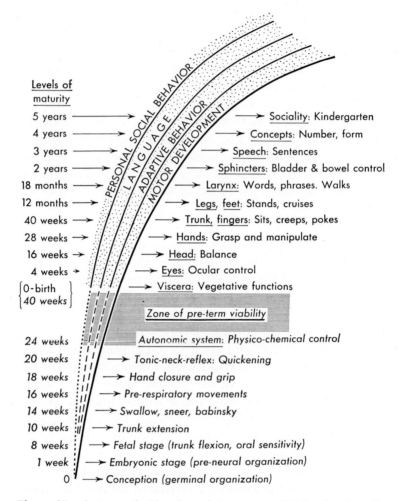

Figure 35. Ontogenetic Trends and Sequences of Behavior Growth.

From *Developmental Diagnosis: Normal and Abnormal Child Development,* by Gesell, A., Amatruda, C. S., p. 9. New York: Paul B. Hoeber, 1947.

potential of activity. The whole organism tends to respond in mass, stimulated, no doubt, by the internal stimuli from the gastro-intestinal tract. The sucking response, for instance, is diffuse and loosely organized at first, but quickly becomes rhythmic, more localized and well controlled. Also, there is little control of head movements at birth; the head responds with generalized reactions.

During the neonatal period, stimulation of any part of the body tends to activate the entire body. Motor responses tend to continue throughout the day, even during sleep. Such stimuli as pain, hunger, or physical discomfort seem to arouse greatest activity. It is estimated that a wide-awake, hungry neonate, for example, is capable of making as many as fifty movements per minute.

The movements of the neonate are in response to stimuli that affect both his reflexes and his general body responses. Among the reflexes important to his life are the pupillary reflex, breathing, sneezing, digestion, and heart action for blood circulation. Other responses basic to the acquisition of skilled motor performance include the movements associated with feeling, eye movements, trunk turning, lifting and turning the head, and movements of hand, arm, foot, and leg. The general direction of motor control represented in the fetus continues in the neonate and later.

MATURATION AND MOTOR CONTROL

Motor abilities involve various types of bodily movements that result from coordinated functioning of nerves and muscles. These movements include not only the gross body movements that involve all parts of the body, but the fine coordinations of the smaller muscles. Skill in any motor activity is possible only when the finer coordinations mesh with the gross body movements to enable the individual to achieve smoothness and efficiency in his everyday activities, such as dressing, eating, completing household chores, driving a car, and doing whatever else is necessary during a normal day's activity.

The kind of motor skill that at one time was needed to fend off an enemy or to insure survival is less needed today than in more primitive cultures. However, highly developed motor skills are crucial to insure satisfaction in social situations or in skilled work activities. The motor activity that starts long before birth is basic to postnatal development of posture, locomotion, and prehension. In motor growth each child follows similar patterns of development, but the rate at which they develop varies among individuals. We now have experimental evidence which indicates that maturation rather than training and experience determines the early rate and pattern of this growth.

Experimental Evidence of Impact of Maturation   Dr. Gesell [1]

[1] Gesell, A., and Thompson, H., "Twins T and C from Infancy to Adolescence: A Biogenetic Study of Individual Differences by the Method of Co-Twin Control," *Genetic Psychology Monographs,* 24: 3–121, 1941.

and his collaborators conducted experiments at Yale University with a pair of identical twins, T and C. These two girls were studied at intervals between the ages of forty-six weeks and fourteen years. Twin T received training for ten minutes daily for a period of six weeks in a motor activity such as stair climbing, and the other twin C received no such training. At the age of fifty-two weeks twin T with training could mount the stairs in twenty-six seconds. One week later, twin C was given two weeks' training and was able to climb the steps in less than half the time required by T at the end of six weeks' training. At the end of fifty-six weeks the motor performance of the two stair-climbing twins was very similar both in time required and in methods employed.

Another experiment with two boys, fraternal twins, was performed by McGraw [2] for a period of three years. The boys, Johnny and Jimmy, were paired in numerous motor activities with the result that skill progress was greater when maturation had taken place for the skill to be developed. Since these were fraternal rather than identical twins, the findings may be somewhat influenced by the slightly different hereditary backgrounds. Nevertheless, maturation proved to be a basic factor in the acquiring of the specific skills. Johnny was given practice in the various skills at an early age. When Jimmy was given an opportunity to practice these skills, his performance in activities characteristic of the human race was very similar to that of Johnny who had had previous practice.

An interesting sidelight results from the fact that one of the authors had in class a student who was a classmate of these twins during their adolescent years. She reported that Johnny, who had received extensive practice in the skill activities of swimming, and climbing an inclined plane, was more graceful and socially aware during his high school years than was Jimmy, who had been permitted to mature without the special training at the early age.

Another study was concerned with the age at which the Hopi Indian child begins to walk. Some Hopi babies usually are kept strapped (except for brief periods) to cradle boards from the day of birth until they are about nine months old. The child, wrapped in a blanket with his hands extended at the sides, is tied to the board with pieces of cloth, thus preventing him from flexing his legs, kicking his feet in the air, or bringing his hands to his mouth. Other Hopi babies are given greater freedom of movement and are not attached to cradle boards.

The study involved 105 babies—63 who had spent the nine months

[2] McGraw, M. B., *Growth: A Study of Johnny and Jimmy.* New York: Appleton-Century-Crofts, Inc., 1935.

in the cradle on the board, and 42 who were permitted freedom of movement. The mean age at which the "strapped" babies began to walk was 14.98 months; for the nonstrapped babies it was 15.07 months.[3] Apparently restriction of movement during the early months of life did not retard motor development when the time came to walk. According to these studies, the development of walking seems to depend largely on maturational factors and is not retarded by inactivity of leg parts during the early months.

Experiments in dealing with such motor responses as bladder control, language development, and fine finger coordination yield evidence that of two twins, the twin whose training begins later (at the maturational level more conducive to skill development) responds more quickly to training. It can be concluded that maturational readiness is a significant factor in the development of motor skills needed in human activity. Thus the development of motor abilities is rooted in the continuing of maturation; little skill development is possible unless the organism has matured sufficiently to be ready and able to engage in the particular activity. See Figure 36 for growth cycles in the patterning of prone behavior of the human infant.

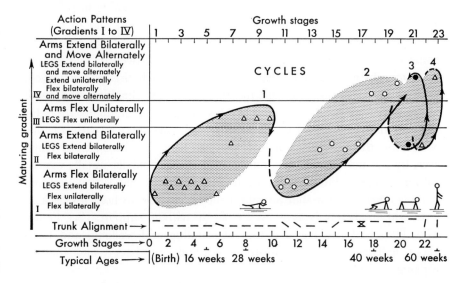

Figure 36. Growth Cycles in the Patterning of Prone Behavior.

From Gesell, A., "The Ontogenesis of Infant Behavior," in *Manual of Child Psychology*, 2nd ed., p. 346, edited by L. Carmichael. New York: John Wiley and Sons, Inc., copyright 1954.

[3] Dennis, W., and Dennis, M. G., "The Effect of Cradling Practices Upon the Onset of Walking in Hopi Children," *Journal of Genetic Psychology*, 56: 77–86, 1940.

GROWTH IN SITTING UP AND WALKING

Much attention has been given to the responses connected with growth in sitting up and walking. Some of the problems and characteristic behavior are reported here.

Experiences in Sitting Up   Although the neonate has a very large head compared with the rest of his body, the muscles of his head and neck are weak. Hence, to keep his head from wobbling, he needs to be handled with care during the first three months. Mothers learn early to place the right hand under the baby's buttocks and the left hand under his head and shoulders to pick him up. The baby soon gains enough strength to hold his head up for a few seconds when lying prone. By the end of two months he is able to turn his head to either side; by the end of three months he holds his head and chest up by pushing his hands and arms. As his nervous system and motor mechanism mature, he can progress from doing this for only a few seconds to maintaining the position for a longer time.

Until the infant is about four to six months of age it is necessary for his mother to turn him from side to side, since he is unable to roll over. This change in position is essential both for his comfort and to prevent strain on the muscles from lying in the same position for a long time. Some babies, however, develop the ability to roll over by the end of three months and cannot safely be left on a couch that is unguarded.

The baby continues to use the muscles of his shoulders and those of the upper part of his trunk. Thus his muscles are gradually strengthened, so that by the end of six months and sometimes as early as four or five months, he is able for brief periods to sit up with support. However, by the time the baby is nine or ten months old he usually can sit without support, but needs to be helped to attain that sitting position. Parents need to know that an infant should be able to hold his back in a straight line before he is allowed to sit up without support. (See Figure 37.) The child's next goal is that of standing and walking, and he is about halfway between the supine position (on back) and that of walking.

The achievement of a sitting posture is the result of the progressive development of the motor responses and the motor areas of the brain that govern movements in the regions of the neck, shoulders, and upper extremities. The line drawings in Figure 38 illustrate the posture phases

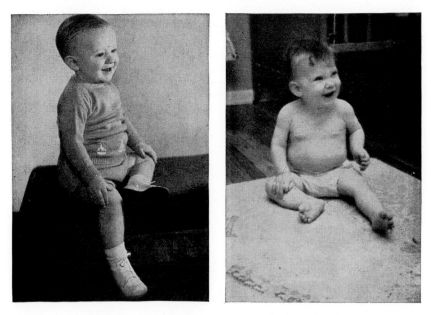

Boy (A)   *Girl (B)*

Figure 37. Boy *A* Poses for His Picture at the Age of One year; Girl *B* Sits Erect for Her Picture at the Age of Nine Months.

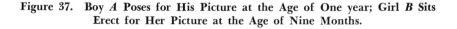

through which the infant passes in his attempt to reach and maintain a sitting position. The ability to change from a prone position to a sitting position and from a sitting position back to a prone position may not be mastered before the end of the tenth or eleventh month.[4]

Some years ago Ragsdale selected behavior items related to the attaining of upright posture of children from the investigations of Gesell, Shirley, Bühler and Hetzer, Bayley, and Thompson, and organized them in a table that indicated the findings of each investigator for the items listed. The investigators are in greater agreement in the sequence of appearance of the behavior than they seem to be in the date of its appearance. The summarized findings are presented in Table 3.

Growth in Walking When an infant is able to change from a prone to a sitting position, he tends to begin to crawl, to creep, or to convey himself toward an object or person of interest. If this object is

---

[4] McGraw, M. B., "Neuro-Motor Maturation of Anti-Gravity Functions as Reflected in the Development of a Sitting Posture," *Journal of Genetic Psychology,* 59: 155–175, 1941.

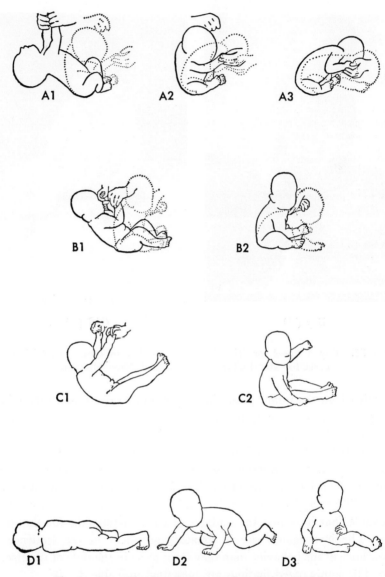

Figure   38.   The Development of a Sitting Position.

A1, A2 and A3 illustrate the passivity of the newborn when raised from a supine to a sitting position. B1 shows infant beginning to take active part in the rising position; B2 dotted line illustrates extension of upper extremities in order to prevent falling forward. C1 indicates a postural reversal from A1; C2 shows maintenance of erect sitting posture. D1 illustrates rolling prone preparatory to the independent assumption of a sitting posture; D3 shows the infant able to maintain erect sitting position without support on upper extremities.

From McGraw, M., *Growth: A Study of Johnny and Jimmy*, p. 91. New York: Appleton-Century-Crofts, Inc., 1935.

TABLE 3
Genesis of the Upright Posture and of Locomotion *

Behavior item	Age in weeks as found by:				
	Gesell	Shirley	Bühler and Hetzer	Bayley	Thompson
Lifts head when held to shoulder	4	—	—	2	—
Lifts head in prone position	4	3	2	—	4
Turns head laterally, prone position	4	—	—	3	—
Makes postural adjustment when lifted	4	—	—	2	—
Head bobbingly erect, upright position	8	—	8	7	8
Lifts head when suspended dorsally	8	—	—	11	—
Lifts chest, prone position	8	9	12	16	—
Holds head erect and steady, upright position	12	—	—	11	16
Elevates self by arms, prone position	12	—	20	14	16
Lifts foot when held erect	—	13	—	—	12
Legs extend recurrently, held erect	—	—	—	—	20
Sits with support	16	—	—	14	16
Lifts head and shoulders, dorsal position	16	—	20	20	—
Definite anticipatory adjustments to being taken up	16	15	—	13	—
Sits with slight support	20	19	—	18	20
Rolls from back to stomach	20	—	—	—	—
Rests momentarily on abdomen and chest, prone position	—	—	20	—	24
Rests on thighs, abdomen, chest, and hands, prone position	—	—	20	—	24
Sits alone momentarily, back rounded	30	25	—	23	24
Sits erect, briefly	32	—	—	—	24
Held erect, stands firmly	—	29	—	—	32
Stands, holding furniture	—	29	—	—	32
Regresses, lying prone	—	40	—	—	40
Rests on thighs, lower abdomen, and hands	—	—	—	—	36
Attains sitting from prone position	—	—	—	—	44
Attains creeping position from sitting	—	—	—	—	44
Pulls self to knees	—	—	—	—	44
Pulls self to standing	40	47	44	—	48
Creeps	—	45	32	38	48
Walks with help	48	45	48	44	—
Lowers self from standing to sitting	48	—	—	—	—
Stands alone	60	62	48	50	52
Walks alone	60	64	48	50	—
Achieves standing unaided	—	—	—	—	56–60
Walks sideways	—	—	—	66	—
Climbs stairs or chair	72	—	—	—	—
Walks backward	84	—	—	68	—
Goes up and down stairs	120	—	—	—	—
Tries to stand on one foot	120	—	—	—	—

* Ragsdale, C. E., "Motor Development of the Child," in Skinner, C. E., and Harriman, P. L. (eds.), *Child Psychology,* p. 79. New York: copyright 1941 by The Macmillan Company.

near him, yet beyond his reach, he is likely to pull himself up to a stand-ing position; this he must be able to do before he can walk. During his creeping experiences the child often comes near an object such as a chair and attempts to pull himself up. Once he achieves the ability to stand, he enjoys it and wants to repeat it. At first, he has trouble return-ing to a sitting position and needs help until he discovers how to do it for himself.

A baby who is placed on the floor may be stimulated to crawl in order to reach a nearby object or person. Babies differ as to the method utilized in locomotion. Some crawl on all fours, others hitch, and still others scoot. A parent needs to be careful that the child does not develop so great a proficiency in crawling that he delays his attempt to walk.

As the child first learns to stand he needs to support himself. Later, discovering that he can stand without support, he attempts to take a few steps. This behavior is encouraged if an object or a person is near him that can add to his confidence, thus avoiding a possible fall. Help is needed during his early faltering stages of walking. When maturation for walking is complete, the child is ready to walk with confidence. The sequential steps in the development of sitting up and walking are illus-trated in Figure 40.

Figure 39.
Mary Stands for Her
Picture on Her First Birthday.

Figure 40.   The Motor Sequence.

Adapted from *The First Two Years*, Vol. II, frontispiece, by Mary M. Shirley. Copyright 1933 by the University of Minnesota Press, Minneapolis, Minn. Reprinted by permission. Copyright renewed 1960.

Shirley studied the developmental sequence of sitting up and walking of twenty-five babies. A summary of her findings are reported in Table 4.

TABLE 4

Sequence for Walking *

I. *First order skills:* Passive postural control

Activity	Median age (weeks)
On stomach, chin up	3
On stomach, chest up	9
Held under arms in erect position, makes stepping movements	13
On back, tenses or stiffens spine for lifting	15
Held erect, keeps knees straight	15
Sits on lap (support at lower ribs and complete head control)	18.5

(This marks the end of the first third of the walking sequence.)

II. *Second order skills:* Postural control of entire trunk and undirected activity

Sits alone momentarily	25
Makes knee push or swimming movements when placed on stomach	25
On back, rolling	29
Held erect, stands firmly with help	29.5
Sits alone one minute	31

(This marks the completion of one-half of the walking sequence.)

III. *Third order skills:* Active efforts at locomotion

Makes some progress on stomach by crawling (i.e., drags or pushes abdomen along on the floor by his arms)	37
Scoots backwards on stomach	39.5

IV. *Fourth order skills:* Locomotion by creeping

Stands, holding to furniture	42
Creeps (abdomen lifted off floor; goes on all fours) (By this stage the child has accomplished two-thirds of the walking sequence.)	44.5
Walks when led	45
Pulls to standing position by holding on to furniture	47

V. *Fifth order skills:* Postural control and coordination for walking

Stands alone	62
Walks alone	64

* Adapted from *The First Two Years: A Study of Twenty-five Babies,* Vol. I, Table III, p. 99, and Chap. 6, by Mary M. Shirley. Copyright 1931 by the University of Minnesota Press, Minneapolis, Minn. Copyright renewed 1959. Reprinted by permission.

The maturational rate for the development of the power to walk varies considerably among children. The normal pattern of development may be interfered with by such factors as physical defects, ill health, or excessive weight. It seems safe to suggest that adults should not try to hasten maturational motor processes. Yet the child's motor development should be watched carefully by a pediatrician so that remedial difficulties are not allowed to persist.

Shortly after the child masters walking skills on an even surface, he learns to walk up and down stairs or sideways, to walk backward, and to run and climb. Ability to stand on one foot briefly, to gallop, to jump with both feet together, or to turn somersaults is achieved by the child by the end of the third year. He continues these motor activities so that, during the fourth year, he becomes skilled in many of his childhood motor activities. For example, his running, hopping, and skipping are skillfully done. By the end of the fifth year he has a high degree of skill in most fundamental forms of locomotion.

DEVELOPMENT OF ARM AND HAND CONTROL

The hands are very valuable in the performance of many motor activities. Motor development in these parts starts early and is observed in the reflex grasping and the arm slashing of the newborn. Arm and hand movements, however, need to be coordinated with such sensory activities as vision, touch, and the kinesthetic sense. The arm and hand responses exhibited during the neonatal period are basic to the many skilled manual activities in which the individual will participate during his developing years.

Arm-hand development appears to follow a more or less regular sequential pattern. Reflex grasping, which is present at birth, begins to decline in the second month. In the reflex grasp the thumb is not used in opposition to the forefinger; it is digital rather than palmar. Partial ability to use the thumb in opposition to the forefinger is present by the fifth month and is well established by the ninth month. Most adults are able to coordinate the thumb with the forefinger; they have developed the palmar grasp in prehension.

Halverson [5] found that twenty-seven of the ninety-seven infants studied under the age of twenty-four weeks were able to support their own weight suspended from a one-centimeter rod grasped with both hands. More infants could support their weight at birth and at four weeks than at later ages. In most instances the reflex did not obtain after twenty-four weeks. The strength of the grip also seemed to be affected by such factors as heightened activity and hunger.

Voluntary Grasping   If arm and hand skill is to develop smoothly, proper coordination is needed between the sensory and the related motor

[5] Halverson, H. M., "An Experimental Study of Prehension in Infants by Means of Systematic Cinema Records," *Genetic Psychology Monographs,* 10: 107–286, 1931.

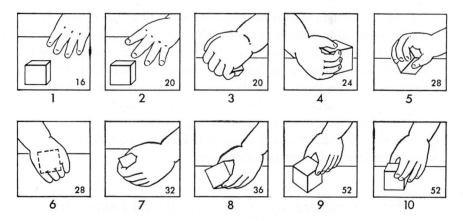

Figure 41. Developmental Progression in Grasping.

From H.M. Halverson, "An Experimental Study of Prehension in Infants by Means of Systematic Cinema Records," *Genet. Psychol. Monogr.* 1931, 10, 107–286, The Journal Press. By permission of the publisher.

parts. The amount of coordination between the eye and the hand during early infancy is minimal. It is not until the fourth week that a baby is able to use his eyes to follow a moving object through an arc of ninety degrees. The hand, especially, is richly supplied with sensory organs. Kinesthetic and tactual patterns, as they function in coordination with visual and auditory patterns, enable the individual to develop manual skills. The hand, through its importance as an exploratory organ, enables the child to make contact with his environment.

The use of the hands for grasping (prehension) was studied by Halverson. His extensive study not only gives a report of the findings but also includes diagrammatical illustrations of the hand and finger positions in the developmental progression in grasping that occur in infants ranging in age between sixteen and fifty-two weeks. Prior to sixteen weeks there is little or no contact, then the action starts with the infant's using the palm, then finger action of a clawing type; later, the finger is used in opposition to the thumb in a pincer movement. See Figure 41.

The behavior responses of an infant grasping a rattle were carefully observed by Curti.[6] Tests were begun at the age of 129 days. The rattle was held directly above and in front of the infant for a period of one minute, or until the infant grabbed it. During the early trials considerable

[6] Curti, Margaret W., *Child Psychology,* p. 95. New York: Longmans, Green and Company, 1938.

diffuse activity of the whole body was in evidence. There was much waving of the arms and kicking of the legs. The number of kicks of the legs involved in a single grasping of the rattle was noted. The general body activity decreased with learning. It was found that the infant, after nine or ten trials, could grasp the rattle quickly with a minimum of bodily kicking movements. In fact, the total number of kicks ranged from about forty at the first trial through eleven at the fifth trial to about six at the seventh trial and two at the thirteenth trial.

Because of the baby's great activity of his hands, it becomes necessary to provide him with objects which he can manipulate. Otherwise he may explore his body, including tugging at his hair and ears, sucking his thumb, grabbing his toes and putting them into his mouth, rubbing his stomach, or exploring his genital organs. Although this is the manner in which the genitals are discovered, no harm is likely to come from this behavior if it is short-lived, as will be the case for the greatest number of children. A few children who start a habit of handling their genitals as a sensuous experience need help to develop other more rewarding motor responses.

Hand Preference When prehension becomes effective for picking

 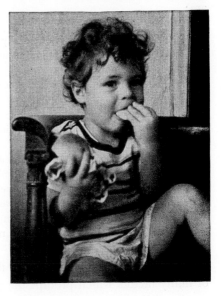

Wide World Photo

Figure 42. Muscular Coordination Shown by a Nine-Month-Old Child as He Reaches for His Father.

Figure 43. Two-Year-Old Bruce Shows Hand Dexterity in His Eating.

up tiny objects and when the eyes and hands become accustomed to work together, the child usually is about six years of age. The baby begins to show a hand preference by using one hand as he picks things up and puts them into his mouth. This is not the time to worry about the activity and the dirt involved; rather should one provide the baby with a clean place to play and the kind of objects which can be manipulated and put into his mouth. The motor response of the arm and hand is to the mouth, and the sucking motion of the lips is to take the object into his mouth. Before the age of two a child can hold an object in one hand as he eats from the other.

Handedness habits of older children have their beginnings in early childhood. The fact that left-handedness persists in spite of consistent opposition to it indicates that the roots are deeper than accidental stimulation. Parents and teachers are encouraged to allow the child great freedom in his choice of the hand he uses in whatever activity he engages, such as eating, throwing a ball, writing, using a key, handling a wrench, or sewing. Although there are a number of problems in this area to which we still do not have the answer, Hildreth suggests a number of reasons why handedness deserves consideration in child training. They are:

1. Achieving handedness is essentially a learning process involving habit formation, spontaneous reactions, postural adjustment, expression of choice, and responding in social situations.

2. The learning and adjustment process begins in infancy and is not completed until adulthood.

3. Emotional conflicts may arise due to the type of training the child receives.

4. There are physiological, neurological, and motor factors to be considered in handedness.

5. Individual differences are very great.

6. Conflicting theories influence training practices.

7. The question of whether handedness is hereditary or environmentally conditioned has never been satisfactorily answered.

8. There appears to be a connection between handedness and speech, as well as between handedness and learning to read, write, and spell.[7]

The hand that is preferred by the child may represent an interplay of many factors which prompt the particular individual to make use of one hand in preference to the other. These conditions may be within the

[7] Hildreth, Gertrude, "The Development and Training of Hand Dominance: I. Characteristics of Handedness," *Journal of Genetic Psychology*, Vol. 75, 1949.

United Press International Photo

Figure 44. Three-Year-Old Bradley Demonstrates Hand and Muscle Dexterity.

individual or in the environment, including the child's relationships with his elders and his playmates. That handedness is a strong tendency is agreed to; the factors that cause it do not merit the same degree of agreement. The questions remain: To what extent is hand preference inherited, caused by physical differences, such as dominance of one hemisphere over the other; caused by chance; or caused by environmental stimuli that emanate from a traditionally right-handed world? We are more concerned here with the fact of handedness and what consideration should be given to it than with further speculation as to its causes.

Gesell studied the time of appearance of the lateral function. He found that not only does laterality apply to hands but it also holds for other body parts. Laterality of function, according to Gesell, appears early in life and is a part of the individuality of the child. Some of his observations are included in the following:

Every infant seems to have what may be called a motor habitude or characteristicness which expresses itself in postural demeanor and modes of movement. . . . One of the most accessible of these is laterality, and even this presented wide variation among the five individuals. By laterality we mean right or left predilection or predominance in motor adjustment. One of our infants (Girl A) showed unmistakable left-handedness as early as twenty-eight weeks. She has remained definitely left-handed for five years. . . . Boy D has been emphatically right-handed. Foot dominance was determined by a careful study of the preferred foot used in prone progression. Boy D showed a right-foot dominance at thirty-six weeks; Boy A, left-foot dominance at forty weeks; Girl B and Boy B, left-foot dominance at forty-eight weeks. This dominance is a well-established trait, but we do not know how late in life it persists.[8]

Hand preference that shows itself as the child reaches for objects is the response that ought to be encouraged by parents and later by teachers. Although the use of the left hand has been less evident in the past, it is making a greater appearance as adult attitude toward its development is furthered. No longer is the child forced to change his handedness in throwing or writing. He is encouraged to use his right hand, but if his tendency to use his left hand persists he is not denied its development.

Handedness does not appear to be complete during the first year. Hence, whatever can be done to encourage the use of the right hand ought to be done during that time. Not only does a child show preference in handedness but also in eye and foot preference. Occasionally an individual shows almost equal preference for either hand. This ambidexterity is revealed among adults in various forms. One obvious example is that of the switch batter in organized baseball. Mickey Mantle, for example, is able to hit with equal effectiveness from either the right or the left side of the home plate. To that extent he is ambidextrous.

Experimental evidence is not clear relative to the effect of forced change of handedness. The major concern of parents and educators, however, is the degree to which a child's speech may be affected by such change-over. The results of studies seem to indicate that speech defects, especially stuttering, are more numerous among left-handed children who had been forced to write with their right hand. Bryngelson and Rutherford,[9] after studying seventy-four stutterers and seventy non-stutterers, report that they found "four times as much ambidexterity in the stuttering group as in the control group, and approximately eight times as much shifting of handedness is experienced by the stutterers." This points to the care that should be exercised in recommending a change-over in handedness.

The left-handed child in school is a problem to the teacher. The desks,

[8] Gesell, Arnold, "Early Evidences of Individuality in the Human Infant," *Scientific Monthly,* Vol. 45, pp. 221–222, 1946.

[9] Bryngelson, B., and Rutherford, B., "A Comparative Study of Laterality of Stutterers and Non-Stutterers," *Journal of Speech and Hearing Disorders,* Vol. 2, pp. 12–16, 1937.

inkwells, lighting arrangements, and other equipment are arranged to accommodate a right-handed learner. The child and the teacher are faced with the problem of adjusting to these conditions. The teacher has learned that continued interference with left-handedness may create difficult emotional and adjustment problems, with the result that the left-handed child becomes less skilled in penmanship and other motor skills than does the right-handed child. The paper for a left-handed writer is in an awkward position for writing. He is forced to write toward his body, thus finding that he always is in the way of a free-swinging arm movement. The child who writes with the right hand uses an arm movement that is away from his body. Thus the adjustments are many for the "lefty" who tries to fit into a right-handed writing world. Mental as well as motor adjustments become his to make and cope with.

Throwing Movements   The infant can throw a ball from a sitting position at about six months of age, give it definite direction at eleven months, and engage in cooperative ball play by thirteen months. Throwing is behavior in which the child likes to engage. Before he can do so he must be able to assume and maintain an upright posture. He also must develop other motor responses such as voluntary grasping, simple reaching, and opening of the hand to release an object before he is able to throw. By the age of two, if given training, the child can toss the ball and play a simple game of catch with a large ball.

Developing Skill in Writing   As with all early stages of the development of a complicated motor skill, mass activity characterizes initial efforts at writing. The child tends to involve the entire body when he gets set to write. He utilizes motor responses of the head, trunk, legs, and feet. Changes also occur in breathing and circulation. As the writing skill gradually is developed, noticeable motor responses are reduced and the writing continues with little overt evidence of these activities even though they are present. The child, however, must continue to focus attention on writing if he wishes to improve his skill in it.

A two-year-old child can hold a pencil between his thumb and fingers. When he is asked to write, he eagerly takes the pencil and moves it back and forth across the paper in relatively straight lines, in circles, or in overlapping curves. Although these movements appear to have no design, most two-year-olds tend to make similar designs. We now present the handwriting of three children, one twenty months of age, one twenty-eight months, and the third thirty-six months. Notice the similarity in the three. (See Figures 45 and 46.)

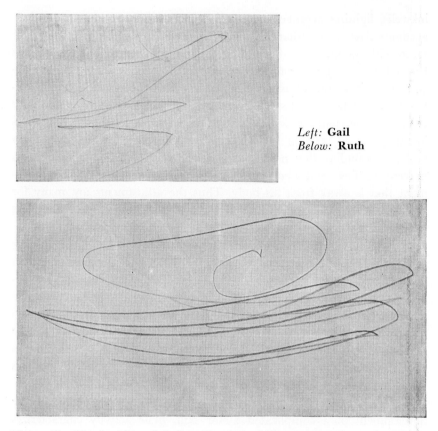

Left: **Gail**
Below: **Ruth**

Figure 45. Handwriting of Gail at the Age of Twenty Months; and of Ruth at the Age of Twenty-Eight Months.

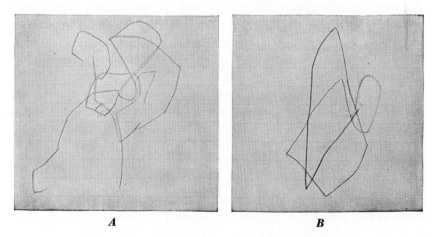

A   *B*

Figure 46. Handwriting of Martin at Age Three
A, Right Hand; B, Left Hand.

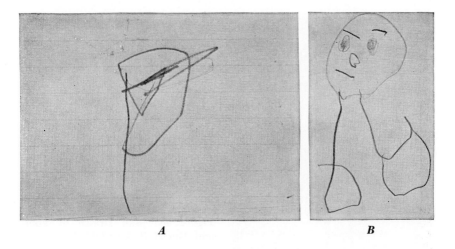

A   B

Figure 47. *A*—A Man Drawn by Three-Year-Old Martin; *B*—A Man Drawn by Bruce At the Age of Three Years and Ten Months.

In Figure 47 are shown the drawings of a man by three-year-olds. We also present samples of drawings of a man by a boy and a girl, each four and one-half years of age. (See Figures 48 and 49.) It is interesting to note that in both examples the hands are attached to the head. Also, the boy added ears and feet, and the girl added hands to the drawings.

GUIDING THE DEVELOPMENT OF MOTOR CONTROL

Motor activity of any kind involves responses to internal or external stimuli. These motor patterns include such *primary* body movements as walking, running, jumping, throwing, dancing, swimming, and skating; and such *secondary* movements as writing, painting, and using tools and implements that require both gross movements and finer muscle coordinations.

Acquisition of even a simple manual skill seems to depend on sensory acuity: tactual, visual, and kinesthetic. In early infancy there is little coordination between the eye and hand. After about forty weeks, however, the baby has acquired sufficient eye-hand coordination so that he can see and touch a small object placed before him. By the end of six years of life, the child is able to manipulate blocks, handle playthings, and effectively use implements for eating and drinking.

Figure 48. Man Drawn by Four-
and One-Half Year-Old James.

Figure 49. Man Drawn by Four-
and One-Half Year-Old Camille.

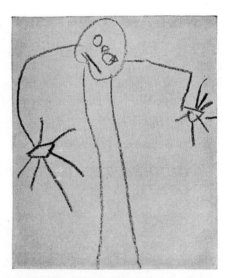

Value of Play in Motor Development The preschool child is
active in play of various kinds. Thus he learns about himself and his world.
He develops motor skills through actively constructing things or by
taking them apart. He learns about other children as he plays with them.
Often he plays by himself in the presence of other children, but sooner
or later he wants to play with them. Play is serious activity to the child
when permitted to choose the activities through which he tries himself
out.

The child displays many repetitive movements during the first few months which basically are play activities. He literally "plays" with his hands, his clothing, his toys, and with the production of sound. He also responds to others in his environment by means of a kind of social play, especially when initiated by the other person. Toward the end of his second year, he engages in imaginary play and imitates the movements of others.

After a time the play of the child is less influenced by his immediate surroundings and becomes less random in character. Up to the age of three the child may prefer playing alone; after this he shows a preference for playmates. He also begins to show an interest in materials which will give him an opportunity to create and construct. Although many of his activities may appear to be "aimless play," they become the practice and drill experiences which he needs in his struggle toward perfecting his motor coordinations. Thus he is provided with the raw materials of manipulation, building, climbing, jumping, and the like, as he attempts to improve his motor skills.

Many play activities in which the child engages involve an element of risk. In skill development, repetition is needed before the child learns

United Press International Photo

Figure 50. Motor Skills Are Developed as Children Roller Skate Together.

Figure 51.
Children Enjoy
Climbing Trees.

to climb stairs, to ride a bicycle, or to construct a mechanism with an erector set. However, if the play spirit prevails, the child is likely to persist until he attains successful achievement. He then is enabled to use his skill to enlarge his play activities. Thus play serves a useful purpose in the development of motor skills.

Value of Correct Practice Basic to the degree of proficiency of motor learning is the extent to which (1) the finer muscular responses are developed and (2) the motor responses become automatic. When the child acquires speed, precision or accuracy, steadiness or control, and strength of response he possesses a high degree of skill. Finer muscular responses are developed only after a long period of correct practice. Not only is practice required, but the practicing needs to be accompanied by an effort to eliminate any errors, a desire to succeed, and confidence that the skill can be perfected.

The aim of practice in motor learning that involves the fine muscles is to habituate correct responses. An individual is helped or hindered in the development of skills by the muscular patterns, acquired earlier, that are associated with the particular skill he is attempting to perfect. For example, habit patterns either aid or interfere with learning progress when an individual attempts to learn to ride a bicycle, repair a watch, type on a typewriter, play a musical instrument, and the like.

The effectiveness of practice in motor learning involves more than mere repetition. The outcomes of motor learning depend on such factors as the nature of the skill to be mastered, the age and special interest of the learner, the circumstances surrounding the practice, the time and place available for practice, the extent of and spacing of the practice periods, and the degree of skill performance desired. The teacher can help the learner focus on each of these, especially on the degree of proficiency desired. The other factors vary somewhat according to abilities and other considerations.

Sufficient and accurate practice of a motor response results eventually in its becoming automatic and relatively independent of the functioning of the higher mental processes, thereby enabling the individual to direct his attention to other aspects of the learning situation. Although drill is essential, practice as mere repetition may create unfavorable attitudes toward the task and thereby defeat the purpose for which it was intended. Practice should be effectively motivated and properly spaced.

Both the length of practice periods and the length of rest periods between them are significant in motor learning. Practice periods for young children should be shorter than for older children and adolescents. The length of practice periods and their spacing should vary not only with the age and ability of the learner, but also with the facilities available and the type of skill to be mastered. Relatively short practice periods, once or twice a day, are likely to be more effective for most learners than extremely long, less frequent periods of practice.

Importance of the Goal   The aim of motor learning that involves the fine muscles is to develop skill in their use. The simpler skills are mastered by utilizing movements already learned and combining these in a workable pattern. Eventually the goal of the learner is to develop good form in the skill. Those motor coordinations that promote proficiency in a particular skill are referred to as *form*. Individual differences play an important role here, since what constitutes good form for one child may not be good form for another. For example, two skilled violinists may hold their bows differently. A skilled performer eventually develops what becomes peculiarly his own form.

The form that the learner hopes to achieve may be patterned after that of successful men and women in a specific activity. Basic aspects of what constitutes good form include the learner's innate ability and his previous experiences. To illustrate, good batting form is indicative of the

United Press International Photo

**Figure 52.   Muscles and Motor Skills
Are Developed through Play.**

successful batter; good tennis form embodies body coordinations by the champion as he makes or returns the service.

Value of Knowledge of Procedures   A skilled person may be unable to explain the reasons for his high degree of skill. It is one thing to be able to give a skilled performance; it is another to be able to explain to a child exactly what is done or the manner in which it is achieved. The would-be teacher may know the reasons for what he does but be unable to find the language with which to express those ideas so that a less trained person can understand them. The skilled golf player is better able to demonstrate what he does than to tell another how he does it; the artist who paints a beautiful picture rarely can convey to another person the important qualities that are basic to his skill. Usually, the best help that can be given to a beginner is for the expert to demonstrate how to do it, and to offer simple suggestions on the developmental level of the learner.

The child who understands what to do as he participates in an activity has his confidence bolstered and is more likely to make an effort to participate in motor learning than is the one who lacks this understanding. Sometimes a child has less knowledge than he realizes; but if he is willing to face the failure needed to discover that he does not know and then increases his efforts to find out, he is well on his way toward learning the required responses. The child who retreats from the activity because he is afraid that he cannot succeed is the one who is likely to have difficulty in mastering the particular skill involved.

A parent, an older sibling, or a teacher can be of assistance in pointing out what to do when a child lacks this knowledge and by suggesting ways of proceeding. A child who shows fear in a learning situation involving motor responses needs help to stimulate him to want to master the skill. Leaders who have had experience with skill-development procedures utilize various approaches to inspire confidence before starting the skill activity. Marble playing develops confidence as well as skill.

The initial attempts at developing a skill rarely are successful. A child who is interested and ready to learn may discover that his first or even his sixth practice attempt is inferior to that of others or falls far below his own expectations. The teacher can do much to encourage the child during these awkward experiences, since he knows that a beginner can be helped to avoid discouragement in the development of motor skills if he realizes that perfection is not achieved during initial stages of practice. The learning of penmanship illustrates this principle. Try as he may, the child is unable to reproduce the model placed before him. Hence handwriting scales are available for the teacher's evaluation of the child's attempt to imitate the model, which is not to be used as an achievement standard for the learner.

Value of Criticism   In his efforts to help a child perfect a skill, the teacher is alert to any incorrect or faulty practices, calls them to the attention of the learner, and does all he can to assist the child to correct them. The teacher who is a skilled performer inspires confidence. Yet, it sometimes is more important that he is able to offer the beginner practical suggestions that will enable him to overcome his mistakes. Unless the teacher is able to give help at the beginning level, he may stimulate emotional blocks in the child that will interefere greatly with effective skill development.

Acme Photo

Figure 53. Champions Showing Their Skill with Marbles.

Normally, progress in skill improvement is likely to be irregular from day to day, in spite of any help that may be given in the form of constructive criticism. In motor development toward skill performance, attention should be directed toward correction of errors in gross movements. The child needs to become oriented to the general nature of the new practice activities before he is able to concentrate on the development of fineness of response. Criticism of the finer elements should be avoided at first. Constructive suggestions tend to encourage and are superior to those that are negative and derogatory. Praise for even a slight improvement acts as a tonic to a child who is interested in increasing his success in a performance. It tends to motivate him toward continuing the practice.

A child who has developed a skill to a high degree of proficiency is relaxed while he is performing. Although beginners are advised to relax, they usually become tense in order to reduce their mistakes, with the result that they actually increase them. Sometimes, if a friend encourages a child to learn a motor skill, the learner becomes more relaxed than if he were receiving formal instruction from an exacting teacher.

Learning Curve in Motor Learning Progress of motor learning can be charted on a graph for each practice. Learning curves indicate the general trend that nearly all motor learning takes. These curves usually show that there is a rapid initial spurt followed by a leveling off and then another rise. The leveling off, referred to as a *plateau* in the learning curve, indicates little or no rise in observable learning in spite of continued practice. Although no measurable gain is evident, it is believed that learning is taking place, however, because, with continued practice, another spurt of performance follows the plateau. During the interval of the leveling off on the curve, undoubtedly mental integration has occurred even though the learning curve does not indicate that fact. The learning curve, with the spurts and plateaus, is illustrated in Figure 54. Represented in the diagram is the improvement in the practice of placing pegs in holes, including the direction taken by motor in conjunction with more abstract learning.

Speed and Accuracy in Motor Learning Whether to emphasize speed at the expense of accuracy continues to confront persons who give instruction in certain motor skills. Both speed and accuracy are

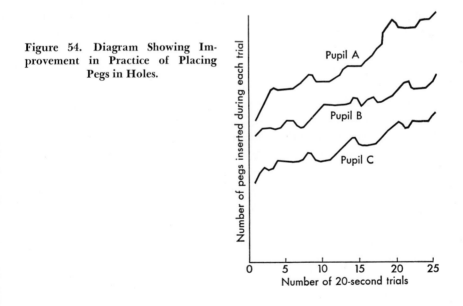

Figure 54. Diagram Showing Improvement in Practice of Placing Pegs in Holes.

important in the learning of such motor responses as eye-movements in reading, handwriting, learning to type, learning to play a musical instrument, or mastering a variety of motor activities. Experience has shown that both speed and accuracy should be considered together from the start of the training. For example, an individual becomes a skilled typist only if consideration is given simultaneously to both speed and accuracy.

When the importance of speed and accuracy is emphasized by the teacher, the child strives to reach these twin goals. Accuracy should not be sacrificed for speed; yet, slow performance does not guarantee accuracy. Beginners should be encouraged to complete the motor pattern at an acceptable speed, regardless of the errors that may be made. Practice of these complete patterns should continue as the individual attempts to eliminate any errors, until definite progress has been achieved. Emphasis should be placed on careful and painstaking execution that leads to the achievement of near perfect results. Hence motor learning should begin with learning by "whole" responses in which attention is given to both speed and accuracy.

Part learning may be needed to refine those weaknesses that have been discovered during the complete performance. For example, the golfer plays a game of golf, yet he spends many hours practicing his drive at one time, and his putting at another. The child attempts to ride a bicycle in toto, rather than to attend to balance alone. At one and the same time, he pedals, steers, and observes where he is headed. Success is his when he achieves coordination of all of them. The ballet dancer, for example, requires much practice before sufficient muscular coordination can be developed for a good performance.

Once motor responses are developed to the point of skill proficiency, the degree to which the habitual behavior remains ready to function depends on the extent to which the individual continues to use those motor activities. The kinesthetic phase of the skill is ever present, although a long period of disuse results in loss of efficiency. Usually a relatively short period of relearning is sufficient to restore the skill at least to its earlier level of proficiency. For example, it is likely that if you learn to ride a bicycle in your childhood, you will be able to ride it even after thirty years of disuse. Even though skills once developed are never lost, they require constant practice if the level of proficiency is to be maintained. The artist, the pianist, the professional golfer, and the baseball player realize the importance of this principle and continue practicing as long as they perform professionally.

As a summary, we present the main findings of many investigations as listed by Ragsdale.

United Press International Photo

Figure 55. Ballet Dancing Is a Difficult Skill to Develop but Is Enjoyed by Boys and Girls.

1. Good equipment and physical surroundings promote efficient learning.

2. Good instruction promotes efficient learning.

3. Learning should be concerned with meaningful units rather than abstracted part activities; the more advanced the learner, the more detailed may be his attack upon the activity.

4. A correct start is essential. This means that the learner must have a general understanding of the goal and of the activity that will attain it; it does *not* mean perfection at the first trial.

5. The learner must be able to get adequate information about his progress, *i.e.*, about his degree of success.

6. Demonstrations are particularly valuable for beginners.

7. Verbal directions should be used sparingly at first, but have more value as an adequate movement vocabulary is built up.

8. Manual guidance is particularly valuable for beginners.

9. Practice periods for a simple skill should be brief; in most motor activities ten to twenty minutes are most efficient for children of high school age; two or three minutes are often enough for preschool children. Concentrated practice should be avoided.

10. Long periods of no improvement are due to such things as boredom, distractions, poor teaching, persistent undesirable habits, radical changes in style, and ill health. They are avoided by good teaching.

11. Strong motivation leads to rapid learning.

12. It is possible to reduce learning efficiency by oversupervision; a large amount of independent activity is necessary for efficient learning.

13. A certain degree of maturity is required for the efficient learning of any

given activity. To attempt to learn an activity in advance of adequate maturity is wasteful.

14. Errors are best eliminated by *positive* instruction; inform the learner what to do rather than what to avoid. . . .

15. [Persistent errors should be studied and eliminated to provide for skilled performance; then turn to attempts to master the *good* performance.]

16. Efficient learning takes advantage of previous learning; it is built upon the facts of transfer of training and motivation.[10]

QUESTIONS AND TOPICS FOR DISCUSSION

1. If possible, observe for five minutes and list the movements of a neonate who is awake. Try to explain the causes of any movements you observed.

2. From the studies presented in this chapter, what do you conclude about the relative significance of maturation and learning in early motor development? How and to what extent can teaching approaches be modified in light of the findings? Give an example.

3. Try to discover from your mother or another adult what your early walking experiences were.

4. To what extent is left-handedness an innate characteristic? What should be done about it?

5. Why are boys popularly considered to be better ball players than girls?

6. Select one of your motor skills, such as bicycling, typing, or singing, in which you have achieved good performance. Trace your learning experiences. Were there any habits that you had to unlearn?

7. Try to teach an elementary school child a skill in which you are proficient. What difficulties do you encounter?

8. Visit a toy shop for children which specializes in special age toys. Report on the toys recommended for ages one through six. What differences do you find in constructor toys, for example?

9. *Special Project:* Have your four selected children draw the figure of a man. Note likenesses and differences.

SELECTED REFERENCES

Fleishman, E. A., "Testing for Psychomotor Abilities by Means of Apparatus Tests," *The Psychological Bulletin,* 50: 241–262, 1953.

Halverson, H. M., "An Experimental Study of Prehension in Infants by Means of Systematic Cinema Records," *Genetic Psy. Monographs,* 10: 107–286, 1931.

[10] Ragsdale, C. E., "Motor Development of the Child," in Skinner, C. E., and Harriman, P. L. (eds.), *Child Psychology,* pp. 102–103. New York: copyright 1941 by The Macmillan Company.

Hartley, R. E., and Goldenson, R. M., *The Complete Book of Children's Play.* New York: Thomas Y. Crowell, 1957.

Hildreth, Gertrude, "The Development of Training in Hand Dominance," *Journal of Genetic Psychology.* In Vol. 75, 1949: "I. Characteristics of Handedness," pp. 197–220; "II. Developmental Tendencies in Handedness," pp. 221–254. In Vol. 76, 1950; "III. Origins of Handedness and Lateral Dominance," pp. 39–100; "IV. Training of Handedness," pp. 101–144.

Jersild, Arthur T., *Child Psychology,* Chapter 5, 5th ed. Englewood Cliffs, N. J.: Prentice-Hall, Inc., 1960.

Jones, Harold E., *Motor Performance and Growth.* Berkeley: University of California Press, 1949.

Martin, K. L., "Handedness: A Review of the Literature on the History of Laterality Preferences," *Journal of Educational Research,* 45: 527–533, 1952.

Munn, Norman L., *The Evolution and Growth of Human Behavior,* Chapters 7 and 10. Boston: Houghton Mifflin Company, 1955.

Olson, W. C., *Child Development,* Chapter 4, 2nd ed. Boston: D. C. Heath and Company, 1959.

Stewart, L. H., "The Expression of Personality in Drawings and Paintings," *Genetic Psychology Monograph,* 51: 45–103, 1955.

Strang, Ruth, *An Introduction to Child Study,* 4th ed. New York: The Macmillan Company, 1959.

6

LANGUAGE DEVELOPMENT: ORAL SPEECH AND VOCABULARY

Effective communication with one's fellows is fundamental to successful participation in life activities. From earliest childhood, the individual possesses the urge to respond by one or another form of expressive behavior to self-stimulating elements of his environment. Responses may take the form of body movement, gesture, grimace, or spoken language. The felt need to give expression to one's wants and interests is innate; the ability to communicate with others through the utilization of the spoken or written word is learned.

The achievement of skill in language follows a generally continuous pattern of development. The sequential steps of progress can be classified roughly as (1) feeble gestures and reflex sounds, (2) babbling, (3) use of a simple spoken vocabulary, (4) relatively meaningful one-word sentences, (5) combination of words into thought units—at first oral and later written, (6) development of skill in reading, and (7) improved mastery of all the tools of communication.

There usually is some overlapping of sequential patterns, with no sharp gaps between the successive steps in language development. The rate of progress, however, may vary from sequence to sequence in the same child and differ among children. Individual differences, both inherent and induced by external conditions, exert a powerful influence on the rate and the limits of individual children's mastery of their language.

SIGNIFICANT INFLUENCES ON LANGUAGE DEVELOPMENT

Although one often hears the term *native language* applied to an individual's utilization of the vernacular, the child does not come naturally by his command of particular language patterns. Some of the influencing factors are peculiar to the individual, such as degree of intelligence and sex; others are the resultants of the kinds of stimulation to which the child is exposed during his formative years. The degree of success he achieves in comprehending and using the spoken or written word depends in great part on (1) his potential ability to acquire mastery of language tools, (2) the language patterns of those about him, and (3) the appropriateness of teaching-learning approaches in the language arts.

Much research has been undertaken to discover the psychological and sociological bases of similarities and differences among children in rate and amount of progress in language usage. Later in the chapter we discuss in some detail the findings of significant studies. At this point we are considering certain general study conclusions that deal with specific factors of influence on the development of skill in communication.

Innate Potentialities Differences among individual developmental patterns are caused in part by differences in native constitution. Progress in the achievement of linguistic skill is closely related to other areas of inborn characteristics, such as intelligence, physical status, motor development, and the sex of the individual. We shall discuss each of these factors briefly.

INTELLIGENCE Intellectual status is a prime factor of a child's degree of language mastery. Individuals differ in their potential ability to gain meaning from language symbols and to put meaning into them. Mentally alert young children usually are what is known as "early talkers." They seem to comprehend what is said to them, recognize objects and people around them, and call these objects and people by correct names. They are able to express themselves in meaningful phrases and simple sentences, and continue to excel less able children in all areas of language skill. Others are slow beginners, but later develop adequate language mastery. Still others, in spite of good learning motivation, continue to find clear understanding and correct usage of symbolic forms to be a difficult task.

Closely associated with differences in expressional abilities are differences in power to think clearly and concisely. In fact, commonly used instruments for the measurement of intelligence rely on verbal responses to spoken or written situational stimulations. Moreover, in daily life an individual's degree of mental activity is judged more or less informally by his linguistic expressions even more perhaps than by other forms of overt behavior. Adults find it difficult to evaluate an infant's mental potentialities mainly because he is not yet able to utilize language symbols.

PHYSICAL STATUS   Physical defects or poor health, insofar as the physical or health condition incites lack of confidence or apathy, may retard the development of effective self-expression. Good health, accompanied by wholesome curiosity, motivates the child to develop interest in the people and things that surround him and the desire to express his reactions to them.

MOTOR DEVELOPMENT   According to some researchers there is a relationship between general motor ability and articulation. Shirley found that after the age of forty-five weeks, babies showed some positive correlation between language development and motor coordination. As a result of her studies, Shirley concluded that, in spite of meager evidence, early vocalization seems to be held in check by rapid motor progress. The appearance of some gross motor abilities and language development have a cyclical relationship.[1]

SEX DIFFERENCES   When the language development of children having equivalent intelligence ratings and the same socio-economic status is studied under similar conditions, it appears that girls have a slight edge over boys. Even as infants, girls tend to vocalize earlier than do their brothers. Moreover, from their early years onward, girls are likely to give longer responses than do boys. The latter's sentences usually are terse; the former's sentences include what to them constitute significant details.

Apart from length of sentence, girls seem to make more rapid linguis-

[1] Shirley, M. M., *The First Two Years: A Study of Twenty-Five Babies,* Vol. II and Vol. III, *Personality Manifestations* (Institute of Child Welfare Monograph, Series No. 8). University of Minnesota Press, Minneapolis, 1933.

tic progress than do boys. In comparisons of same-age children's vocabularies, girls excel boys, as they also do in the comprehension of speech at an early age. If other inherent and environmental conditions are equal, girls tend to talk more than boys and to be more successful in beginning reading.

Speech defects, such as stammering and stuttering, are more common among boys than among girls. The greater incidence among males of reading and speech disabilities may be caused by the fact that, although girls achieve linguistic maturity earlier than do boys, members of both sexes having the same chronological age are exposed to similar language learning situations for which the boys are not yet constitutionally ready.

Parents who are unaware of sex differences in language development tend to become unduly concerned by the fact that a little son does not seem to keep pace with his sister or sisters. A young mother, for example, who kept a detailed record of "firsts" in the early life of her little daughter, was proud of the baby's apparent quickness of development in comparison with her neighbors' same-age children, but was ashamed of her son's slow progress.

Environmental and Cultural Influences Since much of a child's linguistic development is achieved through imitation of the language patterns to which he is exposed, environmental conditions and cultural background are extremely important motivators of the kind and amount of progress in language skill he can be expected to attain. Home and school share in providing models and other factors of influence that finally will determine the degree of effectiveness of language usage which can be expected of a developing boy or girl in light of his intellectual capabilities.

HOME INFLUENCE Parents and other family members exert considerable influence on a child's developing language patterns. Some adults seem to believe that young children cannot understand the meaning of polysyllabic words pronounced correctly. Hence they resort to so-called "baby talk," a practice that may interfere with the child's establishment of correct habits of pronunciation. Moreover, in some homes, speech patterns are incorrect or sloppy. A child from such a home is likely to bring to his formal schooling patterns of speech and grammatical usage which are satisfying to himself but socially unacceptable.

The number of children in a family and the age place of a child among siblings affect linguistic development. It would seem, for example, that a single child has more need to satisfy his wants by communicating with adults and older siblings than do twins who can gain satisfaction from communicating with each other by gesturing and other forms of expression, especially during preschool years. An only child or an oldest child can gain linguistic power from his contacts with adults that may not be experienced by younger children of a large family, since they may depend on siblings near their own age for satisfaction of their expressive needs.

Family background is an important factor of language development. The child is fortunate if his home offers many cultural advantages. When parents present models of correct speech and encourage their child to use reasonably careful speech, the development of good language habits by the child is accelerated. Contrariwise, the child reared in a home representing little more than the acquisition of life necessities, with relatively apathetic parental attitudes toward his developmental progress, may experience retarded language growth as a result of his meager cultural surroundings.

The kinds of experiences provided for children tend either to accelerate or retard linguistic progress. It would seem that travel and other stimulating activities motivate vocabulary building. This may account in part for the fact that children of parents in the upper socio-economic brackets generally are linguistically superior to children of less privileged families. In this connection it also might be noted that children who are reared in orphanages or other institutions usually are more retarded in their language development than are children of poor and uncultured parents. Even though institutionalized children are likely to be the products of low economic home surroundings, the marked retardation is closely associated with meagerness of environmental stimulation.

Another factor that can affect a child's linguistic progress is a bilingual environment. Whether bilingualism in the home hinders or improves language development still is a moot question. If the first language patterns have been well established before the young child is introduced to a second language, he may benefit from the two experiences in a way that would not occur if he delayed learning the second language until the teen years.

The child of foreign-born parents who are accustomed to use their mother tongue in the home rather than English usually is at a great disadvantage in an English-speaking group, especially when he first enters school. Unless the foreign language is common to the majority of the neighborhood children, his classmates are likely to tease him about his English deficiencies. Peer-age attitudes can give rise to emotional disturbance and stuttering unless the teacher is sympathetic toward the non-

English speaking child and helps him gain an understanding of and express himself in simple English. In such situations the other children, taking their cue from the teacher, often share in assisting their classmate to improve his knowledge of the language.

INFLUENCE OF THE SCHOOL   The effect of nursery school experiences on language development differs among children. The only child whose parents' socio-economic status is relatively high has become accustomed to adult-child communication. Hence he may seem not to enjoy mingling with same-age children during play or eating periods. Children from lower socio-economic homes in which there are other siblings may have had fewer preschool opportunities to talk with adults; they, therefore, are more likely to be willing to communicate with other nursery children.

Elementary school entrants differ from one another not only in their inherent ability to profit from instruction in the language arts but also in language habits resulting from their particular preschool background. An entrant's language development may be retarded because English usage in the home and in the immediate neighborhood has been inferior. Therefore, not only must he build upon his previously gained skill, but he must be helped to alter or unlearn certain fixed language habits, such as incorrect grammatical structure, inappropriate use of words, inaccurate pronounciation, and similar language errors.

One of the primary functions of teachers is to motivate some children to continue to build upon already developed good language patterns and to help other less fortunate young people improve or change completely the poor habits they had acquired earlier. To this end, the teachers themselves must possess language habits that are worthy of imitation. They also need to be alert to their pupils' language difficulties, since competence in any learning area depends on clear thinking and facility in precise, fluent expression. Appropriate educational approaches to vocabulary building, reading mastery, and skill in oral and written expression will be discussed later.

BEGINNINGS OF COMMUNICATION

Communication involves the utilization of four vocabularies: listening, speaking, reading, and writing. An adult possessing exceptional skill in the language arts may believe that he has equal command of all four vocabularies. The truth probably is that his mastery of the listening and reading vocabularies is greater than that of the other two. He also may be more fluent in oral communication than in written composition, no matter how expert he is in the latter. Adult performance in the vernacular has its roots in young childhood experiences in language understanding and expression.

Studies of Speech Development There have been many studies of language development that attempted to trace linguistic progress from infancy through the first four or five years of life. Some of these studies began with prelinguistic utterances; others started with the first intelligible word spoken. Early studies, going back to the 1890's, utilized relatively casual observation of the responses of individual children. Consequently, such biographical reports, especially those kept by parents, were generally unscientific, although they offered some valuable information which served as the bases of later research. Biographical studies of many groups of children in which more objective results were obtained through the utilization of finer techniques of obtaining and recording data have yielded a wealth of material about language development.[2]

It is generally agreed that there is a close relationship between language and thought. Jean Piaget, a researcher in the field from Switzerland, stressed this relationship.[3] As a result of his analysis of children's speech development, Piaget concluded that their attempts at communication can be categorized as egocentric and socialized. According to his findings, about 38 per cent of a young child's vocalization is egocentric, giving evidence of his concern with himself and of talking to himself. A relatively later development is socialized speech "in which the child addresses his hearer, considers his point of view, tries to influence him, or actually exchanges ideas with him." [4]

Later investigators tend to disagree with Piaget's high percentage of egocentric speech among young children. McCarthy, for example, in her study of language development found that egocentric speech as interpreted by Piaget includes, on the average, about 3.6 per cent for chil-

[2] See Leopold, W. F., "Speech Development of a Bilingual Child: A Linguist's Record": Vol. I, "Vocabulary Growth in the First Two Years" (1939); Vol. II, "Sound Learning in the First Two Years" (1947); Vol. IV, "Diary from Age Two" (1949); and "Bibliography of Child Language" (1952). *Northwestern University Studies of Humanities*, Northwestern University Press, Evanston, Ill.

Also see Lewis, M. M., *Infant Speech: A Study of the Beginnings of Language*, 2nd ed., New York, Humanities Press, 1951; and *Twenty-eighth Yearbook of the National Society for the Study of Education*, Chicago, University of Chicago Press, 1929.

[3] Piaget, Jean, *The Language and Thought of the Child* (translated by M. Warden). New York: Harcourt, Brace and Company, 1926.

[4] *Ibid.*, pp. 9–10.

dren between the ages of one and one-and-one-half years.[5] Regardless of a child's vocalization that can be regarded as egocentric, the fact that he vocalizes to himself about himself is a valuable asset in the development of language as an adjunct to thinking. Although this form of speech is a sign of immaturity, as he names things to himself, such as "baby," "choo-choo," "milk," "bye-bye," and the like, he is gaining personal experiences that serve a useful function in socialized thinking and language.

Prelinguistic Communication Some psychologists interpret the birth cry as the neonate's first attempt at vocalization; it is regarded more generally, however, as a simple reflex, having no personal intent. In fact, as far as is known, all of an infant's apparent responses to environmental conditions—his feeble gestures and early vocalizations—are reflexes instigated by all-over, felt needs. Many of the earliest sounds resemble the aspirate *h*, probably associated with the infant's gasping for breath. By the end of the first month of life, body movements, screaming, and crying begin to show some differentiation as expressions of hunger, wetness, cold, pain, or general body discomfort.

The first few months are characterized by the occurrence of different kinds of explosive vocalizations. These sounds, commonly referred to as *cooings*, are unlearned but constitute the beginnings of basic speech sounds. Cooings at first resemble vowel sounds, such as *a, aa, ugh*. Between the third and the eighth months, vowel sounds are combined with consonants and are repeated with some slight inflection, such as *uggle-uggle, erdah-erdah, oddle-oddle, ma-ma, da-da*. These *babblings* are sound combinations that represent a gradually developing pattern of vocalization.

Naive parents are likely to interpret *ma-ma* and *da-da* as indications that the baby recognizes his mother and father. The parents tend to repeat these babblings in the child's hearing; he comes to associate them with his parents or with any other person who ministers to his needs. Although the infant's first screaming, crying, and body movements are expressions of discomfort, his later cooings are likely to express feelings of comfort and relaxation.

Body Movements and Gestures Before a young child can give vent to his feelings through intelligible speech, he tends to use body movements and gestures to make his wants known. At first these move-

---

[5] McCarthy, Dorothea, "The Language Development of the Preschool Child," *Institute of Child Welfare Monograph Series*, No. 4, Minneapolis, 1930.

ments are feeble. As he gains greater control of body parts, responses to environmental stimuli become stronger and more definite.

The child wriggles and squirms to free himself from restrictions, such as being held too tightly. If he has had enough food or if the food is too hot or too cold, he turns his head away, puckers his face, closes his lips, or pushes the food away with vehement gestures of his hands. The grimaces and movements of rejection may be accompanied by crying and spitting or spewing action. The baby gives expression to feelings of pleasantness and relaxation by smiling and perhaps holding out his arms to be taken out of his crib and held by an adult. These outgoing responses usually are accompanied by soft cooings.

Language Development during the First Two Years During a child's first year, cooings gradually give way to or are accompanied by simple vocalizations that become increasingly intelligible. These are followed, in relative sequence, by greater understanding of gestures and commands, by imitation of gestures, and by one-word and then two- or more word sentences.

Developmental Studies Reports of studies show considerable uniformity in age of responses observed during the first few months. There is greater discrepancy, however, among responses toward the end of the two-year period. These differences probably are caused by differences in investigators' criteria in interpreting childish "jargon."

Many pages could be devoted to an analysis of studies of early linguistic development. McCarthy has prepared a table of eight such studies. The findings of researchers concerning 126 items are listed according to the age in months at which they first were observed. A careful study of these data can help the reader trace to-be-expected linguistic development in young children. (See Table 5.)

Cautions in Interpretation of Data As one reviews the data included in Table 5, it must be kept in mind that individual children differ in their rate of linguistic progress. Innate and environmental factors of influence discussed earlier in the chapter can affect the developmental pattern of a single child. Hence the age sequences presented in the table refer to expected trends as these are evidenced by the various young children studied rather than a growth pattern of a baby known to the reader. There is danger in a parent's or any other adult's accepting the results of studies as a kind of *sine qua non* of behavior. In fact, as we noted earlier, the various studies included in the table differ among themselves as to the exact age of the appearance of a particular item.

TABLE 5

Composite Table Showing Age in Months at Which Selected Language Items Are Reported in Eight Major Studies of Infant Development *

	Strictly longitudinal		Principally cross-sectional					
	Bayley (1933)	Shirley (1933)	C. Bühler (1930)	C. Bühler and Hetzer (1935)	Gesell, Thompson, and Amatruda (1938)	Gesell and Thompson (1934)	Gesell (1925)	Cattell (1940)
1 Vocal grunt								
2 Differential cries for discomfort, pain, and hunger		0.25						
3 Vocalizes small throaty noises	1.5				1.3	1		
4 Vocalizations								
5 Makes several different vocalizations								
6 Makes several vocalizations		2				2	4	
7 One syllable								
8 Vocalizes *ah, uh, eh*					1.3			
See Items 26–33.								
9 Attends readily to speaking voice	1.3					2		
10 Reacts positively to human voice				2				
11 Responds to voice								
12 Turns head on sound of voice					4			
13 Voice, attends (supine)								2
14 Voice, turns to (sitting)								4
15 Cooing			2				4	2
16 Coos								
17 Babbles or coos			3	3	3			
18 Returning glance with smiling or cooing							6	
19 Coos to music								
See Item 22.								
20 Two syllables		3						
21 Gives vocal expression to feelings of pleasure	5.9							
22 Actively vocalizes pleasure with crowing or cooing						3		
23 Vocalizes pleasure						6		
See Items 15–19, 36–37, 43–44.								

* Reprinted with permission from McCarthy, Dorothea, "Language Development in Children," in L. Carmichael (ed.), *Manual of Child Psychology*, 2nd ed., pp. 499–502. New York: John Wiley and Sons, Inc., 1954. Copyright 1954 by John Wiley and Sons, Inc.

TABLE 5—Continued

Composite Table Showing Age in Months at Which Selected Language Items Are Reported in Eight Major Studies of Infant Development

	Strictly longitudinal		Principally cross-sectional					
	Bayley (1933)	Shirley (1933)	C. Bühler (1930)	C. Bühler and Hetzer (1935)	Gesell, Thompson, and Amatruda (1938)	Gesell and Thompson (1934)	Gesell (1925)	Cattell (1940)
24 Vocalizes to social stimulus	3.1							
25 Responds vocally when socially stimulated See Items 38, 60.						4		
26 Vocalizes in self-initiated sound play								
27 Articulates many syllables in spontaneous vocalizations	6.3					4		
28 Vocalizes several well-defined syllables						6	6	
29 Says several syllables								
30 Vocalizes *ma* or *mu*					6.5			
31 Vocalizes *da*					7			
32 Two syllables—2d repetition of 1st—*mama* or *dada*	8				7			
33 Says *da-da* or equivalent	8.5					9		
34 Gives vocal expression of eagerness								
35 Vocalizes eagerness	5.6					5		
36 Vocalizes displeasure on withdrawal of coveted object								
37 Vocalizes displeasure	5.9					5		
38 "Talks" to a person See Items 25, 60.		6						
39 Distinguishes between friendly and angry talking			6					
40 Imitating sounds *re-re-re*—immediate or delayed response			6					
41 Imitates sounds								9
42 Incipient or rudimentary imitation of sounds See Items 65, 66, 68.						10		
43 Vocalizes satisfaction	6.5							
44 Vocalizing satisfaction in attaining an object See Items 21–23.						7		

TABLE 5—Continued

Composite Table Showing Age in Months at Which Selected Language Items Are Reported in Eight Major Studies of Infant Development

	Strictly longitudinal		Principally cross-sectional					
	Bayley (1933)	Shirley (1933)	C. Bühler (1930)	C. Bühler and Hetzer (1935)	Gesell, Thompson, and Amatruda (1938)	Gesell and Thompson (1934)	Gesell (1925)	Cattell (1940)
45 Singing tones								
46 Vocalizes recognition 47 Gives vocal expression to recognition	7.4	7.3				8		
48 Single consonants See Items 30, 31.		8						
49 Adjusts to words See Items 55, 62.					8			9
50 Vocalizes in interjectional manner 51 Local interjection	8.1					8		
52 Listens to familiar words See Item 61.	8.5							
53 Listens with selective interest to familiar words See Item 62.						9		
54 Understands gestures 55 Responds to bye-bye 56 Can wave bye-bye and often can say it			9		9		12	
57 Expressive sounds 58 Expressive jargon 59 Uses expressive jargon 60 Uses jargon conversationally	13.5	9				15 18		
61 Differentiates words See Item 52. 62 Makes conditioned adjustment to certain words See Items 69–77.	9.8					10		

TABLE 5—Continued

Composite Table Showing Age in Months at Which Selected Language Items Are Reported in Eight Major Studies of Infant Development

	Strictly longitudinal		Principally cross-sectional					
	Bayley (1933)	Shirley (1933)	C. Bühler (1930)	C. Bühler and Hetzer (1935)	Gesell, Thompson, and Amatruda (1938)	Gesell and Thompson (1934)	Gesell (1925)	Cattell (1940)
63 Vocalizes in cup-spoon situation					10			
64 Vocalizes in 2-cube situation					10			
65 Imitating syllables, *mama, papa, dada*	11.7		11					
66 Imitates words 40–42, 68. See Items 40–42, 68.								
67 One word		14						11
68 First imitative words (*bow-wow*, etc.) See Items 40–42, 65, 66.		15						
69 Adjusts to commands	11.5				10			
70 Inhibits on command								
71 Adjusts to simple commands								
72 Comprehends simple verbal commissions								
73 Places cube in or over-cup on command								
74 Understanding simple commands			15–17	13–15				
75 Understanding a demand ("Give me that" with gesture)						12	12	
76 Understanding a command ("Sit down" or "lie down" or "stand up", with gesture)			21–23			12		
77 Putting watch to ear on command 1 See Items 62, 95.			21–23					
78 Responds to inhibitory words					12			
79 Understanding a prohibition				16–18				
80 Understanding a forbidding			18–20					
81 Says 2 words	12.9							
82 Says 2 words or more						12	12	
83 Says 2 words besides *mama* and *dada*					12		12	12

TABLE 5—Continued

Composite Table Showing Age in Months at Which Selected Language Items Are Reported in Eight Major Studies of Infant Development

	Strictly longitudinal		Principally cross-sectional					
	Bayley (1933)	Shirley (1933)	C. Bühler (1930)	C. Bühler and Hetzer (1935)	Gesell, Thompson, and Amatruda (1938)	Gesell and Thompson (1934)	Gesell (1925)	Cattell (1940)
84 Vocalizes when looking in mirror					12			
85 Says 3 words or more					13	15		13–14
86 Says 4 words or more					13	18	18	15–16
87 Words, 5								
88 Names 1 object (ball, pencil, cup, watch, scissors)	17.4			19–24				
89 Names picture in book (dog)		19						
90 Naming 1 object or more	18.7							
91 Names 1 picture		22.5				21		
92 Names picture in book (baby)								
93 Asks with words See Items 101–103.							18	17–18
94 Says "Hello," "Thank you," or equivalent						18	18	
95 Points to nose, eyes, or hair							18	
96 Comprehends simple questions See Items 69–77.								
97 Names Gesell watch on fifth picture See Item 113.	19.4							
98 Names 2 objects	19.6							
99 Repeats things said				30		21		
100 Repeats 4 syllables (2 words)								
101 Joins 2 words in speech						21		21–22
102 Words, combines						24		
103 Uses words in combination See Item 93.								

TABLE 5—Continued

Composite Table Showing Age in Months at Which Selected Language Items are Reported in Eight Major Studies of Infant Development

	Strictly longitudinal		Principally cross-sectional					
	Bayley (1933)	Shirley (1933)	C. Bühler (1930)	C. Bühler Hetzer and (1935)	Gesell, Thompson, Amatruda and (1938)	Gesell Thompson and (1934)	Gesell (1925)	Cattell (1940)
104 Names 3 pictures	21.2							23–24
105 Picture vocabulary 3								23–24
106 Names 3 objects	21.5							
107 Names 3 objects in picture							36	23–24
108 Identifies 4 objects by name						24		
109 Names 3 of 5 objects								
See Items 104–107.								
110 Names familiar objects like key, penny, watch	24.4						24	
111 Points to 5 objects on card						24		
112 Names 5 pictures						30		
113 Names Gesell watch and picture	24.5							
See Item 97.								
114 Points to 7 of 10 simple pictures	25.1						24	28–30
115 Points to 7 pictures						30		25–27
116 Picture vocabulary 7 (1937 Stanford-Binet)	32.9							25–27
117 Names 7 pictures								
118 Pictures, points to 6								25–27
119 First pronoun		23						
120 Uses pronouns past and plural							36	
121 First phrase		23						
See Items 124–126.								
122 First sentence		23						
123 Uses simple sentences and phrases							24	
124 Distinguishes in and under								
125 Understands 2 prepositions	25						24	
126 Understands 3 prepositions	28							

VOCABULARY AND LENGTH OF RESPONSE

The baby's "first word" may seem to be an earth-shaking event in the lives of doting young parents. Cold facts reveal that it is difficult to determine when a word is known. The exact age of its occurrence may range from eight months for superior babies of high socio-economic status to twenty months in cases of pathological retardation. On the average, however, the first intelligible word usually is spoken by the age of ten or eleven months. Writers in the field generally agree that the first word is a monosyllable that may be duplicated, such as "tick-tick," "ma-ma," "da-da," or "bye-bye." Early vocalizations, like "bye-bye," tend to be imitations of adult-made sounds accompanied by gestures that put meaning into the word for the baby.

Growth of Vocabulary The first known words characteristically are nouns or interjections. The baby may use a noun to connote various meanings or emotional reactions. For example, the vocalization of the word "milk" accompanied by voice intonation and gesture may imply "Where is the milk?" "I want milk" or "There is the milk." A single word functions as an expression of the child's immediate need, wish, or feeling.

After the child has learned to use single words satisfactorily, he can be expected to increase his vocabulary rather slowly at first, then rapidly through the preschool years. Degree of intelligence as well as the kind and amount of environmental stimulation afforded him determines the extent of vocabulary growth. Cumulative studies of vocabularies during the preschool years are fairly satisfactory. Since experiential factors affect the later development of vocabulary, it is difficult to trace its exact progress.

According to McCarthy three basic difficulties have contributed to the confused state of the literature on children's vocabularies. These are: (1) the difficulty of determining the proper criterion for *knowing* a word, (2) failure to *define* the word as a unit of measurement, and (3) inadequacy of methods in selecting words from the dictionary for vocabulary tests.[6]

One of the studies in vocabulary development that appears to be more definite than some others is that conducted by Medorah E. Smith.[7]

[6] McCarthy, Dorothea, *op. cit.*, pp. 528–529.

[7] Smith, Medorah E., "An Investigation of the Development of the Sentence and the Extent of the Vocabulary in Young Children," *University of Iowa Studies, Child Welfare*, 3, No. 5, University of Iowa Press, 1926.

Smith devised a vocabulary test by selecting words from Thorndike's list of the 10,000 words frequently found in writing samples. She standardized this test for children of one to six years of age, determining their understanding of the meaning of the words by the utilization of pictures and questions. In Table 6 are reported the results of Smith's study. Although her findings appear to present an accurate picture of growth trends during preschool years, it must be remembered that no provision is made for discovering knowledge of words that were not included in Thorndike's list.

TABLE 6

Average Size of Vocabularies of Children in Relation to Age *

Age Years	Months	Number of children	Number of words	Gain
	8	13	0	
	10	17	1	1
1	0	52	3	2
1	3	19	19	16
1	6	14	22	3
1	9	14	118	96
2	0	25	272	154
2	6	14	446	174
3	0	20	896	450
3	6	26	1222	326
4	0	26	1540	318
4	6	32	1870	330
5	0	20	2072	202
5	6	27	2289	217
6	0	9	2562	273

* Smith, *op. cit.*, p. 316.

Medorah Smith's study dealt with vocabulary development during the preschool years. Mary Katherine Smith performed a study of vocabulary growth through elementary and high school.[8] She stated as her purposes of the study:

1. To determine the criteria of knowledge and the procedures necessary for measuring the absolute size of vocabulary among subjects below college level and particularly at the lower ages.

2. To employ these procedures in determining the individual differences in size of vocabulary over the range from the first to twelfth grades inclusive.

3. To determine the central tendencies and variables of these measurements for a description of the growth of vocabulary during this period.

[8] Smith, Mary K., "Measurement of the Size of General English Vocabulary through the Elementary Grades and High School," *Genetic Psychology Monograph*, 24: 311–345, 1941.

4. To provide tentative norms in the absolute size of vocabulary for this range of age and grade levels.[9]

The investigator constructed a test from a sampling of Funk and Wagnall's *New Standard Dictionary of the English Language* (1937 ed.). The test consisted of three parts:

Part 1: 173 multiple choice items made up of basic general terms, approximately in order of difficulty.

Part 2: 158 words, proper words or rare words. The subject was to select those words he knew and write their definitions.

Part 3: 40 derived words, variations in parts of speech, and compound and technical terms in order of difficulty.[10] In order to obtain the actual size of vocabulary, measurement was made only of the number of words for which the subject had some effective knowledge. Children in grades 1, 2, and 3 of the elementary school were tested individually and orally. Those in the middle elementary grades needed some help in reading. Older subjects received only directions for proceeding and occasional aid in reading. Any given correct meaning of a word was accepted.

The subjects of the study were 867 pupils from two schools in Ohio and one school in Illinois. The findings according to age of school population are presented in Figure 56.

Smith found that although there was overlapping of scores from age to age and grade to grade, there is progressive growth in average size of vocabulary, but the increase is not regular. Some of the factors that might influence children's rate of growth include extent of reading; experiences (conversation, trips); methods of teaching words, such as word drills, analysis of words; composition writing and the like. It also must be kept in mind that this study is based on a relatively small number of subjects for each of the respective grades. The largest number for any grade was 114 in the ninth grade, with 44 in the first grade, and 64 in the twelfth. Although this study probably presents no more than a *minimal* vocabulary for each of the age levels, it gives some indication of the vocabulary growth that can be expected during preadult years.

Length of Response   We have noted earlier that the very young child uses word sentences that usually take the form of nouns. The meaning of the sentence-word is indicated by the appropriate gestures or voice intonation. The growth in vocabularly is accompanied by the use of longer responses, including various parts of speech.

[9] Smith, *op. cit.*, p. 319.
[10] *Ibid.*, p. 319.

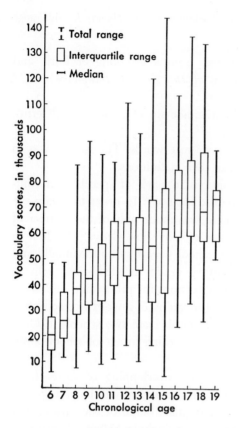

Figure 56. Total Vocabulary Scores of Chronological Age Groups.

Florence Young conducted a study of four groups of seventy-four children (regular boys, relief boys, regular girls, and relief girls, respectively) ranging in age from 30 to 65 months, with a mean of 47.6 months.[11] The children studied had percentile ranks of 70 to 46 on the Merrill-Palmer Scale of Mental Tests.

Young's method of procedure was to observe the language behavior of each of the seventy-four subjects for six hours. In addition to her conclusion that socio-economic status and family condition are important factors of language development, she found that at thirty months of age the mean length of response is 3.2 words, and at sixty months 5.2 words.[12] Her results also gave evidence of the fact that the number of words spoken during a ten-minute period is greater for girls than for boys, as indicated in Table 7.

[11] Young, Florence M., "An Analysis of Certain Variables in a Developmental Study of Language," *Genetic Psychology Monographs,* 23: 3–142, 1941.
[12] *Ibid.,* pp. 123–124.

TABLE 7

Number of Words Spoken in 10-Minute Periods *

Group	Words spoken
Regular boys	46.91
Relief boys	40.02
Regular girls	60.77
Relief girls	47.27

* *Ibid.*, pp. 123–124.

Another finding of this study has to do with the parts of speech used by the children. There appeared to be a decrease with age in the use of nouns and interjections and increase in pronouns, adjectives, verbs, and certain relational words. In this study, pronouns and verbs yielded the largest percentage at all ages. (See Table 8.)

TABLE 8

Parts of Speech Used by Children *

Parts of speech	Per cent of use
Nouns	16.0
Pronouns	25.0
Verbs	29.2
Adverbs	10.9
Adjectives	7.1
Conjunctions	1.7
Prepositions	4.3
Articles	2.4
Interjections	2.8

* *Ibid.*, pp. 125–126.

Many other studies have been conducted to determine mean length of sentence in spoken language at various ages.[13] According to McCarthy, "In general, it may be seen that the child of 18 months is still essentially in the 1-word-sentence stage and that he is just beginning to combine words. A year later, sentences of 2 or 3 words are most typical, and by 3½ years complete sentences averaging about 4 words each are used. By 6½ years the mean length of sentence is about 5 words, and by early elementary school years it appears to level off at about 7 words." [14]

In conjunction with quantitative analysis of sentence usage, researchers also have given attention to the qualitative study of grammatical form and sentence structure. Since the latter are significant aspects of written composition, we discuss them in greater detail in

[13] See Dorothea McCarthy for a report of these studies, *op. cit.*, pp. 542–551.
[14] McCarthy, Dorothea, *op. cit.*, p. 550.

Chapter 7. At this point we shall illustrate the qualitative approach by comparing the age findings of McCarthy, Davis, and Hahn.[15] (See Table 9.)

SPEECH DIFFICULTIES

Psychologists and educators have been engaged in considerable research concerning the causes of evidenced speech disorders and the possible relationship between faulty speech and emotional disturbance or personality deviation. Slow maturation, inadequate learning, and environmental conditions resulting in the onset of emotional tensions or other forms of emotional maladjustment often are accompanied by socially unacceptable speech or difficulties of articulation. We shall review briefly some common forms of speech inadequacies.

Faulty Speech during the Preschool Years The young child may develop incorrect speech habits or unintelligible speech partly because of slow maturation but more generally as a result of poor or inadequate environmental stimulation. Childish errors may be caused by omission of letters, such as *thow* for *throw, weet taters* for *sweet potatoes,* or inability to pronounce letters correctly, e.g., *dederbs* for *preserves.* If the young child is exposed to incorrect grammar in the home or immediate neighborhood, he may continue through adulthood to use incorrectly, for example, the pronoun forms *I* and *me* or *who* and *whom* and the double negative.

Earlier we noted that some parents seem to believe that young children cannot understand adult-used words if they are pronounced correctly. Hence they resort to a kind of abbreviated language in addressing a little boy or girl. If or when the child imitates this so-called "baby" talk, it often is regarded as cunning by the adults, and a little girl especially is encouraged to continue the incorrect speech pattern. Such habits formed in young childhood may cause embarrassment to the user in his later life. Generally, however, faulty speech habits acquired during the preschool period can be overcome as a result of consistent correction.

[15] McCarthy, D., "The Language Development of the Preschool Child," *Institute of Child Welfare Monograph Series,* No. 4, Minneapolis, 1930; Day, E. J., "The Development of Language in Twins: I. A Comparison of Twins and Single children," *Child Development,* 3, 179–199, 1932; Davis, E. A., "The Development of Linguistic Skill in Twins, Singletons with Siblings, and only Children from Age 5 to 10 Years," *Institute of Child Welfare Monograph Series,* No. 14, University of Minnesota Press, 1932; Hahn, E., "Analyses of the Content and Form of the Speech of First Grade Children," *Quarterly Journal of Speech,* 34, 361–366, 1948.

TABLE 9

Mean Percentages of Total Responses in Each Construction Category at Various Age Levels in Three Comparable Studies *

Age in years	Investigator		Type of sentence											
			Functionally complete		Simple		Simple with phrase		Compound and complex		Elaborated		Incomplete	
	Singletons	Twins	Single-tons	Twins	Single-tons	Twins	Single-tons	Twins	Single-tons	Twins	Single-tons	Twins	Single-tons	Twins
1½	McCarthy	Day †	78.4	70.0	9.6	7.5	0.0	2.0	0.0	.2	0.0	0.0	11.9	19.7
2	McCarthy		53.8		17.3		1.4		.9		.6		25.1	
2½	McCarthy	Day	35.3	48.0	38.7	23.0	5.3	4.0	1.5	.5	1.2	.3	18.1	24.6
3	McCarthy		27.2		45.1		8.7		1.5		1.3		16.2	
3½	McCarthy	Day	30.6	48.0	35.3	28.0	11.4	7.5	6.5	1.5	2.3	.9	13.9	13.3
4	McCarthy		32.0		39.4		10.9		6.1		4.5		6.8	
4½	McCarthy		31.2		36.5		10.4		7.0		5.9		8.8	
5		Day		49.0		24.0		7.0		3.6		1.0		15.4
5½	E. A. Davis		39.4	38.0	29.4	31.4	7.8	7.8	4.6	4.6	3.6	2.8	15.0	15.4
6½	E. A. Davis		32.0	28.6	30.8	32.2	9.8	10.8	5.4	7.4	5.6	5.8	16.4	15.2
6½	Shire		16.4		29.7		21.3		8.4		8.2		15.8	
6½	Hahn Adult situation		22.0‡‡		33.2		17.0§		25.5		2.4‡‡		††	
	Class situation		9.‡‡		27.8		23.2§		34.8		10.9‡‡		††	
9½	E. A. Davis		33.6	34.8	18.8	22.2	11.4	10.8	6.8	5.4	10.0	10.2	19.4	16.6

† Figures from Day have been estimated from graphs.
‡‡ Hahn uses only the category of "non-sentences" which probably includes both incomplete sentences and functionally complete ones here classed as functionally complete.
§ Hahn's elaborated sentences involved two or more independent units with one or more subordinate clauses. Cf. McCarthy's definition (1930, p. 44).

* From McCarthy, Dorothea, *op. cit.*, p. 553.

Moncur, J. P., "Symptoms of Maladjustment Differentiating Young Stutterers from Non-Stutterers," *Child Development,* 26: 91–96, 1955.

Natchez, Gladys, *Personality Patterns and Oral Reading: A Study of Overt Behavior in the Reading Situation as it Reveals Reactions of Dependence, Aggression, and Withdrawal in Children.* New York: New York University Press, 1959.

Piaget, J., *Language and Thought of the Child.* London: Routledge and Kegan Paul, 1926.

Travis, L. E. (ed.), *Handbook of Speech Pathology.* New York: Appleton-Century-Crofts, Inc., 1957.

7

LANGUAGE DEVELOPMENT: LISTENING, READING, AND WRITTEN EXPRESSION

THE VARIOUS ASPECTS of language development do not progress in isolation. As the child acquires skill in oral expression, he also is learning to become an effective listener, begins to read simple written or printed material, and later starts to gain mastery of written expression. In this chapter we shall discuss the developmental patterns involved in these three media of communication.

UNDERSTANDING OF SPOKEN LANGUAGE

To acquire an understanding of oral language necessitates the development of the power to listen intelligently to the spoken word and put meaning into each word heard. The acquiring of listening skill progresses gradually and depends upon maturation and training.

Development of Skill in Listening   For one or more reasons adults as well as children often fail to gain complete understanding of that to which they are supposed to be listening, even though they show a receptive attitude. Sometimes attention is divided; the person believes that he is listening to what is being said by another, but thoughts about other matters distract him and he finds himself only partly conscious of the import of the words that he hears. Often a person hears only what he wants to hear. An emotional bias or block may cause him to misinterpret the connotation of the words of the speaker and accompanying voice intonation or gestures. Many times the listener is unacquainted with the terminology used and is left with confused understanding or almost complete misunderstanding.

Children's Listening Difficulties   Children often find it difficult to follow adult speech intelligently, since their elders seem to assume that immature young people possess background experiences similar to their own. Let us assume, for example, that a young child through experience has put meaning into the word symbols for "cow," "dog," "bread," "butter"; he can name a piece of *wood;* he knows what it means to *slip* on an icy pavement. Should he therefore be expected to recognize, without further explanation or actual experience with them, that adults are referring to flowers or blossoms when, in conversation, they use the terms "buttercup," "dogwood," "cowslip," or "bread-and-butter"? These and many other words that constitute the daily vocabulary of older children and adults may be the source of much confused thinking to the little boy or girl who tries to give them a literal meaning.

Another source of communication difficulty between young children and their elders is the latter's inadequate handling of the former's questions. The young child who is becoming aware of the world about him tends to be a veritable question box. He seems constantly to be asking the *why, what, how,* and *where* of everything in his immediate environment or concerning his relationships with others. Some questions are unanswerable; others are asked by the child to hear himself talk, since he either gives the answer himself or does not wait for it before he asks another question. Two mistakes made by adults are (1) to engage in a long, complicated explanation which children are unlikely to understand, and (2) to refrain from responding to the question by telling the child that they are busy or that he is too young to understand. The wise parent or other adult answers the child's questions simply but briefly, without extraneous comments.

Helping Children Develop Skill in Listening   Psychologists and educators recognize the need of teaching young people not only to understand and respond correctly to what is said by others in conversations with associates and in classroom situations but also to evaluate intelligently all the one-way communication by which they are stimulated, for example, through the media of radio and television. Adults, especially parents and teachers, tend to admonish children to "pay attention" or to "listen carefully," sometimes without realizing that listening, like reading, involves more than the assumption of an attentive attitude or body position.

That to which a child is expected to listen needs to be associated with his background of experience and to motivate him toward constructive thinking. The child who is reared in an enriched home, neighborhood, school, or wider environment is much more likely to profit from spoken language than one brought up under meager social conditions. Moreover, no matter how alert a child is or how stimulating his surroundings, the acquiring of listening skill follows a sequential pattern of development.

The skilled listener has learned to enjoy listening. He recognizes the fact that communication is a two-way process and appreciates the value of listening as an aid to learning. He is attentive to oral directions and is able to follow them if they are within his range of comprehension. The good listener does not draw conclusions until he has listened carefully to and digested what has been said, keeping an open mind, maintaining an intelligent attitude, and raising pertinent questions when these are needed to clear his thinking.

The realization that children need to be trained to become efficient listeners is not a new goal of education. In 1928 Paul Rankin directed attention to its importance.[1] Before the recent past, however, reading received greater emphasis as an area of learning than did listening. We now recognize the complex nature of skill in listening and are attempting to assist children in the mastery of the various skills involved in good listening. Pratt and Greene list the skills as:

I. Word perception
   A. Recall of word meanings
   B. Deduction of meanings of unknown words
II. Comprehension of ideas
   A. Noting details

[1] Rankin, Paul T., "The Importance of Listening Ability," *English Journal* (College Edition), Vol. 17, October, 1928, pp. 623–630.

    B. Following directions

    C. Organizing into main and subordinate ideas

    D. Selecting information pertinent to a specific topic

    E. Detecting clues that show the speaker's trend of thought

III. Using ideas to build understanding

    A. Evaluating an expressed point of view or fact in relation to previous learning

    B. Making justifiable inferences.[2]

Parents who are aware of these various listening skills can apply them during children's preschool years. It is the function of school people, however, to organize a program of listening education that is based on the following principles of learning:

1. *Children learn what they practice.* Unless positive steps are taken to teach listening, it is fair to assume that the learning may be negative.

2. *Children need to understand what it is that they are trying to learn.* Talking about listening will help them to understand that it is like reading in some ways, but unlike it in other ways.

3. *Children need to become aware of their ability to listen.* Listening has been taken for granted for so long that it is best to begin any program of instruction by administering a standardized test, or a teacher-made test, as a means of motivating children to set up individual and group goals for the improvement of listening.

4. *Children need opportunities to discover that they can improve their listening ability.* It is difficult to tell children exactly what they must do to improve their listening ability. However, if they are given an adequate number of opportunities to listen for various purposes and to evaluate the results of their efforts, they will discover those things which make a real difference in their comprehension.

5. *Oral reading should be taught so that it fosters good listening.* When children read new material in a well-prepared manner to their classmates, they are providing good listening experiences. When these experiences are followed by discussions and other activities, they provide the listener with an opportunity to react.

6. *Oral language is taught with an emphasis upon communication.* Young children should have many opportunities to express ideas orally to their classmates and to be judged by what they communicate, not by how they speak. When the emphasis is upon communication of ideas, children will become concerned with what they say and whether it is understood by their listeners. As the communication process becomes understood, there will be a need to teach children to use better posture, a more pleasing voice, and accurate grammar.

7. *Children have opportunities to listen to difficult material read to them by the teacher.* Elementary-school children usually can comprehend materials read to them, which are one or more years above their reading level. Content materials read by the teacher, or by a child who is a good oral reader, will provide excellent listening experiences.

[2] Pratt, Edward, and Greene, Harry A., "Training Children to Listen," *A Monograph for Elementary Teachers,* pp. 2–3. Evanston: Row, Peterson and Company, copyright 1955.

8. *Individual differences in listening should be recognized.* It is common practice for teachers to repeat directions and instructions so that the slowest child in the room will comprehend. This teaches brighter children not to listen the first time but to adjust to the pattern followed by the teacher. Children will become better listeners if instructional talking is done at a higher-than-average level to challenge all children. If a few children comprehend less well, they should be helped to improve their listening in a separate grouping.[3]

DEVELOPMENT OF READING SKILL

The acquisition of skill in reading is closely associated with the development of adequate understanding and use of spoken language. Although reading is commonly regarded as the ability to obtain ideas from the printed or written page, a better description of reading might be the power of an individual to put meaning into symbols to which he responds visually in much the same way as he has learned to give thought to language symbols to which he responds through hearing. As with the gaining of skill in oral language, the development of reading skill depends on maturational progress and environmental stimulation.

Preschool Reading Experiences Learning to read generally is associated with the child's formal schooling. Yet, preschool experiences that include a rich background of sensory experiences and many opportunities for the kind of first-hand acquaintance with activities that aid concept development (see Chapter 8) are preparatory steps in learning to read. These provide the bases for the generalizations that children are increasingly able to form. They put meaning into the word symbols used to read, and make reading an exciting experience for children. In too many kindergartens, for example, emphasis upon reading readiness is almost completely in the form of "workbooks" matching pictures and ideas, with little or no appreciation of their larger implications. This is only one aspect of preparation for reading and should be recognized as such.

In addition to his other life activities, the young child's preschool experiences with picture viewing and listening to stories either told to him or read to him by adults serve as preparatory steps in the whole pattern of learning to read. Most young children delight in having simple stories within their power of comprehension told or read to them by a sympa-

[3] Lewis, Maurice S., "Teaching Children to Listen." Reprinted from the April 1960 issue of *Education*. Copyright 1960 by the Bobbs-Merrill Company, Inc., Indianapolis, Indiana.

thetic adult, especially if they are sitting on the adult's lap and seemingly following a story read to them from a well-illustrated story book. Some children seem to have photographic memories. They want to hear the same story over and over, and correct any accidental changes of words in the retelling or rereading.

Many children before the age of three years can identify simple pictures that are free of extraneous details. The eighteen-month-old child, for example, can identify a picture of a dog which he has seen previously, and say, "Bow-wow." About six months later, he should be able to identify pictures of animals, objects, or people with which he has had experience. By the end of the third year he usually can name letters in alphabet books or on blocks. During the next two years the child progresses to the extent that, by the age of five, he usually can recognize his first name in written form and identify signs such as *go* and *stop* as well as the symbols *hot* and *cold* on faucets. While a story is being read to him, he may be able to follow with his finger both the pictures and the text. He is beginning to gain some comprehension of word symbols.

Parents in the higher socio-economic brackets sometimes are so eager to demonstrate the superior learning progress of their young child that they attempt to teach him to read before he enters school. They are proud of the fact that he may have mastered the alphabet. Although gifted children often learn to read before school age, parental emphasis on learning to read during early years may be a strain on the nervous system and interfere with later reading progress.

Reading Readiness and Disabilities Elementary school entrants differ in their ability to learn to read. Preschool experience is a significant factor of reading readiness. The child who has enjoyed rich environmental experiences, such as a home in which parents stimulate childish interest in talking and vocabulary building, and where the older members of the family do much reading, is likely to recognize the social value of learning to read, unless he has received too much prodding by parents in this area of development. Contrariwise, a child of lower social class may have been denied the advantages of upper class children.

Teachers in the primary grades are faced with the problem of introducing children having widely different backgrounds to the beginnings of reading mastery. Although previous language experiences are extremely important, other factors operate in determining children's evidenced learning readiness. Degree of maturation is significant. Not all six-year-olds are equally mature for their age. It is a known fact, for example, that little boys mature more slowly than do little girls. This difference shows itself in the fact that primary grade girls progress more quickly in learning to read than do boys. More boys than girls need to be referred to reading clinics.

According to Strang, by the age of six a child should have had experience with words and books. She says:

It is an advantage to children in learning to read to have had experience with words and books:

To recognize signs and follow simple printed directions like "Go" and "Stop."

To be familiar with the phraseology of stories; this helps children anticipate meaning more readily when they begin to read.

To look at the book while someone reads to them; thus they will get the feeling of correct eye movement from left to right and from one line to the next and may begin to recognize words that frequently recur.[4]

The child who at an early age has become an avid watcher of television programs is likely to become so interested in picture and vocal presentations that he finds it difficult to become interested in written or printed material. Mastery of reading material, except that which is accompanied by many illustrations from which he can deduce the meaning of the story, does not represent a worthwhile goal. More serious is the situation of the child whose reading progress is interfered with by emotional disturbances, excessive fear of or withdrawal from social situations. Failure to progress as rapidly in his learning as fellow classmates may cause greater retardation in reading.

In an increasing number of schools, reading readiness tests are administered to children in the early grades to discover possible causes of differences in performance. Reading readiness tests include such items as shown in the following example (see Figure 57):

Some school entrants are found to be still too immature to profit from regular reading instruction. Such children are permitted to advance at a slower pace than that of more mature pupils. Cases of emotional maladjustment are referred to psychological clinics where emotionally rooted causes are diagnosed and therapeutic and remedial techniques are applied.

According to some theories serious reading disability can be caused by factors other than emotional disturbance. The disability may have a neurological base. Brain dominance may be mixed; the child does not perceive words as normal children do. One example is the reading of the word "was" as "saw," and vice versa. Another theory stresses the un-

---

[4] Strang, Ruth, *An Introduction to Child Study*, 4th ed., p. 277. New York: The Macmillan Company, 1959.

Examples from New York Reading Readiness Test

TEST 1:   Concepts

1. Look at my book. Look at all the pictures in the top row. (Point.) Now look at them in your book—the pencil, the box of crayons, the book, the scissors, the cup. Mark just the cup and not anything else. Mark it just like this. (Illustrate at the blackboard by drawing a diagonal or vertical line on the picture cup. *Help those who have any difficulty. Show them how to mark the cup, if necessary.*)

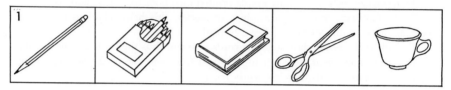

(P. 4) **8.** Look at the last row. (Pause.) Mark the mixing bowl. (10 seconds)

(P. 7) **20.** Look at all the pictures in the next row. (Point.) Find the picture that does not belong with the others in the row and mark it. (10 seconds)

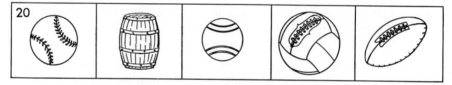

(P. 11) **3.** The child is to draw a line under the word *drum* wherever it appears. **4.** The child is to draw a line under the word *book*.

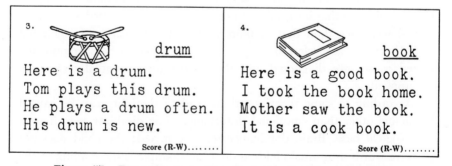

Figure 57. Examples from New York Reading Readiness Test.

From *Manual of Directions for New York Reading Readiness Test,* Forms A and B. Copyright 1947, by Board of Education of the City of New York, pp. 3, 4, 7, 8.

favorable effect of immaturity on readiness to read. Failure to make expected progress results in loss of interest in reading and feelings of inadequacy. Whatever the cause, patience and cooperation on the part of both clinician and patient (subject) are needed in cases of severe reading retardation to effect successful therapy.

Regardless of any child's learning readiness, Russell's summarization of six psychological principles pertaining to reading are worthy of consideration.

1. All children go through similar stages of development as reading abilities mature.

2. Development of reading abilities is a continuous and gradual process.

3. Although children go through similar patterns of continuous development there is a wide variation in the times individuals reach certain points in reading achievement.

4. Although reading is a continuous development, at various levels different needs and interests tend to accelerate certain phases of growth in reading abilities and attitudes.

5. In general, there is a positive relationship between reading achievement and general physical, mental, and social development, and among the various reading achievements themselves.

6. The effect of environmental influences related to reading varies with the stage of maturation reached by the child.[5]

Instructional Approaches Educators are interested in the use of correct teaching procedures. They know that the kind of teaching approach utilized affects the ease with which children learn to read.

BEGINNING TECHNIQUES At one time reading instruction began with the memorization of the alphabet, and oral reading was stressed. This technique gave way to the introduction of the phonic method, in which words were identified as (1) sounding alike (*sing, ring, bring*), (2) beginning with the same letter (*book, bill, buy*), and (3) having parts that look alike (*bough, through, though*). At present, excellent results seem to be achieved by first associating object with word, e.g., pointing to a picture of a dog, writing the word on the chalkboard in a sentence, and saying it. The word recognition technique can be followed or accompanied by the phonetic method. The alphabet is taught later.

Some children learn easily by tracing the word. Since children differ in their learning readiness, various approaches should be used freely: auditory, visual, phonetic, and manual. Unfortunately, the teacher of a

---

[5] Russell, David H., "Reading and Child Development," *Forty-eighth Yearbook of the National Society for the Study of Education*, pp. 16–18. Chicago: University of Chicago Press, 1949.

large class finds it difficult, if not impossible, to utilize the best approach for each individual child.

EYE MOVEMENT   The teacher of reading is concerned with eye movement. He recognizes reading as a kind of visual exploration in which the reader's eyes travel across the page in jumps, recognition of words or combination of words occurring during the pauses. Photographic recordings of reading activity show that reading reactions include:

1. Duration of eye fixations, or rate of recognition.
2. Number of words recognized in one attention span, or span of recognition.
3. Regression units per line, or rhythmic progress.
4. In oral reading, the number of letter spaces between the reading material on which the reader's eyes are fixating and what he is vocalizing, or the eye-voice span.

Good and poor readers can be discovered from reading graphs. As compared with the retarded reader, the skilled reader gives evidence of shorter duration of fixations, fewer fixations of the eyes, and more definite reading rhythm.

SILENT VERSUS ORAL READING   Earlier procedures in "reading lessons," which consisted of having each child in turn stand and read aloud a passage from a reader which the other pupils were supposed to follow silently, have disappeared in most schools. The primary purposes of reading are to obtain information, acquaint oneself with the point of view of writers, and gain enjoyment. Hence in modern schools emphasis is placed on the development of power to comprehend printed or written material through silent reading. Appropriate passages are assigned for reading, followed by the answering, either orally or in writing, of pertinent questions asked by the teacher. In the early grades exercises of this kind can take on the characteristics of a classroom game. Later, the silent reading can become the basis of active discussions, or the carrying out of constructive projects.

Oral reading is not neglected. Rather does it become a social activity. One pupil can read a story for the enjoyment of his classmates. If the child knows ahead of time that he is to entertain the others, he is likely to prepare himself by reading the material in advance, familiarizing himself with new or difficult words (both pronunciation and meaning), and practicing the reading for proper phrasing and intonation. This form of reading activity often serves a young person as a challenge to improve his reading ability. A similar project that is especially useful with stories having considerable conversation is to have the pupils role-play it. Among secondary as well as elementary school pupils, the enacting of a play or story encourages the development of reading skill.

Reading Interests [6] Children's reading interests differ according to maturity level, intelligence, sex, available materials, and the influence of adults and peer associates. Basically, children learn to read what they are expected to read, but background experiences and certain age and sex differences play their part.

Prior to the age of five years both boys and girls enjoy hearing stories about nature and animals and everyday happenings. They tend to want simple, factual stories, but also like rhymes and jingles, such as Mother Goose rhymes. Toward the end of this period they usually thrill to fairy tales. Their imaginations are stimulated by the fanciful as well as the factual. Sensitive children may become terrified by stories of ogres and witches, however. Some years ago Walt Disney produced a motion picture version of "Snow White and the Seven Dwarfs." Some children saw it repeatedly and enjoyed each viewing; others were so filled with fear by the incidents pictured that they could not sleep for several nights after viewing the picture.

As children mature, differences are apparent in the reading tastes of the two sexes. Boys, especially during the elementary school years, prefer stories of adventure and excitement, sports and inventions. Girls are likely to read stories about home life, with a beginning interest in sentimental fiction. Young people of junior and senior high school age tend to become increasingly interested in biography, history, and reading materials dealing with natural and social phenomena. At present, both children and adolescents read fanciful as well as factual writings concerning space travel, nuclear warfare, and related material. Although girls continue their interest in romantic stories and often become avid readers of the classics and poetry, they also evince interest in books and magazine articles generally regarded as favored by boys. The opposite does not hold, however; few growing boys read so-called "girls' books."

Many young people, from early childhood on, appear to be devoted to comic books. This reading interest bothers some adults. It is a fact that some comic books are undesirable: the paper is of poor quality, color combinations are inartistic, some drawings of human figures are grotesque, and the story sequence is absurd. Many comic strips are improving, how-

[6] For a more detailed discussion see Chapter 13, "Formation of Interests and Attitudes."

ever, in both quality of content and in manner of execution. These are intended to represent American folklore and history. They may stress blood and thunder activity, present fantastic situations, and utilize colloquial language. Yet they include threads of fundamental truths that have value for the youngster whose development is being furthered even as he projects himself into the life of Superman or other heroic figures. As is the case with fairy tales, children differ in their reactions to comic books. The child who is encouraged to engage in a well-balanced program of zestful work and relaxing play will not devote an undue amount of time to reading comics. It is the lonely, inactive child who may come to find his greatest thrills and fears through self-projection into the world of fantasy.

Much concern is experienced by many adults with the effect of excessive involvement with television on children's reading habits. A similar situation prevailed during the early days of motion pictures and radio. Although these one-way media of communication may provide certain emotional stimulation in the form of mystery programs and Westerns that are disapproved by adults for children's consumption, we are not dealing with such matters at this point. The question is whether the formation of good reading habits is being retarded or inhibited by time spent watching television. We have referred earlier to the possible effect of televiewing on young children's interest in learning to read. It probably is a fact that about 25 per cent of young people devote time to motion picture attendance and television programs that otherwise could be given to reading or other forms of relaxing activity. Yet, according to publishers of books for children and book stores, modern young people are reading more and better books than they have in any period of the past. Public and school libraries report similar experiences. Credit probably goes to parents and school people for encouraging children and adolescents to satisfy their urge to acquaint themselves through all available media with the world about them.

DEVELOPMENT OF SKILL IN WRITTEN LANGUAGE

The primary factor of written language is, of course, the ability to present ideas that are worthy of putting into written form. In order to express one's thoughts clearly, succinctly, and intelligibly, development of skill is needed in grammatical construction and punctuation, in correct spelling and in legible penmanship. We first shall discuss briefly the mechanics of written composition and then consider content.

Development of Skill in Penmanship Young children differ in the age at which they begin to "scribble" with crayon or chalk. At first, muscular control is lacking, but indiscriminate markings gradually come to be forms that have meaning for the child, especially when in the nursery school he is encouraged to express his ideas by drawing or scribbling on large sheets of paper. By the age of five years, he usually has developed some manipulatory control and a recognition of the association between visual and kinesthetic sensations. He uses free-arm movements, often accompanied by facial grimaces, and his scribblings are large, covering the entire page. Later, the child gains greater control of his muscles and he is able to imitate simple copy that requires more refined, smaller movements.

Adults differ widely in legibility of penmanship. This difference is caused partly by the relative effectiveness of early training and partly by degree of development of muscular control. The acquisition of legible handwriting comprises the mastery of a complex sensori-motor skill that includes (1) the gradual development of dexterity in the use of arm, hand, wrist, and fingers, (2) improvement of perception, and (3) increased memory for details.

Acquisition of Skill in Spelling Much of a child's writing vocabulary is acquired through his reading experiences. This is especially true in the area of words used in common life experiences. It does not mean, however, that the child can spell correctly every word that he can read and of which he knows the meaning. People vary in their spelling ability. In general, a person's speaking and reading vocabulary is larger than his writing vocabulary.

The acquisition of a spelling vocabulary is an individual matter. To learn to spell a word correctly involves perceiving the relationship that exists between the sound of the word and its written form, the interassociation of its parts, and its meaning. Children tend to have little difficulty in learning to spell correctly even long words that can be spelled phonetically, i.e., written according to the sound of each syllable. Some basic words of one or two syllables are misspelled by adults as well as children. The spelling of such words should be learned as early as possible so that they become fixed. Other words probably are mastered best when they are learned in context, rather than in isolated word lists. Mentally alert children usually become accurate spellers if they give attention to details. Some brilliant individuals are notoriously poor spellers because they lack interest in spelling mastery; some slow learners exhibit considerable ability in learning to spell by rote memorization—they may know the correct form of a word but fail to comprehend its meaning.

Conformity to Grammatical Usage A child's written structure usually follows the form of expression used in oral language. The young person who, during the preschool period, has been exposed to correct grammatical usage usually carries his habit patterns over into his written composition. More flexibility of construction is permitted in spoken language than in written, however. Hence the elementary school child needs to be guided toward expressing his ideas in clear, terse form, giving attention to sentence and paragraph sequences, appropriate terminology, and other elements of comprehensible written material.

Harrell made a comparative study of the length of written and oral compositions of boys and girls by chronological age. The results of his findings are presented in Figures 58, 59, and 60.[7] These were later corroborated by Dorothea McCarthy.[8]

Emphasis on the writing of short, simple sentences containing no more than one idea is needed during early learning in written language. There is difference of opinion concerning the value of a detailed study of grammar. At one time, considerable attention was given to the rote memorization and the application of many complicated grammatical rules. There then was a shift to stress on more or less imitation of good models and habit development, with a minimum of concentration on rules.

Recently, many educators have decided that the young person is helped to improve his writing if he knows, for example, why he should follow certain basic rules of agreement of subject and verb or of noun and pronoun, and of relationship between main and subordinate clauses. Consequently, in many schools the study of grammar has returned, but is treated from a practical or functional viewpoint, rather than as a formal study of rules that may be memorized but not understood. The most effective way to combine a study of grammar with its practical application and at what stage of individual maturation this combination will have best results still are moot questions.

Development of Power to Express Ideas in Written Form One might suppose that the bringing of the world closer together through the

[7] Harrell, Lester E., "A Comparison of the Development of Oral and Written Language in School-Age Children," *Monographs of the Society for Research in Child Development,* 22: No. 66, pp. 29, 48, and 51, 1957.

[8] McCarthy, Dorothea, "Research in Language Development: Retrospect and Prospect," *Monographs of the Society for Research in Child Development,* 24: No. 74, pp. 3–24, 1958.

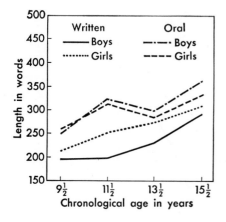

Figure 58. Mean Composition Length of Written and Oral Stories by Chronological Age and Sex.

From Harrell, Lester E., "A Comparison of the Development of Oral and Written Language in School-Age Children," *Monographs of the Society for Research in Child Development*, 22: No. 66, p. 29, 1957.

Figure 59. Percentages of the Total Number of Clauses of Noun, Adjective, and Adverb Clauses.

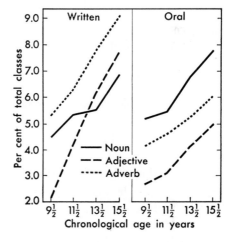

From *Ibid*, p. 48.

various modern media of communication would lessen the need for people to express their thoughts in writing. The amount of mail received daily by the man in business or the woman in the home, however, and the increasing number of books and other publications that are available testify to our continued interest in communicating with our fellows by means of the printed or written word. Written expression serves various purposes: letter-writing, note-taking, narration of a series of events, summarization of material read, description of places, people or things, statements of points of view, or advertising of one's wares.

As a child, the individual's purpose in writing probably is associated almost entirely with daily experiences in his immediate environment. Yet, effective early training will serve as a foundation upon which can be built later more involved usage of the tools of written expression. No

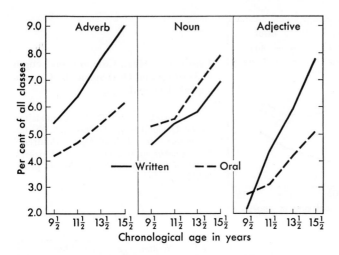

Figure 60. Comparison of Each Subordinate Clause
Type in Written and Oral Stories.

From *Ibid,* p. 51.

matter how simple a young person's attempt at written expression may
be, he must have something to say that is worth reading and say it in
correct grammatical form. This constitutes a difficult task for the average
child.

The child may have interesting ideas but lack mastery of the mechanics of writing, or he may have developed relatively correct form but have
little or nothing to say. In either case, one activity interferes with the
other, and he needs careful teacher guidance lest he become a sterile
or rambling writer. Instruction in composition includes the directing of
attention to both the content and the style or mechanics of the written
material.

As in oral language, even with the same or similar learning experiences, children differ in their ability to express themselves adequately in
written form. Boys usually express themselves less fluently than do girls,
possibly because the former devote less time to reading than the latter
and are more interested in strenuous activities. Members of the same
grade or class, whether they be boys or girls, tend to evidence wide differences in their written expression. To illustrate this point we present
samples of pupils' writing in the form of notes to their teacher who was
absent from school for a week because of illness. These children are
fourth-graders having superior intelligence. The notes are identified by
sex. The reader will observe the difference in amount of detail among

the letters and the fact that several expressed themselves in verse. Spelling and punctuation are those of the children.

Boy. "We hope you feel better. We miss you. We are sorry you got sick. Your pupil,"

Girl. "I was very sorry to hear you are sick. I hope you get well very soon. In school we accomplished much work. We wrote compositions about our trip to the Museum. I miss you very much. I am looking forward to seeing you back in school soon. Sincerely,"

Boy. "How do you feel? I am very sorry you did not come to school today. I hope you will feel better. I feel fine, though I have a little cold. I was sorry because we did not practice the play. I hope you come to school tomorrow. Your pupil,"

Girl. "When I walked into the classroom on Monday morning I was disappointed to find that you were absent. I immediately knew that you were ill, and began to wonder if you caught a cold in the Museum on Friday because it was terribly cold there. I hope that you will be better and come back to school soon because I miss you, Best wishes,"

Girl. "I'm sorry to hear that you're sick. When I came in this morning I was happy because I was going to get furniture, but when I found out that you were sick I could have cried, but I held it back just in time.
"Please don't stay home too long because things are very different when you're around. Hope you get better soon. Sincerely yours,"

Boy. "How are you feeling: I hope you feel all right. Mrs. —— is taking charge of us. She is a nice teacher. Today we finished reading *Mary Poppins.* I liked it very much. Tomorrow we're going to start another Mary Poppins book. Did you know that I was going to move? I will this Thursday to White Plains, N. Y. My mother is going to buy me a convertible to sleep on. I am very sorry you were absent. So was everyone else sorry. I hope you come back tomorrow.
From one of your pupils,"

Boy. "If you come back right away,
Welcome home, we would say.
We like you very much,
Because you have the golden touch.
All the children are very sad,
And, in a way, a little mad.
We never raise a fuss,
Because you're very nice to us.
What is your condition good or bad?
We hope it's good or we'll be sad.
Stay in bed and get better fast,

And hope that this sickness will be your last.
I hope you change for better not worse
Because, if you don't stay in bed you'll need a nurse.
                    Best wishes,"

Girl. "I hear you have a cold today,
     Well I'm going to make it go away.
     For I don't like you to be sick,
     Nor to lie in bed while you hear the clock tick.
     I'd sure like you back in school,
     So you can teach us the golden rule.
     So by now I've got to go,
     And I hope tomorrow you're not feeling low.
                    Sincerely,"

There is some to-be-expected uniformity of expression in these letters. However, one can recognize some of the personality differences among the children. Also evident is the fact that some of them write more easily and in greater detail than do others. Consultation with the teacher of the class disclosed that several of the more fluent writers are among the less vocal in class discussion. Contrariwise, the writer of the first note is quite a talker and much more uninhibited in oral expression than in written. It also may be noted that the boy who wrote letter number seven probably was unaware of the fact that the line, "And hope that this sickness will be your last," lends itself to two interpretations.

QUESTIONS AND TOPICS FOR DISCUSSION

1. Listen to a radio newscast. After it is completed, write a summary of what was given. Check with someone else who also was listening to it. What omissions did you find? How do you explain them?
2. The next time you attend a meeting at which a paper is read, take notes of the important points during the reading. Then compare your notes with the paper itself. How do you explain omissions or incorrect notations?
3. Why do playing children often fail to respond to a mother's call for lunch?
4. What are some of the advantages and disadvantages of children's learning to read before they enter elementary school?
5. Among the children of your acquaintance, what effect does television viewing seem to have on their reading interests?
6. Discuss in class: "Development of reading abilities is a continuous and gradual process."

7. What were your favorite stories during childhood? During adolescence? How did your reading interests compare with those of peer-age associates?

8. *Special Project:* A. With your two young subjects, do the following: (1) Read to them a story, appropriate to their age, and have them answer questions about it. Report their responses. (2) Ask them to tell you a story. Note their use of language forms.

B. With your older subjects, do the following: (1) Give them directions for completing a simple project. Note how well they carry out instructions. (2) Ask them what their favorite reading material is and why they like it. (3) Have them write a story. Let them choose the subject, but offer suggestions if they ask for them. Report the length of the story, and the use of nouns, adjectives, and adverbs.

SELECTED REFERENCES

Adams, Bess P., *About Books and Children.* New York: Henry Holt and Company, 1953.

Ames, L. B., and Ilg, F. L., "Developmental Trends in Writing Behavior," *Journal of Genetic Psychology,* 79: 26–46, 1951.

Barbara, D. A., *The Art of Listening.* Springfield, Ill.: Charles C. Thomas, 1958.

Cole, Luella, *Handwriting for Left-Handed Children.* Indianapolis: The Bobbs-Merrill Company, 1955.

Collier, M. J., and Gaier, E. L., "Adult Reactions to Preferred Childhood Stories," *Child Development,* 29: 97–103, 1958.

Ephron, B. K., *Emotional Difficulties in Reading.* New York: Julian Press, 1953.

Frank, J., *Your Child's Reading Today.* Garden City: Doubleday Company, 1953.

Huber, M. B., *Story and Verse for Children.* New York: The Macmillan Company, 1955.

McCarthy, Dorothea, "Language Development in Children," in L. Carmichael (ed.), *Manual of Child Psychology,* 2nd ed., pp. 492–630. New York: John Wiley and Sons, Inc., 1954.

McKim, M. G., *Guiding Growth in Reading in the Modern Elementary School.* New York: The Macmillan Company, 1955.

Willy, P., and Sizemone, R. A., "Reading the Comics: A Summary of Studies and an Evaluation," *Elementary English,* 31: 501–506, 1954.

8

DEVELOPMENT

OF UNDERSTANDING

IN THE BROADEST connotation of the term, *understanding* implies the development of meaning. In Chapters 6 and 7 we referred to the understanding of language patterns. Used in this framework, the word can be interpreted to indicate that the hearer or reader has learned to put meaning into the words, phrases, or sentences of a language. From a more general viewpoint, *to understand* implies (1) to receive and to appreciate the nature of the elements of a matter under consideration, and (2) to have a full, clear knowledge or mastery of a situation or condition. Understanding is the sum total of the mental powers by which knowledge is acquired, retained, and extended. It constitutes a complex of physical and mental activity.

PHYSICAL BASES OF MENTAL ACTIVITY

We are wont to differentiate between the body and the mind as though they were two separate entities. More correctly, the word "mind" represents an abstract collective term for any mental state or activity which, in turn, depends on the functioning of the physical constitution.

Physical and Mental Growth Physical growth refers specifically to changes in body structure and increasing adaptation of body organs to developing body needs. Mental growth is concerned more definitely with the development of adaptive behavior, in light of environmental conditions, toward the fulfillment of desired purposes or goals.

From infancy onward, physical and mental growth increases with chronological age. The results of cross-sectional age-group studies of children indicate, however, that there are wide variations in growth patterns, both within the same child and among children. Certain areas of body growth such as height and weight, for example, do not parallel mental growth. Children who are well developed physically may be retarded mentally. Although the reverse also is true, mentally superior children tend to attain good physical growth as well. Some children fail to achieve either physical or mental growth that is considered "normal" for their chronological age.

Relation of Brain Growth to Mental Development Mental activity depends on the functioning of the brain and nervous system. Hence neurological growth is an important factor of effective mentality. The pattern of the nervous system is complete at birth, but its functional development continues throughout life. The weight of the brain at birth is greater in relation to total body weight than it will be at any future stage of body growth. This does not mean that the brain does not continue to increase in rate and amount of growth during the child's developing years. The greatest rate of brain growth occurs during the early years. By age five, the brain has attained 80 per cent of its maximum weight; this percentage increases to 90 per cent by age nine; maximum brain weight usually is reached by the age of twenty. The actual number of brain cells is fixed at birth, but the cells themselves continue to grow until maturity.

The main parts of the brain include the cerebrum, the cerebellum, the medulla, the thalamus, and the pons varoli. We are especially interested in the cerebrum, which is the center of conscious activity and learning, and which functions in intelligent behavior. The brain always functions as a unit, although the cortical areas are differentiated in function. It is generally accepted that specific sensory functions are performed in certain areas of the cortex, and motor functions in others. The areas of cortical function are shown in Figure 61.

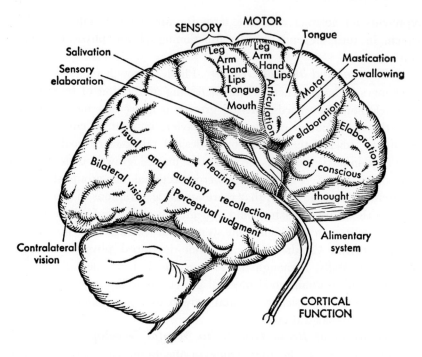

Figure 61. Brain, Showing Cortical Function.

This illustration will serve as a summary restatement of conclusions, some hypothetical, e.g., the elaboration zones, others firmly established. The suggestion that the anterior portion of the occipital cortex is related to both fields of vision, rather than to one alone, is derived from the results of stimulation.

From Penfield, W., and Rasmussen, T., *The Cerebral Cortex of Man.* New York: copyright 1950 by The Macmillan Company.

The cortex has three layers: the *infragranular*, the *granular*, and the *supragranular*. Each layer serves specific functions. The infragranular, reaching about 80 per cent of its growth at birth, controls reflexes and unlearned responses, such as the knee jerk and the eye blink. The granular layer, attaining 75 per cent of its growth at birth, is concerned with the conduction of sensory impressions. Degree of mental ability is closely associated with the functioning of the supragranular layer which has achieved only about 50 per cent of its growth at birth.

The child's mental progress follows the developmental patterns set by the three layers of the cortex. The infant can engage in reflex and related responses. As we suggest in our discussion of sensory mechanisms, his developing senses help acquaint him with his environment. As the supragranular layer grows, the child first acquires the power to engage in simple mental activities; later, with the approach to full maturity, he achieves skill in abstract thinking.

The Sensory Mechanisms   Although all the cells of the organism possess some degree of irritability, certain nerves are highly sensitive to appropriate stimulation. When particular physical forces or substances activate the specialized end organs of sensory nerves, respective sensations are experienced. Nerve impulses produce activity in the brain that eventually finds its way to muscles or glands, with resulting behavior changes.

Sense organs are highly complex mechanisms.[1] The development of the sensory processes as the means whereby an individual is enabled to achieve an understanding of the world about him and of his own behavior is discussed later in the chapter. At this point is presented a classification of the various sense organs, their activating stimuli and the resulting sensations. (See Table 10.)

TABLE 10

Sense Organs, Their Stimulation, Sensations, and Organic Action *

Sense organ	Stimulus	Sensation	Organic action
Eye	Light waves	Visual	Sight
Ear	Air waves	Auditory	Hearing
Tongue	Soluble liquids	Gustatory	Taste
Nose	Gaseous particles	Olfactory	Smell
Skin	Mechanical, thermal, electric, chemical	Cutaneous	Pressure, pain, heat, cold
Muscle or joint	Change of movement	Kinesthetic	Pressure and movement
Alimentary canal, etc.	Membrane tissue conditions	Organic	Hunger, thirst, euphoria (feeling of well-being)
Semicircular canal (inner ear), body muscles	Movement and muscle tension	Equilibrum	Balance

* Crow, L. D., and Crow, Alice, *An Outline of General Psychology*, p. 79. Paterson, N. J.: copyright 1959 by Littlefield, Adams and Company.

Other Physical Bases of Mental Activity   The normal functioning of the nervous system and of the sensory mechanisms is fundamental

[1] Morgan, Clifford T., *Introduction to Psychology*, Part 5. New York: McGraw-Hill Book Company, Inc., 1956.

to the development of understanding. The physical processes represent the activities of an integrated whole, however. Hence the part played by the muscles, glands, and other physical organs in the activity of mental responses must be kept in mind as we consider the development of understanding and its effect on human behavior.

THE COMPONENTS OF UNDERSTANDING

Mental activity resulting in an understanding of self and of the world about one is a complex process. Interpreted broadly, the attainment of understanding includes sensation (the receiving of sensory impulses), perception, imagery, memory, conceptualization, judgment (discrimination), reasoning, and problem solving. A factor exerting considerable influence on the effectiveness of an individual's power of understanding is his degree of mental acuity or his intelligence. Before we discuss the functioning aspects of intelligence and the stages in the development of understanding, we shall attempt to interpret briefly the various components of mental activity.

THE FORMATION OF PERCEPTS

The sense organs often are referred to as the gateways to learning and understanding. Sensation is the first response to the stimulation of sensory nerve ends. A "pure" sensation, however, is no more than a bare quality of experience. In order to function for the benefit of the individual it must be identified and interpreted in an experiential framework.

Meaning of Perception It is only during infancy that "pure" sensations are experienced; all later sensory experiences are associated with one another in the nervous system. The individual builds a sensory background, consisting of sensory discrimination (auditory, visual, olfactory, etc.) and sensory recognition (object, person, or condition). *The organization and interpretation of sensations in light of previous experiences are known as perception.* Objects, persons, situations, or conditions which are recognized or identified while they are being sensed can be said to be perceived.

To the degree that an individual's sensory mechanisms are functioning adequately, active interpretation based on integration continues in the cerebrum. Perception includes both the sensory function and learning. During our waking hours we constantly are responding to sensory stimuli and experiencing perceptions. The fusing of percepts makes our experiences more meaningful.

Factors Affecting Perception   The quality and extent of an individual's perception depend on factors such as sense organ sensitivity, kind and amount of sensory stimulation, previous experience and training, attitudes and feelings, degree of attention to and concentration upon the details of the sensory experiences, and functioning of the integrative process. Faulty perceptions are common and can be caused by the malfunctioning of any of the factors listed.

EFFECT OF PAST EXPERIENCE AND ATTITUDE   Past experiences make for or militate against the accuracy of present perceptions. The young child perceives an orange as a brightly colored, round object having sweet juice. To the housewife, the orange is a fruit which usually is served for breakfast and which varies in quality and price during successive seasons of the year. The owner of an orange grove views the fruit as a means of earning a living; he is perceptive about proper growing conditions, packing and distribution.

Existing attitudes or feelings also affect perception. The ringing of a telephone bell is responded to differently by the young girl who is expecting a call from a close friend, a woman who is busy preparing dinner, or a man who fears that the call may bring bad business or personal news. Different individuals or the same individuals at different times interpret sensory stimuli differently. Personal likes and dislikes, age, sex, and social or occupational interests often determine the way in which stimuli situations are perceived.

Many examples could be cited to indicate differences in interpretation of common objects, conditions, and situations. We have referred to the possible effect on different people of the ringing of the telephone bell. Similar differences can be discovered, for example, in attitudes toward the daily newspaper. To the child it means the comics. A young man may turn first to the sports page, the middle-aged man is interested in the business section and stock report, his wife turns first to the woman's page, while grandpa or grandma scans the obituaries. The news of the day may receive scant attention.

SIGNIFICANCE OF ATTENTION   An individual's past experience, training, and attitude at the moment tend to influence the extent to which he selects sensory stimuli to which he attends. Attention is the process of focusing on certain elements or aspects of a stimulus situation

Figure 62.   The Vase and the Faces. Look at this picture. Can you see the vase? Can you also see the two faces?

and neglecting others. (See Figures 62 and 63.) A child or older person may deliberately give his attention to or concentrate on an outside force, or on his thoughts and emotional state to the exclusion of something else. This is known as *voluntary attention*. While he is engaged in such activity, however, he may be distracted from it by the intrusion of a sensory stimulus such as a loud noise, a sudden pain, or other element that claims his attention either momentarily or for a longer period of time. This type of reaction is termed *involuntary attention*. As a result of training or great interest a person may experience still another kind of attention— habitual attention, whereby a certain aspect of a situation or condition usually is perceived. When, for example, a family sits down to a meal, the mother has learned through experience to make certain that everything needed is on the table; the hungry children concentrate on the food that is being served.

IMPORTANCE OF CHARACTERISTICS OF STIMULI   Throughout his life, an individual attends to certain sensory stimuli in light of their characteristics, such as size, intensity, change, motion, repetition, and unusualness or strikingness. A child tends to perceive a large building or sign, for example, more readily than a smaller one, unless the latter has other unusual characteristics such as color or shape. Similarly, the more intense a stimulus is the greater is the attention given it. A loud sound, a bright light or color, or a strong odor attracts one's attention more easily than does a weaker stimulus.

Repetition of a stimulus at frequent intervals, such as the continued ringing of a bell or the repeated flashing of a light, is more likely to gain a person's attention than one stimulation that is not intense. Too many repetitions, however, may cause the perceiver to disregard the stimulus.

Other things being equal, moving objects catch the eye more quickly than stationary ones. Television advertisers recognize the value of motion in attracting the attention of the viewer.

STATE OF THE INDIVIDUAL   What a young person is likely to perceive in his environment is influenced by his physical condition, the social situation in which he finds himself, or his interest at the moment. An individual's attention may be distracted from what he is doing by a sudden cramp in his leg, a toothache or other body pain, or a feeling of discomfort. A new or unaccustomed situation may include factors to which an individual might not attend unless his attention is directed to them by others. The worker is warned of the possible danger to himself of careless manipulation of complicated machinery. A child can be helped by his parents and teachers to attend to certain details of behavior that are important for him to follow, including the giving of special attention to significant aspects of a learning situation, and socially acceptable deportment while eating or in the company of other people.

A powerful attention-getter is one's interest in that which serves as a sensory stimulus. Past experience is a strong motivator of attention. As we noted earlier, a person tends to perceive in any situation those elements which are associated with his developed interests. A chair, for ex-

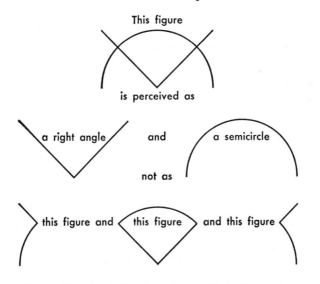

Figure 63. Good Continuation in Unit Formation.

From Baldwin, Alfred L., *Behavior and Development in Childhood*, p. 63. New York: copyright 1955 by Drydren-Holt Company. By permission of Holt, Rinehart and Winston, Inc.

ample, may be perceived differently by various people. A furniture maker may attend to its construction; an interior decorator is interested in its fitness in the room; a tired man may select it because it looks comfortable; the owner of the chair may be sentimentally attached to it.

Past experience as a motivator of interest exerts a tremendous influence on percept formation. The close relationship which exists between interest and perception is evidenced in the learning process. The master teacher, as he attempts to help his pupils gain skill in perception, constantly builds new percepts on those with which younger individuals have had pleasant experiences.

The influence of mental set and attention on perception is better understood when we realize that attention tends to shift quickly from one stimulus to another. A person does not engage in two or more mental activities at the same time. Rather does his attention shift from one to another. Although many sensory stimuli seem to demand attention at the same time, the individual who has learned to concentrate effectively is able to bring his attention back to the matter at hand in spite of the fact that other stimuli temporarily come into his focus of attention; he has good power of concentration.

Moreover, much is taken for granted in the perceptual process. To the extent that we have developed certain habits of perception, we can gain a perception of the whole even though some elements are missing. The mind fills in the gaps or disregards them. We come to recognize that if we know a person well, we can recognize him by his voice or footsteps even though we do not see him. We may fail to notice that a familiar word is misspelled. Any disparity in impressions gained by way of the sensory mechanisms is corrected through mental integration and interpretation.

Errors in Perception   Past experiences with quality of stimuli, extent of distance, and size of objects cause us to be confronted with the necessity of correcting possible errors of perception. Experience with the direction of sound, and with the actual and relative sizes of objects if removed from us in distance, for example, helps us form correct perceptions of sensory materials. Mental set affects perception. We may be so attentive to one element of a situation that we miss another equally important detail. Someone may ask us, for instance, "Which is correct: 8 and 9 *is* 16 or 8 and 9 *are* 16?" We may attend only to the grammatical structure and fail to recognize the arithmetical error. Strong emotion also can cause a distortion of perception. In a highly emotionalized state, one is likely to perceive that which is associated with his emotionalized interest.

Although errors of perception (*illusions*) may result from the physical condition of the sense organ, the sensitivity of the receptors, or extent of learning background, many of them are caused by strong mental set or emotional status. For example, a person who is eagerly awaiting a telephone call mistakes the ringing of the door bell for the sound of a telephone bell; a gravestone can be mistaken for a ghost by a highly emotionalized person walking through or alongside a graveyard at night; the voice or footsteps of an acquaintance may be misinterpreted as belonging to a beloved relative who is absent or who has died. Illusions such as these are common and are not serious unless they are experienced continually and are symptoms of mental illness. Various kinds of illusions are illustrated in Figure 64.

THE BUILDING OF CONCEPTS

Conceptualization can be interpreted to mean that the mind is capable of forming abstract ideas (concepts) independently of concrete existence. Through the process of mental integration, percepts become mental images and result in concepts.

Mental Imagery Imagery is the art of forming images. In our discussion of perception, we referred to the part played by past experience in the development of new percepts. To the extent that contributing factors are favorable (normally functioning sensory mechanisms, attention, and attitude) a percept can become a remembered image or a mental picture. An image can be defined as a representation in the mind not perceived at the moment through the senses, or a product of the reproductive imagination or memory of things seen, heard, touched, or experienced through other sensory activity, including the accompanying emotionalized attitudes. The accuracy of a mental image depends on the amount and correctness of perceived details. In perception, certain aspects of the stimulus may receive so much attention that others are not responded to. When the object is present to the senses, the neglected details can be checked; this process is not possible with the mental image. An individual may believe, for example, that he has a perfect image of an American beauty rose. He recalls its general form and color, but if he is asked to state the number of its petals, he probably will need to view an actual sample and count the petals. Much of our imagery is faulty except in those instances in which a special interest prompts us to include all the elements of the originally perceived sensory stimulus. Moreover, memory

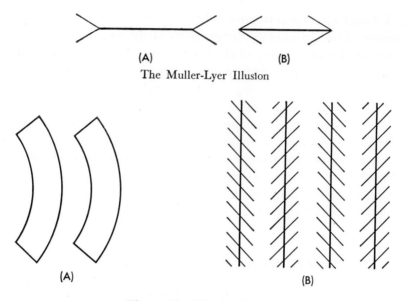

(A)   (B)

The Muller-Lyer Illusion

(A)   (B)

Figure 64. Visual Illusions.

A. Wundt's Illusion; **B.** Zollner's Illusion; **C.** Hering's Illusion; **D.** Poggendorf's Illusion.

may fail us. Although the first image is relatively accurate, with the passage of time some of the seemingly less significant aspects of the image may be forgotten.

Concept Formation   A concept is an abstract idea or notion, combining elements into the idea of one object. Concepts are formed through the integration of many images resulting from adequate percepts. Hence concepts are built out of experience. The richer and more varied an individual's experiences are the more complete are his concepts. Terms such as "morality," "ethical values," "beauty," "loyalty," "cooperation," and the like are abstractions that take on increased meaning as they are applied to many widely differing situations. The child, for example, has no understanding of the meaning of morality, but he has learned that he is *good* when he obeys his parents, and *bad* if he does something disapproved by them. It often is said that beauty lies in the eye of the beholder. Differences in standards of supposedly artistic production attest to the truth of this statement. Many instances of struggles between divided loyalties are examples of relative rather than absolute interpretation of the concept of loyalty. A long process of extensive and intensive experi-

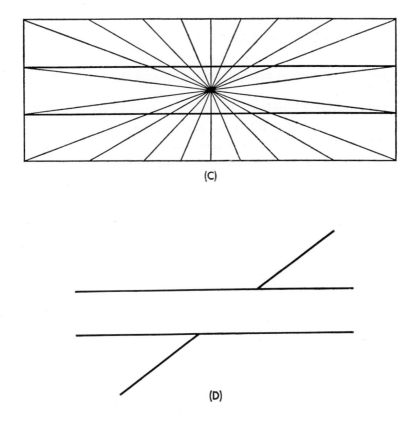

(C)

(D)

ence is needed to gain a recognition of a concept as an abstract general-ization that is applicable to an appropriate total of inner and outer behavior.

Although language is used to communicate ideas, every individual develops his own concepts. Adequate communication is established among the members of a group when concepts or generalizations expressed in language symbols (words or phrases) possess the same or similar conno-tation for each member of the group. Lack of comprehension or misun-derstanding occurs when the background experiences differ so widely that individuals appear to be talking at cross-purposes. One example of this kind of misconception is found in the difference in meaning at-tached to the word "freedom" which to most people implies following one's own interests within the framework of social approval, but to some connotes the right to engage in "license," or uninhibited behavior, re-gardless of the welfare of others.

THE THINKING PROCESS

Ideation or mental manipulation of images or concepts is referred to as *thinking*.

Function of Thinking   To think is to form by the mental process or to examine mentally. When we are thinking we are manipulating ideas (thoughts), emerging as a result of previous sensory experiences (percepts) which have been identified, interpreted, and remembered. Cognition, the act or power of apprehending or knowing, is closely allied to thinking.

The thinking process includes perception, imagery, conceptualization, the utilization of language symbols, and subvocal speech. Awareness of stimuli present to the senses and memory of past experiences are involved in the thought processes and are aimed at a goal that may be clear and specific or relatively indefinite and vague.

Thinking Levels   Interpreting the term "problem" broadly, all thinking includes some aspects of problem solving. Differences in thinking depend on the nature of the problem situation, the end in view, and the approach utilized. The levels of thinking are: reverie or daydreaming, aesthetic appreciation, acquiring of information, reflective thinking, and creative thinking. The goal to be attained differs with the level.

In *reverie* or *daydreaming,* one is motivated by interest and association to leave the world of reality temporarily for that of fantasy. Ideas are permitted to succeed one another in a pleasing sequence, with little or no conscious control of their practical significance.

Aesthetic appreciation is the emotionalized channeling of mental responses in the direction of an evaluation or appraisal of beauty in one or another form. One "loses" himself in a beautiful sunrise or sunset, or an emotionally satisfying artistic production. The end result is the enjoyment to be derived from the stimulus situation.

The thought processes involved in *acquiring information* are pointed toward a definite and specific purpose. The individual becomes aware of his need for certain information. He engages in mental activity aimed at seeking, assimilating, and recalling new facts or experiences that have extrinsic or intrinsic value.

The most complex and difficult level of thinking is reflective or creative. In reflective thinking, usually referred to as *reasoning* or *problem solving,* the thinking activity is set in motion by the need to solve a difficulty. The thinking process of collecting and manipulating relevant experiences, which is continued until a solution is found, is called *inductive reasoning*. When the thinking process attempts to discover the extent to which a general principle applies to particular phenomena or instances, it is called *deductive reasoning*. Creative thinking differs from reflective thinking in that, when one is creating mentally, experiences are projected toward the formation of new ideas or concepts.

The stages of creative thinking include (1) a period of *preparation* during which the various aspects of the situation are investigated and preparatory materials organized, (2) the period of *incubation,* varying in length, during which vague ideas are taking form, and (3) a more or less sudden *insight* or *illumination*. All constructive thinking, however, utilizes the same mental processes: experience, association, and expression.

INTELLECTUAL STATUS AND UNDERSTANDING

The degree to which an individual achieves a valid understanding of himself, his surroundings, or his relationships with other people depends in good part on his level of intelligence. Hence, at this point, we shall discuss briefly the role of intelligence in the development of understanding.

Meaning of Intelligence Imagination, attention, memory, reasoning, and other forms of mental activity can be regarded as various aspects of a person's intelligence. The functioning of these complex mental processes cannot be observed directly but are manifested in behavior. For this reason many psychologists prefer to use the term *intelligent behavior* rather than intelligence. In seeking an explanation of the higher mental processes, however, researchers have attempted to discover the basic factors that comprise the integrated whole which is known as *intelligence*. One of the early twentieth-century workers in the field, Alfred Binet, considered intelligence to consist of "comprehension, invention, direction, and criticism." Another early but significant definition of intelligence is that of William Stern, who states that "intelligence is a general capacity of an individual consciously to adjust his thinking to new requirements. It is a general mental adaptability to new problems and conditions." [2]

Various psychologists have attempted to analyze the components of

[2] Stern, W., *Psychological Methods of Testing Intelligence,* p. 3. Baltimore: Warwick and York, Inc., copyright 1914.

intelligence. Thorndike [3] interpreted intelligence as the "power of good responses from the point of view of truth or fact." He classified abilities as (1) *abstract* (linguistic), (2) *mechanical,* and (3) *social.* He held that "quality of intellect depends on quantity of connections of neural connections." Carl Spearman [4] promulgated a two-factor theory of intelligence: *general ability* and *special abilities.* Spearman's two-factor theory was extended by Thurstone [5] into a multiple factor theory, including thirteen factors. Thurstone regarded seven of these as primary mental abilities: (1) number facility, (2) memory, (3) ability in verbal relations, (4) ability to visualize space, (5) ability to deduce from presented data, (6) speed of perception, and (7) problem solving. In light of the various studies of the nature of intelligence, Stoddard [6] described it as "the ability to undertake activities that are characterized by (1) difficulty, (2) complexity, (3) abstractness, (4) economy (speed), (5) adaptiveness to a goal, (6) social value, and (7) the emergence of originals (inventiveness)." Later, Wechsler summarized the function of intelligence as "the aggregate or global capacity of the individual to act purposefully, to think rationally, and to deal effectively with his environment." [7]

It will be recognized from the foregoing interpretations of the term that intelligence connotes the ability to abstract, compare, and generalize. According to his degree of intelligence, an individual makes more or less successful adaptations to new situations, manages his affairs more or less effectively, and varies in the adequacy with which he solves problems that confront him. Intelligent behavior is characterized by goal-directed and well-organized activity, adaptability, speed of reaction, and a rich background of experience.

Factors of Possible Differences in Intelligence   Scientific studies have yielded some tentative conclusions concerning differences in intelligence. Many of the research findings have been obtained through the administration of tests which will be discussed briefly later, and by

[3] Thorndike, E. L., "Intelligence and Its Measurement," *J. of Educ. Psy.,* 12: 123–147 and 195–216, 1921.

[4] Spearman, Carl, *The Nature of Intelligence and the Principles of Cognition.* New York: The Macmillan Company, 1923.

[5] Thurstone, L. L., *Primary Mental Abilities.* Chicago: University of Chicago Press, 1938.

[6] Stoddard, G. D., "On the Meaning of Intelligence," *Psychological Review,* 48: 235, 1941.

[7] Wechsler, D., *The Measurement of Adult Intelligence,* 4th ed., p. 9. Baltimore: The Williams and Wilkins Company, 1958.

the observation of behavior in controlled situations. As we consider such differences, however, it must be kept in mind that factors other than mental ability *per se* can account for variations in intelligent behavior.

THE EFFECT OF HEREDITY AND ENVIRONMENT   In Chapter 3 were discussed the biological and cultural factors of child development. Insofar as psychologists can determine, both heredity and environmental factors exert a significant influence on intelligence status. Studies of family lines through several generations offer some evidence that parents and children and siblings tend to resemble one another in their intelligence level. The findings of these studies are not so conclusive as the hereditarians would like to believe, however. Environmental stimulation exerts an effective influence on mental development. Twins reared apart, for example, may show differing degrees of mental acuity. Children who spend their early years in economically and socially underprivileged homes seem to perform more intelligently if or when their living conditions are improved.

Socio-economic status or cultural background is not completely responsible for an individual's evidenced intelligence any more than is heredity. Although environmental conditions are effective in bringing about small changes, naturally bright children tend to be superior in spite of nonstimulating experiences. Children who from an early age appear to be mentally retarded cannot be expected to develop superior intelligence, no matter how rich their environment may be.

THE SEX FACTOR   The popular belief that males are more intelligent than females has been found by psychologists to be a false assumption. There is a wider range of differences within either sex than between the sexes. The results of administered intelligence tests and of observation do indicate that boys seem to excel in the ability to detect similarities and in mathematics, and that girls perform more successfully in aesthetic appreciation, memory, and language usage. Here, again, differences within a sex occur as well as differences between the sexes. Moreover, apparent differences in certain areas of performance between the sexes might well be traced to differences in opportunity rather than to extreme differences in innate ability.

THE FACTOR OF AGE   As is the case in height and weight, intelligence presents a trend toward increasing diversity with growth. According to Nancy Bayley, "There is ample evidence that mental ages in normal samples tend to become more variable with age." In her study of increasing diversity in intelligence, she was faced with the problem of setting up comparable units. Bayley describes her study procedure as follows:

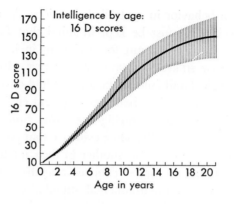

Figure 65.   Curve Showing the Mean and SD Intelligence Scores of the Berkeley Growth Study of Children from Birth to 21 Years. Scores from several different tests were converted into units based on the mean and SD of the 16-year test scores.

From Bayley, Nancy, "Individual Patterns of Development," *Child Development*, 27: No. 1, p. 66, 1956.

In working with the Berkeley Growth Study scores on intelligence tests the problem was further complicated by the need to compare scores from several different tests, having different methods of scoring. This has been done by the device of relating all scores to the mean and SD earned by this group on the Wechsler-Bellevue scale at 16 years. By adjusting the means and SD's earned on the Stanford-Binet and the Terman-McNemar tests at adjacent ages, all scores for the three scales and for all ages, were converted into units of deviation tentatively, the 16-D score. . . . [See Figure 65.]

In Figure [66] are individual curves for 5 boys selected to represent wide differences in adult intelligence. . . . Superimposed on these general trends are the fluctuations that may be related to differences in motivation or drive or to other factors such as emotional distractions, or differences in the content of the tests used at different ages. Figure [67] shows the same thing for 5 girls. When we see how closely alike the scores are in the first two years, it seems obvious that this is at least one reason why it is impossible to predict later intelligence from scores in infancy.[8]

A popular belief is that intelligence decreases with increasing age beyond early adulthood. The facts do not uphold this assumption. It is true that normal mental development or growth in intelligence continues

[8] Bayley, Nancy, "Individual Patterns of Development," *Child Development*, 27: 65–68. March, 1956, No. 1.

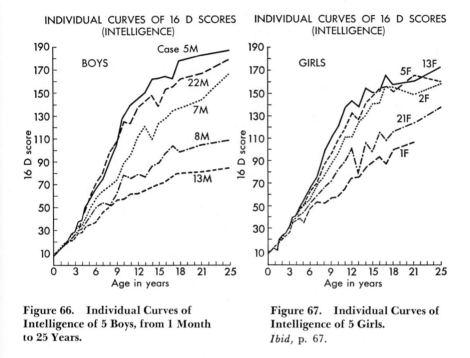

INDIVIDUAL CURVES OF 16 D SCORES (INTELLIGENCE)

INDIVIDUAL CURVES OF 16 D SCORES (INTELLIGENCE)

Figure 66.   Individual Curves of Intelligence of 5 Boys, from 1 Month to 25 Years.

Figure 67.   Individual Curves of Intelligence of 5 Girls.
Ibid, p. 67.

at a relatively even pace through adolescence into early adulthood. The slower child may reach his final level early, the mentally more alert individual may continue to develop mental acuity well into the twenties. Although actual growth of intelligence ceases, continuing experience may cause a person to organize his mental processes in such a way that he appears to gain in innate intelligence or seems to be less able than he was at an earlier age to respond effectively to novel situations.

Some individuals who have been accustomed to meet mental challenges continue to perform effectively throughout old age. Others who have allowed themselves to become routinized in their day-by-day activities may believe that they have lost earlier evidenced mental power, until or unless they encounter a challenging situation which, often to their surprise, they are able to master. Further, older men and women sometimes are heard to bewail the fact that their memory is not so good as it once was. The truth of the matter probably is that they have so many more things to remember as they become involved in life activities that they forget unimportant details, concentrating on what to them is worthwhile at the moment. Unless physical difficulties, such as disease or the results of accidents, interfere with the functioning of the mental processes, normal or superior intelligence status tends to remain relatively constant.

INTELLIGENCE AND RACE   Contrary to popular opinion, it would seem that there is a greater spread of intelligence among people having a common racial background than there is between races. Since individual intelligence ratings are obtained for the most part from the administration of tests of intelligence, cultural factors and common experiences not only are reflected in the construction of standardized tests but also influence performance on the tests. Hence the testing results of children who have been reared in the same environment, regardless of their racial heritage, tend to follow similar curves of distribution. The children in the United States who represent the first generation of the foreign-born are likely, however, to have slightly lower mental ability than those whose parents are themselves native born.

UTILIZATION OF INTELLIGENCE TESTS

An individual's degree of intelligence probably can be ascertained most effectively by observing his behavior in novel situations that demand quick and accurate thinking accompanied by success-achieving performance. This is a time-consuming process, however. School people who need to place children in appropriate classes, and organizations that are responsible for selecting personnel, need to discover as soon and as well as they can the range of mental ability of the learners with whom they are dealing. The construction of standardized testing instruments has been undertaken to meet this need.

The Beginnings of Intelligence Measurement   Early in the twentieth century Alfred Binet, a French psychologist, was called upon to devise a measuring instrument to discover, if possible, the reason for the school failure of some French children. After devising several preliminary scales, in 1911 Binet, in cooperation with Theophile Simon, constructed an individual intelligence scale (administered to one child at a time) containing eighty-one items which included verbal and performance tasks. This test was intended to measure degrees of intelligence from age three through adulthood.

A revised form in English of the Binet-Simon Scale was published as the *Stanford Revision* in 1916. This scale was revised in 1937 by Terman and Merrill, and again in 1960 with the help of Samuel R. Pinneau.

Since its first construction the Stanford Intelligence Scale has been widely used for the measurement of intelligence. Considerable training in its administration and interpretation is needed.

The testing of intelligence in group situations had its beginning during World War I. In order to place American servicemen in appropriate positions in the army, it was necessary to discover their potential abilities and experiential background. Consequently, a group of psychologists devised the *Army Alpha Tests* for men who could read English, and a performance test, the *Army Beta,* for nonreaders. These tests served as models for the many *group intelligence tests* that later were devised for use with school children.

Later Development Since their early beginnings, many intelligence tests have been constructed and administered. Most of them are group tests that vary considerably in their validity (testing what they are supposed to test) and in their reliability (yielding similar results in successive administrations).

Widely used individual tests are those devised by David Wechsler: the Wechsler-Bellevue Intelligence Scale (WBIS) published in 1929, the Wechsler Intelligence Scale for Children (WISC) in 1949 (see Figure 68), and the Wechsler Adult Intelligence Scale (WAIS) in 1955. Wechsler included both verbal and performance material in his tests. The WAIS, for example, consists of the following subtests: [9]

Verbal Tests	*Performance Tests*
1. Information	7. Digit Symbol
2. Comprehension	8. Picture Completion
3. Arithmetic	9. Block Design
4. Similarities	10. Picture Arrangement
5. Digit Span	11. Object Assembly
6. Vocabulary	

Interpretation of Intelligence Test Scores Various approaches are utilized to give meaning to the results obtained from the administration of intelligence tests, the most commonly used being *mental age, intelligence quotient,* and *percentile rank.* Binet interpreted the raw score earned by a testee according to expected performance at given age levels as the *mental age.* Terman related an individual's mental age (MA) as

[9] Wechsler, David, *Manual for the Wechsler Adult Intelligence Scale.* New York: The Psychological Corporation, 1955.

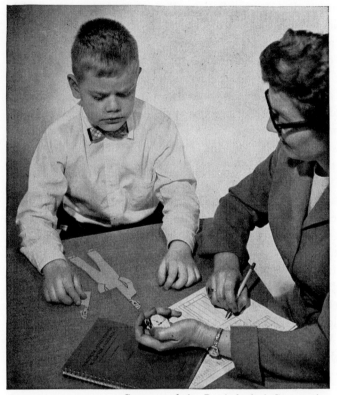

Courtesy of the Psychological Corporation

Figure 68. Administration of the Wechsler Intelligence Scale for Children (WISC).

obtained from the administration of the Stanford Binet Scale to his chronological age (CA). This relationship is expressed as the *intelligence quotient* (IQ). The formula employed is

$$\frac{MA \ \text{(months)}}{CA \ \text{(months)}} \times 100 = IQ.$$

If the MA and CA are the same, the IQ will be 100, or average; an MA higher than the CA is predictive of better than average intelligence; an MA lower than the CA denotes inferior intelligence.

According to the results of the administration of the Terman-Merrill Revision of the Stanford Binet Scale of Intelligence, the spread of intelligence is as follows:

TABLE 11

Classification of Intelligence Quotients

Classification	IQ
Near genius or genius	140 and above
Very superior	130–139
Superior	120–129
Above average	110–119
Normal or average	90–109
Below average	80– 89
Dull or borderline	70– 79
Feeble-minded: moron, imbecile, idiot	69– and below

Another device for interpreting intelligence scores is *percentile rank-ing*. The raw scores are expanded or compressed to a range of 100; the highest score earned in a group is indicated in the 100 level, and the others downward in rank order. The 50th percentile represents the median or average, *i.e.*, for an individual's raw intelligence score to fall at the median means that half of the individuals tested by the particular test scored higher than he does and the others have scores lower than his. Tests such as the American Council on Education Psychological Exami-nations use percentile norms for interpretative purposes. The relation between the normal curve of distribution and percentile equivalents is illustrated in Figure 69.

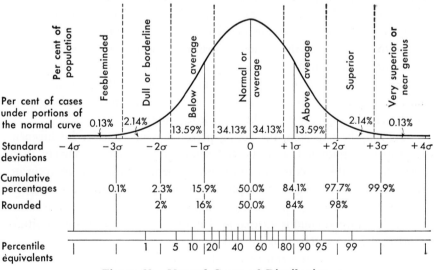

Figure 69.   **Normal Curve of Distribution.**

From *Test Service Bulletin*, No. 48. Jan. 1955. New York: The Psychological Corp. Distribution labels have been superimposed by the Authors.

Value of the Measurement of Intelligence Well-standardized intelligence tests have considerable predictive value, especially if attention is given to individual performance on the various types of items which comprise the test. For example, each of two children of the same age may earn an intelligence quotient of 115 as the result of the administration to them of the same intelligence test. The way in which they achieved the same IQ may give evidence of differing specific abilities, however, if the responses are analyzed, item by item. One may have performed excellently in number but less well in word analogies; the other's performance may have been the reverse. Similar differences can be found in responses to other tasks included in the test. (See Figure 70.)

General performance as indicated by the over-all result yields a general measure of predictability; the discovery of specific strengths and weaknesses is extremely important. Hence psychologists and school people are tending to view the results of intelligence testing as a general picture of an individual's mental status, and to employ other measuring instruments to achieve a better appreciation of his specialized abilities. Among these other instruments can be included tests of specific aptitudes, reading comprehension, mathematical potentiality, and the like.

It would seem to be a truism to state that an individual's power of understanding is dependent on his degree of mental alertness. Yet, as adults attempt to guide a child's learning to think accurately and objectively, they need to know the extent to which a particular child is potentially able to progress in the development of understanding. Through the administration of the various instruments devised to measure degree of mental acuity can be discovered the child's relative classification from the extremely gifted through intermediary stages to the very much retarded. Teaching approaches and learning materials then can be geared to the child's capacity to profit from instruction.

As may be expected, the young person having superior intelligence, if properly stimulated, can succeed more quickly and effectively than mentally less able children to form correct perceptions, achieve accurate images, build meaningful concepts, and develop the power to engage in purposeful, long-range problem solving. Contrariwise, the very slow or mentally retarded child is incapable of mastering any except simple situations that involve the thinking process.

Since most children can be classified as supposedly "normally intelligent" or deviating only slightly from an accepted norm, many of all young people's learning experiences are directed toward what is considered to be normal for their age group. It is imperative, therefore, that

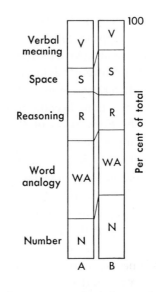

Figure 70.
Each Child Has the Same IQ (115), but
the Two Children Differ in Their Primary
Mental Abilities.

adults discover early those children who deviate to a marked degree from the average in intelligence, and provide experiences for them that will encourage the best realization of their innate capacity to perform.

STAGES IN THE DEVELOPMENT OF UNDERSTANDING

The development of understanding does not proceed in an orderly fashion, beginning with sensation and then continuing, with growing maturity, step by step, along a progressive pattern of perception and imagery, followed by conceptualization, and ending with problem solving and creative thinking. Although sensation is basic to the other steps in developing understanding, all the elements of thinking are present from an early age, and build upon one another. We now shall trace the developmental stages in the thinking process as it progresses in the normally intelligent child, cautioning the reader, however, to remember that the thinking pattern of the mentally superior or of the mentally slow tends to be accelerated or retarded, respectively.

Development during the Early Years   An infant possesses all his sense organs at birth. He responds to light during the first few weeks of life, turning his eyes toward the light and becoming disturbed by a strong light. The extent of his hearing is not known, although loud sounds may elicit changes in respiration and body movements. The taste of sweet solutions seems to be liked and that of salty solutions rejected. The young baby also appears to be sensitive to pain and pressure, hunger and thirst, and heat and cold. His responses to pleasant and unpleasant stimuli at first are diffuse, involving body movements, facial changes, smiling and crying. Later, he seems to be able to differentiate among his sensations, and his reactions become more localized and definite.

The Formation of Percepts   Although the child's first sensations are no more than awareness, he gradually comes to put meaning into things that are in his immediate environment. It can be said that he is beginning to form percepts. He associates percepts, which usually are of general outlines and often inaccurate, with other percepts. He also makes simple judgments concerning them, especially in relation to himself.

As early as the age of six months the baby shows some signs of self-awareness. He seems to recognize himself in relation to those who care for his needs; he turns away from strangers. By the end of the first year he looks for and perhaps tries to retrieve a toy or a spoon that he has dropped. If, in his presence, an object of interest to him is hidden under a chair cushion, for example, he will find it.

During this early period of life, however, memory is short, rarely covering more than a period of one month. The child gradually comes to understand and to remember that some things can be eaten, although at first anything that is small enough to be put into his mouth goes in until he learns that some enticing bits of matter are not for eating. In a similar way he discovers that some moving objects that attract his attention can be played with, such as a ball or his father's moving foot, and that others are not to be handled. Until the child is able to talk, the simple reasoning about himself and the elements of his environment shows itself in his behavior toward them.

Children gradually become able to interpret their sensory experiences so as to recognize subtle likenesses and differences in form, size, and color of objects. Form discrimination, beginning in the first six months, is aided, as the child grows older, through experiences with forms of different sizes and shapes. During the first two years, form rather than color is the basis of discrimination. From then until about the age of four and a half years, color as a key to discrimination appears to predominate. From that age onward, discrimination is likely to be by form rather than by color. *Intensity* of form or color is an important factor of choice, however.

Perception of gross size begins during the first year of life. Fine discrimination in size is acquired gradually and is more likely to occur if the objects compared have the same form. Some young children give evidence of good discrimination between objects in light of form, color, and size. Two little girls, Amy (three and one-half) and her sister, Joan (twenty-one months old), and their parents were served ginger ale at a friend's home. The adults were given tall glasses and the children were given water tumblers, each glass having a brightly colored jacket—Amy's a bright blue and Joan's a deep orange. When Amy picked up Joan's glass, the latter objected, pointing to the jacket and saying, "Mine." Then the children's father took Joan's glass while she was not watching and changed her orange jacket for his yellow one. He extended his larger glass with the orange jacket to her saying, "Here is your ginger ale." Joan looked at the two glasses, refused the larger glass and took the smaller one. The forms of the glasses were the same, the jacket colors and the sizes were different. Her second decision was on the basis of size, rather than color difference.

Perception of position and spatial relationships is a learned activity and begins with general percepts. During the first year the baby learns the meaning of "up"; if he is in his crib and wants to leave it, he will raise his arms and say "up" or "baby up." The meaning of "down" comes later. The terms "nearer" and "farther" probably are not understood until about the age of four years. The two-year-old child, if asked where he sleeps, usually answers "at home." The answers "in my bed" and "in the bedroom" come later. Absolute positions like "over" and "under" or "before" and "behind" at first are general but, during the period from the third year to the fifth year, are qualified to become "way up" or "way down," "nearer" or "farther," and the like. It is during the third year, when the total vocabulary is increasing, that children appear to begin to perceive and use words to describe an increased number of space relationships.

By the time a child reaches his sixth year, he has learned to perceive short distances, and has become more precise in his use of the words "back," "from," and "over." He can distinguish between quick and slow motion, and can recognize objects in relation to other objects and to himself. He also acquires greater skill in matching forms, and distinguishing between two lines of different length or two objects of different weight. Many children become adept at putting together the parts of simple, sometimes relatively complex, picture puzzles, block formations, or building sets.

The Formation of Concepts   The young child's concepts of form, size, and space are abstractions which are built on his experiences with real objects. At first, since he tends to ignore the details of perceptions or meaningful sensations, his concepts develop as generalities and he fails to discriminate among details. Any adult who cares for the child's needs in the absence of his parents may be Mama or Daddy; any furry animal is a doggie or a bunny. During his later preschool years the child's widening experience with different people or things, his improving memory, and his increased facility with language usage help him develop more accurate concepts of the elements of his environment. Adults often make the mistake, however, of assuming that the child's concept of an object or condition is similar to theirs.

The child's first concepts of distance are limited to his immediate environment. Hence places remote from his home have no meaning. It is only gradually that he learns to find his way if he leaves his house or the block on which he lives. The six-year-old usually must be accompanied many times by an older person on his trips to and from school, even though the building is in close proximity to his home street. Linear measures are conceived in relation to home experiences. It is not until he is introduced in school to the use of the ruler that he has any definite conception of the length of an inch, foot, or yard. To obtain a clear understanding of the length of a mile is almost impossible for a child and difficult even for an adult. The verbalization of "twenty city blocks to a mile" may seem to help but does not necessarily produce a completely accurate concept.

Orientation in time is difficult for the young child. Since he lives in the present, the concepts of yesterday and tomorrow are vague terms until he is at least three years old. Before that age he may have gained some understanding of "now," "before now," and "after now," usually in relationship to sleep. Even then he verbalizes the terms "yesterday," "today," and "tomorrow." Yesterday came before he went to sleep and tomorrow is when he awakens from any sleeping period, regardless of whether it is an afternoon nap or a night's sleep. The six-year-old may not be able to name the days of the week, except as certain days are associated with special events, such as going to Sunday School on Sunday. By his seventh year he knows what a month is, but he cannot name the months of the year until he is eight. The child also finds it difficult to learn to "tell time." He needs much practice. The child may not be able to comprehend large time units until he is twelve or older. Moreover, to the average young child a *minute* is no longer than a moment.

Number concepts also are difficult for the child to master, although he seems to gain an understanding of *bigness, littleness, muchness,* and *moreness* fairly early. When he begins to use words, he is likely to say "more" if he has finished eating food which he likes. He also may stretch his arms upward, saying "so big." The concept of exact number comes later. The two-year-old can distinguish between "one" and "more" or "many." The number *two* has meaning to the three-year-old. He gradually learns to count objects, but this is done at first by naming them, as one, two, three, four, and the like. Before they enter school, some children are taught by their elders to count to twenty or higher, but this usually is mere verbalization. The child may omit a number in the sequence; he cannot distinguish between the concepts of fifteen and seventeen, for example.

Progress in concept formation for the child is the process of gaining a clearer picture of earlier concepts, thereby adding depth and extent to their meanings. Many abstractions that are relatively meaningful to adults are beyond the child's capacity of understanding. Preschool children have difficulty with terms such as "God" and "death." The child of religious parents is likely to be told by them that God is everywhere and that he rewards a good child and punishes a naughty one. The idea of being everywhere is beyond the child's understanding, since his thinking still is limited to the concrete and he knows that his parents, his friends, and he himself can be in only one place at a time. The rewarding and punishing aspect causes the child to confuse God with his father, or, if he has seen pictures of God as having a long, white beard, to identify him with Santa Claus. Also, death as a final departure from the family or social circle is difficult for the child to understand. He is likely to think that a person who has died has gone away for a time, but will return eventually. Usually, it is only when a beloved member of the immediate family dies that a child comes to realize that death means an irreparable loss. (See Chapter 17, "Development of Moral and Religious Values.")

Beginning at about six months of age, a child gradually increases in self-awareness. The baby gives evidence of the concept of himself as an individual. He enjoys looking at himself and seems to derive pleasure from playing with his toes or other parts of his body. When he begins to vocalize intelligibly, he is likely to refer to himself as "nice baby." By the age of three years he has learned, with proper motivation, to identify parts of his body, know whether he is a boy or a girl, and know his first and last name. The four-year-old child is likely to know much about himself and to be interested in his appearance. A little girl, especially, takes great pride in her clothes. A favorite pastime of a girl is to "dress up" in her mother's clothes and apply cosmetics indiscriminately.

The developing child frequently views himself as two different selves—the objective and the subjective. He knows that features of his body—height, color of hair, and facial contours—are more or less different from those of other children or adults. He also is aware of his inner self—his thoughts, attitudes, and feelings. His concept of the inner self cannot be perceived except through his behavior. Sometimes the child's recognition of these two selves may continue to cause him to be confused. He wonders who or what he really is. For example, little Ann's mother, who was a Sunday School teacher, was very fond of one of her fifteen-year-old pupils. This bothered Ann very much. With a child's natural self-centeredness, she decided that she must be a changeling (a term the meaning of which she had just learned), because her *real* mother could not give an older girl the attention that rightfully belonged to her own little daughter.

Growth in Reasoning and Problem Solving   The young child's lack of experience causes his reasoning or attempts at solving a problem to seem to the adult to be erroneous or even far-fetched. Early in life the child gains some idea of cause and result relationships. He discovers that to touch or handle some objects or to throw things on the floor receives adult disapproval. Hence he associates parental frowns, the slapping of his little hands, or other forms of punishment with his engaging in this or that "wrong" action. The child becomes confused, however, if certain acts which seem to him no different from others which he performs are greeted with smiles of approbation while others receive disapproval. Especially bewildering is parental inconsistency—at one time a certain form of behavior is punished, but at another time it is disregarded or even approved. Another deterrent to a child's building definite cause-and-effect relationships is fostered by difference in attitudes between his parents, for example. His father may ignore or actually encourage behavior which his mother disapproves. Hence he learns that cause and effect vary with people. As he grows older he may learn to pit parent against parent. He thereby is gaining skill in reasoning that will serve his immediate purposes. This developed attitude may continue to color the child's thinking and problem solving well beyond childhood.

The child's mental processes function much in the same way as do adults' problem solving activities. Because of his immaturity, however, he often cannot comprehend all the implications of the raw mental materials which he is attempting to manipulate. He does not recognize the significant inferences inherent in the problem. Inadequate understanding of the problem causes him to evolve erroneous conclusions. Too often adults, not realizing the child's normal inadequacies, conclude that he is mentally retarded, stupid or uninterested.

Increasing Maturity and Development of Understanding Between the ages of seven and eleven, the child begins to engage in logical thinking. Although he still is somewhat self-centered, he is able to get outside himself and recognize cause-and-effect relationships in the world about him. Natural phenomena take on added meaning. The seasons of the year become real concepts, representing weather and temperature changes. Yet the seasons may be identified more definitely in light of personal interests: summer means vacation from school, play and trips from home; winter brings the Christmas gifts and fun. Boys, especially, tend to associate the seasons with different kinds of sports. Many childish evaluations of things and conditions continue through much of some people's adult experiences.

During later childhood and early adolescence, the young person is likely to be extremely curious about his world. He is intrigued by all the different people and things that stimulate his senses. He wants to experiment and, through his experiences, build new and satisfying concepts. He looks for cause-and-effect relationships and enjoys solving problems that arise in his daily life. Previous experiences still tend to affect the accuracy of his conclusions, however.

The elementary school child gains much satisfaction from comparing his thoughts and feelings with those of his peer-age associates. Although he may ask adults many questions concerning matters which are not clear to him, he seems to believe that other children of his own age are more understanding than are most adults. He may be fearful of adults' laughter when he expresses an opinion that to him is very serious but to them may be amusing. He no longer is a baby and wants his ideas to be accorded the respect he thinks they deserve.

One can learn much from children's conversation among themselves when they are talking freely. For example, one of the writers was walking along the street behind a group of nine- and ten-year-olds who were returning home from school. They were discussing Mother's Day and the gifts that they had made in school for their mothers. One of the children was heard to make the comment: "It's nice to have a Mother's Day when you show how much you love your mother, but there should be a 'Children's Day.' You know what I mean? A day when you could say anything you like without being punished. That would be fun!"

This child not only was giving voice to her secret desire, but also disclosed her parents' interest in her behavior. The chances are that this little girl did not offer her suggestion to her parents.

The accuracy and richness of an older child's percepts, concepts, and understanding are dependent in good measure on the kind of experiential stimulations he received in his earlier years as well as on his degree of mental acuity. A bright child reared in a home where, from earliest childhood, he has experienced many different and stimulating situations and has been encouraged to think and make simple decisions under adult guidance, can be expected to develop good habits of thinking that will serve him well throughout his life.

QUESTIONS AND TOPICS FOR DISCUSSION

1. Compare the relation that exists between the physical and mental growth of children with whom you are acquainted.
2. Justify the statement that the sense organs are the gateways to understanding. Select one of the senses and show ways in which a person is handicapped if the sense organ does not function adequately.
3. Study the illustrations in the chapter. Report your responses to them.
4. Trace the relationships between perception and imagery.
5. Select a concept, such as massiveness, generosity, or pulchritude. What does the term mean to you? How did you develop the concept?
6. Sit comfortably in an easy chair and allow your thoughts to wander at will for about five minutes (have someone time you). Then try to recall your thoughts. How do you explain them?
7. Read a short poem by Keats. How did it affect you? Why?
8. After you have read this chapter, make note of any new facts you learned. What were they? How much of the chapter material was already known to you? Where did you get the information?
9. Recall a common, everyday problem that you have solved recently and list the steps you took in its solution.
10. You are more or less intelligent than you were five years ago. Agree or disagree and explain.
11. *Special Project:* If possible, obtain the intelligence quotients of your four subjects. To what extent does their behavior give evidence of their intellectual status? Make specific notes. Discover and report at least two differences in understanding between the two younger and the two older children.

SELECTED REFERENCES

Bayley, Nancy, "On Growth of Intelligence," *American Psychologist,* 10: 805–818, 1955.

Combs, Arthur W., and Snygg, Donald, *Individual Behavior: A Perceptual Approach to Behavior,* rev. ed. New York: Harper and Brothers, 1959.

Eells, K., *et al., Intelligence and Cultural Differences.* Chicago: University of Chicago Press, 1951.

Griffiths, R., *The Abilities of Babies: A Study in Mental Measurement.* New York: McGraw-Hill Book Company, Inc., 1954.

Hirst, R. J., *The Problems of Perception.* New York: The Macmillan Company, 1959.

Lowenfeld, V., *Creative and Mental Growth,* 3rd ed. New York: The Macmillan Company, 1957.

Navarra, J. G., *The Development of Scientific Concepts in a Young Child.* New York: Bureau of Publications, Teachers College, 1955.

Piaget, J., *The Origins of Intelligence in Children.* New York: International Universities Press, 1952.

Piaget, J., and Inhelder, B., *The Growth of Logical Thinking from Childhood to Adolescence.* New York: Basic Books, Inc., 1958.

Russell, D. H., *Children's Thinking.* Boston: Ginn and Company, 1956.

Terman, L. M., and Merrill, Maud A., *Stanford-Binet Intelligence Scale: Manual for the Third Revision Form L-M.* Boston: Houghton Mifflin Company, 1960.

Wechsler, David, *The Range of Human Capacities.* Baltimore: The Williams and Wilkins Company, 1952.

9

THE PATTERNING
OF CHILDREN'S
IMAGINATION

BETWEEN THE AGES of about three through twelve, the child tends to live in two worlds—the real and the fanciful. He is highly imaginative. As his percepts and concepts gradually are developed, he is moved to manipulate them to meet his immediate desires and interests. To the extent that his real world is bound by the limitations of adult controls and environmental circumstances, he can project through his imagination his wants and interests beyond the bounds of reality.

THE WORLD OF MAKE-BELIEVE

Since the young child's experiences are limited, he does not have sufficient knowledge of reality to construct ideas that meet the test of actuality and that are at the same time satisfying to himself. Although he only partially understands situations and conditions, he is stimulated by his developing interests to manipulate ideas in such a way that the end result meets his emotional needs without the utilization of all relevant data. He neither realizes nor cares that the outcomes of make-believe may be far removed from actual fact. It is only as he matures sufficiently and receives patient and intelligent adult guidance that he eventually comes to appreciate the relationship that exists between fact and fantasy.

The Role of Fantasy Make-believe may take the form of fantasy, or the projecting of oneself into situations that are far removed from everyday life experiences. The young child's imagination is stirred by nursery rhymes that are read to him. He has never seen a cow jump over the moon, for example, but he receives much emotional satisfaction from visualizing the possibility. Later, as he reads about the exploits of the heroes and heroines in fairy tales and of mythological characters, and views motion picture and television programs, he tends to identify himself with them. He is the one who defies the power of the wicked witch, goblin, or fearsome creature who threatens his safety or the life of one he loves. He is not always successful in solving his problems in real life. In the world of fantasy the good and just (himself) always prevail.

Most boys prefer accounts of adventure, and girls thrill to romantic stories. Usually, emotion-arousing tales not only provide them with excitement but also motivate them to enact heroic and dramatic roles that they may not fully understand. Too great involvement in the world of fantasy is likely to arouse personally unachievable ambitions. Both younger and older children thereby may be stimulated, as they fail in attempted exploits, to retreat still further from the world of reality into one of continued fantasy. The tendency to confuse the real and the fanciful may persist into adult life. Contrariwise, insofar as a maturing young child gradually can appreciate consciously the relationship of fantasy to realism, engaging in some wish-fulfilling activities will sharpen his imaginative powers and prepare him for the fulfillment of worthwhile creative projects during adulthood.

Make-Believe in Play Activities Play activity serves several purposes, such as giving pleasure, absorbing the whole attention, providing some degree of creativity, and not being concerned *per se* with the end result of the activity. Imaginative play or make believe is highly satisfying to the child, especially during the preschool and the primary school years. He manipulates his toys at will, endowing them with qualities they do not possess. In play situations he imitates the everyday activities of his elders. A girl of this age also enjoys dressing in her mother's clothes. Note the shoes in Figure 71. Through these media the child learns a great deal

United Press International Photo

Figure 71. Three-Year-Old Caroline Kennedy Interrupts a Conference of Her Father, President John F. Kennedy, to Show Him How She Can Walk in Her Mother's High Heel Shoes.

about the world around him and unconsciously is preparing himself for participation in real life responsibilities.

Fantasy and make-believe are closely associated with concept development. Children not only find release of feeling in make-believe, but it has distinct value for them in clarifying their concepts of what their world is like and how it operates. Through make-believe activities, they are helped to appreciate their own sex role and learn what society expects from them. In dramatic play, a child constantly is giving the future a dry run, trying it on for size, as it were, as can be seen in Figure 72.

YOUNG CHILDREN'S PLAY The very young child usually plays alone. His blocks and other toys assume a variety of meanings for him. As a little boy plays with his blocks, they take on the form variously of a train, a house, and the like. The little girl's dolls are her babies. She gives them names, cares for their needs, and talks to them, often admonishing them to be good children—all of this in imitation of her mother's or another woman's behavior in relation to herself or younger children. In these forms of make-believe, the toys always do what their little owner desires, otherwise they are punished. Hence these make-believe activities are extremely satisfying.

As the child gains some understanding of the various activities that constitute the household's customary activities, the little boy, more especially the little girl, imitates some of them in play. Five-year-old Ethel, for example, was intrigued by her mother's marketing experiences. Using a dining room chair with the seat as her counter and the open back to divide her imaginary customers from herself, she would spend long periods in selling groceries. She carried on lengthy conversations with the women who came to buy, advising them what to purchase while measuring carefully and making change. In all of this activity, she performed as she believed adult women did. Sometimes her mother was amazed by the child's ability to imitate the voices and mannerisms of the clerks and customers whom the child had observed when she accompanied her mother on shopping trips.

Little children give vent to their emotionalized feelings in their free play. Through a child's make-believe, adults can gain insight into his attitudes toward family relationships and his social adjustments. The child, for instance, may have ambivalent feelings toward the members of his family. He may act out his hostilities, fears, or aggression in his play with a doll family. In his play, as he imitates the activities of the members of the family (especially parental behavior toward himself and other siblings) he talks to the various dolls, calling them by their appropriate names, and telling them how he feels toward them. In extreme cases of aggression he may throw a particular doll on the floor and step on it. Such activity apparently helps to release tension and is extremely satisfying to the child who suffers more or less conscious frustrations inspired by his awareness of limitations set by his elders on the fulfillment of his childish desires.

MAKE-BELIEVE PLAY OF OLDER CHILDREN The make-believe activities of the younger preschool child center around specific materials. The older child, either alone or in the company of playmates, supplies imaginary materials. As boys, for example, play "cops and robbers," they use an imaginary gun, and as they crook their fingers, they cry, "Bang-bang." Little girls plan and carry out a tea party. They engage in social chit-chat, while they drink tea from toy dishes and eat imaginary cake. Through all of the make-believe they imitate in detail the behavior of their mothers in similar situations.

In like fashion, children may act out their school experiences. This form of make-believe affords an opportunity for younger and older children to play together. One older child is the teacher, another may be the principal, while the younger children are the pupils. It might be a good thing on occasions for school people to view themselves through the eyes of young people, as their voices and mannerisms are imitated by the boys and girls. In the play situation the children do many of the things they would like to do in school but dare not. Sometimes, if the pupils are too docile, the child teacher insists upon more aggressive behavior so that proper punishment can be applied. Rarely do the children supply actual books, pencils, and paper. They seem to gain sufficient satisfaction from working with imaginary materials.

Another form of play that is popular, especially among children who have experienced various illnesses, is that of doctor-patient relationships. Either a younger child or a doll is seriously ill. The doctor (a boy) is called by the patient's child-parent to diagnose the illness and treat the patient. The various activities are acted out. As often as not, the patient is so ill that the doctor must experiment with many kinds of treatment.

**Figure 72.
Five-Year-Old Linda
Showers and Bathes
Her Doll.**

United Press International Photo

Figure 73. Boys Stop Their Swing-ing Activities Long Enough for a Picture.

The members of the family engage in emotionalized behavior, begging the doctor to save the child's life. Here again equipment, medication, and the like are imaginary. The children sometimes appear to take great pleasure in their role-playing, bringing the entire situation to a logical conclusion: either the patient recovers and there is great rejoicing, or he dies and the children enact their conception of sorrowful arrange-ments for the funeral.

Occasionally, adults are brought into the make-believe play. To be accepted in the situation, however, the older person must follow the lead of the children. If the adult is invited to be the parent or teacher, for example, he must play his role according to the children's dictation. Any deviation from expected behavior is thoroughly criticized. By sharing in children's make-believe or watching them carefully, older people can gain considerable understanding of the way in which a child's mind tends to function during this period of social development.

IMAGINARY COMPANIONS It is a common practice for a child to have an imaginary companion, either another child or an animal, such as a dog. The child talks to and about this companion. He often endows the imaginary child or animal with many virtues which are absent in his real associates. It has been a common belief that it is the lonely child who is most likely to create an imaginary companion for himself. This is not altogether true. A bright child is more likely than a slow child to engage in this form of make-believe, in spite of the fact that he may have same-age associates with whom he plays freely. It is a different kind of relationship, however. The child's imaginary companion is his own; there need not be any separation between the two; the child receives an emotional satisfaction from this association with a kind of alter ego that may not be possible even with a very close real friend.

Adults often are bothered by a child's imaginary companion. They may believe that its "existence" is a sign of something wrong with the child. Kin Platt, for example, in his "Mr. and Mrs." cartoons, devoted several issues of the series to the troubles of "Mr." with a neighbor's child whom he was accustomed to meet with the youngster's imaginary dog that the man was expected to treat as if he were real.

Perhaps the best approach of adults to this phenomenon is to accept the imaginary companion and talk about it seriously with the child, with the assurance that, with increasing maturity and involvement in many real activities, this form of make-believe (like others) gradually will be forgotten. At the same time, however, the adult must be careful not to overplay the existence of the imaginary companion to the extent that the child is encouraged, for example, to place the blame for his own misdeeds on the influence of the figment of his imagination. Neither should the adult ridicule the companion or punish the child for imagining him. This adult attitude may cause the young person to become even more involved, using his relationship with the other as a means of comfort in an unpleasant experience.

Exaggeration   The child tends to want attention from his associates. He wants to make an impression on the members of his peer-age group as well as on adults. His father is the best and most important father in the neighborhood. His family can do things that others cannot. Insofar as he cannot impress his companions with his own superior achievements, he tends to exaggerate the activities of his close relatives. He is in the class of the individual who, feeling himself to be inadequate, boasts of his "illustrious ancestors."

Children's lies often fall into a similar category. Youngsters tend to think in big terms. Two cats in the areaway become a hundred or even a thousand cats. A dime is a fortune. Children from the ages of three to six find it difficult to distinguish between fact and fancy. Their urge to capture attention may cause them to tell lies which they themselves seem to believe. If the family does not appear to be sufficiently appreciative of a kindergartener's or a first grader's reports of his school successes, he may announce that the teacher is unfair to him, punishing him for misdeeds which he did not commit. In this way he can focus family attention on himself. This is satisfying, even though his accusation is found to be untrue. He finds reason enough in excusing his action by the comment, "I had to make you pay attention to me."

It is best for parents and other adults to refrain from viewing too seriously a child's exaggerations or "tall stories." An attitude of sympathetic amusement, accompanied by a question such as, "Do you really want me to believe what you say?" or a suggestion that the child and adult check the facts, usually results in the child's admitting that "I was only fooling."

There are occasions when a child's lies are rooted in fear of punishment for the performance of an act that he believes will receive parental disapproval. A sensitive child accidentally may break a family's prized possession, for example. His remorse, coupled with fear of consequences, may cause him to deny any knowledge of the broken object. He even may attempt to place the blame on someone else. Too-strict parents often find themselves in situations of this kind. They are likely to make matters worse by accusing the child of deliberately engaging in a misdeed. Teachers also may fail to recognize the underlying reason for children's cheating. Best results usually are achieved in situations such as these if the adult attempts to find the actual cause of the dishonest behavior of the child, and to help him face unpleasant situations honestly, secure in the knowledge that his conduct will receive fair and just treatment. Moreover, adults can do much to prevent children's getting into mischief without meaning to do so, thereby helping them develop attitudes of frankness and truthfulness.

Imaginary Illness Somewhat related to exaggeration and lying is a child's tendency to "pretend" temporary or more lasting forms of illness as a means of avoiding an unpleasant chore or situation. We all probably have encountered instances of children's morning sickness which can keep them at home on a school day and thereby save them the embarrassment of going to school unprepared for the day's work. Miraculous recoveries usually are made later in the day, and play activities are engaged in with

considerable zest. The child who uses this technique to meet an immediate, to him serious, crisis is not mature enough to realize that he has
not solved his problem; he has merely delayed retribution.

More serious is the condition of an older child or young adolescent
whose home, school, or social experiences have become so intolerable,
sometimes through no fault of his own, that he believes himself unable
to face his difficulties. He then may take refuge in the imagined development of one or another form of illness. He actually may suffer disturbing
symptoms of the sickness. He is deceiving himself as well as those whom
he regards as responsible for his condition. If malingering is permitted to
occur during the growing-up years, the individual concerned may continue to use this technique during adulthood as a means of shirking responsibilities.

A young person who is suspected of feigning illness should be submitted to a thorough physical examination. If no organic disturbance is
found, an attempt should be made by a responsible adult to discover
the basic cause of the victim's condition. Any reasonable obstacle to his
normal ability to perform should be removed, and he himself should be
helped to make a more realistic adjustment to problem situations. In
severe cases, prolonged, patient, and sympathetic assistance may be needed
to bring about the willingness to face facts with understanding.

THE DREAM WORLD

Both daydreams and dreams during sleep are common experiences
of children. Through their dreams they often can satisfy their interests
and urges in a way that is denied them in actual experiences.

Dreams during Sleep   Various points of view have been expressed
in attempts to interpret children's dreams. Some psychologists hold that
dreams are related to those emotional or exciting happenings that occur
during waking hours. According to some psychiatrists, through his dreams
the child can give vent to his needs, desires, hopes, fears, and hostilities.
In his dream world he manipulates his ideas either in a satisfying or a
frustrating fashion. The child may confuse the dream with reality, he
fills in gaps, but his dream may be limited by his lack of experience in
appreciating logical relationships between cause and effect.

Jane, a bright, highly sensitive seven-year-old girl, had become very
much disturbed by a story she had heard about the father of one of her

little friends who supposedly had left home because he and the mother "always fought." One night, as the child was preparing for bed, she heard her father and mother engaging in a mild disagreement. Jane fell asleep but awakened to find tears running down her cheeks. She jumped out of bed, ran to her parents' room, and threw herself into her father's arms, crying, "Daddy, daddy, I'm so glad you're here. I dreamed you had run away because Mommy and you were fighting." The emotionalized attitudes stimulated by the experience of her little friend had gained so much influence over her imagination that in her dream she herself was living through a similar experience.

From the age of two years through adolescence many children seem to have disturbing dreams. Especially do these occur if a child has had annoying or exciting experiences during the day. The tense, overexcited child may continue to have similar emotional reactions in his dreams. Their presence is attested to by the kicking off of bedclothes, tossing and turning, and crying or screaming. Contrariwise, the child who goes to bed in a tranquil state of mind is likely to have pleasant dreams. He may be seen to smile or heard to laugh in his sleep. Any movements he makes during the night are quiet and nondisturbing.

Some children report that they may awaken during a dream (pleasant or unpleasant) and recall it distinctly. In fact, they may find it difficult to distinguish between the dream and reality. In some instances the dream continues after they have again fallen asleep. Like adults, however, if the child sleeps through until morning, he may have a vague memory of his dream, but is unable to fill in details unless the dream was extremely vivid or occurred just before waking. It must be admitted, however, that there is much about the dream world of both children and adults that still defies explanation.

Daydreaming   There are few children who do not engage more or less frequently in daydreaming. As in make-believe play, in daydreams the child, through the exercise of his imagination, can achieve many satisfactions that are denied him in real life. Problems can be solved according to his best interests. Success in achievement is his for the asking.

As the child becomes acquainted, through stories read to him or by himself, with the heroes and heroines of fancy or fact, it is normal for him to identify himself with these glamorous creatures. In his daydream he is not hampered by cold facts. He allows his imagination to soar to great heights. If he gets himself into a situation from which he cannot extricate himself, it is an easy matter to shift the scene to one in which noble exploits are possible. Usually, childhood dreams of conquest and power give way during adolescence to what may seem to the dreamer more realistic achievement of romance, luxury, or financial gain.

Daydreams may take on the form of a serial novel. A woman known for her creative writing reported to the writers that from the ages of about ten to eighteen she was accustomed to tell herself success stories before she fell asleep at night. She added a chapter each night (revising when necessary), until she had reached the pinnacle of success in one type of achievement, whereupon she would start another. In order of age, according to her report, the daydreams dealt with school experience: the performance of courageous feats, such as the rescue of a drowning person and the like, that could bring fame to herself and her family; romantic conquests; the winning of a fortune so that she could become a great philanthropist; finally, the becoming of a world-renowned musical virtuoso, in spite of the fact that she had little or no musical ability, but a tremendous admiration for a friend who had considerable musical talent. This woman admitted that in her daydreams she usually wanted herself to be the heroine, but that sometimes she could not avoid giving this honor to a beloved associate and basking in the reflected glory of the other's achievements.

Daydreaming that is related to a young person's changing ambitions is not necessarily harmful. In fact, the daydream can be constructive in that it may inspire the dreamer to do something definite about achieving a desired goal. He may become fired *to do* instead of to dream. Although one desirable quality of the daydream to the dreamer is that it is a private form of activity, he often is impelled to discuss his hopes and dreams with a sympathetic, tactful adult. The latter thereby is enabled to help the young person to translate his dream into achievable actuality that can be extremely self-satisfying. There is danger in daydreaming, however, if the individual indulges in emotionally satisfying dreams to the exclusion of attempts to meet day-by-day problems of adjustment in a realistic way. The life of fantasy, then, can persist and, instead of helping in the solution of life problems, instigate the experiencing of deep inner conflict which can be met only through still greater utilization of destructive imaginings. (See also Chapter 18.)

CREATIVITY IN CHILDHOOD

Properly used, fantasy, make-believe, and daydreaming are fundamental elements in the development of creative ability. Insofar as the child's imagination can be channeled into paths that combine the real and the fanciful, he can be guided toward evolving or creating novel aspects of known phenomena.

The Meaning and Value of Creativity   Since the child's imagination seeks expression, he needs opportunities to participate in activities which have value for himself and others as he fulfills his urge to express his creative abilities in a recognizable form. What he creates may be concerned with the realm of thinking or with the development of something new through media such as music, the dance, representative art, or imaginative writing. In any case, emotional reaction and satisfaction accompany the act of creation. According to Dorothy Barclay:

> A true creation will be an object, a process, or an atmosphere that will, at the mundane level, help others to cope more comfortably with life. In the highest sense, it will help others to find beauty and meaning in their lives and in their surroundings, to see and to understand the world about them. [1]

As the child creates something new and different, he is not concerned with the effect of his creation on the lives of other people, but he himself is gaining emotional satisfaction from his efforts at self-expression. The young child's product may be unrealistic and crude. Nevertheless, what he has produced has definite meaning for him. Moreover, during the early stages of a child's attempts at creativity, the process—the free play of his imagination—is important. Later, as the child's activity takes on a purpose that is more in keeping with realism, he becomes more concerned with the kind and ultimate worth of his production. He then recognizes the need to combine freedom of expression with the following of appropriate rules for performance. Basically, however, for a child to create, his activity must be stimulated by an emotionalized urge to engage in the project. In fact, his behavior may be motivated by the felt need to obtain release from pent-up emotions.

The young child may give vent to his feelings by covering a sheet of paper with meaningless scribbling. This activity is highly satisfying to him. The older child, adolescent, or adult sometimes, almost unconsciously, may engage in aimless doodlings that appear to have no other objective than that of relieving emotional tensions. In the strict connotation of the term "creation," such purposeless activities do not represent creativity, although from such beginnings may emerge eventually what can be accepted as more or less artistic productions.

[1] Barclay, Dorothy, "Creativity and the Child," *The New York Times Magazine*, p. 64, February 28, 1960.

Two points of view are extant concerning the possession of a creative ability. Some people believe that the ability to create is a special talent that does not show itself until adolescence or adulthood, that little or no training is needed, and that "artists" are likely to have different or "queer" personalities. There are some individuals who accept the belief that to create means to "express oneseslf," without inhibition. Any impulsive deviation in action or in thought by a child, for example, is assumed to be a creative act and should be encouraged.[2]

We have come to realize that every child possesses to some degree the ability to create, but that not every impulsive or uninhibited act or word is an expression of creativity. To produce the new and the different requires, as we suggested in Chapter 8, a felt need and a definite purpose, a background of experience as preparation, and usually much hard work during the period of incubation so that illumination may be achieved and the value of the product verified.

Development of Creativity   Even among small children, creative expression derives from mental exploration. The child needs to be given opportunities to manipulate freely not only objects in his environment, such as toys, pencils, paint brushes, and simple instruments or machines, but also his simple ideas. We have stressed the child's power to imitate the behavior of others. This is a useful asset, but equally valuable to him are self-initiated activity, flexibility, and freedom to discover forms of expression with which he can identify himself and from which he gains emotional satisfaction.

EARLY BEGINNINGS OF CREATIVITY   The very young child derives satisfaction from the manipulation of blocks. The infant touches a block or picks it up. By the end of the first year he is able to place blocks next to each other. According to the studies of Gesell and others of young children's behavior with blocks, definite conclusions were formulated.[3] If ten cubes are placed on a table and the child is seated in a chair at the table, the fifteen-month-old child stands and attends to the blocks for a short time only; the eighteen-month-old child remains seated and attends to the cubes for a longer period, while he picks up the cubes, holds them in each hand, and replaces them on the table, sometimes scattering them. The two-year-old, remaining seated, tends to place the blocks in a row, or scatter them; the three-year-old is likely to arrange the blocks in hori-

---

[2] See Millard, C. V., *Child Growth and Development in the Elementary School Years,* rev. ed. Boston: D. C. Heath and Company, 1958.

[3] Gesell, Arnold, *et al., The First Five Years of Life,* pp. 109–111. New York: Harper and Brothers, 1940.

zontal rows, occasionally attempting to build a tower. Four- and five-year-olds build complicated structures, sometimes having three dimensions. A complicated structure is called a house, a building, a church, or anything else that suits their fancy. Increase in maturation and experience is evidenced in the developing pattern of cube handling.

The preschool child gives expression to his growing curiosity and imagination in his treatment of his toys. He attempts to superimpose one toy on another, he may squeeze a doll or take a toy apart and try to put it together again. At first his scribblings have no form, then he engages in longitudinal scribbling, and later he attempts to give it form and names it a house, a man, or a flower. He is annoyed if adults cannot recognize the object he has drawn.

CREATIVITY DURING EARLY SCHOOL YEARS   In the nursery school, kindergarten, and early grades of the elementary school, the child is encouraged to express his imagination through painting, drawing, the art crafts, singing, dancing, and storytelling. *Finger painting* with colored mud on a table covered with oilcloth is a popular form of activity, especially in the nursery school. The child is motivated to pour some of the soft mud on the table and then with hands and arms to the elbow, work out intriguing designs. Through the use of this technique the young child is enabled to give expression to his emotions and imaginative interests. Similar purposes can be served by having children paint with water on the chalkboard, using wide bristle brushes.

Later, nursery school and kindergarten teachers introduce the children to easel painting with ready-mixed paints and large brushes. At first they use one color only, and then red, blue, green, and violet. Later, orange and yellow are included. It usually is not until the third or fourth grade that children are permitted to mix their own paints. Painting on paper with smaller brushes, at tables or desks, is attempted in the later grades. (See Figure 74.)

Children enjoy experimenting with color and form. There is considerable difference, of course, in their products. Some children are more successful than others in giving expression to their imagination and in including desirable details. These differences show themselves also in children's attempts to draw objects or create designs, first with crayons and later with soft pencils.

Children also enjoy craft activities. They revel in playing with lumps of clay, as they mold the clay into what at first may be fantastic forms, but that later take on some similarity to real objects. Paper-cutting and construction, carving objects out of soft wood, and puppet-making pro-

United Press International Photo

Figure 74. Young Artists at Work.

gressively afford the imaginative child opportunities to engage in expressional interests.

During the child's early school years, he is encouraged to devote much of his time to various forms of rhythmic expression, such as folk and social dancing, singing, and the playing of simple musical instruments. As a group, children are sensitive to musical rhythm. The baby enjoys being sung to sleep. The very young child may attempt to imitate an adult's singing, even crooning himself to sleep.

Nursery school and kindergarten children like to develop simple dances to music played by the teacher. They also improvise dance steps to radio or television music. They enjoy singing simple songs, especially if the music has a quick tempo, or the song seems to tell a story that can be "acted out" by the children as they sing. Here, again, children differ in their ability to perform. Some seem to be more sensitive than others to correct time, pitch, timbre, and tone quality. Although most children can be helped to perform adequately in simple rhythmic expression, most psychologists believe that individuals differ in the possession of musical ability and rhythmic expression.

LATER CREATIVE DEVELOPMENT   Individual differences in creative abilities show themselves rather definitely during later elementary and secondary school years. These differences are caused partly by individual depth and breadth of imagination, and partly by greater or lesser skill in the manipulation of materials of expression. To some degree, however, the extent of young people's interest and skill in creative production is directly related to the attitudes of the teacher and his skill in motivation of the learner.

Regardless of the area of creation—representative art, rhythmic expression, creative writing, or object construction—the creator needs to express himself freely and, at the same time, give attention to the formal details of correct production. Neither aspect can be sacrificed for the other if a worthwhile result is to be achieved.

Some teachers become so concerned about the skill phase of the creative act that they discourage the free play of imagination or the spirit of inventiveness. Other teachers may stress the creative phase and accept slovenly or inaccurate performance. Either attitude is likely to interfere with a pupil's best efforts and performance, especially one who is not sure of himself in a particular medium of expression. It is the teacher himself who is creative and who has experienced difficulties in producing worthwhile outcomes of his imagination who is able, in his guidance of youthful endeavors, to encourage skilled performance without dimming or killing the creative flame. Such teachers, unfortunately, are relatively rare, but where they exist they sometimes can motivate young people to create superbly.

QUESTIONS AND TOPICS FOR DISCUSSION

1. Try to recall your childhood experiences in fantasy. What were your accustomed flights of imagination?
2. What kinds of stories did you enjoy as a child? Explain.
3. In what ways does the telling of "tall stories" satisfy the child's ego?
4. How can hypochondria be related to childhood experiences?
5. Try to recall some of your dreams during sleep. How do you explain any similarity that exists in your dreams?
6. Have you ever experienced a daydream that was constructive? Explain the situation.

7. If you have a creative interest, when did it begin and what have you done or are doing to develop it?

8. What training are you receiving that will fit you to help children develop creative ability?

9. *Special Project:* Discover the kinds of stories your subjects enjoy. Who are their heroes or heroines? What are their favorite play activities? Give the subjects appropriate materials for creative activities. What age and sex differences do you find in their practices and products?

SELECTED REFERENCES

DeMartino, M. F. (ed.), *Dreams and Personality Dynamics.* Springfield, Ill.: Charles C Thomas, 1959.

Freud, Sigmund, *The Interpretation of Dreams.* New York: Modern Library, 1950.

Hadfield, J. A., *Dreams and Nightmares.* London: Penguin Books, 1954.

Hartley, R. E., *et al., Understanding Children's Play.* New York: Columbia University Press, 1952.

Johnson, J., *Home Play for the Preschool Child.* New York: Harper and Brothers, 1957.

O'Brien, Mary, and Sibley, L., "Developing Creativity in Children's Use of Imagination," in F. Ligon *et al., Character Research Project,* Union College, Schenectady, 1953.

Patrick, C., *What Is Creative Thinking?* New York: Philosophical Library, Inc., 1955.

Piaget, J., "Play, Dreams and Imitation in Children," *New Education Fellowship,* 1951.

Tauber, Edward S., and Green, M. R., *Prelogical Experience: An Inquiry into Dreams and Other Creative Processes.* New York: Basic Books, Inc., 1959.

Wilt, M. E., *Creativity in the Elementary School.* New York: Appleton-Century-Crofts, Inc., 1959.

I O

THE DEVELOPMENT OF CHILDREN'S EMOTIONS

THE AFFECTIVE PHASE of life is extremely important in the child's total developmental pattern. Progress in every other aspect of his integrated personality—physical, motor, intellectual, and social—is accompanied by feeling tones and emotional experiences. The child's behavior tends to be motivated by the effect upon him of inner responses that usually are referred to as joy, sorrow, anger, jealousy, resentment, fear, worry, anxiety, awe, or any combination of these states. A child may not be able to express verbally his inner reactions, nor does he always understand their effect upon his thoughts and actions. Emotions exercise a potent influence on his life pattern, however.

BASIC NATURE OF THE EMOTIONS

The kind of emotional reactions experienced by a child depends on the extent to which his desires or interests are satisfied or frustrated, and on the amount of understanding he possesses of his relationship to the people, objects, and conditions that comprise his environment. If we subscribe to the belief that emotion is the background for behavior mo-

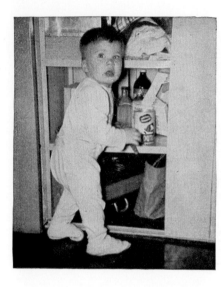

Figure 75. A Fourteen-Month-Old Child Shows a Guilty Expression When Caught in the Act.

tivation, it is necessary that adults understand the basic nature of emotional experience in order to gain insight into children's developing personality patterns.

Meaning of Emotion   The term "emotion" is associated with the Latin verb *emovere* which, translated, means *to stir, to agitate, to move.* Hence an emotion can be referred to as *a stirred-up state of agitation,* or *a temporary disorganization of responses.* One must keep in mind, however, that the degree of agitation varies with the intensity of the emotional state. In extreme anger or fear, for example, there may be considerable disorganization of response, but in a milder emotional state, such as tenderness, the organism may be less "stirred-up."

Physiological Changes   The emotional experience is facilitated by the internal secretions of the endocrine glands as they affect the autonomic nervous system, making possible the rapid physiological changes that occur. During an emotional state, the secretions of the adrenal glands, for example, relax the smooth muscles, send blood to the surface of the body, release glycogen into the blood stream, change the rate of heartbeat, and change the size of the blood vessels. Normal functioning of the endocrine glands enables the individual to experience emotional stability.

Physical and physiological changes during an emotional experience do not produce the emotion but are evidences of it and are a part of the overt phase of it. Physiological accompaniments of emotions have been studied through chemical tests of blood or changes in body function. Among the types of instruments used in such tests are: the *pneumograph* (respiration), *sphygmomanometer* (blood pressure), *sphygmograph* (pulse), *plethysmograph* (blood volume), *electrocardiograph* (heart-muscle activity), and *psychogalvanometer* (resistance of skin or sweat gland activity).

Although many physiological changes accompany emotion, little is yet known about the distinct physiological characteristics of respective emotions. Strong emotions provoke greater physiological effects or concomitants than do the weaker emotional states. When an individual is in a state of optimum physiological balance, the metabolic functions of the visceral organs are carried out in a definite rhythm. Serenity and contentment favor the continuance of normal, healthy bodily functions; excitement tends to upset the equilibrium. The body is readied to fight or to run; blood pressure is increased; digestion ceases; the heart beats more rapidly; and the tonus of the skeletal muscles is raised.

Aspects of an Emotion To the extent that a child is emotionally moved, the physiologist can measure increase in the blood changes, decrease in the flow of saliva, change in heart rate and forcing of extra blood into the extremities of the body, alteration in endocrinal secretion, and interference with digestive movements. To the lay observer are noticeable other changes, such as flushing or paling, more rapid breathing, choking of voice, flow of tears, and perhaps bulging of the eyes and trembling of the hands or entire body. These physiological changes are accompaniments of the emotional state; they do not produce the emotion. As the physiological changes take place, however, the emotional process may be quickened.

Viewed subjectively, emotions are accompanied by strong or vague, pleasant or unpleasant feelings. Extreme fear can be described, for example, as possessing a strong, unpleasant feeling tone; anxiety may be vague but unpleasant. Great love is strong but usually pleasant; a more generalized emotionalized state, such as tenderness, may be vague but pleasant. On the subjective side can be included an awareness or perception of that which has aroused the emotion. The child may fail to perceive correctly the basic cause of his feelings that can instigate certain kinds of behavior, such as fleeing from a fear stimulus (if possible), moving toward the person or object that arouses an attitude of tenderness, or attempting to fight or attack anyone or anything that causes anger or jealousy. It also can be said that emotionalized behavior can be well organized or highly disorganized and explosive.

Causal Factors of Emotions   When we consider the factors that are active in the arousal of an emotion, we tend to emphasize the stimulating effect of people, objects, conditions, or circumstances in one's environment. Actually, factors within the individual himself also operate to arouse an emotion which, once aroused, will determine its intensity. Among these inner stimuli are included his attitudes, desires, interests and ideals, the state of his health, and his degree of self-understanding and self-control.

The same stimulus may arouse a particularly strong emotional feeling at one time and, at another time, arouse another emotion or not affect him emotionally. For example, if a woman is busily engaged in completing a household chore, she may become angered by a neighbor's dropping in for a chat; if she is relaxing with no special task awaiting her attention, she may be delighted to see her neighbor; at other times, during the course of daily activities, she may have no special feelings about stopping to talk over neighborhood affairs. Similarly, different persons may respond with different emotionalized attitudes toward the same stimulating situation. Two children are playing in the park while their mothers are sitting near them. A woman passes by and starts to talk to the children. One child, delighted by the attention she is receiving, enters into conversation with the woman; the other child, fearful of the strange woman, runs to her mother and attempts to hide behind her.

An emotion is likely to continue as long as the stimulus is present and is recognized as a motivator of a certain kind of reaction. With its removal or a better understanding of its import, the emotional state diminishes or another emotion takes its place. Fear, for example, may give way to anger; angry annoyance may be superseded by more pleasant feelings when the object of the anger is re-examined in light of the individual's greater understanding of it. Jersild evaluates the significance of the emotions thus:

Emotion is involved in the whole business of living. The most obvious occasions for emotion are those involving bodily harm or threat of violence or of being overwhelmed. But emotion may also be elicited by any condition which thwarts or threatens or which furthers or enhances the gratification of a person's needs, as he perceives them, or the realization of his goals, or which blocks or expedites a disposition to action or behavior tendency (recognized or unrecognized, "conscious" or "unconscious") which he has acquired in the process of adapting himself to the demands of life.[1]

[1] Jersild, Arthur T., "Emotional Development," in L. Carmichael (ed.), *Manual of Child Psychology*, 2nd ed., p. 834. New York: John Wiley and Sons, Inc., copyright 1954.

As we study the emotional development of the child, it is important that we consider both the objective stimuli that serve as emotion arousers and the subjective factors that cause the child, at various stages of his progressive growth, to respond emotionally to the elements of his environment. His temporary and more lasting needs, desires, interests, and motives are closely associated with his emotional experiences. Personal satisfactions or thwartings are likely to arouse in him accompanying emotionalized behavior that, according to his degree of progressing maturation and the results of learning, give evidence of lesser or greater amount of emotional control.

The significance of the subjective aspect of emotions must not be minimized. Inner motivations are implicit in this discussion of the developing emotions. They are treated at length in Chapter 12. It probably is sufficient here to call attention to the fact that the child's emotional state is closely related to his physical well-being and to his degree of social adjustment. Emotional satisfaction inherent in tenderness promotes adequate functioning of body organs. It also encourages outgoing attitudes on the part of the child in his relationships with adults and other children. Tension is released and normal growth is fostered. Contrariwise, strains and frustrations caused by fear or anger-producing stimuli are likely to inhibit growth and cause the child to retreat from satisfying social relationships.

Children's Emotions and Adult Attitudes   The general pattern of a child's emotional development is determined in part by his experiences with the adults in his environment. The child who receives loving and understanding care is likely to be generally happy and outgoing. Too great emphasis on childish responsibilities or undue stress on adult-conceived ambitions for the child may result in the latter's developing a fearful or resentful attitude.

A pilot study of some of the child-rearing antecedents of dependent and aggressive children, for example, led to the following conclusions:

. . . First, that the kind and amount of frustration and punishment expressed by the child are major determinants of the properties of both the dependency and the aggression drives; second, that there are radical sex differences in the processes by which these drives are developed, differences that are probably a function of the differential identifications of boys and girls with their mothers; and third, that there are deep and pervasive differences in maternal treatment of boys and girls after the first year of life.[2]

[2] Sears, R. R., Whiting, J. W. M., Nowlis, V., and Sears, P. S., "Some Child-Rearing Antecedents of Aggression and Dependency in Young Children," *Genetic Psychology Monographs,* 47: 233–234, 1953.

Baldwin [3] and his colleagues attempted to find a behavioral measure sensitive to differential audience situations that could be a first step in the measurement of individual differences in pride and shame. They concluded that achievement can be conceptualized as an internalized value similar to conscience. Because of the loss of love, children's failure may lead to feelings of self-contempt. These feelings result from antecedent threats of loss of self-respect. A question is raised concerning whether social approval may not be more important as an antecedent condition to acquiring need achievement than it is as an on-the-spot controlling condition in children's daily behavior.

Many modern psychologists accept Watson's categorization of primary emotions such as fear, rage, and love as the basis for many gradations, nuances, and mixtures. There are various degrees of fear, including awe, worry, and anxiety; rage may include relatively slight annoyance and milder or more destructive anger; love shows itself in tender feelings toward persons, objects, or situations. In describing the emotional development of a child we usually trace the progress of his involvement in emotional states such as fear, anger, and tenderness, and their possible attributes.

THE CHILD'S EMOTIONAL PROGRESS

The newborn child possesses the potentialities of so-called emotionalized behavior. The arousal of definite patterns of emotions is a matter of developmental progress, however.

Infant Reactions For an individual to experience an emotional reaction in the fullest connotation of the term, it is necessary for him to perceive the stimulus and understand his behavior as well as that of others in his environment. Since the cerebral cortex of the infant is not yet developed to the extent that he can experience such understandings, emotion as experienced by the older person is not possible.

If the seat of the emotions is the hypothalamus, it is possible for the infant to experience emotion before the higher centers are developed. Some psychologists, such as Rank,[4] for example, believing that the child can suffer a severe traumatic experience at birth, claim that the indi-

---

[3] Baldwin, Alfred L., "Pride and Shame in Children," *Newsletter, Division Developmental Psychology,* American Psychological Association, Fall, 1959.

[4] Rank, O., *Modern Education: A Critique of Its Fundamental Ideas.* New York: Alfred Knopf and Company, 1932.

vidual may continue to experience anxiety throughout his life as a result of the birth trauma.

It is difficult to determine the extent to which an infant responds according to what in later life is recognized as a state of emotion. His reactions when stimulated by supposedly emotion-arousing stimuli are diffuse, including weak, all-over movements of his little body. In the newborn infant there is a general gross expression of emotionalism and a drive toward regaining or maintaining the optimum physiological balance.

The infant who is healthy and comfortable sleeps most of the time, indicating that he is satisfied. After a few weeks he commences to smile, coo, and gurgle, and engage in simple motor activities. The emotion which accompanies this normal state of affairs is one of pleasure, relaxation or contentment. When the balance is lost, however, the infant cries and struggles. The muscles become tense, the face contorted, and the blood pressure raised. These familiar signs indicate to the mother that something is wrong with her child, and she sets about to restore the balance.

The infant who is ill, in pain, or hungry is stirred up in a definite sense of the term. The behavior then is directed toward the removal of the disagreeable condition. It does not take the infant long to learn that adults give him welcomed help when he displays these signs. Thus, he displays these indications of a stirred-up condition, not because his physiological equilibrium has been upset, but because his mother does pleasing things for him. He learns how to gain greatest satisfaction for himself by getting help and attention from others. As an infant he responds "all over" to the situations that confront him; as he matures, however, he acquires the ability to gain greater control of his overt behavior and comes to express his emotions in more subtle and refined ways.

As a result of their studies of infant behavior (aged from birth to a few months), Watson and Morgan [5] concluded that the emotions of fear, rage, and love, that could just as well be called X, Y, and Z, are elicited respectively by certain forms of stimulation. A *fear* reaction, caused by a sudden loss of support or a loud noise, is likely to result in grasping at random, catching the breath, blinking the eyelids, and crying. *Rage* reactions are instigated by a person's holding tightly the body or a limb, or by other forms of hampering body movement. Consequent behavior includes all or some of the following reactions: striking or slashing movements of the limbs, stiffening of the body, drawing up and down of

[5] Watson, J. B., and Morgan, J. J. B., "Emotional Reaction and Psychological Experimentation," *American Journal of Psychology,* 28: 163–174, 1917.

legs, crying and screaming, and holding of the breath. What may be described as the *love* response is elicited by patting or gently rocking the infant, shaking or tickling him, or stroking erogenous zones. The to-be-expected responses are cessation of crying, attempted smiling, gurgling and cooing, sometimes accompanied in the later months by the extending of the arms.[6]

In light of some later studies psychologists have failed to confirm Watson and Morgan's findings concerning the very young neonate's emotional reactions. Sherman and Sherman have this to say:

> Any form of *sudden* stimulation, such as dropping, loud noises, restraint, pain, or a rush of air on the face, produces in the young infant aimless activity of most of the musculature, accompanied by crying. The stimuli must be sufficiently strong, however, to produce a reaction. When an infant below four or five days of age is dropped one or two feet it frequently shows no perceptible response, except for vague movements of the arms and legs. The younger the infant the stronger must be the stimulus. This is also true for so-called "pleasurable" stimuli, such as stroking or petting, to which many newborn infants show no overt reaction.[7]

Moreover, adults listening to a baby's crying without knowing the cause of the behavior are likely not to be able to evaluate the situation. If they are aware of the circumstances that stimulate the crying they tend to make correct judgments. In light of an experiment which they conducted, the Shermans concluded:

> Most persons judge the emotional behavior of an individual in terms of the stimuli which have produced the reactions. They have learned the names of a number of emotions and have learned to evaluate various emotional responses in terms of the stimulating conditions which have aroused them. If the situation confronting an individual is estimated to be one which arouses an aggressive reaction, the resulting response is named "anger," but if it is considered dangerous to his welfare, the response will be called "fear." In this way the differentiation of emotions is based upon a knowledge of the character of the stimulating circumstances rather than upon differences in overt behavior.[8]

Dennis, however, found that when, for example, the bodily activity of two fraternal female twins at one month of age was restricted they responded about two-thirds of the time according to Watson's reporting.[9]

[6] Watson, *op. cit.*, pp. 199–202.

[7] Sherman, M., and Sherman, I. C., *The Process of Human Behavior,* p. 145. New York: W. W. Norton and Company, copyright 1929.

[8] *Ibid.,* pp. 142–143.

[9] Dennis, Wayne, "Infant Reactions to Restraint: An Evaluation of Watson's Theory," *Trans. N. Y. Academy of Science,* 2, pp. 202–218, 1940.

Hunt, Clarke, and Hunt [10] conducted experiments in which they studied infants between the ages of eight days and eighteen months as they responded to the sound of revolver shots. Although they did not find evidence of fear responses among all these young children, they did invoke the "startle" response as a result of the sound of shots. A startle response includes the eye blink and body movements similar to the Moro reflex. Recent research among psychologists raises questions concerning the extent to which supposedly emotional reactions are among the infants' unlearned repertory of responses. Munn concludes his discussion of very young children's emotionalized behavior thus:

. . . we may say that "fear," "rage," and "love" responses described by Watson and Morgan do not appear in all or even in most young infants. The only unlearned response of emotional significance which appears in all normal infants as well as in all older children and adults is the "startle pattern." This pattern may eventually be the "mass activity," the "aimless activity of most of the musculature," and the "undifferentiated emotion of excitement" mentioned as primary by other investigators. At least it should, from the above discussion, be clear that very young infants fail to exhibit a variety of emotional responses recognizable to adults as such.[11]

Developing Emotional Patterns Some emotional patterns develop during babyhood. Both maturation and learning or conditioning bring about the possession and display of definite emotional states. Growing control of his body parts, increasing power to perceive and to discriminate, and developing ability to engage in new activities are accompanied by greater differentiation in the child's earlier all-over affective responses.

As a result of her study of children's reactions during the first two years of life Bridges constructed a scale of the progressive stages of to-be-expected emotionalized experiences of the baby from birth through twenty-four months. (See Figure 76.) It can be observed that, beginning with a so-called all-over excitement at birth, the child gradually progresses through various stages to the point at which he possesses an extended repertory of emotionalized behavior. It must be remembered, however, that the chart portrays a general pattern of behavior. Children differ in the ages at which they give evidence of the listed emotions. As in other areas of development, some children are accelerated, others

[10] Hunt, W. A., Clarke, F. M., and Hunt, E. B., "Studies of the Startle Pattern; IV Infants," *Journal of Psychology,* 2: 339–352, 1936.
[11] Munn, N. L., *The Evolution and Growth of Human Behavior,* p. 396. Boston: Houghton Mifflin Company, copyright 1955.

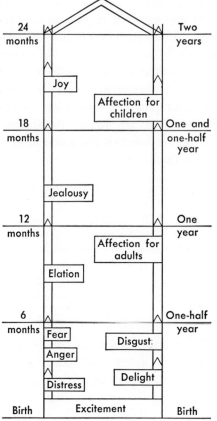

Figure 76. Time Chart Showing Changes and Differentiation of Emotional Reaction during the First Two Years after Birth.

Based on data in "Emotional Development in Early Years," by Bridges, K.M.B., *Child Development*, March, 1932, 3, 324–341.

are retarded. Temperamental qualities that tend to characterize an individual through life also affect the kind of emotional reactions displayed by young children and the age of their appearance.

Maturation and Conditioning   Many of a young child's emotional reactions are learned as he is conditioned by the examples of adult behavior and the influence of the situations in which he finds himself. Conditioning is not possible, however, until the child has achieved an appropriate stage in his maturational process to be "ready" for the learning to be effective. This interrelationship between maturation and learning can be illustrated in various ways. The young child does not necessarily fear snakes, rabbits, dogs, or other animals or conditions. An unfortunate experience when he is old enough to perceive the element of danger to himself may change his attitude.

A snake that moves rapidly toward a child, a dog that jumps at him in his play and throws him down, or any other sudden or strong stimulus that interferes with the child's *status quo* may arouse an emotional reaction and accompanying overt behavior of avoidance or attack. Later, more pleasant experiences with the disturbing stimulus, however, may recondition the child's attitude toward it. Greater maturity as well as the external stimulation plays a role in the reconditioning process.

Tangible and More Subtle Stimuli   As the young child experiences a continuing, widening scope of effective stimuli, he tends, during his early years, to respond to tangible conditions and events that affect him directly. The behavior toward him of the people in his environment, his contact with objects and situations stimulate him to respond directly and immediately with an appropriate emotional reaction. As the stimulus is removed or changed so does his behavior change. The young child may give evidence of anger or fear by crying one minute, and the next respond to a new or changed stimulus by smiling or laughing. For example, a child may become very angry when his mother removes a toy with which he is playing. He attempts to hit her or grab the toy from her; he may cry or scream with rage. If the mother replaces the removed toy by another one liked by the child or in other ways diverts his attention from his loss, he is likely to forget his anger, and engage in pleasurable, affectionate behavior.

As the child's ability to conceptualize increases, he becomes responsive to symbols or signs that are associated with the encouragement of or hindrance to his desires or interests. If an adult relative of the child, for example, is accustomed to visit his home frequently, each time bringing him a small gift, he learns to look forward to the visits of the beloved person, with much anticipation of what will be brought for him. If the relative then stops the practice of bringing him gifts, the child may develop a deep resentment of the adult which may continue long after he has forgotten the original cause of it.

As the child increases in maturity and responds to inner and outer stimuli with greater understanding of their relation to himself, his emotional reactions are affected by the moods which derive from the influence upon him of existing conditions and circumstances. Parents and teachers know that weather conditions exert an influence on children's degree of impulsiveness of action, loudness of voice, and degree of controllability.

On a dark, dreary day, children tend to be noisy and restless in school, sometimes resisting the teacher's efforts to interest them in learning tasks. Hot, humid weather often causes them to be apathetic or easily angered. On a sunny, crisp day, children seem to be filled with the joy of living. They usually are amenable to adult suggestion, are prone to engage in zestful activity and, altogether, give evidence of happiness and an outgoing pleasant attitude. Of course, there are other elements in a particular child's environment that negate the influence of weather conditions alone. Home difficulties, poor health, or real or imagined frustrations may have a potent effect on a child, regardless of other conditions.

Later Development of Emotions   As the child progresses from infancy through adolescence he refines the expression of his emotions. The gradual influence of maturation and training results in the transition from general gross behavior to more definite and individual emotional expression. With adult guidance, the child is likely to outgrow some babyish angers, jealousies, fears, pleasures and joys, childhood temper tantrums, avoidance of real or imagined fear arousers, or squeals of delight. These gradually give way to the more subdued and adultlike, but still definite, forms of expression that are likely to receive greater social approval.

With increase of age comes self and social discovery. Opportunities for self-realization and social realization become extremely important. The emotions still play an important role in the life of the developing young person. His loves, fears, and hates may be extremely intense and endure for long periods of time. There is an interweaving of the emotions and other aspects of development.

Rarely does the older child or adolescent hurl things when he is angry. Instead, he throws words in the form of sarcasm, sneers, and belittling remarks at the person whom he considers to be the cause of his emotional state. Growing boys, even more than girls, are expected to be brave and "grown-up" in possible fear-producing situations, and the young person may attempt to suppress any display of his fears. This may exert a devastating and lasting influence on his inner life to the extent that he represses their expression.

In our culture open demonstrations of affection tend to be frowned upon. Hence boys especially, who as youngsters were accustomed to kiss their parents before going to bed at night or welcomed parental embraces, feel that they must be matter-of-fact in their relations with adult members of the family. In fact, their own desire to give expression to their feelings of affection can lead to attitudes of great embarrassment. Although young people's emotional expressions probably change gradually from the explosive and gross to the subtle and indirect, their emotional states will become less transitory and more even and enduring in expression.

The Achievement of Emotional Maturity New interests and knowledge and changing attitudes toward life cause stimuli that formerly aroused the emotions to lose their potency, but others are substituted for them. Older children and adolescents often express great amusement as they recall incidents in their earlier years that had been accompanied by emotional concomitants. These young people rarely appreciate the fact, however, that adults sometimes are amused and sometimes concerned by the kinds of stimuli that affect the emotions during the later stages of development. During the later years of growing up, the individual's total pattern of emotions is influenced by his progressive appreciation of values and ideals and by his growing interest in and responsiveness to the points of view and ideals of other people, to the functioning of cultural institutions, and to the recognition of his own responsibility for the welfare of himself and others.

Emotional maturity is not easily achieved. Some adults who can perform well under favorable conditions seem to go to pieces emotionally if they encounter problem situations that appear to defy solution. Contrariwise, there are young people who seem to attain a degree of emotional control that goes far beyond what normally could be expected for their age status. The emotionally mature or stable individual, regardless of his age, is the one who has the ability to overcome tension, to disregard certain emotion stimulators that affect the young, and to view himself objectively, as he evaluates his assets and liabilities and strives toward an improved integration of his thoughts, his emotional attitudes, and his overt behavior.

Jersild has compiled a list of some of the trends and tendencies involved in the process of physical, motor, intellectual, social, and emotional development that have been known to indicate emotional maturity. We quote:

A change from helplessness to a greatly increased capacity for self-help, with a consequent progressive freedom from the frustrations and fears that beset a helpless creature.

A shift from abject dependence on others to increasing balanced independence, with consequent opening of channels for enjoyment of self-help and an increasing degree of psychological as well as physical self-support.

A shift from capacity to appreciate and react only to the immediate present to increasing capacity to encompass the past and to anticipate the future, with resulting changes in anticipation of both good and ill.

Increasing intellectual capacity, including increased capacity for dealing with aspects of life on a symbolic level, increased ability to plan; increased "attention span," bringing increased ability to see beyond and to be immune to momentary or intermediate frustrations; increased intellectual perspective and an increased ability to take a panoramic view of things.

A change from a disposition to be physically very active to an increased capacity during adolescence and later to tolerate and to enjoy sedentary pursuits.

A shift from social life centered only on the parents to a social life that encompasses one's peers and which also includes a capacity not simply to tolerate but to appreciate persons who are considerably older and considerably younger than oneself.

A change from being a creature who at first receives much, gives little, to one who is capable of giving as well as receiving, and capable of learning to get enjoyment from giving.

Development of capacity to identify oneself with a larger social group, and the ability to participate emotionally in the fortunes of the larger group.

Development from the status of being the child of the family to the status, ultimately, of being able to have children of one's own and, along with this development, a capacity to exercise the feelings and attitudes involved in being a parent psychologically, whether or not one is a parent biologically.

Progressive sexual development and the capacity after puberty for enjoying mature sex experiences.

An increased capacity for bearing the inevitable sufferings and pains connected with life and growth without feeling abused.

An increased capacity for sympathy and compassion as one assimilates the meaning for self and others of the joys and vicissitudes of life.[12]

In our earlier discussion of the emotions we considered some of the objective and subjective factors inherent in the arousal of emotional states. We now shall direct our attention to the various emotional states which children experience.

FEAR AND ANXIETY

Apprehension, fear, worry, and anxiety are rooted in feelings of insecurity. An individual of any age either may encounter a particular situation which he cannot handle at the time or may be filled with dire forebodings concerning the more or less general pattern of one or another area of his day-by-day experiences. In either case, he becomes emotionally disturbed and unable to function normally.

Causes and Expression of Fear   The external causes of fear and the inner states that make children susceptible to fear are so many and

[12] Jersild, A. T., *op. cit.,* pp. 861–862.

diverse that it is difficult to give any clear picture of what may be expected to arouse it. We know that very young children respond with unlearned behavior that can be regarded as expressive of fear when they are stimulated by loss of support, a loud noise, or any other sudden, intense sensory experience.

Another fear producer is the appearance in the child's immediate environment of a person, object, or condition that is strange or unfamiliar. Whether the child perceives the disturbing situation as strange depends on what he has learned to accept as familiar or what he can take in his stride. If the baby has been accustomed to have the members of his family treat him gently and move quietly about him, he will exhibit strong fear reactions if a strange visitor approaches him noisily and engages in excited "baby talk," as she playfully points at him with her finger. A more quiet approach and a friendly smile may cause a momentary disturbance which soon subsides. Whether the child is comfortably relaxed at the time of the visit is another factor affecting his reaction to the situation.

Psychologists disagree concerning the extent to which fear of animals, of the dark, or of being alone is innate or learned. Most children do not give evidence of such fears until they are about two years old. From that age onward, children differ in their reactions to these possible fear-arousing stimuli. In many instances they reflect the attitudes of their elders. They are sensitive to the admonishments of parents and to the fears that are possessed by their elders even to a slight degree.

Adults who are not affected emotionally by supposed fear producers or who encourage children to accept such situations wield a favorable influence over children. A child in whose home there is a gentle, not-too-large dog is likely to accept him as a member of the family, petting him and playing with him. If he meets a strange large dog that responds to the child's friendly advances by jumping at him, the child is likely to develop at least a temporary fear of all dogs, including his own dog and other animals. It is not until he is helped by adults to recognize the fact that some animals act differently from others and are to be avoided that he is able to combine caution with friendliness.

Apparently, fear of the dark is not innate. Most psychologists agree that before the age of about two years, children do not evince fear of the dark, unless they are alone and assailed by strange noises, or experience other disturbances in the dark. Even an older child may come to fear the dark because of untoward circumstances. For example, a seven-year-old boy, who was accustomed to having the light turned off in his room as he was falling asleep, was awakened suddenly one night, without knowing what had awakened him. The moonlight touched his familiar toys, causing them to look strange and eerie. Fortunately, the relationship between his parents and himself was such that he was able confidently to grope his way to their room and receive the comfort and security he needed. Soon he fell asleep again and was carried back to his room by his father. The next morning the three of them discussed the situation seriously and the reason for his fear was explained to him, without his being accused of being a baby. He was very proud of the fact that when he awoke again during the night some weeks later, feeling a little afraid, he got up and touched his toys. Then, finding that they had not changed to strange creatures, he returned to bed and to sleep. The situation might have been quite different had his parents been less understanding.

A child's fear of being alone or being separated from parents usually is rooted in other factors that intensify the fear. Children differ in their reactions to such situations. During the first year or so, most children are not bothered by being alone unless they are accustomed to receiving a great deal of attention from their elders. Such children, as they grow older, find it difficult to stay in bed alone, while their parents still are awake and about. Curiosity as well as fear of being alone may cause such children to demand attention. A little girl of four and her three-year-old brother, for example, would go to bed quietly enough at their accustomed bedtime. They started to develop the habit of tip-toeing half-way down the stairs to watch their elders in the living room. When they were discovered, their plea would be that they were afraid of being alone in the dark. Since they showed no evidence of fear in their behavior, however, they soon were encouraged, through the application of reasonable penalties, to stay in bed and go to sleep.

A child may experience a shock that causes him to become, tempo-rarily at least, extremely dependent on his parents. Little Ethel was a confident child during her first two years. Her parents could put her in her crib and leave the room or even the house without her becoming disturbed. In fact, she often stood up in her crib and waved at them as they left her. When she was about thirty months old, the family was in an automobile accident in which her upper lip was cut. The experience of the pain and a stay in the hospital resulted in a complete change of attitude. She became so tense and fearful that, for several years there-after, she could not tolerate being left alone during the day or night.

As children grow older, some of their earlier fears remain, espe-cially as carry-overs of experiences in which they were badly frightened, even though they were not harmed. Although some concrete fears continue, many of the fear-producing situations of the older child are born in their imagination, such as imaginary creatures. As a result of their reading and viewing of motion pictures and television programs, eleven- and twelve-year-old children report some of the things that "worry" them because of the fear of harm to themselves or close relatives. These include fire, holdups, burglars, accidents, sickness, and death, even though no one whom they know well has had any experience with such misfortunes.

Children's school experiences often become fear-inducing stimuli. It is quite common for a child who is achieving success in his school work to be afraid of failing a test, of being demoted, of earning the disapproval of his teacher, or of failing to gain the friendship of his schoolmates. Sometimes the less probable it is that any such catastrophe will occur, the greater does the fear seem to become. It sometimes appears to serve as a self-protective covering against loss of prestige in the school community. This type of fear often continues well into adolescent and young adult life. Some college students become extremely apprehensive about their chances of maintaining desired status among instructors and college mates.

We need to attempt to distinguish here between what may be termed "healthy" fears and "morbid" fears. A child needs to learn early that some situations are dangerous and should be avoided. He must be aware of the fact that he may be harmed if he touches a hot stove, steps out into the middle of traffic, or puts himself into any other danger-producing situation. This is the development of reasonable caution and is not accompanied by inner or overt symptoms of the fear emotion. He also needs to learn so to behave that he does not harm someone else. Emotionalized fear results when or if the child finds himself in a dangerous situation that exists or is imagined to be productive of hurt but is not able to do anything about it. Morbid fears are irrational fears. They usually have little or no basis in fact but can cause considerable suffering on the part of the victim. Severe irrational fears are called *phobias*.

Anxiety   Basically, fear and anxiety are similar in that both are aroused by some recognition of elements of danger to oneself. They differ, however, in that in fear there is a more or less clearly perceived cause for the aroused emotional state, but anxiety is associated with a feeling of uneasiness instigated by circumstances that the individual is unable to define objectively. The emotional reaction tends to be vague or diffused. Something is threatening a person but he is not quite certain what it is.

In a particular situation, the victim of anxiety is likely to say to himself, "Something is likely to happen. I don't know what it may be, but I'm worried about it." A mother, for example, is anxious about the safe return home of her adolescent daughter who is out on a date. The mother approves of the girl's escort; objectively, she is aware of the fact that nothing untoward is likely to happen, but she is uneasy until the girl has returned. The mother's anxiety becomes intensified if her daughter's return is delayed. The woman cannot do anything positive about the situation, but she may develop a severe headache or other ailment, which disappears when the girl finally arrives. (See Figure 77.)

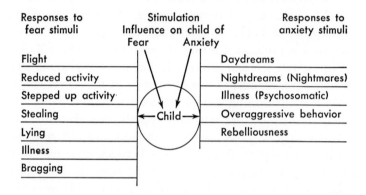

Figure 77. Different Ways a Child Responds to (A) Fear-Producing Stimuli, and (B) Anxiety-Producing Stimuli.

The form in which anxiety shows itself differs among individuals. The following incident indicates differences in expressions of anxiety. During his family's stay at their summer home on a lake, a nineteen-year-old boy was sent by a large motorboat on an errand early one evening. He had taken this trip many times, returning within an hour. Concern began to be evidenced when dusk fell and he had not returned. As the hours passed, the members of the family and several visitors became extremely anxious. The mother lay on the couch, pretending she was asleep but watching the clock; the father busied himself with odd jobs, iterating that the boy probably had met someone and was chatting. One member of the group continued to go to the shore with a flashlight to search for the boat; another suggested following the boy with another boat; still another recommended that someone go by car to his supposed destination. It is worth noting that no one actually followed him, however. When the boy returned at midnight, everyone relieved his emotional tension by starting to scold him for worrying the family by his long absence late at night. This attitude changed to one of approving pride when the boy reported that he had been detained by the fact that he had helped a boat that had been in distress and that he too was bothered by his delay but could not report to his family.

Some people seem almost unconsciously to enjoy being anxious about something. They are somewhat like the man who is afraid to stay in the house because the roof, which is in good condition, may fall in; he also is afraid to go outside lest he be struck by an automobile. Instead of fleeing from possible danger, inner conflict can cause a person to seek the kind of situation in which his anxious state is rooted. An older child or adolescent is concerned about his prestige in his group. He experiences a vague anxiety that he may do or say something that could harm his self-esteem. For example, a sixteen-year-old girl, writing in her diary, says "I have to invite a boy to 'sweet 16.' I might ask Harvey but I'm afraid he will say 'No.' Then he'll have something to tell his friends." A possible loss of face is a powerful fear among adolescents.

Many young people are anxious about their vocational plans. They are eager to engage in an occupational field that will meet their ambition, but they are anxious about the possibility of receiving needed training, obtaining a desired assignment, and then earning success on the job. The anxious state may cause one individual to become aggressive in his approach, and encourage another to spend his time in "worrying" about possible obstacles, without doing anything constructive about the situation. Moreover, the anticipation of danger may act as a cautionary measure against the production of fear.

The worries of preadolescents are in the areas of school activities and home relationships. Later their worries are extended to such life areas as social relationships, vocational choice, religion, and health. The worries of 658 fifteen- and sixteen-year-old high school students (352 girls and 306 boys) were investigated by the authors. These pupils were given an opportunity to list their worries during the teen years according to the seven life areas listed in Table 12.

These investigators found some differences existing between the sexes. Girls seem to worry more than boys about their ability to measure up to what may be expected of them. Boys seem to worry more than girls about such things as laziness, growing old, and living in undesirable homes.

Psychologists disagree about the causes of anxiety and its development. Most writers believe that the very young child's imagination does

TABLE 12

Adolescent Worries in Various Life Areas *

Life area	Male worries	Female worries
School life	Homework Getting along with teachers Tests Marks Failure Reciting in class Grade for parents' sake College entrance Being accepted	Homework Getting along with teachers Tests Marks Failure Reciting in class Parents' attitude toward grade Being accepted College entrance
Home life	Arguments with sister or brother Arguments with parents Arguments between parents Strict parents Conflict with parents Arguments about dating Treated unjustly	Younger brothers get what they want Parental domination Parents object to going steady Conflicts with parents Fear of mother Conflicts on values Arguments in home
Boy-girl relationships	How to get a date Girls I like don't like me Girls cost too much How to be invited to parties Mother objects to my going steady How to have a girl go steady Inability to dance Does girl love me? Girls of another religion How to forget girl who jilted me	How to meet new friends Boys I like don't like me How to be popular Boys are too demanding I would like to go steady Loss of boy friend Behavior of boy friend Sexual relations to maintain Girls who try to steal boy friend How to get over love for boy How to refuse a date tactfully
Friends	Are they true friends? Friends may not like me To be worthy of good friends How to make friends To be popular	Are friends true friends? Not to let friends down To be popular How to be a leader in a group Feelings of inferiority
Vocational choice	State of indecision How to get a job	State of indecision How to get into show business
Religion	Should I marry out of my religion? Indecision Not attending religious services	Should I marry out of my religion? Doubt about religious values Fear parents will discover that I wish to change my religion
Health	How to grow more How to lose weight Pimples Disease	Thinness and smallness Fear of losing good health Disease Illness tendencies

* By permission from *Adolescent Development and Adjustment,* Crow, Lester D., and Crow, Alice, p. 151. New York: copyright 1956 by McGraw-Hill Book Company, Inc.

not yet function adequately to project itself toward the possibility of danger. Freudians, however, claim that the term "anxiety" (*angst*) can be applied to early mental levels and is a phase of fear development.

Phobias A strong, persistent, and irrational state of anxiety about a possible danger situation is termed a *phobia*. Various writers contend that some of children's strong "fears" of the dark, of wild animals, or of dangerous people or conditions are products of the imagination and have no basis in actual experience. Such fears partake of the nature of subjective fears.

There are some apparently irrational fears, however, that represent the aftermath of fears instigated in the past by actual danger situations. For example, a seven-year-old boy was locked accidentally in a small shed in which there were nests of active wasps. Although he called for help, he was severely stung by them before he was released. The memory of his extreme suffering was so great that now, at the age of thirty-five, he still exhibits unreasonable fear at the sight of a wasp. So intense has been his phobia, that recently when he was painting a house, the sight of a wasp flying above him caused him to jump off a twenty-foot ladder, in spite of the fact that the fall might have injured him far more severely than a wasp sting.

From one point of view, phobias can be regarded as pathological fears that are symbolic and may affect an individual during most of his life. It is possible for an individual to develop a phobia without knowing the original fear situation that started it. The phobia may be intensified by the individual's attempt to conceal his abnormal emotional state. Contrariwise, if he is able to discover its origin, is frank about his feelings, and has pleasant experiences in the supposedly fear-producing situation, the intensity of the phobia may be lessened or it may be eliminated.

Some of the more common phobias that are associated with unpleasant experiences and have strong irrational states are: *nyctophobia* (fear of the dark); *acrophobia* (fear of high places); *mysophobia* (fear of dirt) *claustrophobia* (fear of closed rooms); *algophobia* (fear of pain); *demophobia* (fear of crowds); *musophobia* (fear of mice); *xenophobia* (fear of strangers.)

ANGER AND HOSTILITY

Most children, as well as adults, experience either mild or more intense feelings of anger, resentment, jealousy, or other forms of aggressive and antisocial reactions. The emotional state is caused by valid objective stimulation or is imagined. In either case, it is likely to result in behavior that can be harmful to the individual experiencing it as well as to others. Like fear, anger is instigated by a situation that is considered to represent a threat. Although the bases of anger or rage, like those of fear, are rooted in feelings of insecurity, anger reactions are aggressive, taking the form of attack rather than avoidance or flight.

Progressive Development of Causation and Expression of Anger   Young children learn early that they may be able to achieve desired goals through angry outbursts or temper tantrums. This attitude tends to continue throughout the life of some individuals, although stimulating situations and forms of expression change with age. Actual or imagined loss of prestige, interference with personal possessions, and thwartings of interests or desires are basic to the arousal of anger, jealousy, or resentment. Sex, age, and temperament are important factors as determinants of the kind and extent of the emotional reactions experienced.

As we know, if a young child's movements are restrained or his desires are thwarted, he is likely to engage in generally explosive behavior. He screams, bites, kicks, or throws things. As he grows older, he directs his angry behavior at a particular person or object. His expressive behavior becomes more subtle in its approach. Ridicule, sarcasm, and innuendo are substituted for the outspoken "I hate you" or the all-over temper tantrum. The young child's attention usually can be diverted from his angry state and its cause; the older child or adolescent may harbor resentment for a long period of time. Sometimes he attempts to refrain from exhibiting his antisocial feelings, thereby intensifying the inner turmoil.

Goodenough conducted a study of anger in young children.[13] She found that, during the first year, routine care, such as bathing or dressing, accounted for one-fourth of exhibited anger responses; another one-fourth was associated with minor physical discomforts; about 6 per cent resulted from the restriction of bodily movements. The causes of anger in two-year-olds fell into the following categories, from most to least: (1) establishment of routine physical habits, (2) conflict with authority over other matters, (3) social relationships, and (4) minor physical discomforts, restriction of bodily movements, or problems arising out of attempts at self-help.

[13] Goodenough, Florence L., *Anger in Young Children*, Institute of Child Welfare, Monograph Series, No. 9. Minneapolis: University of Minnesota, 1931.

Between the ages of two and three, the chief provocations were difficulties with playmates, conflicts with authority, and establishment of routine physical habits. From three to four years, two outstanding causes of difficulties were disagreements with playmates and conflict with authority. For the four-year-old and older, the most frequent source of provocation continued to be in the area of social relationships, with less emphasis on habit formation and conflict with authority.

Goodenough's findings were based on parents' reports of their young children's anger reactions. Hence the validity of the study results was influenced by the emotional atmosphere that prevailed in the home. The children of anxious, conflict-ridden parents were more likely to display aggressive behavior than occurred in more serene homes where the parents themselves were able to control their emotions.

Older Children's Anger   Studies of anger in older children seem to indicate that, as young folks' social environment widens, anger, resentment, and general annoyance are associated with their social relationships outside the home. Hicks and Hayes studied the behavior of 250 junior high school pupils, between the ages of eleven and sixteen.[14] They found the following, in order of frequency, to be the most provocative of anger: being teased, people being unfair to them, a sibling taking their property, or imposing on them, people lying to them, things not going right, people being sarcastic, and people being bossy.[15] It will be noted that except for difficulties with siblings, these causes of anger are tied to the attitudes exhibited toward them by people in and outside the home.

Older boys and girls tend to be very much annoyed when their growing independence is questioned, their pride hurt, or their self-respect threatened. In a study by Block of relationships between mothers and their junior and senior high school children, the findings disclosed that young people tend to resent having siblings held up as models, being restricted in their behavior, taking younger brothers or sisters with them wherever they go, and being subjected to parental nagging.[16]

Some of the factors that encourage a child's susceptibility to the experiencing of anger are (1) poor health or fatigue, (2) the presence of many adults in the home, (3) the display by family members of critical, overanxious, or uncertain attitudes toward him, (4) the assignment of

[14] Hicks, J. A., and Hayes, M., "Study of the Characteristics of 250 Junior High School Children," *Child Development,* 9: 219–242, 1938.

[15] *Ibid.,* p. 233.

[16] Block, V. L., "Conflicts of Adolescents with Their Mothers," *Journal of Abnormal Social Psychology,* 32: 193–306, 1937.

difficult or impossible tasks, and (5) physical and psychological restrictions.[17]

As we have noted earlier, modes of expressing hostility or anger change with increasing age. Crying, a common expression of annoyance

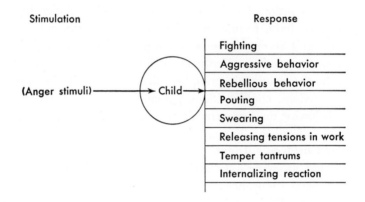

Stimulation   Response

(Anger stimuli)————→ Child—→

Fighting

Aggressive behavior

Rebellious behavior

Pouting

Swearing

Releasing tensions in work

Temper tantrums

Internalizing reaction

Figure 78. Different Ways a Child Responds to Anger-Producing Stimuli.

among young children, becomes less evident with age. Direct attack also gives way to verbally expressed aggression, swearing, teasing, and sometimes bullying. If social pressures make it undesirable to vent his spleen on the subject of his anger, the child may transfer his angry behavior to inanimate objects. A boy, for example, may resent a parent's display of authority toward him. He dare not "take out" his anger on the parent, so he goes for a walk and kicks at stones in his path as he mutters imprecations about adult injustice.

Extremely hostile or antisocial attitudes may be exhibited in the form of prejudice, cruelty, or delinquent acts. The disturbed emotional state also can show itself in physical symptoms. Jersild makes this comment:

Numerous writers have explored the theory that illness may serve as an escape from frustration. The interplay between psychological and biochemical factors in connection with asthma and other allergic reactions has likewise received considerable attention. Among other troubles, arthritis and other rheumatic diseases frequently appear to have a psychogenic origin and represent, according to one theory, a reaction to suppressed hostility.[18]

[17] Jersild, Arthur T., "Emotional Development," in L. Carmichael (ed.), *Manual of Child Development*, 2nd ed., New York, copyright 1954 by John Wiley and Sons, Inc.

[18] *Ibid.*, p. 889.

JEALOUSY

The term "jealousy" commonly is applied to a combination of fear, anger, and affection with feelings of inferiority. Jealousy is an accompaniment of experiencing social relationships. It represents a resentful attitude, usually associated with one's experiences with other people. Jealousy originates in the actual or imagined loss of the good will or affection of another or in the attaining by another of a much desired goal. Jealousy may be expressed in direct attack, but a more subtle approach is more common, especially among older children and adolescents. Furthermore, the jealousy may be sporadic, showing itself only in the presence of the conditions that arouse it, or it may take the form of a deep, continued obsessive resentment.

In the home an older child has been the center of parental attention until the birth of a baby sister or brother. Unless the child has been prepared carefully for the arrival of the sibling and, after its birth, encouraged to help in the care of *our* new baby, he or she is likely to become extremely jealous of the newcomer. Some of the behavior symptoms of the emotional state are: demanding help in dressing and undressing, refusing to eat unless he is fed, and similar attitudes of helplessness. In brief, the child seems to regress to an earlier stage of development, thereby competing with the younger child for his share of parental attention. He also may ignore the baby, make faces at him, or actually attack him.

Among older children sibling rivalry can take the form of teasing, quarreling, ridicule, boasting, use of sarcasm, and sometimes tale-bearing. In most instances, however, no matter how resentful a child may be of a sibling, he will defend the child against any expressed or implied criticism of him by persons outside the home.

Children often display attitudes of jealousy in school situations. They resent classmates who seem to be more successful than they are in academic or sports activities. They are especially resentful of any members of their class who appear to be favored by the teacher. So-called teacher's pets may be ignored or treated cruelly by their peer associates. A jealous school child can compensate for his disturbed emotional state by attracting attention to himself through aggressive behavior, loud speech, telling tall tales of imagined feats of courage engaged in by himself or members of his family, recounting stories of superior home conditions, or inciting younger children to participate in acts of mischief.

THE TENDER EMOTIONS

Outgoing reactions directed toward persons, objects, or situations that are satisfying or pleasant represent the expressing of a tender emotion. The display of affectionate behavior has been found to begin during the first year of life and expresses itself in smiles, gurgles, and cooings.

Developmental Pattern of Tender Emotions   The child's first display of tenderness is confined to persons or objects in his home. The baby finds satisfaction in being held and fondled; he goes to sleep with his teddy bear or other favorite toy clasped in his little arms. He becomes very much attached to pets in the home. When the child becomes aware of the presence of other same-age babies in his environment, he is likely to engage in affectionate behavior, embracing another baby, perhaps kissing him and offering him his favorite toy.

As a child grows older and experiences an increasing number of associations outside the home, he lavishes his affection on people who give him attention or minister to his wants. The growing child needs the feeling of security that grows out of adults' display of affectionate behavior toward him. He gains great satisfaction from the realization that he is

Figure 79.   The Cast on the Broken Leg Does Not Deter Amy from Enjoying Life.

Figure 80.   Boys Enjoy Horseback Riding as an Individual
as Well as a Social Experience.

wanted and liked by others of his own age and older. Not only should
the child appreciate the receiving of affection; he also should learn to
exhibit attitudes of affection toward others and concern for their welfare.

Outgoing attitudes can be developed in the home as children imitate
parental examples, and assist in the care of younger children and pets.
Although occasional and mild hostilities or resentments are common in
the close associations of the home, family loyalties usually are strong and
tend to carry over into outside relationships, such as the school, the club,
or other community organizations. Many friendships formed during
childhood continue through the life span of the individuals concerned.
An individual's feelings of self-esteem and self-appreciation can be
strengthened by his affection, respect, and appreciation for friends and
associates.

The affection-giving and affection-receiving child usually experiences great joy in living. His feelings of security enable him to play and
work with others, free from the experiencing of serious resentment or
jealousy. It is interesting to note age changes in the sources of great
pleasure or joy experienced by children and young people. In Table 13
are summarized some broad categories of the circumstances that were
described by different age children as constituting "one of the happiest
days" of their lives. Figures 79, 80, and 81 illustrate a few of these high-
lights.

Compassion and Sympathy   Included among the tender emotions are compassion and sympathy. Although these two emotional reactions are closely allied, the term "compassion" usually denotes a general, outgoing appreciation of other people's deep emotional stirrings that may be basic to exhibited fears, hostilities, anger, delight, or other emotionalized attitude. The compassionate person understands himself and the roots of his own emotional experiences. He can put himself into another person's position. The compassionate parent and teacher understand that a young person's apparently unpredictable behavior often is motivated by certain fundamental emotional processes of development.

TABLE 13

Frequency of Responses in Various Categories When Children Described "One of the Happiest Days of My Life" *

(The values represent percentage of children giving one or more responses in each category)

Number	Grades 1–3 Ages 6–9		Grades 4–6 Ages 9–12		Grades 7–9 Ages 12–15		Grades 10–12 Ages 15–18	
	Boys 363	Girls 331	Boys 309	Girls 343	Boys 282	Girls 290	Boys 159	Girls 171
Receiving or having or otherwise enjoying material things, gifts, toys, money, living quarters	8.7	8.1	10.4	7.2	10.1	4.5	5.6	3.1
Holidays, festive occasions, birthdays, Christmas, etc.	39.1	40.5	32.4	38.9	6.3	10.1	0.6	6.5
Sports, games, hiking, hunting, bicycling, etc.	10.2	6.4	9.1	5.5	12.4	5.8	13.0	7.3
Going to miscellaneous places of recreation, going to camps, traveling, going to resorts, to parks	9.6	9.0	10.1	11.4	9.7	13.9	30.2	6.9
Self-improvement, success in school, educational opportunity, evidence of vocational competence, getting a job	2.4	2.3	2.9	1.9	4.8	4.1	13.6	15.9
Happenings connected with school, including last day, end of school, going to a certain school	3.6	3.4	5.4	4.3	14.0	11.1	7.0	5.4
Relationship with people (explicitly described), companionship, being with certain friend, return home of relatives, etc.	7.7	15.9	8.0	15.8	10.5	22.0	8.7	19.9
Residing in, moving to, a certain city or community	1.3	1.0	0.8	2.9	0.9	2.9	1.4	5.0
Benefits befalling others, or mankind in general, including end of war	0.6	0.8	3.2	2.8	2.2	2.6	7.9	9.7

*** Reproduced, by permission, from Jersild and Tasch (1949). The table omits several categories including hobbies, movies and radio programs, art activities, etc., mentioned by only small percentages of children.

* *Ibid.,* p. 191.

The adult then is enabled by his understanding to help ease the younger person's course of maturation.

Compassion represents a generalized attitude; *sympathy* is a fellow-feeling for another when the latter is experiencing an immediate emotional upset that may be pleasant or annoying. A child may not be mature enough to be compassionate, but he can sympathize with an older or younger individual or an animal.

Children by the age of three or four exhibit sympathy through their action and words. They are likely to respond to injuries treated with iodine, bandages, swellings, accidental falls, attacks on the person, crying, deprivations, having to stay in bed, and the like. Their sympathetic behavior may take the form of comforting, helping, trying to remove the cause of the difficulty, and other more or less organized anxious behavior.[19] As children mature, their sympathetic responses become increasingly active. In general, however, youngsters vary in their show of sympathy in light of their own experiences.

Children's Laughter and Humor   Beginning during the first year of life, the child tends to express the experiencing of a pleasant emotional state through smiling and laughter. The laughter of a healthy, contented baby can be aroused by his observing unexpected or unusual activities of another person that can be described as a kind of "horse-play": shaking a finger or the head before the eyes of the child, grimacing or engaging in other "odd" body movements, playing peek-a-boo, or tickling the child mildly.

Various studies have been made of the causes of laughter in young children. According to Justin's summary of various theories of laughter, among children from three to six years of age, the situational groupings are: surprise-defeated expectations, superiority-degradation, incongruity and contrasts, social smile as stimulus, relief from strain, and play. In her own checking of these theories, Justin found that, although in all the situations tested, some children laughed, the most effective laughter producers were the surprise situations and social smile.[20]

The playing of any simple game usually stimulates the young child to engage in gales of laughter. Bodily activity in a social situation is highly enjoyable. Preschool children also tend to find cartoons of the Walt

[19] Murphy, L. B., *Social Behavior and Child Personality*. New York: Columbia University Press, 1937.

[20] Justin, Florence, "A Genetic Study of Laughter Provoking Stimuli," *Child Development*, 3: 114–136, 1932.

**Figure 81.   Children Enjoy Being Part of the Royal Court
of the Campus Queen.**

Disney type extremely amusing. It must be remembered, however, that
stimuli which are laughter-provoking for the healthy, relaxed child may
be the cause of fear in less well-adjusted children. It also has been found
that children of superior intelligence are more easily moved to laughter,
especially by incongruities, than are less intelligent children.

Studies have indicated that a sense of humor develops according to
the child's emotional and intellectual progress. Through the elementary
school years, incongruity is a common cause of laughter, but the preadolescent responds to deviations from the normal and the discomfiture
of others. Some children's jokes are likely to receive adult disapproval.[21]

Elementary school children experience great satisfaction from
"matching" jokes. To be considered the best jokester in the group is a
matter of great pride. This attitude can be illustrated by the following
incident. A bright fourth-year elementary school class recently had an
end-of-term party. Each member of the class was expected to recount
his favorite jokes. The developed sense of humor of these nine- and ten-

[21] Jersild, Arthur T., *Child Psychology*, 5th ed., pp. 250–254. Englewood Cliffs,
N. J.: Prentice-Hall, Inc., 1960.

year-olds can be evaluated in light of their selection of the following as the "best" jokes.

Dentist: Why are you making a face? I haven't touched you.
Boy: I know, but you're standing on my toe.

Boy: I was writing dirty words on the sidewalk. When I got home my father hit me. If I tell you where he hit me, he'll hit me again.

Question: Three men were on a boat. They wanted to play cards. Why couldn't they?
Answer: They were sitting on the deck.

Question: What is an ice cube?
Answer: A cool, cool square.

Teacher: Billy, how do you spell Mississippi?
Billy: The river or the State?

A man and his daughter were riding in their wagon. They were going to buy furniture and had a lot of money with them. On the way they were held up and the horse and wagon were taken. The father was very sad, but the daughter said happily, "Look father, I saved the money. When I saw the bandits coming I put it in my mouth." Her father praised her. Then he said, "If your mother had been with us, we could have saved the horse and wagon."

THE DEVELOPMENT OF EMOTIONAL CONTROL

Earlier in the chapter we referred to the importance of achieving emotional maturity. At any stage of development the experiencing of strong emotional feelings, whether pleasant or unpleasant, can be detrimental to an individual's personality pattern. Hence it is essential to his general well-being that he acquire intelligent understanding of the role of emotions in his life and use them for his own benefit as well as for the welfare of others. Children need the help of emotionally mature adults to achieve such understanding.

Control of Fear Reactions We know that children are great imitators of adult behavior. Consequently, adults who are responsible for child-rearing themselves need to exhibit confident attitudes in situations that can serve as fear arousers for the child. Too often the young child is exposed to the behavior of fearful adults. The mother, for example, who becomes frightened by thunder and lightning is almost certain to pass this form of fear to her child. Fear of animals or of other possible dangers also can be acquired through adult example.

Social imitation has been found to have value as a fear controller. Another method often used successfully is the process of conditioning or reconditioning. An object, condition, or situation has aroused fear because of accompanying elements of the total picture. A large dog playfully knocks a child down; the latter becomes frightened of all animals. The child trips and hurts himself in the dark; he associates the frightening situation with the lack of light and transfers the fear from tripping to being in darkness. By exposing the child to dogs in pleasing situations or having the child enjoy satisfying conditions in spite of darkness, he gradually can be reconditioned to them, thereby losing his fear of them. Explanation of reasons for not being afraid of supposed fear arousers also may be helpful, but usually is not so successful as confident imitation or conditioning.

Since fear usually is rooted in lack of correct information, one approach to fear elimination is to provide the child or adolescent with experiences from which unknown factors are removed or modified. The acquiring of certain skills which encourage self-confidence aids in preventing or overcoming fear of a new or difficult situation.

Many instances could be cited to indicate that previous learnings are valuable as fear modifiers. For example, as one aspect of training at West Point, the boys are required to climb a rope to a high platform and then jump feet first into a pool. The directions are to fold the arms, hold the nose closed with one hand, and jump. Most of the boys "freeze" with fright and are unable to jump. The boys who are able to perform this feat are successful because as youngsters they had had considerable experience with water sports, and had engaged in similar activities, even though the height of the diving board was not so great as the one used at the Point.

Adults need to be careful that their method of eliminating fear does not deal merely with its outward display. A child may come to understand that an exhibition of fear is babyish. He therefore controls his behavior in a fear-arousing situation, but the anxiety remains. The fear is repressed but not eliminated. Social disapproval may influence the individual to the extent that he refrains from outer manifestations of his fear state, but his inner suffering is intensified. The fear may develop into a phobia that is difficult to overcome. The situation may become serious enough to necessitate the application of psychoanalysis and psychotherapy. The individual may have forgotten the original cause of his great fear. He needs help not only in tracing its causation but also in developing greater self-confidence in mastering it.

Enjoyable activity and successful achievement are excellent tension-reducers. Moreover, intelligent fear or caution, of course, is necessary as a defense against any harmful elements in an individual's environment. Fear of consequences as a result of engaging in socially undesirable behavior also is a cautionary measure that should be learned early by a child. Too great permissiveness that encourages self-centered aggressiveness or too rigid control that leads to timidity may be equally harmful to the growing child.

Control of Anger Reactions One of the most important factors in adults' attempts to help a child overcome displays of rage, temper tantrums, or other forms of angry behavior is consistency of disapproval. No constructive results are achieved if a child is reprimanded or punished for throwing things in anger on one day if, on another day, such behavior is ignored or is the source of adult amusement. Moreover, it is essential that adults who are responsible for training a child be emotionally controlled themselves and exhibit well-controlled, calm behavior. Too often mothers especially tend to meet temper tantrum with temper tantrum, or threaten the child with severe punishment to be administered by the father on his return to the home.

One helpful approach to aiding a child "come out" of an angry state is to divert his attention from the anger-arousing situation to one that is unlike it and likely to stimulate pleasurable feelings. As we have noted earlier, angry behavior usually is stimulated by the child's appreciation of a situation as a threat to himself or his self-esteem. Thwarting conditions can be lessened or eliminated for the child who experiences regular sleeping and eating regimes and who is afforded many opportunities to engage in constructive work and play activities.

It probably is impossible for parents and other adults to grant a child's every wish or desire. Many things must be denied him. A denial should be accompanied by the giving of reasons which the child can understand, and by suggestions concerning more desirable means of gratification. There are times, however, when a child's anger is justified. An adult either does or says something that the child rightfully may regard as unfair. Unless the adult is able to recognize his own failure, attempts at quieting the child or reasoning with him are likely to be fruitless. Better results are achieved if the adult involved admits his fault and asks the child's forgiveness. Children tend to forgive and forget easily if causes of anger and resentment are brought out into the open and handled objectively. This attitude also is helpful in dealing with a child's jealousy. It is natural for any child to suffer occasional feelings of jealousy in his home, school, and social relationships. The development of an habitual jealous attitude can be avoided if, during his early years, a child has experienced fair and objective treatment in his home.

Intelligent Expression of the Tender Emotions The old saying to the effect that the head should rule the heart applies particularly to expressions of the tender emotions. Although concern for the welfare of others is characteristic of love, compassion, and sympathy, this interest can be carried to an extreme unless it is expressed in intelligent behavior. Sentiment, not sentimentality, leads to beneficial results for both the giver and the receiver. The sentimental person weeps, actually or figuratively, for the ills of the world but does nothing constructive about remedying them. An individual who is truly concerned about the welfare of another tends to do whatever he can to ameliorate unfavorable conditions or to give succor in time of distress.

The overindulgent parent is an example of the kind of person who harms rather than helps his child who is the object of his great affection. A mother, because of her great love for her little son or daughter, may assume complete responsibility for the child's welfare and seems to be unwilling or unable to deny the fulfillment of any childish desire.

A child reared in the home of overindulgent parents is likely to become extremely self-centered, developing an adult attitude of expecting everyone outside the home to defer to his wishes. The product of such rearing often lacks the experiencing of outgoing tender emotions. In his dealings with other people, care of his own interests dominates his behavior, even at the expense of others' welfare. He thereby is denied the joy of giving to others and doing kind and thoughtful acts.

A child who, during his early years, experiences affection and respect from the members of his family usually responds in kind. It is good for a child to share in family responsibilities within the limits of his developing ability to do so. To care for a pet or help parents in the care of younger children in the family enables the growing person to become less concerned with selfish interests than would be possible if his interests always received priority. Exposure to consistent displays of family loyalty and affection is likely to motivate a child to become an outgoing, kind adult, unless in his later developing years he becomes the victim of unpleasant experiences with uncooperative and generally suspicious associates.

QUESTIONS AND TOPICS FOR DISCUSSION

1. How do you react when you are angry? Afraid?
2. Watch the behavior of an angry person. What do you notice about his appearance and actions?
3. What differences are there in your expressions of emotional behavior as a child and at present? Have you become more or less given to emotional outbursts with increasing age? How do you account for any differences you find?
4. What is your pet "peeve"? Why? What do you do about it?
5. Which of the listings of emotional states included in this chapter do you consider to be most adequate? Why? Would you list emotions differently? How?
6. If possible, for one hour watch the reactions of an infant who is awake. What emotional responses do you think you have observed? Explain your judgments.
7. Give specific examples of ways in which one emotional state can be changed to another: (1) in a child, (2) in an adolescent, (3) in an adult. On what level would the shift probably be most effective? Why? Most difficult? Why?
8. Do you consider yourself to be emotionally mature? On what do you base your judgment of yourself?
9. Read carefully Jersild's compilation of steps in emotional development. Select those which you consider to be most important; least important. Evaluate your own emotional growth according to the trends listed.
10. Name at least ten cautionary fears that children should develop.
11. List at least five anxiety-arousing situations for an elementary school child; for a young adolescent.
12. If you have experienced a phobia, or if an associate has, try to trace its origin.
13. How would you as a parent or teacher handle a child who engages in temper tantrums?
14. Note and report on humorous stories you hear children tell.
15. *Special Project:* Report any emotional differences that you have observed in your four subjects. Be specific concerning their anger, fear, and affection responses.

SELECTED REFERENCES

Arnold, Magda B., *Emotion and Personality*. New York: Columbia University Press, 1960.

Bender, L., *Aggression, Hostility and Anxiety in Children*. Springfield, Ill.: Charles C Thomas, 1953.

Bennett, Edward, *The Search for Emotional Security*. New York: The Ronald Press Company, 1959.

Caplan, G. (ed.), *Emotional Problems of Early Childhood*. New York: Basic Books, Inc., 1955.

Flint, Betty M., *The Security of Infants*. Toronto: University of Toronto Press, 1959.

Jersild, Arthur T., "Emotional Development," in L. Carmichael (ed.), *Manual of Child Development,* 2nd ed., pp. 833–917. New York: John Wiley and Sons, Inc., 1954.

Liebman, Samuel (ed.), *Emotional Problems of Childhood*. Philadelphia: J. B. Lippincott, 1959.

May, R., *The Meaning of Anxiety*. New York: The Ronald Press Company, 1950.

Montagu, A. (ed.), *The Meaning of Love*. New York: Julian Press, 1953.

Wolfenstein, M., *Children's Humor: A Psychological Analysis*. Glencoe, Ill.: Free Press, 1954.

I I

SOCIAL DEVELOPMENT

THE NEWBORN INFANT is an organism possessing certain potentialities that have varying degrees of readiness to function in the environment in which he finds himself. At birth, he exhibits neither social, asocial nor unsocial traits. At that point he is nonsocial. His social development, soon under way, is determined by his biological inheritance and those qualities that make possible the modifiability of his behavior as he interacts with others in his environment. Fortunately, no matter what his inheritance, each child possesses important potentialities for growth and development and a high degree of modifiability of traits.

NATURE AND NEED OF SOCIAL BEHAVIOR

We live in a world of people; we not only are influenced by them but exert our own influence on them. The ability to live with or to get along with others sometimes is as important to an individual's happiness and success as the mental ability which he displays in adjusting to his physical environment. The importance of getting along with those with whom one lives, studies, or works becomes clear when it is realized that good social adjustment improves physical health, adds to enjoyment in play, encourages school success, and increases productivity in work,

Factors of Influence   The social individual wants to be with people, meet group standards, and do things with others rather than alone. A child must learn his social behavior, since he is not born a social person. Social ability can be acquired only as a result of being with people. Hence each child needs to be given opportunities to be with various types of individuals during his formative years. This is so important that it should not be left to chance. To help the child achieve the development of social habits and attitudes requires careful planning on the part of adults. Since there are interactions between the child and the individuals in the social group or groups with whom he associates, it is essential that some selection be made of the members of any one of these groups. At first, this guidance must come from adults who are more experienced in this area than is the child.

Mental, physical, and emotional aspects of development are closely associated with social development. The interrelationships among them are so significant that what has been learned pertaining to general growth and development should be applied to social development. The child's degree of mental acuity influences the interpretation which he places on the attitudes or overt behavior of others. The child displays anger if his wants are not satisfied; he responds with affectionate behavior when they are satisfied. Likewise, the emotional attitudes of adults who attend the child are affected by his behavior responses. The child who early develops satisfactory social habits is likely to be equipped to meet those social situations with which he will be confronted in later life.

A child is a social being and is unhappy if he is isolated from others. However, he may play cooperatively with other children at one time and become shy or aggressive with these same children in a different setting. One child may prefer to be with his mother; another may be happier with siblings or friends. The child constantly is surrounded by social forces by which his behavior is conditioned. These stimuli affect him favorably or unfavorably long before he is able to make social choices for himself. The social forces in his environment include such factors as sex status, social status of the family, school atmosphere, and religious affiliation. The influence of these is discussed in Chapters 19 and 20. Gradually, the child learns to adapt his behavior to that of the various individuals or groups in the society in which he is maturing.

The individual and the group coexist through an overlapping of interests, feelings, attitudes, and common understandings. Social culture is not something that is apart from the individuals of which it is composed and it does not operate independently of other influences. The experiences of the individual in interacting with the members of the group are aspects of a complex entity. Any period of social development is evaluated in terms of what has gone before and what is to follow. The social maturation of the child is better understood when we know something about such factors as his behavior in meeting new situations, his mental acuity, his emotional status, his physiological maturation, his home life, and his schooling.

   The Developmental Process   As the life needs of the neonate are fulfilled for him by those upon whom he depends, he begins to respond to them as persons. For a long time the child is dependent upon someone for his survival. This period of dependence provides the child with an opportunity for maturation as adults care for his needs. As survival needs are met, he begins to respond to those who provide for his welfare. At first, the important persons in his social environment are his mother or nurse, and perhaps his father.

   The child's early responses to cither his mother or his nurse are rather meager. His social behavior reflects the various rseponses he makes in his endeavor to satisfy his body needs. As his sense organs become more receptive to stimulation through their maturation and use and as he lives one day after another, social behavior becomes more evident. The stimuli necessary to evoke social responses change from specific and intense satisfiers of physical needs to the more subtle behavior motivators, such as approval, the use of language, and self-interest or interest in others. Personal-social relationships are taking place.

   Social behavior is developing when the mother cares for and handles the infant. As she nurses the newborn baby, the mother stimulates him socially. When the baby becomes restless and cries, he is dried, kept warm, and talked to, with the hope that he will respond with behavior that is satisfying. Although the changes that are taking place in the child are not discernible at first, they are revealed through such behavior as gurgling, cooing, smiling, and movements of the arms and legs. Gradually, the infant becomes aware that it is an individual who stimulates his feeling of satisfaction. The mother's touch, her facial expression, and her tone of voice are constant stimuli that develop patterns of behavior which help the infant relate to the mother and appreciate her. As the infant integrates his social experiences, he passes from one social relationship to another, without maintaining a sustained response to any one person.

   The child discriminates among kinds of social learning at an early age. This is achieved through the many social experiences that are his as he grows and develops in an expanding environment. He soon learns to differentiate between the touch of his mother's hand and that of another person; he recognizes her tone of voice, her fondling, her presence as opposed to that of another person. Each time a stranger enters his environment, he is presented with a new set of social stimuli to which he needs to give meaning. At first, they are obscure to him; later they are interpreted in light of the behavior of the newcomer. Thus is his social understanding increased.

Cultural Influences   The attitudes of adults and other children found in a rural district or an urban community and the general mores of the social order are among the factors that will give direction to the child's social behavior. Often he develops citizenship attitudes and becomes a particular kind of citizen without realizing how it happened. Thus culture becomes a regulator of behavior among the members of a single society.[1]

The social values of any group influence the behavior of the members of the group. In a typical American community the upper class focusses on leisure pursuits and family background; the upper middle class stresses the importance of money and status; the lower middle class emphasizes the value of achieving social gains through collective action; and the lowest class may be content to enjoy meager wealth or achievement.[2] Family and peer group pressures help in maintaining class status. If a child wishes to be accepted by members of another social class, he must be willing to accept the ideals, beliefs, values, and attitudes of individuals of the social class with which he wishes to be identified. When he strives to meet the conditions required to enter a higher class he is known as a social "climber."

In a study of lower-class children concerning the relationships between aggression and popularity of seventy-four white boys ranging in age between ten and thirteen years, Lesser found that directly provoked physical aggression and unprovoked verbal aggression are disapproved, and indirect aggression of all forms is strongly disapproved.[3] The influence of the peer group as a socializing agency depends upon many variables. Young children are capable of making fine discriminations among the responses of their age-mates. In the socializing process these responses are approved or disapproved, or rewarded or punished differentially by means of peer group behavior. This sensitivity appears to operate either within the class group or between social classes.

[1] Bagby, P. H., "Culture and the Causes of Culture," *American Anthropology,* 59: 535–554, 1953.

[2] Goldschmidt, W., "Social Class in America—A Critical Review," *American Anthropology,* 52: 483–498, 1950.

[3] Lesser, Gerald S., "The Relationships between Various Forms of Aggression and Popularity among Lower-class Children," *Journal of Educational Psychology,* 50: 20–25, 1959.

SEQUENCE OF SOCIAL DEVELOPMENT

Social interaction starts early. Social behavior develops as soon as adults begin to cuddle the infant. The mother communicates more than nourishment, for example, to the child when she nurses him; she conveys her feelings of affection or rejection to him. A mother who enjoys motherhood feels warm toward the infant as she dries, feeds, talks to, and otherwise cares for him. This gives the child a favorable emotional atmosphere to start life. He is given a feeling of security and a chance to respond with behavior that indicates satisfaction.

Early Social Responses There is much social communication between the child and the mother during the early weeks of feeding. The feelings of the mother are reflected in how she holds and cuddles the infant and the extent to which he is permitted to satisfy both his hunger and his pleasure in sucking as he is being fed. Consciously or unconsciously, the infant is concerned almost completely with the satisfaction of bodily wants. Yet, as these are being satisfied, he responds to the behavior of those about him whose responsibility it is to supply his wants. Crying and mass activity are the earliest forms of behavior that can be considered as social since they call forth a response by others.

During the first month, infants respond to relatively few stimuli of a social nature. As maturation necessary for receptivity to both physical and social stimuli occurs, babies are undergoing necessary preparation for the social behavior that will be theirs to enjoy. Stimuli that activate behavior may be either internal or external. For example, if an infant stops crying when an adult enters the room or when he speaks to him, it is no assurance that the presence of the adult or the sound of his voice has achieved the change in overt behavior. Many times, in the absence of similar stimuli, the infant may stop crying, indicating that the behavior can result from hearing any noise, changing his position, or receiving pressure relief.

During the second month, an infant gives evidence that he is actively aware of adults who care for him. He seems, however, to be unaware of the presence of other babies who may be near him in the room. He responds to persons who make an effort to stimulate him in one or another social way. He responds to a smile of his mother or another familiar person. By this time he stares at faces that are near, and begins to differentiate among the individuals in his home, becoming more demanding in getting attention from them.

By the end of the third month, the infant attends, if only for a moment, to a block placed on the table before him. Although there is little of the social in this, the presence of a person or the sound of his voice may stimulate the infant to turn his head or his eyes toward the direction of the stimulus. When stimulated by another person, a smile can be evoked, although it may not be in response to a smile by that person. The infant has not yet learned that the smile of the adult is what evolves his smile, since his smile response can be elicited when he is stimulated by an angry face or a distorted facial expression. Maturation for making these responses is progressing rapidly, but the responses themselves are learned. By this time, a few infants are able to discriminate between facial expressions, tones, and gestures of adults.

By the fifth month, the infant is fast becoming a socialized human being as compared with his twenty-day-old self. He not only smiles in reply to another's smile but may cry at other social stimuli. He is developing powers of perception that enable him to interpret the expressive behavior of an increasing number of adults. He recognizes the type of ministration to his needs which his mother or nurse is giving or about to give. He is becoming aware of the sounds and sight of persons, is participating in smiling, crying, and grabbing, and, in general, is interacting with the various forces in his immediate environment.

As the child gains in strength and maturation, he may, by the end of the seventh month, be expected to enjoy the game of peek-a-boo, or "hide your face." He follows any object that is placed in motion, and will smile when a person uses his hands to cut off the view of his face. His maturation now is sufficient to enable him to balance his head without support; he can sit for ten minutes or more when supported. If offered a hand, he will grasp it and attempt to pull himself to a sitting position. He enjoys being bounced on a bed, on his mother's or father's knee, or sometimes on the knee of a friend. He gradually is gaining interest in people and things. He plays longer with one toy than with another, and indicates through his laughter that he enjoys the attention of others. He is contributing as well as receiving social stimuli. His increasing capacity to utilize social stimuli enables him to enlarge the scope as well as the number of social responses emanating from the respective situations.

From the eighth to the tenth month, the infant begins to display more aggressive behavior toward adults. He will pull an adult's hair, grab his nose, tug at his clothes or other personal features. He shows ability to imitate some vocal sounds. Everyone is becoming aware of the fact that he is conscious of other human beings as persons. Previously the infant was not interested in another baby who was placed in close proximity to him. He now shows an awareness of the other child and may crave the attention given to the other. He may object to sharing his toy with another baby or protest having a toy taken away from him. Objects in motion catch his attention. If a seated adult swings a foot of his crossed legs, the child, with his eyes, will follow the motion for a long time.

Development of Specific Responses during the First Year   Social responses that start early in life and have received considerable attention by those who have studied social development in children are those of smiling and laughter.

SMILING AND LAUGHTER   Smiling and laughter seem to follow a developmental sequence. A smile can be evoked in various ways. For example, when a human being bends over or comes within the line of vision of an infant of two months of age, a smile is likely to appear on his face. If the infant is between the ages of two and six months of age he is likely to smile whether the adult smiles, grimaces, or makes use of a mask. These smiles appear to be activated by the total configuration of the stimuli from the face, especially if motion is given to the lips or the head.[4]

Washburn, who studied smiling and laughing responses of infants during the first year of life, found that laughter occurred later than smiling. Great differences were found to exist among children in their frequency of response. However, the method which elicits smiling also can elicit laughing. Physical proximity is the usual stimulus to elicit smiling. Smiling is conditioned to certain stimuli by the end of fifty-two weeks but laughter seems not to be a conditioned response. Washburn describes the smiling behavior between the twelfth and fifty-second weeks as follows:

Twelve weeks
Twitching of lips and other facial muscles preceding smiling.
Round, open mouth.
Protrusion of chin (incidence and degree decreasing up to 40 weeks).
Vocalizations monosyllabic—"ah" (decreasing up to 40 weeks).
Hands are moved up and down over center of body and come to rest in the mouth region. } These forms of activity are not confined to smiling, though typically present in the last stage of the smile.
Knees are drawn up toward the abdomen, with rolling of body.
Mobilized attention with reduction of bodily activity precedes smiling (decreasing up to 44 weeks).

Twenty weeks
Upward retraction of corners of the mouth are frequent.

[4] See Spitz, R. A., "The Smiling Response," *Genetic Psychology Monographs,* **34:** 57–125, 1946.

Crescent-shaped mouth first seen.

Shortened nose, wrinkles on bridge of nose, first observed.

"Peach-stone" chin appears.

Dissyllabic as well as monosyllabic vocalizations—"ha," "ahgh," "ah-goo," "garg-ling," "squeal."

"Waving" of arms and successive kicking of legs, especially in the last stage of the smile.

Leaning toward source of stimulation begins (depending upon degree of development of eye-hand coordinations).

Thirty-two weeks

Retraction displaces "opening" of the mouth with consequently greater bulging and raising of cheeks.

Horizontally elliptical mouth most typical.

Tongue protrusion at its height.

Exposure of gums begins.

Eyes often half-closed rather than narrowed slightly.

Wrinkles or curves at outer canthi of eyes frequent.

Chin drawn in to neck.

"Coy" smiles (head bowed or bent to one side, glance directed upward) first observed.

Vocalizations—prolonged "ah." Varied jargon-like sounds.

Bubbles blown, especially in the last stage of the smile.

Fifty-two weeks

Greater effect of "control" in the above forms of behavior; less bodily activity.

More individualization in subjects' smiles.

Double naso-labial fold first seen.[5]

Brackett [6] found that, among nursery school children, laughter is a predominantly social form of behavior displayed more frequently when children are interacting. Children prefer other children who laugh, and they confine their laughter to a few particular children. Laughter of younger children usually involves one other person, while laughter of older children involves two or more other individuals. The laughing responses tend to remain consistent for one-year periods; children who laugh a great deal at the start of the year continue to do so later.

Kenderdine [7] found that the frequency of children's laughter depends first on situations involving motion of self, next on those situations children believe to be socially acceptable, and finally on humorous situations. Children with high intelligence quotients laugh more frequently than do those with low.

[5] Washburn, Ruth W., "A Study of the Smiling and Laughing of Infants in the First Year of Life," *Genetic Psychology Monographs,* 6: 527–528, 1929.

[6] Brackett, C. W., "Laughing and Crying of Preschool Children," *Journal of Experimental Education,* 2: 119–126, 1933.

[7] Kenderdine, M., "Laughter in the Preschool Child," *Child Development,* 2: 228–230, 1931.

Dennis [8] studied the smiling and laughter responses of female twins between the ages of two and fourteen months of age under conditions of restricted practice and of minimum social stimulation. He reports that smiling and laughter were neither caused by imitative behavior nor the result of a social learning process; that social behavior is the result of a maturative process rather than a learning process. The twins began to smile and laugh without specific stimulation from the experimenters.

VARIOUS SOCIAL RESPONSES DURING THE FIRST YEAR   Many types of infant responses have been studied. Those made to adults are of significance. As the baby matures through his first year, he develops ways of responding to adults in his environment. These adults are individuals who either satisfy or thwart the infant's desires or urges, thus establishing certain attitudes toward them on the part of the child. With the development of the ability to walk, the baby meets many children. These meetings afford an opportunity for social experiences which seem to produce little in the way of observable behavior. Significant differences, however, exist among infants in the display of social behavior toward one another. Bühler [9] has reported certain observations concerning the responses of infants to adults (see Table 14) and infants to other infants (see Table 15).

TABLE 14

Responses of Infants to Adults, Observed in Sixty Per Cent or More of the Cases *

	Age in months
Returns glance of adult with smiling	1 to 2
Is quieted by touching	1 to 2
Cries when adult who was attending him leaves	2 to 3
Smiles back at adult	2 to 3
Disturbed when approached	2 to 3
Returns approaching glance with "lalling"	3 to 4
Displeasure when loses glance of adult	3 to 4
Quieted by caressing	4 to 5
Disturbed by the sight of people	4 to 5
Striving for attention by "lalling"	7 to 8
Stretches out hands toward adults	7 to 8
Cries when adult stops talking	7 to 8
Strives for attention by movements	8 to 9
Pulls on the clothes of adults	9 to 10
Offers adult an object	9 to 10
Imitates movements of adult with a plaything	9 to 10
Organizes play activity	10 to 11

8 Dennis, Wayne, "Infant Development under Conditions of Restricted Practice and of Minimum Social Stimulation," *Genetic Psychology Monographs*, 23: 143–191, 1941.

9 * Bühler, Charlotte, *The First Year of Life*, pp. 56 and 57. New York: The John Day Company, 1930.

TABLE 15

Responses of Infants to Other Infants, Observed in Sixty Per Cent or More of the Cases [**]

	Age in months
Observes other child	4 to 5
Smiles at other child	4 to 5
Cries if other child receives attention	8 to 9
Offers toy to other child	8 to 9
"Lalls" to other child	8 to 9
Imitates movements of another child	9 to 10
Opposes toy being taken away	9 to 10
Organized play activity	10 to 11
Strives for attention by means of "lalling"	10 to 11
Ill-humor if another child moves away	10 to 11
Setting aside toy and turning toward another child	11 to 12

In their study of the temporal order of appearance of social responses in babies, Gesell and Thompson observed the number of responses of specific behavior items of babies at given ages between four and fifty-six weeks of age. (See Table 16.) They found that significant changes take place with age. The variation in percentages of babies who display specific responses at respective ages is indicative of the great variation that exists among the individual babies. To the age of about sixteen weeks, however, all babies exhibited no response to strangers.

The Preschool and Kindergarten Child A year-old-child is ready to expand his social contacts. Although he has the power of locomotion, his social behavior still is limited. He can wave and say "bye-bye" or play hide-and-seek behind a paper or a chair. By two, he understands and can obey certain commands, knows the names of certain objects or parts of the body, or calls the attention of another person to an object in which he is interested. He can hold a spoon with which to eat and a glass from which to drink. The training he has received up to this point has been toward egocentricity or self-centeredness. He has demanded and received personal attention. He therefore needs training and experience in living with others and giving consideration to the interests and needs of others. In a study of changes in egocentricity of nursery school children, Ezekiel [10] reports that there is a positive correlation be-

[**] Bühler, Charlotte, *The First Year of Life*, pp. 56 and 57. New York: The John Day Company, copyright 1930. Used by permission of the author.

[10] Ezekiel, L. F., "Changes in Egocentricity of Nursery School Children," *Child Development*, 2: 74–75, 1931.

TABLE 16

Temporal Order of Appearance of Social Behavior Items in Babies *

| | Babies' ages in weeks | | | | | | | | | | | | | | |
Behavior items	4	6	8	12	16	20	24	28	32	36	40	44	48	52	56
	Percentages of babies showing responses at given ages														
Responds to smiling and talking	8	62	63												
Visually pursues moving person	12	69	74												
Knows mother	3	21	30	81	92										
Sobers at strangers	0	3	4	35	56										
Turns head on sound of voice	0	3	26	42	50	100									
Accepts strangers	100	100	100	100	80	61	52	59	41	39	39	26	18	18	14
Withdraws from strangers	0	0	0	0	19	8	24	16	47	42	19	48	44	30	9
Adjusts to words					0	8	12	16	47	68	75	94	82	89	73
Responds to "bye-bye"						3	3	3	13	35	53	65	38	59	27
Adjusts to commands						0	0	3	22	23	31	55	56	73	50
Responds to inhibitory words						0	0	3	25	23	28	45	44	52	23
Responds to "So big"						0	0	0	6	7	8	26	18	34	0
Elicits attention						0	0	0	9	16	14	26	27	53	50
Plays pat-a-cake						0	3	6	19	23	25	42	27	50	9
Plays peek-a-boo						6	6	0	9	13	11	13	9	25	9

* By permission from Gesell, A., and Thompson, H., *Infant Behavior: Its Genesis and Growth*, p. 258. Copyright 1934 by McGraw-Hill Book Company, Inc.

tween the age of the child when he enters a new social situation and his type of egocentricity. He found that during the first three months, few significant changes were made by those children who were predominantly egocentric, but egocentric and aggressive behavior was displayed by unaggressive children.

The preschool child is an active, independent, and adventurous individual. Although his interests are fleeting, he enjoys exploring many situations. Often he is caught between his father who encourages the tendency to experiment and to discover things for himself, and his mother who has a greater tendency to restrain or limit his scope of activities. During this period the child displays tendencies toward negativism by responding to almost every parental request with a "no." The result is that, although he gains a feeling of independence, his parents become exasperated. Parents need to make proper use of parental authority and yet exercise proper control. This is a trying period for both the parents and the child.

The child who is imaginative at this period is likely to have many phantasies. He has imaginative playmates, makes up stories, and puts on his mother's shoes or his older sibling's clothes. These are wholesome behavior practices. On the negative side, however, are possible feelings of being in danger when left alone. He may develop a fear of aloneness and even abandonment and tell false tales for which he may receive severe reprimands from his parents. It is difficult for parents to distinguish between phantasies and actual falsehoods, and they often punish their child for acceptable projections of the imagination.

The nursery school child is egocentric and tends to think of things as his own. He refers to them as "my pencil," "my ball," "my house," "my book," and so on. He may even take objects from another child for his own use. He needs help in the development of social attitudes and behavior. He can be given assistance in developing a sense of right and wrong. He is given experiences that afford satisfaction and heighten his feeling of himself as an individual.

Teachers of the young child need to be temperamentally able to accept his dependence upon them and to give the child a sense of security which will bring satisfaction to him. A child should neither be kept a baby too long nor rushed into becoming self-reliant too rapidly. A nursery school child usually has one friend, sometimes two, with whom he identifies, if only for short periods. Sometimes he has an imaginary companion.

The type of companion a child selects or the type of child selected by another child has long been the concern of those who work with young children. Some children are extremely diffident and tend to keep to themselves, while other children are more social-minded and move aggressively into any group. The child's ability to function in a group results from his earlier training and experience rather than from other factors. Hence the child who receives training in group living is likely to adjust without too much frustration in new social situations which he meets from time to time.

When children are permitted to form groups without adult interference, they usually select the members from children who are near their homes or in their nursery or kindergarten group. When left to themselves, race, color, sex, poverty, or riches seldom become factors in the selection of their companions. In a study of companionships of preschool children, Hagman [11] reports that individual children varied greatly in their selection of companions. Some chose those similar to themselves; others chose companions who had very dissimilar characteristics. Some reacted to a companion during more than 40 per cent of the opportunities provided; others reacted to less than 5 per cent of them. Two-year-olds showed no sex preference, but four-year-olds preferred to be with their own sex. The two-year-olds spent 50 per cent of their time in companionship reactions; the four-year-olds spent 58 per cent.

Four- and five-year-old children begin to display sympathetic behavior toward their same-age group. They play together; they display aggressive behavior at one moment and cooperative behavior at the next. They also begin to assume the roles of leader and follower. Competitive or cooperative behavior is affected by the attitudes of others in the home and community. If cooperation is stressed, the children become less competitive; if competition is a part of the social mores, rivalry becomes a strong motivator of behavior. This varies with individuals and with groups.

Adequate play situations and equipment are valuable to the social growth of children. Toys and play equipment that are graded according to age are available. These materials should be selected with care by parents and school people so that both physical and social growth may be promoted by their use.

Nursery school and kindergarten experiences are important in the lives of developing children. The teacher, as a mother substitute, guides the children away from egocentric behavior to that which is more social.

11 Hagman, E. P., "The Companionship of Preschool Children," *Studies in Child Welfare*, Vol. 7, No. 4. Iowa City: University of Iowa, 1933.

The influence of attendance at a nursery school was studied by Hatt-wick.[12] He reports significant findings pertaining to social adjustment. He found that the children studied became more sociable only after long periods of attendance, but that traits such as fear of strangers and avoid-ance of other children diminished quickly. He also found that the children who attended the nursery school from the time they were three years of age had acquired acceptable social habits by four years of age. These children showed an increase in ability to express themselves, and a de-crease in tension, wiggling, and play with fingers.

The social behavior of the preschool child is well summarized in a statement by G. Murphy, L. B. Murphy, and T. M. Newcomb.

1. Between the ages of two and five years, the variety of social behavior patterns increases from year to year.

2. Among two- and three-year-olds, there are substantial positive correlations between practically all overt social behavior patterns, including those which adults think of as desirable and as undesirable.

3. Resistance and negativism may commonly be expected to reach a peak at three years, more or less independent of economic group or geographical location. This probably means merely that in our culture the conflict of the child's readiness to expand with the restrictions imposed by adults is almost universal for this age.

4. Friendship and integrated patterns of cooperation begin at three or four and expand from that time on into more complicated or organized forms.

5. The quality and amount of cooperation or conflict are affected by the set-up of the group: number of children in relation to space and play material, age range of children, personality of dominant children, amount of teacher direction, and personality of teachers.

6. Personality reactions to home situations, especially parents' attitudes toward the child, carry over into general tendencies toward withdrawal (children of over-protective parents) or aggression (children rejecting parents), appearing in other situations.

7. Children vary in the extent to which behavior in any one situation is a basis for prediction of behavior in any other situation. Some children are relatively con-sistent from situation to situation and others vary sharply; where variations occur, they follow consistent patterns that can be understood when seen in relation to the total personality of the child.[13]

The Elementary School Child   By this time the child has lost interest in playing alone. He wants to expand his social environment to include many friends. He no longer prefers to accompany his parents

[12] Hattwick, B. W., "The Influence of Nursery School Attendance upon the Be-havior and Personality of the Preschool Child," *Journal of Experimental Education,* 5: 180–190, 1936.

[13] Murphy, G., Murphy, L. B., and Newcomb, T. M., *Experimental Social Psy-chology,* pp. 617–618. New York: Harper and Brothers, copyright 1937.

Wide World Photo

Figure 82. Children Enjoying a Birthday Party.

on trips to the park or to visit relatives to the exclusion of his friends. He has turned from his former interest in individual games to the type of play activity that involves the group; play without companions is rarely satisfying. He is entering the age when social awareness develops very rapidly. Birthday parties are always welcome. (See Figure 82.)

As the child participates in the activities of his peers, he must learn how to meet his new associates and obtain satisfaction from being with them. This is accomplished through his having many experiences in a variety of situations. He desires to be in a group of the same age, the members of which exhibit interests similar to his own. He must learn how to treat these people outside the home since they are destined shortly to replace his family as the dominant influence over his behavior and attitudes. Note the unusual cafe for children shown in Figure 83.

The need for learning to meet new people in new situations is an ever-present problem. Many boys and girls have deep-seated fear of social situations and sometimes worry about the resolution of this problem. One girl had great concern about being accepted by a desired and admired group. She wanted to be recognized by the members and to share in its activities, but was shy about joining it. Another elementary school child found it difficult to make friends with the pupils in a new school. Although there was a particular group to which this boy wanted to belong, he found that it was not easy to make friends of the members in it. He found that the easiest and most satisfying place to make new friends was in the school among the members of his class. The strong urge for friendship and peer approval during this age tends to stimulate the kind of cooperative behavior that will earn this approval. Children enjoy all kinds of activities at this age.

A child's friends usually are chosen from children of the same sex who live near his home, are in his class at school, and are similar in intelligence. The friendships of boys seem to be more enduring than are those of girls. Quarrels, however, are common among friends of either sex. Boys tend to be more aggressive. They attempt either to settle their disagreements "on the spot," or to sever the friendship completely. Girls'

United Press International Photo

Figure 83. Supervised Activity of Children in London, England.

quarrels are just as intense as those of boys, but girls often engage in bickering; they display jealousy or feelings of personal hurt.

Because of divergent interests between the ages of eight and ten, boys and girls tend to reduce the extent to which they formerly had played together. In fact, they now often show antagonism in the form of teasing and tormenting each other. After the age of ten, however, children tend to begin to choose members of the opposite sex. According to a recent study in which the incomplete-sentence technique was used with children between the sixth and twelfth grades, it was found that the favorable attitude or preference of girls toward boys increases between the sixth and ninth grades, while the preference of girls for girls decreases between the sixth and twelfth grades. Boys, however, tend to prefer boys to girls from the tenth to the twelfth grades. See Figure 84 for various attitude trends of one sex toward the other.

This study also was concerned with the attitudes of children toward their parents. Positively and negatively toned responses of both boys and girls toward mother and father are presented in 4c and 4d of Figure 84. The percentage of children expressing preference for mother or father are given in 4e of the same figure.

GANGS OR CLUBS The child needs and seeks friends among his peers. This need for social satisfaction is rooted in the human urge to be with others rather than to be alone. To satisfy this urge, children enter into many kinds of social activities. They form clubs and organize gangs and secret societies. In the early stages or during his transition from the pregang stage of early childhood to the gang stage of late childhood, the child often goes from one group to another, thus bridging the gap that leads to the gang stage.

Gangs are usually organized along sex lines. The boys will have their gangs and the girls will have their social clubs. The activities in which both boys' and girls' groups engage are numerous and vary from community to community and with the age of the members. They include such activities as sports, quiet games, social activities, going to the theatre, watching television, annoying other groups, fighting, stealing, later gambling, drinking, and smoking, and a long list of others, depending on the nature of the group and its location. These groups often are short-lived.

The drive that impels children into gang activities can be channeled into well-organized and supervised clubs where the individuals can give wholesome expression to their social needs. A boys' club, for example,

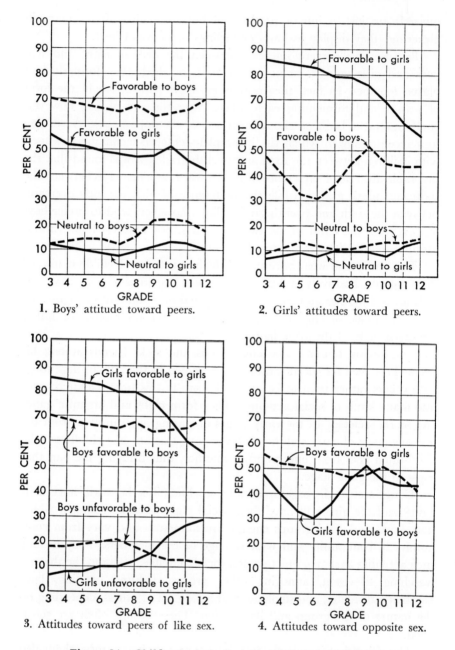

Figure 84. Children's Attitudes toward Peers and Parents.

From Harris, Dale B., and Tseng, Sing Chu, "Children's Attitudes toward Peers and Parents as Revealed by Sentence Completions," *Child Development*, 23: pp. 403–409, December, 1957.

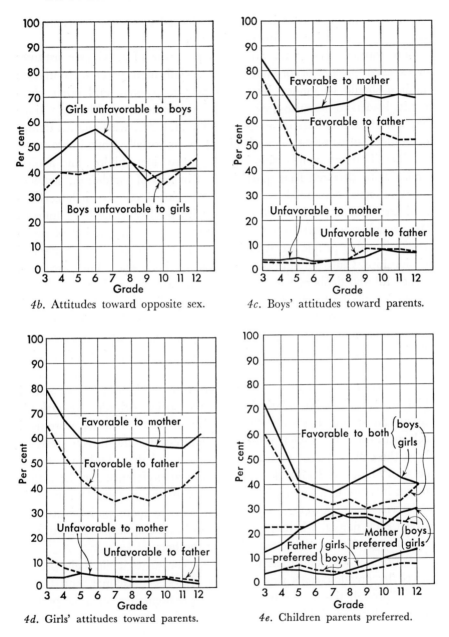

4b. Attitudes toward opposite sex.

4c. Boys' attitudes toward parents.

4d. Girls' attitudes toward parents.

4e. Children parents preferred.

can be referred to as a gang if it is a group to which the individuals want to belong. Its activities can be enshrouded in secrecy. Eligibility restrictions for membership can be imposed, thus giving each member a feeling of exclusiveness. Passwords, badges, rules for membership, and special meeting places tend to provide desired emotional overtones for the members of active groups of this type.

The formation of groups with their programs of activities constitutes an excellent means of promoting the socialization process. Immature children should be guided by school people, parents, and other community leaders to organize their groups for socially acceptable goals, since they are great imitators of adult behavior and otherwise might attempt to simulate unrealistic stories of adventure or socially undesirable adult activities. Through membership in such groups older children and adolescents can be deterred from participation in acts of vandalism, stealing, or sex offenses. Antisocial attitudes of behavior developed in late childhood are likely to persist, and interfere with positive social development. The prepubescent years usually represent a satisfactory period of social growth if young people receive wise but indirect guidance of their social relationships. Clubs should be encouraged for both sexes. They are more purposeful and deliberate in their aims than are informal groups. These should include both school clubs and other well-established groups such as Boy and Girl Scouts, 4 H clubs, and young people's religious groups. Participation in group living exemplified by attendance at a summer camp also is a worthwhile social experience. (See Chapter 20 for a discussion of the summer camp.)

ATTITUDE OF CHILDREN TOWARD PARENTS   The elementary school child tends to exhibit relatively desirable social attitudes toward his parents. According to a study [14] by Harris and Tseng, in which were used such methods as incomplete sentences, picture-story, and direct questions about the child's parent preference, it was found that children between the ages of five and nine show a decrease in preference for the father and an increase in a favorable attitude toward the mother. During their adolescent years, however, boys seem to have a more positive attitude toward each parent, whereas girls seem to have a more positive attitude toward their fathers than toward their mothers.

Another study concerned with family control of child behavior as viewed by preadolescents was made by Hawkes, Burchinal, and Gardner.[15] Through the use of two types of questionnaires an attempt was made to discover children's attitudes toward various means of control

[14] Harris and Tseng, *op. cit.*, pp. 401–411.

[15] Hawkes, G. R., Burchinal, L. G., and Gardner, B., "Pre-Adolescents' Views of Some of Their Relations with Their Parents," *Child Development*, 28: 393–399, December, 1957.

of their behavior commonly used by their parents. The findings indicate that boys and girls in the fifth grade in rural and small town areas are reasonably well satisfied with the relationships between themselves and their parents. Nevertheless, boys expressed a greater criticism of home conditions and family relationships than did girls; both, however, believed that they had better relationships with their mothers than with their fathers.

Similar findings were shown in a study made by Koch [16] concerning sibling attitudes held toward each other and toward their parents.

The Young Adolescent By the time the child reaches early adolescence, he has formed many habits, attitudes, and ideals which will either hinder or help his further social development. He has learned the meaning of bad and good and has been able to distinguish right from wrong in social situations. If he has developed these social habits before the age of six, they are likely to continue to function under the guidance of teachers, parents, and other leaders during his adolescent years. Although social and moral standards vary from time to time and among different cultures, the adolescent knows what is right even if he does not always practice it. He may not, however, reveal the fact that he has the knowledge of what is right and wrong in respective situations.

The adolescent soon discovers that the rights of others are to be respected if he wishes to gain and keep friends. The behavior he displays toward another will evoke definite responses from the other person. If he wishes to win the other's friendship he will try to do or to say that which will win approval. He observes what is said by the other person and becomes an active imitator of desirable traits or mannerisms. As he mingles with his peers, his feeling of belongingness increases until it becomes a most important possession. It may become so strong that family considerations are neglected as he meets the demands (real or imagined) of his peers. He may insist upon wearing shorts to school, for example, thus defying his parents' wishes, but gaining peer approval.

The adolescent displays a desire for close friendship with other teenagers. He wants a friend of his own age to whom he can speak freely concerning his problems, hopes, and ambitions, and who will show sympathy toward his mounting troubles and conflicts. During early adolescence the confidant is likely to be a member of the same sex. The

[16] Koch, Helen L., "The Relation of Certain Formal Attributes of Siblings to Attitudes Held toward Each Other and toward Their Parents," *Monographs of the Society of Research in Child Development,* 25: No. 78, 3–124, 1960.

older adolescent, however, usually seeks a member of the opposite sex as his friend, although same-sex friendships may continue. Friendships are started that may be maintained through adulthood.

In their selection of friends of the opposite sex, adolescents give attention to specific personal characteristics. According to the findings of a study made by the authors, based on the responses of more than 4,000 young adolescents, both boys and girls place considerable emphasis on the display of positive, socially acceptable behavior traits by members of the opposite sex. The social qualities which were stressed by both sexes included sincerity, consideration for others, good manners, friendliness, reasonable modesty about oneself, and self-control.[17]

Adolescents have many social worries which they usually keep to themselves. Fortunately, these worries are alleviated in one or another way before they do any damage to the developing personality. A college girl, for example, reflecting on her adolescent worries, reports: "I had many social worries during my adolescence. I was very tall in comparison with the boys in my classes. I wore glasses. I was thought to be gifted, and I had a minor case of acne. I feared meeting boys socially, with the result of 'no dates.' Three years went by before the problem was solved. Suddenly the boys 'shot up' and I accepted the wearing of glasses. I associated with individuals who got me blind dates until I achieved enough courage so that I did not need that type of date. For a long time, I felt socially unwanted. Finally, I was able to enter into almost any kind of situation comfortably."

Another girl suggested: "One big worry at school was being approved of by the bright kids in my class. I was always considered the slow one at home, and I really always thought someone had made a mistake when I was placed in an honor class at school. Mother would tell me that my sister actually belonged there, not I. Also, I could never understand why people liked me, and was afraid that they would tire of me. One of my aunts continually reminded me that she was afraid that I would never marry. Although I was not yet fifteen, it caused me to start worrying about it."

Many studies of adolescent attitudes have yielded similar results. Most adolescents have a clear idea of the personality traits which they wish to find in their friends. They try to display the kinds of traits admired by members of the opposite sex. In their attempt to increase their

[17] Crow, Lester D., "Teen-Age Traits, Interests and Worries," *The Educational Forum*, pp. 423–428, May, 1956.

popularity with girls, boys tend to give attention to dress and participation in school activities; they become active and interested in what is happening, are polite and friendly, and try not to annoy others. In order to interest boys, girls become careful of their appearance, are sincere and friendly, avoid being catty and going to expensive places on dates, show an interest in their elders, participate in school activities, and become good conversationalists.

Adults are concerned about adolescents' development of acceptable social habits. It takes many trial-and-error experiences before young people finally succeed in gaining the social maturity they crave. They avoid making social errors in the presence of others. Fear of ridicule is a strong motivator of their behavior. As they strive to meet adult standards, they fear ridicule from their peers if they falter in any way. This is the time, however, for them to exercise their latent abilities in the development of personal and social relationships.

The Leader and the Isolate Leadership qualities begin to show in young children. Children like to have a leader whom they can follow. They rally around one of their members who displays leadership qualities. To them a good leader has superior physical stature, recognized mental acuity, interest in the welfare of the members of the group, and willingness to cooperate with any worthwhile plans of the group. This type of individual is both admired and imitated. The gang or the club offers an opportunity for individuals to develop leadership qualities as the individual gives direction to the activities of the group.

Some children have difficulty in relating with individuals in a group. The child who finds it difficult to make friends in a particular group sometimes is alone in the group and becomes an *isolate*. Most human beings are gregarious; to be alone or unwanted by others is distasteful. The leader of any group of children, whether in school, in camp, on the playground, or in any other situation, can discover much about each individual by observing his behavior in a group of children. This can be facilitated by using a systematic approach in the nature of a *sociogram*.

THE SOCIOGRAM The purpose of a sociogram is to aid in the discovery of those children who need assistance in social living. Sociograms can be constructed by asking the members of a class a variety of questions dealing with social relationships. These might include the naming of a child's best friend, or the classmate with whom he would like to sit, work with on a report, or walk with on a trip to the museum. The socio-

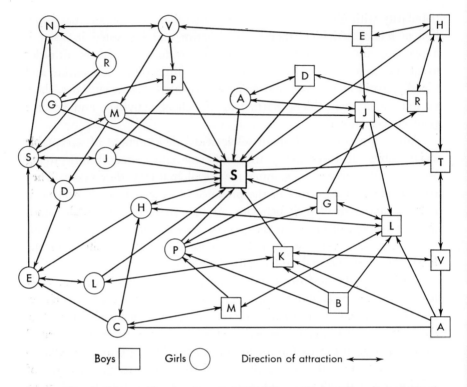

Boys ☐   **Girls** ◯   Direction of attraction ◄──────►

Figure 85. Sociogram Showing Best Friends (Three Choices) in a Fourth-Grade Class.

gram in Figure 85 illustrates the responses of a fourth-grade class to the question, "Who are your three best friends in this class?" The girls are represented by the circles, the boys by the squares. No one in the class is a complete isolate but several were not chosen by many pupils.

The sociogram illustrates various facts about the members of the class. The teacher can get much help from a study of the friendships that are revealed in the chart. Easily discernible is the fact that the most popular child in the class is a boy (S), who appears to be a friend of both boys and girls. Boys J and L and girls S and E also rate high in popularity. There was one child (Boy B), however, who was not chosen as a friend by anyone and may have isolate tendencies. Also, boy A and girls R and G were selected by only one member of the class each. Chosen by two as friends were girls L, M, and J and boys D, E, R, and M. With this information available, the teacher can provide opportunities in social training so that greater acceptance can develop among all members of the class.

THE MEASUREMENT OF SOCIAL MATURITY

The development of a device that can measure social maturity of a growing child is not simple or easy. The child lives in a complicated environment of people and things, with the forces of heredity and inner drives aiding him in his social adjustment. At first, he is at the mercy of these people and forces, but he becomes less and less helpless, until finally he becomes self-sufficient and able to make decisions for himself. As he learns to make use of the forces in his environment, he is able to attain a creditable achievement in whatever direction he chooses. The developmental changes through which he progresses in his growth and development from birth to maturity have been charted by Edgar A. Doll in the form of a scale called the *Vineland Social Maturity Scale* (Figure 86).[18]

The scale measures the level and degree of social competence of maturing individuals. The items of the scale are arranged in order of difficulty. The scale consists of social and motor performances keyed according to such behavior traits as self-help, self-direction, occupation, communication, locomotion, and socialization for the different levels of development or maturation. Along with the scale, we are interposing sketches which Dr. Doll prepared for a booklet, *Your Child Grows Up*.[19] These illustrate some of the behavior practices suggested in the scale, and at the same time portray the interrelationships of the mental, emotional, and social factors of child development.

[18] The Vineland Social Maturity Scale was originally published in the *Journal of Orthopsychiatry* in April, 1935, as Experimental Form A. Experimental Form B was published in the same journal the following year. Bibliographical details are as follows:

Doll, E. A., "A Genetic Scale of Social Maturity," *Amer. Jour. Orthopsychiatry*, 5 (April, 1935), 180–188.

———, "The Vineland Social Maturity Scale: Manual of Directions," *Training School Bull.*, 32: 1–7, 25–32, 48–55, 68–74 (March, April, May, and June, 1935). Also *Revised Condensed Manual of Directions, Series 1936, No. 3*, April, 1936.

———, "The Inheritance of Social Competence," *Jour. Hered.*, XXVIII, No. 5 (May, 1937).

[19] *Your Child Grows Up*, John Hancock Mutual Life Insurance Company, Boston, Mass. Used with permission.

THE VINELAND SOCIAL MATURITY SCALE [1]

The Roman numerals divide the scale into chronological ages for which the various "steps" are normal.

The revised scale is reprinted herewith to the age VI. Each item of the Scale has been given a categorical designation which is indicated by the following letters:

S H G—self-help general
S H E—self-help eating
S H D—self-help dressing
S D—self-direction
O—occupation
C—communication
L—locomotion
S—socialization

CATEGORIES	ITEMS	AGE 0–I
C	1.	"Crows"; laughs
H G	2.	Balances head
S H G	3.	Grasps objects within reach
S	4.	Reaches for familiar persons
S H G	5.	Rolls over
S H G	6.	Reaches for nearby objects
O	7.	Occupies self unattended
S H G	8.	Sits unsupported
S H G	9.	Pulls self upright
C	10.	"Talks"; imitates sounds
S H E	11.	Drinks from cup or glass assisted
L	12.	Moves about on floor
S H G	13.	Grasps with thumb and finger
S	14.	Demands personal attention
S H G	15.	Stands alone
S H E	16.	Does not drool
C	17.	Follows simple instructions

[1] Excerpts of the *Vineland Social Maturity Scale* through age VI. Reprinted by permission of *Educational Test Bureau*, Educational Publishers, Inc., Minneapolis, Minn.

SEQUENTIAL DEVELOPMENT ILLUSTRATED *

Before the 1st Birthday . . .

Sits up unsupported and steadily. Pulls self up to standing position, holding on for support; balance may be a bit "wobbly," but stands alone on firm surface.

* **Figure 86. Pictorial Representation of Social Development.** Based on the Vineland Social Security Scale.

From *Your Child Grows Up, op. cit.* pp. 10–22. By permission of John Hancock Mutual Life Insurance Company.

"Helps" with undressing by removing socks and shoes (if untied).

Uses short sentences, and has vocabulary of twenty-five words or more —not mere "parrot talk."

Imitates sounds and attempts to say words which only his parents understand. Follows such simple instructions as coming when called, pointing out pictures or objects when asked.

Names familiar objects for practical purposes.

Climbs up stairs without help, gets about house and yard with only occasional oversight. Gives up baby carriage to walk, or ride in go-cart.

Before the 2nd Birthday . . .

AGE I—II

L 18. Walks about room unattended
O 19. Marks with pencil or crayon
S H E 20. Masticates food
S H D 21. Pulls off socks
O 22. Transfers objects
S H G 23. Overcomes simple obstacles
O 24. Fetches or carries familiar objects
S H E 25. Drinks from cup or glass unassisted
S H G 26. Gives up baby carriage
S 27. Plays with other children
S H E 28. Eats with spoon
L 29. Goes about house or yard
S H E 30. Discriminates edible substances
C 31. Uses names of familiar objects
L 32. Walks upstairs unassisted
S H E 33. Unwraps candy
C 34. Talks in short sentences

Eats with spoon from bowl or cup, without help or too much spilling.

Chooses between suitable food and substances unfit for eating. Removes wrappers from candy.

Performs useful little errands such as bringing named objects from nearby places. Opens closed doors, climbs up on chairs to reach, removes simple obstacles from his path. Uses basket to carry things.

Before the 3rd Birthday . . .

AGE II–III

S H G   35. Asks to go to toilet
    O   36. Initiates own play activities
S H D   37. Removes coat or dress
S H E   38. Eats with fork
S H E   39. Gets drink unassisted
S H D   40. Dries own hands
S H G   41. Avoids simple hazards
S H D   42. Puts on coat or dress unassisted
    O   43. Cuts with scissors
    C   44. Relates experiences

Occupies self without "looking

after" at own play such as drawing with crayon, building with blocks, dressing dolls, looking at pictures.

Uses blunt-end scissors in cutting paper and cloth—is not destructive.

Uses fork without much spilling, and eats solid food that does not require cutting. Can get drink of water unassisted, turning water tap on and off. Dries own hands if washed.

Gives simple account of own experiences and tells stories that can be understood. By action or speech makes known desire to go to toilet—seldom has daytime "accidents."

Avoids simple hazards. "Comes in

out of rain." Is careful about falling when on stairs and high places, avoids sharp edges, broken glass, etc., and should keep out of streets.

Before the 4th Birthday . . .

AGE III–IV

L 45. Walks downstairs one step per tread

S 46. Plays coopera- tively at kinder- garten level

S H D 47. Buttons coat or dress

O 48. Helps at little household tasks

S 49. "Performs" for others

S H D 50. Washes hands un- aided

Washes hands acceptably without help and dries them without soiling towel. Puts on and buttons coat or dress, but may need help otherwise in dressing.

Walks down stairs without help, one

step at a time. Runs, skips, marches, and shows some sense of simple rhythm.

Takes part in such group activities as simple kindergarten games; joins in simple play tea parties, and ac- tivities requiring no skill. "Performs" for others upon request.

"Helps" in small way about the house, such as running short errands, picking up things, feeding pets, dust- ing.

Before the 5th Birthday . . .

AGE IV–V

S H G 51. Cares for self at toilet

S H D 52. Washes face unas- sisted

L 53. Goes about neigh- borhood unat- tended

S H D 54. Dresses self except tying

O 55. Uses pencil or cra-
       yon for drawing
S 56. Plays competitive
       exercise games

Dresses self except for tying laces, ribbons, or ties. Does all own buttoning, but clothing is laid out. May need help with muffler, rubbers, or overshoes, and with specially difficult or close-fitting clothes.

of children of same age such games as tag, hide-and-seek, jump-rope, hopscotch, marbles, etc.

Draws with pencil and crayon simple, but recognizable forms as man, house, animal, landscape.

Before the 6th Birthday . . .

AGE V–VI

O 57. Uses skates, sled,
       wagon
C 58. Prints simple words
S 59. Plays simple table
       games
S D 60. Is trusted with
       money
L 61. Goes to school un-
       attended

Washes face, except ears (!) acceptably and dries his face without help. Goes to toilet alone and without help, unfastens own clothes, no daytime "accidents."

Goes about neighborhood unattended; may be restricted as to areas or "deadlines" so that his whereabouts are known, but is "on his own" within this limitation. Plays in small groups

Takes care of self unsupervised, outside own yard; manages roller

skates, sled, wagon, velocipede, scooter, or other play vehicle.

Plays simple table games with others that require taking turns, observing rules, attaining goals, and does so without undue squabbling. (Games include tiddleywinks, parchesi, dominoes, etc.)

Goes to school unattended. He may go with friends, but no one is in di-

rect charge of him. "On his own" outside his neighborhood. Learns to print simple words of three or four letters without copy—and his own first name. Does so without direction.

Is trusted with small sums of money to make clearly-stated purchases. He carries out directions in returning purchases, but he may not be able to make change.

Before the 7th Birthday . . .

Takes bath without supervision; but may be assisted in preparing tub, washing ears, drying hair, and "touching up."

Writes (not prints) legibly with

pencil a dozen or more simple words, correctly spelled. Does so at own desire, or from dictation, but does not need copy.

Before the 8th Birthday . . .

Takes part in group play; boys prefer games that do not require much skill, such as unorganized baseball, or basketball, follow-the-leader, fox and hounds, hiking and bicycle riding. Girls prefer playing house, school, nurse-doctor, and other imitations of home and social affairs.

Reads ordinary clock or watch correctly to nearest quarter hour and actually uses clock for practical purposes.

Before the 10th Birthday . . .

Goes about home community freely, alone or with friends. There may be forbidden areas, but the restrictions do not confine the child's activities to his nearby neighborhood.

Looks after all his own needs at table; helps himself, ordinarily prepares such items as baked potatoes, boiled eggs, difficult cuts of meat.

Buys useful articles and exercises some choice in making purchases. Is responsible for safety of articles, money, and correct change. Does this independently or can be relied upon to follow directions.

Runs useful errands; is trusted as a messenger, or to carry out orders to or from not too distant points, and under clear instructions.

Before the 11th Birthday . . .

Writes occasional short letters to friends or relatives on own initiative, or following mild suggestions. Does so without help except perhaps in spelling unfamiliar words. Addresses envelope and makes ready for mailing.

Uses telephone for practical pur-

poses; looks up number, makes call, and carries on sensible, purposeful conversation. Does not attempt long distance calls and automatic dialing may be difficult unless in long usage.

Does occasional or brief work on own initiative about the home or neighborhood, for which small sums are paid or merit payment, such as "odd jobs," housework, helping in care of children, selling magazines.

Responds to magazine, radio, or other advertising by mailing coupons, requesting samples, sending for literature, and ordering from catalogues.

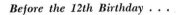

Before the 12th Birthday . . .

Makes useful articles or does easy

repair work. Cooks or sews in small way; does a little gardening; raises pets; writes brief stories; produces simple paintings or drawings.

Is sometimes left alone at home or at work for an hour or so, and is successful in looking after his own needs or those of other children left in his care.

Reads for practical information or own enjoyment stories or news items in papers, magazine articles, library book stories of adventure and romance.

Washes and dries own hair; is re-

sponsible for a thorough job of cleaning hair, but may need reminding to do so.

Before the 15th Birthday . . .

Writes business and social letters that are more than a matter of routine; gives serious information, significant news, and acknowledges instructions. Among friends discusses general news, sports, events, and follows these matters.

Goes outside limits of his home town, and makes his own arrangements. Is "on his own," and able to find his way about unfamiliar places. Is given responsibility for all daytime movements without accounting in advance for his plans.

Uses money with common sense. Plans for future needs rather than spending all for mere immediate enjoyment, so is ready for own spending money (either allowance or earned). Usually purchases clothes, including dresses, suits, overcoats, hats. May

Shows personal interest in the opposite sex; is interested in *a* boy or *a* girl, as well as in all boys or girls. Calls or receives callers; but "dates" may be restricted as to time, place, or circumstances.

receive advice, but makes own sensible decisions.

QUESTIONS AND TOPICS FOR DISCUSSION

1. How is a child's intelligence level related to his social development? Be specific.
2. Trace a child's social awareness from infancy through the preschool years.
3. Give examples to illustrate the statement, "The social values of any group influence the behavior of the members of the group."
4. In what kinds of behavior may a "social climber" engage?
5. What are some of the social reactions of the nursery school child?
6. What criteria do young children use in selecting their friends?
7. Which of your friendships, if any, started during your childhood years? How do you explain such long-time friendships?
8. How do elementary school boys and girls differ in their relations with other young people? What was your experience during this age period?
9. In what ways do neighborhood conditions affect children's group activities? Give examples.
10. What are some of the things a young person may do to win peer-group approval?
11. Do you agree with the list of traits admired by young people in their friends as presented by the authors? Justify your answer.
12. What were your social worries during adolescence?
13. State the advantages and disadvantages of using the sociogram approach.
14. *Special Project:* Note the friends of your four subjects. On what basis do they seem to have been selected? To what extent do they form groups or gangs? What are the accustomed activities of their groups?

SELECTED REFERENCES

Bossard, James H., *The Sociology of Child Development*, rev. ed. New York: Harper and Brothers, 1954.

Combs, A. W., and Snygg, D., *Individual Behavior: A Perceptual Approach to Behavior*, 2nd ed. New York: Harper and Brothers, 1959.

Doll, Edgar A., *The Measurement of Social Competence*. Minneapolis: Educational Test Bureau, University of Minnesota, 1953.

Estvan, F. J., and Estvan, Elizabeth W., *The Child's World: His Social Perception*. New York: G. P. Putnam's Sons, 1959.

Heider, F., *The Psychology of Interpersonal Relations*. New York: John Wiley and Sons, Inc., 1958.

Hollingshead, A. B., *Elmstown's Youth*. New York: John Wiley and Sons, Inc., 1949.

Jennings, Helen H., *Leadership and Isolation: A Study of Personality in Interpersonal Relations*. New York: Longmans, Green and Company, 1954.

Kennedy, Paulina M., *Acceptance of Self and Acceptance of Others as Interdependent Variables in Interpersonal Relations*. Washington, D. C.: Catholic University of America Press, 1958.

McDavid, John W., "Imitative Behavior in Preschool Children," *Psychological Monographs*, 1959, No. 486.

White House Conference on Child and Youth, *Children in a Changing World*, U. S. Department of Health, Education and Welfare, 1960.

Winnicott, D. W., *The Child and the Outside World: Studies in Developing Relationships*, edited by Janet Hardenberg. New York: Basic Books, Inc., 1957.

12

MOTIVATION OF
CHILD BEHAVIOR

IN PREVIOUS CHAPTERS we have discussed some of the ways in which a child develops the ability to respond to environmental stimulation. We have considered the *how* of his behavior. Knowing what he says and does as he adjusts to the people, things, and conditions surrounding him does not necessarily imply, however, that the *why* of his behavior is recognized.

MOTIVATION OF BEHAVIOR

A growing child's experiences involve motivating or causative factors that, as they are integrated, produce appropriate responses. The underlying reasons for individuals to behave as they do in differing situations can be interpreted as the dynamics of behavior. The child's reaction pattern is not static, but constantly is ready and able to change. In this chapter consideration is given to those needs, cravings, drives, urges, purposes and goals that serve as motivating forces and are fundamental to the dynamic nature of human behavior.

Motivational Processes Inner tensions brought about by internal interacting forces and external influences direct and energize tension-releasing behavior. Motives operating from within cause the child to react in such ways that he achieves satisfaction of his needs, wants, and purposes. From infancy on, every child possesses a disposition that is peculiarly his own. Hence it is essential that adults responsible for child-rearing have a functional understanding of a child's motives for behavior. Usually, the influences of relatives or friends are reflected in his motives. Yet the child cannot be regarded as composed merely of a plastic substance that can be molded according to adult will. Although the young child is relatively raw material, he has inherited certain potential tendencies from his forebears and is well on the way toward a realization of these potentialities. They show themselves in his resistance to fitting into parent-desired molds and in his attempts to build characteristic forms of behavior that are outgrowths of inner motivations.

The child is motivated to respond differently to situations that are new and strange from those that are known—he is either attracted or repelled. Rewards and punishments also serve as motivators of differing reactions, according to the intensity of the satisfaction or annoyance induced by their application.

It is difficult to assert with confidence just what should be included in a study of motivation. Paul Young attempts to explain the motivating process as follows:

If motivation is viewed as a process, there are at least three aspects that must be considered in defining the concept. First, motivation may be viewed as the process of arousing and sustaining action. This includes physiological activation through sensory stimulation, inner chemical sensitization, direct brain action, and through other means. Second, motivation may be viewed as the process of regulating and directing behavior, especially channeling behavior toward goals. This aspect includes regulation through neural structures, direction by purposive sets and orientations, and regulation by environmental conditions. Third, motivation may be viewed not as a contemporary event but as a disposition or psychological state that persists over a period of time. This view implies the existence of a stable organism which carries about with him certain attitudes, evaluative dispositions, intents to act, interests, and sentiments, as well as latent abilities, skills, and habit structures.[1]

Topological Motivation   Motivation has been defined to include movements, stresses, and strains in a circumscribed relational field. A child's behavior is influenced by his own characteristics and his perception of existing conditions. A little girl, for example, who, during early

[1] Young, Paul T., "The Role of Affective Processes in Learning and Motivation," *Psychological Review*, Vol. 66: No. 2, March, 1959, p. 117.

childhood, associated only with adults is more likely to be shy and with-drawing among nursery school children than she would be if she had enjoyed the company either of brothers and sisters or of same-age play-mates.

If a child is in a situation to which he is sensitive, he tends to be motivated to behave in a way that will help him make a personally satis-fying adjustment. Ragsdale has prepared diagrams to indicate the possi-ble operation of what he refers to as "field forces." These diagrams are presented here.[2] (See Figure 87.)

SIGNIFICANCE OF INNER DRIVES

Needs, urges, and drives are the terms applied to those motivators in which, as they are conditioned by environmental influences, are rooted the potentialities of action. All phases of a child's life pattern are affected by the functioning of his drives.

Interpretation of Drive Various attempts have been made to define the term "drive." A drive can be regarded as any inner force that motivates behavior. According to some psychologists, the basic human drive is self-realization. According to Ausubel, "drive is *not* a persistent afferent or humoral *stimulus* but a *multiple determined neurobehavioral state coextensive with the lowering of response thresholds.* It is necessary, in other words, to distinguish between drive as a transitory state of altered reactivity, and the various determinants (including stimuli) that induce it."[3] A tendency toward particular responses, if unlearned and engaged in for immediate satisfaction, is referred to variously as a need, want, urge, desire, motive, or mental set.

Since a tendency implies persistence, it can be considered to be a pre-disposition. It causes the activity to continue in spite of possible variations in environmental stimuli, and may take the nature of a purpose or goal that seeks fulfillment. A young child, for example, is motivated by curiosity about his surroundings to pick up, manipulate, or put into his mouth anything in his immediate environment that intrigues him. If certain interesting objects are removed from his reach, his drive to in-vestigate causes him to find others to handle. Adults then are faced with the problem of removing all *taboo* objects from his grasp, or to try to

[2] From Ragsdale, C. C., "Growth in Motivation during Childhood," in *Child Psy-chology,* Skinner and Harriman (eds.). New York: The Macmillan Company, pp. 124–126, 1941.

[3] Ausubel, D. P., *Theory and Problems of Child Development,* p. 224. New York: Grune and Stratton, Inc., copyright 1958. By permission of author and publisher.

help him understand that some objects are not to be handled and that others can be utilized in play.

The awareness of a need sets up in the child a drive to satisfy it. This inner active force may affect the child's feelings, thinking, actions, and sense of values. It is possible, however, for a child to desire something that he does not need. After a satisfying meal, the child is "hungry" for candy. The situation is complicated for him if he knows where the

Figure 87.   Diagrams Showing Some Possibilities in the Operation of Field Forces.

ATTRACTION

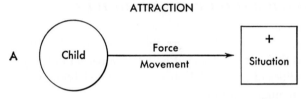

The child's activity may be in a straight line leading to identification of himself and the situation; he is attracted.

REPULSION

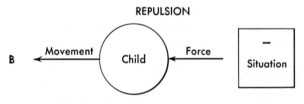

The child's activity may be in a straight line away from the situation; he is repelled.

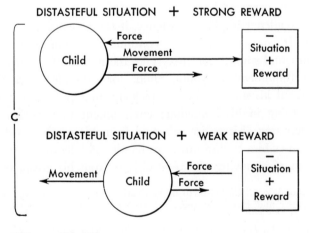

Ibid, pp. 124–126.

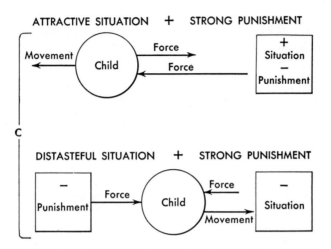

The situation may contain opposing forces, in which case the direction and force of the child's movement are determined by the resultant of the forces.

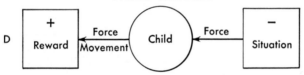

When the situation contains opposing forces, the child may succeed in separating it into two aspects in such a way that he can flee the one and approach the other.

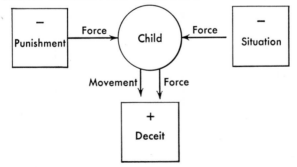

USING DECEIT TO FLEE SITUATION AND ATTAIN REWARD

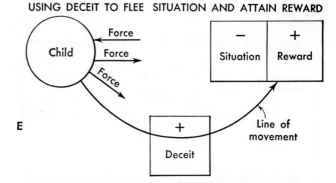

E

When the situation contains opposing forces, the child may be able to introduce a third force, deceit, acting at an angle to the other forces, thus escaping both situation and punishment or attaining a regard while avoiding the situation.

BLOCKED MOVEMENT

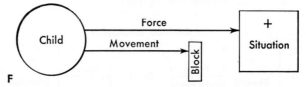

F

Forces my be adequate to initiate activity, but the movement may by blocked by other factors, such as lack of knowledge of progress.

INSULATION AGAINST FORCES

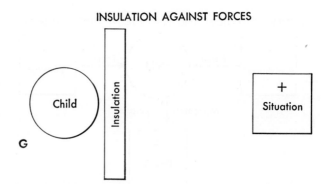

G

The child may be insulated from the action of some forces because he fails to perceive the situation on account of ignorance, immaturity, preoccupation, or sensory defect.

candy is, but is not supposed to take any without permission. He then is beset by conflicting urges: to enjoy the eating of the desired candy, or avoid parental disapproval.

A child may experience conflicts similar to the one described as he is stimulated by two opposing drives to action and must decide between the values to be achieved by following one of them in preference to the other. The final choice usually depends on the mental awareness of a definite purpose or goal. Each reaction in a series of reactions is motivated by purpose and mental readiness in sequential order. Two-year-old Raymond, for example, was visiting with his parents in the home of friends. Since he is a healthy, active youngster, he proceeded to run around the room to his great delight but to the annoyance of the adults. His father picked him up and placed him on a chair, admonishing him to stay there. His drive toward activity was so great that he continued to move his hands and feet in concert, and to contort his face into grimaces. He did not cry, however. He kept a watchful eye on his father and, when the latter was not looking at him, got up backwards on his knees, preparatory to sliding off the chair. A glance from his father was sufficient to bring him back to a sitting position, which he maintained until the drive for greater activity became too strong. He suddenly lunged from the chair, and ran to his father, iterating with persuasive smiles, "Daddy play." To what extent had Raymond thought through the relative value of obeying his father and of engaging in strenuous activity?

One characteristic of a child's motivation is that it must be evaluated according to the kind of behavior produced rather than to be observed directly. Hence the extent or level of a child's drive to action can be determined by an adult only in the light of (1) the persistence of the behavior, such as the child's continued search for hidden objects, (2) the energy output, such as a child's efforts to lift a heavy object, and (3) the application of various approaches to achieve a desired purpose, as when a child attempts to gain the attention of an associate, first by smiling at him, then by offering him his favorite toy, and finally, if the other approaches fail, by slapping, pinching, or biting him.

Nature of Drives The force of the drive that instigates a particular form of behavior tends to be accompanied by emotional reactions that are rooted in previous experience. The emotional factor tends to affect the strength and persistence of the influence exerted on overt behavior. Although it probably is a fact that behavior is activated throughout the life span of an individual by differing, persisting drives, psychologists find it difficult to explain all human needs, urges, and drives, or to determine how they are stimulated and what their relative strength may be. An oft-cited list of drives is that constructed by Cattell in 1950 as the possible basic motivators of behavior.

PRELIMINARY LIST OF DRIVES

I. Organic needs:

> To seek air; to avoid physical pain, heat, cold; to seek water; to urinate and defecate.

II. Propensities which are organic, viscerogenic, appetitive:

1. (a) To seek stimulation, exercise, activity when well rested.
   (b) To play.
2. To avoid stimulation, lie down, sleep, and rest when tired.
3. To seek food. This may be functionally connected with storing food, with restless wandering (as in the herbivorous animals), or with hunting readiness (as in carnivorous).
4. To court and mate (sex drive).
5. To feed, protect, and shelter the young.
6. To reject and avoid noxious substances.

III. Propensities showing no clear organic rhythm, nonappetitive:

7. To escape from violent impression by (a) flight, (b) "freezing" to the spot.
8. To defer, obey, abase oneself in the presence of superiority and dominance behavior in others.
9. To appeal, cry aloud, and seek help when utterly baffled.
10. To acquire, collect, possess, and defend whatever is found useful or attractive.
11. To explore strange places and things or manipulate and pull to pieces strange objects.
12. To remain in or seek the company of one's fellows. . . .
13. To assert oneself, achieve, domineer, lead, display oneself.
14. To resent resistance to the expression of any propensity; to attack and destroy such resistance.
15. To laugh and destroy tension in certain tension-provoking situations.
16. (Questionable.) To construct shelter and implements.[4]

Children's Needs   According to modern theorists, primary needs have to do with the maintenance of body equilibrium. If there is inner imbalance of an organism, activity is aroused which attempts to restore equilibrium or homeostasis. For its proper development, body tissue requires adequate oxygen supply, maintenance of healthful body temperature, food and drink. Secondary needs include a feeling of belonging and of being wanted, security, and satisfying accomplishment or success.

[4] By permission from *Personality*, by R. B. Cattell, copyright 1950, McGraw-Hill Book Company, Inc.

These fundamental needs of children must be fulfilled, but care should be taken that young people do not concentrate only on the satisfaction of their own needs, wants, and urges. They also need to learn to consider the needs and drives of others. Breckenridge and Vincent present the needs of children very well when they say the following concerning the balancing of needs:

Progressive educators have long practiced the adaptation of teaching programs to fit at least the most outstanding of the "basic needs" of childhood. They have long taught that work with children proves wasteful unless programs are adjusted to the *individual* needs of *individual* children. Progressive educators have helped greatly to adapt schoolroom teaching and teaching by parents at home to the "basic needs" of children. They have not always remembered, however, the other aspect of genuinely successful education, namely, that the child must be trained to adapt his drives to the patterns of society. This requires a nice balance between understanding or moulding the environment to fit the child on the one hand, and discipline or training in self-control and consideration of others on the other hand. . . .

Old-fashioned parents and formal educators, motivated by the children-should-be-seen-and-not-heard philosophy, leaned much too far in the direction of forcing adult patterns upon children, ignoring many of their basic needs and building up antagonisms or neuroticism as a result. Then the pendulum swung too far in the other direction in a few ultra-progressive schools or homes, with the result that children received no discipline, their whims were catered to and their "individualities" were permitted to flourish uncurbed. It soon became evident that uncurbed drives are no better than completely suppressed ones. No child who has failed to learn how to control his drives in order to live smoothly with other people can be called an educated child.[5]

In light of the preceding discussion, we now shall discuss children's needs and drives according to their classification as (1) physiological or biological needs and (2) social drives or urges.

PHYSIOLOGICAL NEEDS AS DRIVES

The neonate has few needs, but some of them (hunger, thirst, and elimination, for example) must be satisfied immediately. The organism possesses mechanisms to initiate appropriate activity when a state of organic equilibrium is lacking and needs to be regained. These reactions continue until the physiological condition is returned to normal. Hence a physiological drive is an organic condition of change in equi-

[5] Breckenridge, M. E., and Vincent, E. L., *Child Development*, 4th ed., pp. 117–118. Philadelphia: W. B. Saunders Company, copyright 1960.

librium that starts a particular series of behavior changes. Needs or drives essential to the well-being of the organism include (1) the satisfaction of hunger, thirst, or sex, (2) proper elimination, (3) securing of an adequate supply of oxygen, (4) maintenance of appropriate temperature, and (5) recovery from fatigue (sleep and rest).

The Hunger and Thirst Drives The need for food and drink persists throughout the life of the individual. The origin of hunger is not fully understood, however. Although hunger pangs apparently are the result of the contractions of stomach muscles, it has been found that the hunger drives can be present without stomach contractions. Hence it is believed by some that a chemical factor may be responsible for the hunger, and that the stomach contractions may be by-products of the hungry state. There also is some evidence of a relationship between the rhythmic occurrence of striped muscle activity and the rhythmic occurrence of hunger.

Hunger is one of the strongest physiological drives. The kind of food children customarily like to eat is determined chiefly by the food tastes they have acquired in the home. Yet, if a child or an older person has been without food for a relatively long time, he usually is not concerned about the kind of food served, or the way it is served. The need for food is so great that any food is welcomed, unless it is completely repugnant. Moreover, consciousness of hunger tends to be more definite if the individual is in a semi-starved state rather than suffering from the effects of total fasting.

Attitudes toward food can have an emotional base. Although the causes of certain food allergies are not completely understood, it is known that they sometimes result from developed attitudes toward food which may have their origin in stomach distress caused by eating them. Environmental conditions while one is eating also may give rise to emotionalized attitudes. For example, a woman who was recovering from an illness and whose appetite was not up to par found herself becoming so disgusted by the large quantities of food consumed by other persons sitting at the table with her that she found it impossible to eat even a small amount. Feelings of nausea made it necessary for her to leave the table and the room.

Children tend to crave more food than is provided by the customary three meals a day eaten by adults, regardless of how substantial the regular meals may be. Their growing bodies seem to require at least a midmorning and midafternoon snack. Moreover, it is generally agreed that children who are the victims of inner repressed resentments or emotional upsets tend to gain much satisfaction and release of tension from overeating. Their emotional maladjustment takes the form of continual hunger pangs.

A drive similar to hunger is that of thirst. A decrease in the secretions of the salivary glands and a deficiency of water in the tissues cause a dryness of the tissues of the mouth. Although the thirst drive is best satisfied by drinking cool, clear water, the chewing of gum also is helpful. Flavored drinks may seem to relieve thirst momentarily, but the sugar content of such drinks militates against the satisfactory quenching of thirst. Furthermore, although the drinking of water gives temporary relief from thirst, throat dryness may be no more than a symptom of a body deficit that requires the balance of moisture in the entire system to be restored to satisfy completely the experiencing of the thirst need.

The Sex Drive In Chapter 15 we shall discuss the development of psychosexual behavior. At this point, therefore, we shall consider only the physical manifestations of the sex drive, noting that it may or may not be essential to the maintaining of physiological equilibrium. Although sexual activity is essential to the survival of mankind, it is not necessary to the life of an individual. Properly controlled sexual activity does contribute to physical and mental health. Its importance is second only to hunger and thirst drives.

The sexual development of the male is affected by the androgens secreted by the gonads, and by the hormones secreted in the pituitary gland. If the androgen supply is not interfered with, the sexual appetite in the male remains fairly stable throughout the adult years. The female's principal sex hormones are the progesterone and estrogen which are secreted by the ovaries. The former is important in pregnancy and the latter controls the sexual appetite. If the testes of the male or the ovaries of the female are removed, the individual may lose much of his sexual appetite.

Since the satisfaction of the sexual drives can be restricted by moral and social codes and by civil law, psychological conflicts can be aroused by denial of desired sexual activity. Hence sex can become a dynamic force in the motivation of an individual's behavior. He may be moved to disregard social disapproval or disease possibilities by the strength of his sex need. He can become so emotionally motivated that he brings harm to himself and to those who become involved in his promiscuous sex activities. During preadolescence and adolescence, a young person's thoughts, emotions, and activities may be very much influenced by the development of sexual appetite. In fact, it is believed by some who have studied the sex drive that later sex conflict can be initiated through the fixed patterning of an infant's nursing experiences. (See Chapter 15.)

The Maintaining of Proper Elimination   The body takes care of the process of elimination through the functioning of special organs. These are activated by internal stimuli. Proper diet and adequate body activity are favorable to normal elimination. One of the rearing problems during the early years is to train the child to develop regular habits, and to want to meet his hunger and thirst needs in such ways that difficulties of elimination are avoided. Training in habits of elimination can start as early as six months and can be well established by the end of one year, although it is likely to be achieved later. The mother who encourages the formation of elimination habits at an early age helps not only herself but the child as well. Adolescents and adults who tend to engage in sedentary activities may need either to change their pattern of living or to take cathartics to activate the process.

Oxygen and Temperature Needs   Air hunger can become a strong drive under certain conditions, although people normally seldom experience it. It is possible for a person who has lived in a lower altitude to move to a high altitude where there is less oxygen content and suffer considerably without being aware of the cause of his difficulty. This is known as *anoxia* (oxygen deficiency). The symptoms of the trouble are confused feelings, dizziness, or a kind of drunkenness. The victim may burst into tears, shout, or engage in fighting for no reason.

Less severe but also unhealthful is lack of sufficient oxygen in classrooms. Unless the school has an air conditioning system that works adequately, the ventilating of a classroom is achieved by opening windows. Since children who, in the winter months, sit near open windows that do not have ventilator shields may be exposed to cold draughts, it is not uncommon for the oxygen in a classroom filled with children to become insufficient for their needs. The problem is intensified by the fact that one becomes accustomed to airlessness. It is only as someone enters the room from the outside or that those in the room begin to feel drowsy that the need for better air is recognized and the room ventilated.

The maintaining of a satisfactory body temperature usually is linked with the supply of sufficient oxygen. The normal temperature of the human body is about 98.6° F. This is maintained by means of a homeostatic process or a constant internal adjustment. A deviation from this norm tends to be a symptom of body imbalance.

At one time it was considered desirable to keep children bundled in many layers of clothing, especially during the cold months, to prevent cold air from touching their delicate little bodies. Present attitudes toward the amount of clothing needed by children appears to be much more sensible. During warm weather, children wear a minimum of clothing so that the air may circulate around their bodies. Most children wear little underwear the year around. In adequately heated houses they are lightly clad, but are protected from the cold when they are out of doors during cold weather.

Fatigue Recovery Relatively strenuous activity is needed by the growing child. Equally important is relaxing sleep when he is healthily fatigued. The child needs sleep to conserve energy for growth. During infancy the child spends most of his time sleeping, awaking for needed feeding and some slight activity. As he matures, his sleeping time is reduced, so that usually by the age of three years he spends about twelve hours in sleep, most of it at night, with at least one daytime nap. By the time a child is old enough to enter the first grade of elementary school, his sleeping time approximates about eleven hours, all of them during the night.

The amount of sleep needed by the older child depends on the kind and amount of activity in which he engages during the day and his own particular sleep needs. The more alert, faster growing child seems to need less sleep than does the slower developer. The sleeping habits of the family also are significant. Constancy in bed-going routines are important. In some homes children are the victims of irregular family patterns. One father of a two-year-old was heard to say, "Tommy is supposed to go to bed at eight-thirty, but you know how it is. Too often it is eleven o'clock before we get him to sleep." The family schedule should be so arranged that, at a reasonably early hour, the child is healthily fatigued (not overexcited) so that he is ready for bed and a good night's sleep.

School-age children and adolescents, as well as adults, sometimes mistake boredom for fatigue. A study or work task may fail to hold the individual's attention. Consequently, he asserts that he is too tired to continue the activity. The same person may then engage, with vigor, in a more appealing type of activity with no signs of fatigue. Contrariwise, a person may become so engrossed in a project that he continues with it far beyond his physical endurance. His motivation is so great that he fails to recognize the signs of great physical fatigue. The results may be harmful, since rest and sleep needed to maintain organic equilibrium are being denied.

SOCIAL DRIVES AND URGES

A child needs to develop a feeling of self-esteem or personal worth. He needs challenging experiences and reasonable freedom to engage in them. His behavior in relation to other persons and to the various situations in which he finds himself is motivated by the desire for recognition, approval, and sympathy, the need for security, and the urge for success, superiority, and adventure. He wants to be like other people but, at the same time, be recognized as an individual different from his associates. He has the drive to adjust to his outside world, the while he is "living happily" with himself. To the degree that his drives come into conflict with his social environment, he needs intelligent and sympathetic adult assistance in learning to control them.

Desire for Recognition and Approval An individual of any age seeks attention from his confreres. To the child the receiving of attention from those who surround him is a characteristic that shows itself early. The baby's crying, more often than not, is a bid for attention to his needs. As he matures, he attempts to gain attention in other ways—by smiling, cooing, patting, and, if these approaches fail, by slapping and biting. He wants to impress others. As he grows older, recognition *per se* is not as satisfying as is approving regard. He may engage in various activities with a kind of playing-to-the-gallery attitude. A nursery school child, observed by one of the writers, appeared to be extremely eager for attention. She invented little tasks which took her past the observer's chair. Each time she smiled, curtsied, and murmured, "Excuse me." This behavior continued as long as the writer smiled and nodded. When the observer's responses ceased, the little girl withdrew to a far corner of the room, turned her back on the visitor, frowned and muttered disapproval of the visitor's refusal to continue the game. So strong was the child's need for approval, however, that soon she was begging the teacher to allow her to dance and sing for the visitor.

Well-administered praise is a powerful motivator of constructive activity. Parents and teachers sometimes fail to utilize commendation intelligently and sincerely. Some adults, in their relations with a child, seem to assume the attitude that all his activities are to be commended lest he feel rejected. The child soon learns to discount the worth of the approval given. Other adults refrain from giving a child any commendation for fear that he might thereby become conceited or vain. This is an extremely depressing experience for the young person. Either attitude is harmful. Justified praise and earned disapproval of unsocial acts help a child interpret more realistically than otherwise would be the case those social values which aid him in obtaining a proper perspective of himself as a social being.

The Need for Sympathy Adult attitudes toward the offering of sympathy to a child when it is needed follow closely the pattern that should be set for the giving of approval. Often what may seem to an adult to be a minor hurt or disappointment takes on the proportions of a great tragedy to the child. He needs the understanding sympathy of the adult.

Physicians and nurses sometimes claim that women can endure pain better than can a man. If this is true, it is not a carry-over from childhood. From early years, little girls, more than boys, tend to receive more sympathetic attention from adults if they fall or otherwise hurt themselves. Boys usually are admonished to be little men and not to cry.

Care can be taken by adults to become aware of a child's attempts to solicit sympathy. A young person may believe that he is not receiving sufficient attention. Consequently, he makes much of a minor injury to receive desired attention. To the extent that his elders are receptive to his crying or other distress symptoms in such situations, he can develop habits of dependence and self-pity that may continue throughout his adult life.

The Need for Security A child's seeking of recognition, approval, and sympathy are rooted in his strong drive to find security in the affection and regard of his elders. He needs to feel that he is wanted and accepted as an esteemed member of his group. This urge tends to encourage the child to act in such ways that he earns the respect and admiration of his associates. Especially is he eager to win the favor of his fellow playmates or schoolmates. If he cannot gain his purpose through constructive achievement, he may attempt to "buy" their friendship by means of gifts or tall tales of family prestige.

Economic security usually is not recognized as a need by the child until he has learned what it means. The age at which this understanding is achieved tends to vary with the economic situation of the family. The child of economically privileged parents may delay the assuming of financial responsibility for his own welfare until early adulthood. In fact, attending college can become a means of continuing parental provision of personal needs and wants. The son or daughter of less favored parents may attempt early, through part-time work, to increase the family income because of the recognition of the needs of the parents or of younger siblings.

The emotional life of the child is affected by his awareness of the degree of economic security experienced by his family. Regardless of conditions, the young person, during his later developmental years, should come to feel personal responsibility for his own welfare. He needs to be given many opportunities to spend money to satisfy his actual personal requirements. An allowance that is in keeping with the financial ability of the family can afford valuable experience to the child as he is guided in his expenditure of it. Early experience with money can be helpful in discovering its value and use.

It is unfortunate if, during his early years, the child is stimulated to worry about money matters. Moreover, the growing child is likely to develop patterns of confident living to the degree that he is assured of security in home and out-of-home relationships, in economic status, and in the ability to cope with day-by-day problems of adjustment.

The Urge for Success and Superiority An important aspect of adjusted living is the satisfaction of the urge for successful achievement. Parents who tend to care for all of a child's needs deny him the opportunity to take responsibility and thereby to experience the pleasure of earning success in his accomplishments. Furthermore, continuing development of success is encouraged by the operation of the success factor during the early life of a child.

A young person thrills to satisfaction engendered by mastering what to him constitutes a challenging problem. The drive to do something better than someone else is a valuable asset to the growing child if it is not carried to extremes. Too often parents fail to recognize the strength of this need. A child, for example, receives a new, relatively complicated toy. He is eager to manipulate it. How great is his disappointment if his father, for instance, decides to take this pleasurable experience for himself by showing the child how it operates! Too often children's Christmas presents offer adults more fun than they do the child. After they have demonstrated the working of toys, older people wonder why the supposed recipient is not challenged as they are by them.

Even during preschool years, a child craves opportunities to excel. This drive, as we have indicated above, tends to continue through adulthood. According to Alfred Adler and other psychologists, superiority in achievement is a dominant drive that is basic to the happiness of most human beings. The child as well as the adult desires activity, but even more than sheer "doing" he craves the power to be master of a situation. Moreover, the individual's feeling is increased to the extent that other persons recognize his superiority to themselves in at least one area of activity.

The possession of an intense urge to be superior may have harmful as well as beneficial results. If a young person is exposed to unequal competition in home, school, or social situations, for example, he may attempt to satisfy his need to excel by cheating, lying, or stealing. Adults must be alert to a particular child's capabilities and provide opportunities for him to earn wanted success in work or play activities that are fitted to his innate abilities, stage of maturation, and background of experience.

The Urge for Adventure Curiosity is a normal human quality. From early childhood onward most individuals have the urge to explore the new and the different. An important aspect of the child's developmental pattern is to broaden his horizon by participation in experiences that increase his knowledge and understanding of the world about him. He uses all his maturing sensory equipment to become acquainted with all the fascinating objects and conditions in his environment. Sometimes his curiosity seems to be insatiable. He observes, he handles, he asks innumerable questions about the *how* and *why* of things and situations. He usually has many opportunities to satisfy this drive. Some of these opportunities are discovered by himself; others are provided for him.

The child has a strong urge to investigate. He builds with his blocks and tears down what he has constructed; he enjoys prying into things; he destroys his toys in order to discover what makes them "tick." Usually the child's desire for adventure is easily satisfied. He tries one adventuresome activity after another. Unless he is denied the privilege of experimenting, his drive follows a relatively harmless path of investigation and discovery. Wise parents and teachers can utilize this commonly felt drive to help the child or adolescent gain considerable knowledge and understanding of his world through personal and vicarious experiences. If the child is thwarted by rigid adults in his efforts to engage in healthful, constructive adventure-seeking, he may be impelled to find his satisfaction in socially undesirable adventurous acts, such as vandalism, truancy from school, or serious delinquent behavior.

THE ACHIEVEMENT OF PURPOSES OR GOALS

Needs, drives, and urges can be regarded as behavior motivators toward the realization of the child's developing life purposes or goals. As we have suggested in earlier discussions, the baby appears to be concerned almost entirely with the satisfaction of his bodily needs, although awareness of his relationships with the persons and objects in his environment is beginning to show itself. Gradually, purposes and goals associated with his physiological and social urges take form. The young child's immediate wants usually are short-lived, however, and vary with existing inner conditions and outer circumstances. It probably is not until the child starts his school experiences that he can be regarded as giving evidence of longer-term purposes that resemble somewhat later-age life goals.

The arousal of a desire to learn constitutes the motivation of purpose in learning. It is the teacher's responsibility to discover and utilize whatever stimuli will assist individual learners to apply the mastery drive to the attaining of success in skill perfection, subject-matter learning, or attitude development. Various approaches can be utilized to encourage satisfying achievement and to avoid the onset of feelings of thwarting or frustration. Some of the techniques available to parents and teachers for assisting young people to engage in purposeful or goal-aimed activity are discussed here briefly.

The Use of Incentives   In child rearing, one of the chief responsibilities of adults is so to plan their courses of action that the child is motivated to discover the underlying purpose of his learning activities and to put forth his best efforts to benefit from his learning experiences. These planned motivations can be referred to as *incentives.*

Incentives usually are classified as (1) *extrinsic,* lying outside the learning or working situations, such as a money reward, a medal, or a "star" in school, and (2) *intrinsic,* lying within the learning or working situation, such as pride in achievement, increase in self-confidence, or attainment of power to engage in related activities. The young child may need to be motivated to engage in certain necessary activities through the offering of extrinsic rewards. He can be encouraged early, however, to recognize the value to himself of behavior motivations through intrinsic incentives. The self-confidence engendered by their application usually motivates the child or adolescent to earn success in his constructive activities. Incentives for young peoples' learning and work projects include, among others developed by ingenious adults, knowledge of results, rewards and punishments, competition, fear of failure, and avoidance of feelings of frustration.

Knowledge of Results   It is important for a younger person to be mentally set to engage in an activity that is aimed at the fulfillment of a desired purpose or goal. Although the very young child may seem to want activity merely for the satisfaction he derives from it, his behavior, even though it may be in the form of make-believe play, gradually comes to be motivated by a purpose. Consequently, the child's learning is facilitated insofar as he is helped to understand toward what goal he is moving and how well he is performing in the realization of his purpose.

As the learner is kept informed concerning his relative progress, he usually is stimulated thereby toward greater learning effort. It often is difficult to evaluate objectively and satisfactorily the degree of progress that has been attained. The most practical medium of evaluation, of course, is demonstrated ability to utilize the skill or material learned. The functional approach to learning, as in the developing use of a language or of mathematical concepts, or in the mastery of a complicated skill, does not lend itself to satisfactory measurement of the successive steps in the continuity of progress. Hence the child may become discouraged from putting forth his best efforts in learning situations that require much integration of processes before efficiency in overt responses becomes apparent.

Reward and Punishment   Reward and punishment are or should be related to the acquiring of some knowledge of achieved results in learning. Many experiments have been conducted in which the strength of animals' biological drives have been studied. The subjects were trained to become aware of rewards in the form of desired food, or of punishment administered by way of a mild electric shock. The reward approach usually is utilized by animal trainers in their attempt to teach an animal to learn a particular behavior habit. On any age level and in most areas of activity, an effective incentive for motivating an individual to continue satisfying performance is achieving a reward in the form of success. Another valuable stimulator of continued effort is the giving of praise for adequate progress in mastering the learning or work task.

Punishment can take the form of reasonable vocal disapproval or mild physical pain. There is some experimental evidence to the effect that the administration of painful punishment is more effective than the mere calling of attention to inadequate results. Whatever form of punishment is applied, the child needs to recognize it as a means of alerting him to corrective changes in his behavior that should be made for which he will receive approval.

Thorndike and others believe that reward is superior to punishment as a motivating force. The consciousness of successful progress in the completion of a project arouses inner satisfactions that prepare the entire body for continued favorable activity. Both reward and punishment should be used with discretion. To encourage improved performance rather than discouragement and resentment, punishment needs to be directed toward inadequate activity, not at the child. The learner's or worker's cooperation can be secured by shifting the emphasis from punishment and disapproval to the stimulation of a feeling of security in right-doing as soon as this change in attitude is feasible.

Competition and Cooperation Children before the age of two years seldom seem to be affected by the motive of competition. From the age of five or six onward through adulthood, competition or rivalry appears to be a significant motivator of an individual's behavior. It sometimes is difficult to shift a child's competition against the achievement record of another to competition against his own past accomplishments. Some teachers attempt to encourage competition with self among their pupils, especially on the secondary school level, by having young people keep a record, in graph form, of their successive ratings in tests, for example, as compared with class averages. The young people then are encouraged to discover possible reasons for variations in their progress.

For competition with associates to have value for the developing individual, it is essential that he be provided opportunities to compete with other young people who are similar to himself in ability to achieve. It is extremely frustrating for a child or older person to find himself in competition with others who have greater ability or wider background experience than himself. Failure to succeed in an inequitable situation can have serious emotional results, even for those children who generally are successful in their accomplishments. Hence adults are charged with the responsibility of setting up situations in which children will be given opportunities to engage in healthful competition with their ability peers.

Modern parents and teachers are emphasizing the value to a child of engaging in cooperative activities with his play and work associates. There need not be an antithesis between competition and cooperation. In most competitive sports, for example, team cooperation is most important. The two competing groups need to be well matched, however, so that there may be equality of performance.

The older child who is given to "bullying" younger children is a poor sport—he neither is cooperative nor a fair competitor. In fact, he is more than likely to withdraw from any attempt to compete with boys of his own age or stage of maturation. Contrariwise, some younger, smaller children refuse to compete with their peers but seem to be driven by their strong competitive spirit to "take on" older, stronger associates. Either type of youngster needs the wise guidance of adults who understand the psychological factors involved. The child's personal integrity must be maintained, but he needs to learn the value of cooperation with his fellows and the limits to which he should go in attempts to meet competition in any area of endeavor.

Fear of Failure Some theorists in the recent past held that a child's adjustment to his life's pattern is best achieved if he is protected from any situation in which he might encounter failure. It was assumed that failure is always a destructive force that can incite in the child negative, unconstructive patterns of behavior. It is true that actual or anticipated failure may result in the cessation of an activity even though some success is possible if the individual were to stay with the project. Yet, unless the child has experienced at least some slight degree of failure in the performance of desired tasks, he not only is unable to savor the sweet rewards of success, but he is denied the opportunity to evaluate his own strengths and weaknesses.

The urge to avoid failure is basic in every phase of an individual's life. This drive has definite educational significance. The attitude of a child's parents and teachers toward what constitutes success or failure influences his own standards. The extent to which he accepts their judgment concerning the quality of his work affects his own attitudes toward them as well as toward the tasks involved. If a younger person has come to believe (rightly or wrongly) that an adult who is critical of his performance is not a good judge or is prejudiced against him, the adult will have little influence on the child's work.

Avoidance of Thwarting and Frustration It seems almost contradictory to claim as we did in the foregoing that it is beneficial for a child to experience some failure and now to seem to assert that the same child should not be exposed to thwarting and frustrating experiences. The difference is a matter of degree. Occasional failure to achieve desired goals that are possible of achievement can be an excellent motivator of improved working habits. For a child to meet a relatively insurmountable obstacle in the attempted satisfaction of a vital need or drive is a destructively frustrating experience that, if the situation persists, can do inestimable harm to the child's personality development.

A child can be said to be frustrated if there is any interference with goal-directed behavior that is severe enough to cause mental or emotional disturbance. A feeling of frustration is rooted in a thwarted need or drive. Although a developing individual may be exposed to many personal or social obstacles as he attempts to reach desired goals, a thwarting situation does not result in frustration unless the child recognizes the obstacle as a threat to self-realization.

The forces that incite frustration differ with age level. The infant can experience all-over feelings of thwarting if he is denied his bottle when he is hungry. The baby may show signs of extreme frustration if a favored toy is out of his reach or he is subjected to toilet training. An older child or adolescent can become emotionally disturbed if his parents, with no apparent reasons, deny him participation in a much desired activity, such as attendance at a party, or if peer-age associates seem to engage in projects which, for one reason or another, are beyond his powers of participation. A high school freshman, for example, was several years younger than her classmates. Because of her physical immaturity, the family physician had deemed it unwise for her to participate in physical activities appropriate for her older school associates. Hence she was excused by the school authorities from participation in regular gymnastic activities. As she sat on the sidelines in the gymnasium and watched her classmates climb ropes and engage in other similar stunts, she felt completely frustrated. She believed that the other girls regarded her as a child, even though she was a leader in academic learning. This emotional experience continued to plague her through later adolescent years and early adulthood. The fact that she possessed superior intelligence did not compensate her for her strong drive to participate in these athletic activities for which she had not been prepared during her earlier years.

Throughout childhood and even into adult years, an individual can be frustrated by conditions and situations that are beyond his power to control but that may interfere seriously with the immediate needs or desires. In retrospect, some of these thwarting incidents may seem relatively unimportant, but at the time of their occurrence they may take on the proportions of a major catastrophe. A few illustrations can be cited: A child who has been looking forward eagerly to a school picnic is inconsolable if inclement weather on the day of the picnic causes it to be postponed; a high school senior hurts his right hand just before the taking of his final examinations and must either forfeit his graduation or try to write with his left hand; an adult has been selected by his professional group to be a delegate to an important convention but instead is forced by the development of a serious illness to go to a hospital.

Some sources of frustration are rooted in social and cultural aspects of experience. Laws and codes established for the general welfare may interfere with a younger or older individual's wishes or desires. A child who is not succeeding well in his school work may become emotionally disturbed because school attendance laws require him to stay in school. An adolescent girl may feel herself to be completely frustrated when her parents, according to Old-World traditions, refuse to permit her to date, as is the custom among her peer associates whose parents are more permissive than hers. The obeying of traffic regulations is irksome to the driver of an automobile who wishes to reach his destination quickly. Equally frustrating to a pedestrian is the "Don't Walk" sign at a street crossing, if no automobiles or trucks are in view and he is in a hurry. Laws governing business practices can be most annoying to the man who believes he can avoid following these rules without hurt to anyone else. Many individuals also experience feelings of frustration if their economic situation (no matter how good it may be) is such that they realize they cannot afford an expensive car, a large, finely furnished home, or any other much desired luxury that is possessed by others who are wealthier than themselves.

The reader probably can enumerate occasions in his own life when serious drives to action were frustrated. The degree to which such experiences have a lasting effect upon an individual's personality pattern depends to a great extent on his ability to accept denial of his strong drives or urges. In Chapter 18 we discuss the mental health approach to thwarting, frustration, and conflict. At this point we suggest that, insofar as is possible, adults attempt so to order the child's environment and guide his developing behavior that unreasonable frustrating experiences are kept to a minimum and that, when thwarting experiences do occur occasionally, the child has sufficient emotional balance to take them in his stride.

QUESTIONS AND TOPICS FOR DISCUSSION

1. What is meant by the dynamics of behavior?
2. Study Ragsdale's diagrams. Illustrate the operation of at least five of them.
3. Explain what is meant by a predisposition. Give examples.
4. Which of Cattell's list of drives have you experienced? To what extent have you been able to satisfy them?
5. Give examples of situations in which children need to be trained to adapt their needs to the pattern of society.
6. What are some of your definite food tastes? How did these develop?
7. What are your present sleeping habits? How do they differ from what they were ten years ago? Five years ago? How do you explain any changes?
8. To what extent have you learned to live happily with yourself?

How does your degree of self-sufficiency affect your relationships with other people?

9. Give examples of some specific needs, wants, or urges displayed by (1) young children, (2) older children, (3) young adolescents.

10. How important to you is the earning of success in achievement? Explain.

11. Give examples of healthful adventure-seeking by a child that may be disapproved by his parents.

12. To what type of incentive are you most likely to respond? Why?

13. *Special Project:* Notice any attention-getting techniques employed by your subjects. What age and sex differences do you find? Have you in any way been able to increase their feelings of security?

SELECTED REFERENCES

Blake, R. H., and Ramsey, G. U., *Perception: An Approach to Personality.* New York: The Ronald Press Company, 1951.

Cantor, N., *Dynamics of Learning,* 3rd ed. Buffalo: Henry Stewart, Inc., 1956.

Crow, L. D., and Crow, A., *Human Development and Learning,* Chapter 6. New York: American Book Company, 1956.

Davis, A., and Havighurst, R. J., *Father of the Man.* Boston: Houghton Mifflin Company, 1947.

McClelland, D. C., *Studies in Motivation.* New York: Appleton-Century-Crofts, Inc., 1955.

Munn, N. L., *The Evolution and Growth of Human Behavior,* Chapter 16. Boston: Houghton Mifflin Company, 1955.

Mussen, P. H., and Jones, M. C., "The Behavior-Inferred Motivations of Late- and Early-Maturing Boys," *Child Development,* 29: 62–67, 1958.

Stellar, E., "The Psychology of Motivation," *Psychological Review,* 61: 5–22, 1954.

Strang, Ruth, *Helping Children Solve Problems.* Chicago: Science Associates, Inc., 1953.

Woodworth, Robert S., *Dynamics of Behavior.* New York: Henry Holt and Company, 1958.

13

FORMATION OF
INTERESTS AND
ATTITUDES

INTERESTS AND ATTITUDES are personal and may be latent or active. They develop from early childhood. They exert an important influence in the life of an individual, and can become the bases of biases and prejudices. A particular interest or attitude is discriminative in that it can motivate a child or older person to follow one course of action rather than another.

Interests and attitudes vary in intensity. To the degree that an interest or an attitude continues to affect the individual pleasantly it is maintained and probably strengthened. If experiences associated with the fulfilment of the interest or attitude are annoying or cause discomfort, however, they lose their power as a motivator of behavior. An attitude tends to be general, deep-rooted, and continuous, but an interest usually is regarded as relatively inconsistent and fleeting. Yet an interest may become so persistent that it takes on some of the characteristics of an attitude.

CHILDREN'S DEVELOPING INTERESTS

Children's developing interests are closely allied to their growing needs, drives, and urges. A particular need or drive tends to be satisfied according to a more or less consistent pattern of behavior. From this mode of reaction often emerges a relatively consistent interest that can be further encouraged by environmental conditions and experiences.

Meaning and Development of Interest   The term "interest" is generally used to explain the reasons for an individual's engaging in one form of activity rather than in another. A child usually is conscious of his interests, and they are related to his power to perform. A child's early interests emerge from his growing capabilities and powers. The younger child usually has little concern about his environment except as he responds to people and objects about him in light of his needs and those things he can and wants to do. It is not until he reaches an appropriate maturational level that he becomes interested in talking, walking, or playing with other children. He cannot be forced to be interested in these activities until he is constitutionally ready.

The arousal of any of the child's developing interests is affected by his physical status, his mental and emotional maturation, and the elements of his social environment. Experience is an important factor in a child's acquisition of interests, which are relatively unstable until adolescence. Interest becomes a motivator of behavior as soon as the young child becomes aware of himself as a person. Consequently, his first interests are centered in himself and his wants.

During the child's early period of struggles for self-realization he appears to be almost completely self-centered. He tends to describe people and things in his environment as his personal possessions. He constantly uses expressions such as *baby's* ball, *my* cup, *my* daddy, *my* mommy, and the like. It is only as he gains greater understanding of his relationships that he gives indication of larger interests that include concern about the activities of family members and play associates, and later of teachers and schoolmates. The child also gradually becomes interested in other people's appraisal of himself and in ways in which he can gain their approval.

A child's interests are broadened with increase in maturity and experience. He acquires an interest in constructing attractive or useful objects, such as airplanes, space ships, stools, birdhouses, and the like. He becomes interested in faraway places and the lives of great people.

He is especially interested in animals as pets as may be seen in Figure 88. In light of the stimulation he receives, he is motivated to develop an interest in scientific research, mechanics, big game hunting, or other areas of challenging activity.

Wide World Photo

Figure 88.   Children Enjoy Playing with Animals.

Factors Affecting Interest Development   Experienced needs and urges, of course, are basic to the kind and extent of developed interests. The child not only has a felt need for food and drink but learns to like them prepared in certain ways, usually as a result of imitating his family's food habits. A child is likely to resist eating something that his elders do not eat, especially if he is admonished that it is good for him. He is especially attracted to food that seems to be eaten with gusto by a favorite adult. One child enjoys milk, but another has no interest in milk unless chocolate syrup is added.

Little girls, earlier than boys, become clothes-conscious. This may be caused partly by the fact that mothers appear to take greater interest in "dressing up" a little daughter than they do their son. Then, again, boys tend to participate in more strenuous sports and resent wearing "sissified" clothes. Their interest in dress and grooming does not really show itself until adolescence when they begin dating. During this latter period of development, both girls and boys are stimulated by their increasing sex urge to develop interest in personal appearance, dancing and other social activities, and perhaps in study to cause them to become more attractive to the members of the opposite sex.

Social motives, in addition to the sex urge, may become motivators of changing interests. Leisure-time interests are rooted in the need to relax from more or less strenuous work activity. Some interests, such as participation in physical and social activities, or pride in home conditions, have prestige value. Interest in self-improvement or study may be aimed at acquiring vocational competence or earning commendation from relatives and friends. In fact, some young people are interested in study for no other reason than that they gain considerable pleasure from engaging in study activities.

The emotional factor can wield a powerful influence on a growing child's development of an interest pattern. Success in an activity is a potent encourager of continued interest. Contrariwise, failure or imagined failure to succeed dampens a young person's interest in a work, study, or play project. A child tends to view with affectionate regard anyone who seems to be interested in him and his doings. He soon loses interest in a person, however, who fails to accord him the attention which he believes to be owed him.

Although success is a strong motivator of interest arousal, a young person soon loses interest in a project that appears to be too easy. He thrills to the challenge of solving problems that require time and energy but that he considers to be within his ability range. The mentally superior pupil, for example, may tend to neglect what he considers "easy" subject matter and be driven by his interest in challenging situations to spend many hours working on a problem that appears to defy solution. The unevenness of performance in school study that too often is found among bright children and young people can be explained in light of the interest factor.

The fact that a young person is expected to achieve adequate competence in all areas of school study may be a cause of hardship for the secondary school pupil, especially one who may perform brilliantly in one field (mathematics or science, for example) but who, because of lack of interest, may fail in another, such as a foreign language, art, or any other subject that does not constitute an interesting challenge for him. Interest that is rooted in a special talent can be a strong motivator of a child's persisent efforts toward productive achievement in a particular field. Yet he needs to be guided toward recognition of his need to develop some interest at least in other areas of endeavor so that he will be fitted for balanced living in his group.

Although a young person should have more than one behavior-motivating interest, there is danger in his developing so many interests that he finds it difficult to concentrate on the adequate fulfillment of any one of them. This is the kind of situation, for example, in which a young person may find himself in relation to his school studies. Instead of having one all-engaging interest as described in the previous paragraph, an older child or adolescent may spread his interests to include all or most of his subjects. He then is likely to become so eager to excel in all of them that he is driven to spend so much time and energy on school work that, unless he is carefully guided, he will deny himself recreational and social activities which he needs. He may even try to broaden his interests to combine excessive study with participation in athletics and social events. If he finds it impossible to keep up with all his interests, he may become discouraged and lose actively motivated interest in all or most of them.

Most childhood interests are relatively fleeting. A baby or young child tends to change from one interest to another. He plays with one toy, and then throws it aside for another. He climbs on a chair, sits there momentarily, and then goes in pursuit of something else that attracts his attention. When he gains good control of his legs and acquires body balance, he walks, he runs, he skips, he jumps; he falls down and picks himself up again. The city child delights in balancing himself along cracks in the pavement or the street curb. The country child scales trees, balances himself on the top edge of a low fence, or jumps from rock to rock. All these activities indicate his interest in physical activity, but he soon tires of any one activity and finds something else to intrigue him.

There are times, however, when even small children persist in an activity for what seems to an adult to be a long time to continue the project without earning success in it. For example, a baby tries to get his toe into his mouth, the older child tries to stand on his head, wriggle his ears, or perform any one of the acrobatic stunts that he views on television. Repeated failure seems to serve as an added impetus to continue, until extreme physical fatigue requires that he stop, or his attention and interest are diverted to something else.

Duration of Interest   The older elementary school child or adolescent often is influenced by his immediate interest in decision-making situations. Will the boy complete his home assignments for school or play ball with his pals? Will the girl finish reading an interesting story or complete a household chore which is her responsibility? Young people as well as their elders experience conflicts of interests. The strength and length of duration of any developed interest varies with degree of maturity and with the extent to which the individual is able to sacrifice immediate interests to more remote benefits.

An interest may become so engrossing that other interests are forgotten temporarily. Nine-year-old Joan, for example, came in from play one late afternoon, announcing that she was starved. She asserted that she just couldn't wait until six o'clock for dinner to be served. Then she suddenly remembered that one of her favorite television programs was about to be shown. So engrossed did she become in the program that, when her mother called her for dinner, she begged to be allowed to stay with the viewing until the end of the picture. Her supposed interest in food had been superseded by her interest in television.

A similar situation is shown in the behavior of a five-year-old child who was so interested in his new train that he refused to stop to greet guests who had arrived to visit the family. Upon persuasion, however, he left his train to say "hello" to his relatives who had come to dinner. When told by his parents that now he might return to his toy he refused to do so, saying, "I want to listen to what you are saying."

Cause of Interest   Many of the significant factors that influence the arousing and maintaining of the various interests experienced by individuals can be determined through observation of cause-and-effect relationships. There are subtle elements within the child's maturing personality and in his surroundings that account for differences in interests, the bases of which are difficult to detect. We must keep this fact in mind as we attempt to explain reasons for children's changing behavior. It is almost impossible, for example, for a teacher to discover with certainty why he is able to stimulate some of his pupils to activity and not others, when he utilizes what seem to him to be excellent motivational approaches.

One or a few pupils may deviate from the norm of a class with no apparent reason. Ronald, a seventh-grade pupil, is a case in point. He was a member of an average class group. Most of his classmates were motivated to perform adequately in their school work. Ronald was not interested in anything except the writing of compositions. Here he excelled. His parents were uneducated; his home conditions were pathetically unfavorable; he himself usually came to school unkempt and poorly clad; he rarely completed school assignments. Moreover, he was ignorant in the field of grammar, and his spelling was unique. He would give evidence of complete boredom during class activities, not even engaging in mischief or other disturbing activities. Yet, during composition periods, he was a changed boy. His accustomed lethargy disappeared. He listened to directions or suggestions with an almost abnormal show of interest. Then he wrote. His ideas were presented logically and forcefully; his style was attention-holding. He gave evidence of superior imaginative abilities.

Ronald could not explain the great difference between his fine performance in this field and his failure to achieve in other areas. In reply to questions about this difference, his answer invariably was, "Writing is fun; the other stuff is a bunch of baloney." Unfortunately, counselors and other school people could not arouse his interest in general school work, and he continued to fail. He left school as soon as age permitted and became a factory worker. According to latest information, he is a leader in his labor union because of his powers of persuasion with his co-workers. Ronald's consuming interest in the expression of ideas cannot be explained according to the more obvious factors of motivation.

SPECIAL AREAS OF INTEREST

Interest aroused through participation in an activity can stimulate an individual to continue in the same activity or others that are similar. Hence interest can both cause and result from experience. The child's interests are developed in relation to other aspects of behavior. It is the responsibility of adults, therefore, to attempt to foster, insofar as they can, those interests in children through the operation of which can be developed constructive modes of behavior that have lasting values.

Play Interests   An inner urge for pleasurable activity arouses the play interest. A child does not have to learn to want to play, but the kind of play in which he engages depends on maturation and experience. The baby, as we have suggested earlier, plays alone or with adults. He then will play alone in the presence of other children. Gradually, he comes to experience the satisfaction of playing with other children, sharing his toys with them. Group play during early childhood is relatively unorganized; the children make up their rules as they go along. It is not until later childhood that established rules of the game become important.

The child craves activity throughout his waking hours. The play interest controls much of this activity, even when he is engaged in a constructive project. To help his mother, for example, in simple household tasks may take on the characteristics of play. Moreover, the child's growing interest in the doings of his parents and of other members of the family causes him to imitate their activities in his play.

As the child expands his social relationships, he utilizes his language and motor responses in play. He exercises his growing abilities spontaneously and at his own selected level of difficulty. He tries out new experiences as, through play, he experiments with the unknown. The utilization of the imagination is a significant factor of the play interest. There is an element of danger in play-initiated climbing, swimming, riding a bicycle, and similar feats. In fact, children, especially boys, often seem to be most interested in forms of play that involve a certain amount of risk.

Children's Games Children's interest in the playing of games varies with level of intelligence, social and economic background, season, and locality. Bright children tend to play more complicated games than do slower children and give more attention to the rules of the game. Mentally superior children usually enjoy indoor games that challenge their imagination, such as checkers and, later, chess. Less able children are more likely to prefer physical sports. This does not mean that bright children have no interest in outdoor play.

Children of higher socio-economic status usually are provided with opportunities to engage in various types of games, both indoor and outdoor. Tennis and ballet dancing, for example, are becoming fairly popular in some suburban areas. Children who live in crowded city areas are dependent on neighborhood community centers for participation in game activities.

The season of the year, of course, influences the kinds of games children play. Thus, rope-skipping and top-twirling are harbingers of Spring. The locale of the children's homes also exercises an influence over the kinds of games and other play in which they are free to engage. Urban children are more restricted in their activity than are children in open areas where they need not be so concerned about annoying neighbors. Most communities, however, are exerting considerable effort to provide space and equipment needed for children's participation in health-fostering games and other sports.

Kindergarten and first-grade children seem to enjoy playing with blocks, painting, and modeling. Older children appear to be more interested in group games. With increasing age, there is a diminution of interest in games demanding large muscle activity, such as tag, and in make-believe play, including playing with doll families, cops and robbers, and cowboys. During the adolescent years many young people become spectators of sports rather than participants.[1]

Work and Play Play tends to dominate an individual's interest throughout his life. He continues to engage in some activities for the sheer pleasure that can be derived from them. Work and play commonly are differentiated according to their motivating purpose. The former is supposed to be activated by the desire to achieve a relatively remote goal; the latter is engaged in for immediate satisfaction. To the extent, however, that a child or older person is extremely interested in the performance of a task, it becomes for him, temporarily at least, play rather than work. It is as he plans further progress in the project that the work aspect is appreciated. There are times when even an unpleasant chore can be viewed by the participant as play, in that he is motivated to engage in a game with himself in the interest of completing it accurately.

Reading Interests One- and two-year-old children enjoy having stories read to them, even though they may be unable to comprehend the meaning of the words. They respond to the sound of the reader's voice, the rhythmic flow of words and the reader's facial expressions. The satisfaction derived from sitting on the reader's lap or snuggled against him adds to the experienced enjoyment. The three- or four-year-old gains pleasure from looking at pictures and identifying them as he manipulates the picture-and-story book. Four-year-olds are much interested in viewing comics as the written material is read aloud. They laugh lustily at grotesque figures and unexpected events in the story portrayed. Children in this age group also tend to evince interest in stories about other children, animal stories, nature stories, and rhymes and jingles.

Reading interests differ among children of elementary school age, according to influencing factors, such as adult persuasion, intelligence status, and available materials. During this period, children are interested in both fanciful and factual literature. Observation of primary children's choice of stories indicates that they like stories that have a plot and a surprise element. Stories about school also hold their interest. Girls especially enjoy stories about other children like themselves and family life; boys like stories about animals that are pets. Interest in comics continues for both sexes, although now they want to read the strips themselves.

[1] For a more detailed discussion of play, see Farwell, L., "Reactions of Kindergarten, First and Second Grade Children to Constructive Play Materials," *Genetic Psychology Monographs*, 8: 431–562, 1930; Lehman, H. C., and Witty, P. A., *The Psychology of Play Activities*, New York: A. S. Barnes, 1927; and Jersild, A. T., *Child Psychology* (4th ed.), New York: Prentice-Hall, Inc., pp. 504–507, 1954.

Older elementary children continue to thrill to fanciful tales of brave heroes and beautiful heroines. They also enjoy stories of factual situations, simply presented and dealing with sports, travel, biography, science, and geography. According to May Lazar,[2] children in grades four through six are interested in reading material that includes action, adventure, animal life, airplanes and other inventions, bravery and sportsmanship, child life, excitement, humor, mystery, realism, and suspense.

As children near junior high school age, boys and girls enjoy stories of boarding school life. Girls' interest in fiction increases and boys become excited by tales of adventure. As Penny[3] asserts, most girls are interested in the *hows* and *whys* of people, and boys are more interested in the *whys* and *hows* of things. This difference in reading interest between the sexes is relatively significant during adolescent years. A boy tends to be interested in reading about adventure, mechanics, science, sports, travel, and the lives of great men. A girl likes stories about other girls, romantic, sometimes sentimental, novels, and poetry.

One should not assume that all children and young people follow the age trends described in the foregoing. Mental age rather than chronological age should be the criterion. Cultural trends also influence reading tastes. An increasing number of girls are evincing interest in the type of reading formerly considered to be boys' choices. General concern about world affairs, scientific discovery, and technological advances are influencing not only the reading choices of young people but also the number of books made available for them, as well as for adults, in these areas of modern interests.

A study of adult reactions to preferred childhood stories made at Louisiana State University revealed that of the 264 students (184 women and 80 men in Educational Psychology) the childhood story interests for women in order of frequency were: fairy tales, fiction, animal stories, religious stories, poetry, and biography; for men the order was reversed for fairy tales and fiction with no reference to poetry, but otherwise the order was the same as for women. In their summary statement, the authors suggest:

Results show that women chose stories stemming from the Oedipal period, involving evil mother figures, benign but active males, and persecuted, passive young women. Their stories had been shared more with loved persons, covered a re-

[2] Lazar, M., *Reading Interests, Activities, and Opportunities of Bright, Average, and Dull Children,* Contributions to Education, No. 707, p. 517. New York: Bureau of Publications, Teachers College, Columbia University, 1937.

[3] Penny, R., "Age and Sex Differences in Motivational Orientation to the Communicative Act," *Child Development,* 29: 163–171, 1958.

stricted number of themes, and had happy, often magical, endings. Men preferred stories encountered independently during the latency period with themes of adventure, problem solution, and self-assertion. Story endings and evaluations of the stories were more obviously reality-oriented in the male group; women figures, though rare, were almost exclusively kind and maternal.[4]

Many studies have been made of the reading interests of children of differing ages. There is a gradual development of changing interest with increasing maturity. As we have indicated, however, certain sex trends, for example, remain relatively constant. There are differences between what adults believe young people *should like* and what the individuals themselves report that they like. Norvell [5] lists the various factors that influence boys' reading interests as compared to girls' both on the elementary school and secondary school levels. See Tables 17 and 18. Norvell also has tabulated prose and poem selections, ranked by popularity by boys and girls of grade 3 and grades 4 to 6. These tabulations are valuable for anyone interested in providing literature for children.

TABLE 17

Various Factors Influencing Boys' Reading Interests *

Favorable	*Unfavorable*	*Neutral*
Adventure with lively or violent action	Description	Brief description required for the story
Physical struggle as found in fighting and rugged games	Didacticism	The supernatural
	Fairies as such	Literary quality
Human characters: men, or boys somewhat older than the reader	Love (romantic)	Women or girls as minor characters
	Other "soft" sentiments, as sympathy, self-sacrifice	
Animals, wild or domestic	Women or girls as leading characters	IN POETRY
Humor	Physical weakness or lack of aggressiveness in male characters	Rhyme and rhythm of a simple type (with older children)
Courage and heroism		
Mystery		
Patriotism	IN POETRY	
Christmas or Thanksgiving Day	Nature	
	Subtle or involved rhyme	
IN POETRY	Namby-pambyism	
Rhyme and rhythm of simple type (with young children)		

* Norvell, George W., *What Boys and Girls Like to Read*, p. 176. Morristown, N. J.: copyright 1958 by Silver Burdett Company.

4 Collier, M. J., and Gaier, E. L., "Adult Reactions to Preferred Childhood Stories," *Child Development*, Vol. 29, No. 1, p. 103, March, 1958.

5 Norvell, G. W., *What Boys and Girls Like to Read*. Morristown, N. J.: Silver Burdett Company, 1958.

TABLE 18

Various Factors Influencing Girls' Reading Interests *

Favorable	Unfavorable	Neutral
Adventure, lively	Bloody or violent action	Brief description required
Home and school life	Description	by the story
Characters: men,	Didacticism	Literary quality
women; boys and girls	Boys and girls younger	
somewhat older than	than the reader (ex-	IN POETRY
the reader; babies	cept babies)	Rhyme and rhythm of
Domestic animals and	Fierce, wild animals	simple type (with
pets		older children)
Love (romantic)	IN POETRY	
Other "soft" sentiments	Nature	
as sympathy, self-sacri-	Subtle or involved rhyme	
fice, generosity	Namby-pambyism	
Mystery		
The supernatural		
Patriotism		
Christmas, Thanksgiving		
Day		
IN POETRY		
Rhyme and rhythm of		
simple type (with		
young children)		

* *Ibid.*, p. 177.

Radio, Television and Motion Picture Interests   Before the advent of television it was estimated that elementary school children spent about one-seventh of their waking hours listening to radio. Now, with close to fifty million television sets in the United States, children as well as adults are giving much of the time formerly devoted to listening to the radio to televiewing. At present, however, many automobiles are equipped with radios. Some children enjoy listening to radio programs on auto trips.

Age and sex influence the kinds of radio and television programs in which children are interested. Young children enjoy dramatizations of make-believe adventures, including fairy tales. As children increase in age, these programs decrease in their power to motivate viewing, and greater differences between the sexes appear. In general, elementary school boys are interested in sports and science, and programs that are marked by adventure, such as "Lone Ranger" or crime. Girls seem to prefer programs that feature their favorite motion picture stars or that deal with domestic drama. More girls are coming to share boys' interest in sports and, to some degree, Westerns. Yet girls seem to show relatively little desire to view programs showing scientific progress; they prefer programs in which the love interest dominates or in which child characters are featured.

Although younger children are intrigued especially by late afternoon and early evening showings designed to excite their interests, older children are relatively universal in their tastes. Adult persuasion has some effect on young people's radio listening and televiewing. They can be motivated to become interested in musical programs that are within their ability to appreciate. Teachers can stimulate their pupils' interest in newscasting and accounts of current world affairs, if through the attention given to such programs the pupils are enabled to participate in interesting class discussions. It is difficult, however, for a teacher to motivate listening to a radio presentation of current events that is scheduled for the same hour during which a stirring television program is presented.

According to Witty and Kinsella [6] favorite television programs change. In 1950 the favorite programs were *Hopalong Cassidy, Howdy Doody,* and *Lone Ranger.* From 1952 to 1955 *I Love Lucy* held first place, but fell to third place in 1957, with *Disneyland* and *Rin-Tin-Tin* taking first and second places, respectively. In 1958 first rankings by elementary school children in Evanston and Skokie, Illinois, went to *Zorro, Disneyland, Bugs Bunny,* and *Shock Theatre* (second place for children in grades 4 to 6).

The average time spent on television by elementary and high school pupils and by parents and teachers as reported for the Chicago area between 1951 and 1958 is given in Table 19.

TABLE 19

Average Hours Spent Weekly with Television *

	1951	1953	1955	1957	1958
Elementary School Pupils	19	23	24	22	20
High School Pupils	14	17	14	12	13
Parents	20	19	21	20	19
Teachers	9	12	12	12	12

* Witty, Paul, and Kinsella, Paul, "Children and TV—A Ninth Report," *Elementary English,* 35: 450–456, November, 1958.

The amount of time devoted by children and adolescents to radio listening and televiewing is affected by the cultural values and the adherence to rules and regulations found in the home. The child whose parents enjoy average or better socio-economic status usually is motivated to engage in so many other interesting activities that his televiewing opportunities are reduced. He participates in after-school activities, such as

[6] Witty, Paul, and Kinsella, Paul, "Children and TV—A Ninth Report," *Elementary English,* 35: 450–456, November, 1958.

religious instruction, lessons in music or dancing, and perhaps special classes in a foreign language. He is motivated by his parents and his own ambitions to prepare his home assignments adequately, to spend some time in the library, and to be a member of a community-sponsored social or recreational group in which he participates in interesting activities with same-age associates. Moreover, this child probably is expected to have dinner with the family rather than to sit in front of the television set while he is eating, and to go to bed at a specified time, before some of the more intriguing programs are presented.

Contrariwise, there are homes in which parents are unable or unwilling to provide other avenues of interest for their son or daughter, or in which there is greater permissiveness concerning personal activities. A child reared in such a home is likely to find that televiewing affords him an outlet for the vicariously experienced enjoyments which he craves. A sixth-grade pupil, for example, was failing in her school work, although she had sufficient intelligence to succeed. She usually came to school heavy-eyed, and was accustomed to fall asleep in class. Her teacher discovered that, although the other members of the family retired at a reasonable hour, she stayed up to watch the late and the late-late shows on television. This is an extreme case, of course, but relatively similar situations occur in some homes.

Contrary to common prediction when television first became popular, interest in reading has not been diminished by televiewing. According to Bennett Cerf, worthwhile juvenile books have increased in sale from 57 million in 1947 to 270 million in 1957.[7] Apparently television has not affected destructively young people's interest in books.

Children's and young people's interest in worthwhile televiewing is being encouraged by the progress that has been made in educational radio and television. The United States Office of Education started to sponsor educational radio in 1931, and educational television in 1944. In 1959 there were forty-three educational television stations. An interesting teaching technique is the experiment in a flying laboratory, begun in September, 1961. The Midwest Program on Airborne Television Instruction (MPATI), which presents learning material for elementary (beginning with the first grade) and secondary schools, has been made available to pupils in schools in parts of Indiana, Illinois, Kentucky, Ohio, Michigan, and Wisconsin. Projects such as these not only are encouraging the provision of an increasing number of interesting and worthwhile programs but also are fast resulting in radio and television broadcasting's

---

[7] Cerf, Bennett, "Books Are Here to Stay," *Saturday Evening Post,* March 22, 1958.

becoming an integral part of our cultural pattern and a significant influence on children's developing behavior.

Although television has tended to decrease interest in motion picture programs, a sufficiently large group of children still attends the "movies" to make their influence felt. Many children visit neighborhood motion picture houses at least once in two weeks; for some it is at least once a week. Most children enjoy comedy, especially of the modified "slapstick" variety now shown. Boys enjoy gangster plots; girls prefer love themes and educational films.

Children can be affected physically and morally by motion pictures that are intended for viewing by adults. According to a study by Healy and Bronner,[8] delinquents studied evidenced more interest in motion pictures than did the nondelinquent group. The motion pictures viewed by the delinquents served as a means of escape from the bitter realities of life, although some admitted that they obtained ideas for their asocial activities from gangster and crime themes.

Many commercial films present the beauties of nature or depict current affairs in an intriguing fashion. These pictures usually are enjoyed by young people. They gain much educational value from an appreciation of geographic wonders and current events. Many schools utilize motion pictures to illustrate points in teaching situations that are excellent motivators of children's interest in learning.

Vocational Interests   We know that few occupational ambitions held in childhood continue through adolescence and early adulthood. Nevertheless, the roots are imbedded in childhood experiences. Stimulated by hero worship for men or women in various fields, or stirred by accounts of persons who have engaged in daring deeds or have earned a high degree of prestige, children tend to be motivated to follow in the vocational footsteps of their current idol. Boys express the urge to be, variously, policemen (especially Mounted Police), firemen, big business tycoons, and, most recently, spacemen. Some little girls, in light of their childhood experiences, want to be teachers, nurses, or mothers of big families. The preadolescent or adolescent girl may secretly nurture the ambition to emulate the vocational example of her favorite woman ideal in motion pictures or on television. We know, however, that these vocational interests usually are short-lived and have little influence on adult vocational choices.

Occasionally we find that a strong childhood ambition does finally

[8] Healy, W., and Bronner, A., "Delinquency as a Mode of Adjustment," in Kuhlen, R. H., and Thompson, G. T., *Psychological Studies in Human Development*, pp. 480–489. New York: Appleton-Century-Crofts, Inc., 1952.

reach fulfillment. Moreover, we decry attempts on the part of parents to determine for their children the latter's occupational field in light of their own interests and ambitions. Yet it is a fact that a young person can be subtly influenced by factors in his home toward the development of interests that can be potent factors, often unrecognized as such, in his future vocational plans. This would be a difficult field of study, but the results might be most enlightening.

In an article dealing with interests, Strong presents some worthwhile ideas concerning the relationships that exist between a worker's interest and his job satisfaction. Of particular value to us in this discussion are his five characteristics of interests. They are:

First, they [interests] are acquired in the sense that feeling becomes associated with the activity. . . .

Second, interests are persistent. Sometimes disliking is replaced by liking and vice versa; many start out disliking olives and acquire a taste, a pleasant feeling for them. But, all in all, interests are surprisingly permanent.

A third characteristic is intensity. One cannot only immediately indicate whether he likes or dislikes an activity but one can also immediately indicate his relative preferences for different activities. . . .

The fourth and fifth characteristics are acceptance-rejection, and readiness to act. . . . Acceptance-rejection implies action, direction, choice. Such preferences typify readiness to act in the sense that a habit or memory is a readiness to act. [A certain situation] is a stimulus and the already acquired interest, habit, memory, whatever one wants to call it, functions. The associated value, or feeling quality, determines whether the activity will be accepted or rejected, whether the organism will go toward or away from, whether it will continue the status quo or discontinue it.[9]

To the extent that these attributes are characteristic of an interest, vocational or otherwise, it can become a definite motivator of behavior.

THE DEVELOPMENT OF ATTITUDES

Although attitudes tend to be more persistent than many interests, they are not static. A child may develop certain attitudes that seem to be relatively habitual; yet, increasing age and newer experiences can instigate changes in formerly exhibited attitudes.

The Attitude Concept Every situation experienced by a child or older person is accompanied by a more or less pleasant or unpleasant feeling tone. An attitude develops from the kind of feeling tone that

9 Strong, E. K., "Satisfactions and Interests," *The American Psychologist,* Vol. 13, No. 8, August, 1958, pp. 452–453.

habitually is associated with a person, a thing, a condition, or a situation. It can be said, therefore, that an attitude is a tendency, an inclination, or a readiness to move toward or away from elements within the individual himself or external to him and reflecting his past experiences with them.

One's attitude toward a situation depends on the extent to which inner stimuli motivate one toward or away from participating in an activity. Attitudes are not taught in the sense that skills are, for example. Rather are they acquired as a result of an understanding and appreciation of stimulating circumstances and accompanying emotional responses. Often, a child is unaware of the attitude that motivates his behavior in a particular situation.

An attitude may be present but temporarily inactive. It then becomes an aspect of one's *disposition*. One child is described as having a sunny disposition, another as being extremely sensitive or "cranky." What is meant is that the first child does not become unduly disturbed by unpleasant happenings, but that the latter seems "to look for trouble." If the child's attitudes are accompanied by strong feeling tones, they are referred to as *sentiments*. Some little girls, for example, "love" ice cream, a favorite toy, or a person who gives them much attention; they "hate" beets, a toy which refuses to operate correctly, or an adult who disapproves of their actions.

The child's developing attitudes are specific and dynamic. They influence his thoughts, interests, and overt behavior. They vary with his changing interests and experiences. Hence they are the fundamental concomitants of his personality pattern in relation to other people. Insofar as a child's attitudes show themselves in his overt behavior, they become the bases of his reputation among associates. Moreover, to the extent that he achieves awareness of what others think of him, his attitudes are affected by this knowledge, either constructively or destructively. For example, a child who is accustomed to receiving approval of his conduct from his elders, especially parents and teachers, is likely to develop outgoing attitudes, accompanied by further efforts to obtain commendation for his actions. Another child, who consciously or unconsciously has engaged in adult-disapproved behavior, may earn the reputation of being mischievous or uncooperative. If he continually is blamed, sometimes unjustly, for whatever goes wrong in his immediate environment, he is likely to give up trying to please what he considers to be unreasonable adult requests. He assumes an attitude of not caring what people think of him; he may engage consciously in undesirable behavior, believing that since he has the name, he might as well enjoy the game.

Sources of Children's Atttiudes A child's thoughts, interests, feelings, and actions constantly are being influenced (1) by experiences in the home, school, and community, and (2) by his exposure to media of communication, such as newspapers, books, radio, television, and motion pictures. Advertisements may have a strong impact on his attitude toward available merchandise. As environmental changes occur, so may the individual's attitudes change from what they formerly were. His new attitude patterns may be acquired consciously or unconsciously. The young child whose needs are cared for by his mother develops an attitude of going to her with troubles. If his mother's illness, for instance, necessitates his having his wants met by another person, he soon shifts his attitude of leaning on his mother to this other person.

CULTURAL INFLUENCES The culture of a people is a potent influence on attitude development. The child acquires his cultural attitudes first from his parents and later from others in his immediate environment. Children's feelings become ambivalent, and there may be a conflict of attitudes if the child too suddenly is exposed to attitudes that differ markedly from those common to his home culture. To illustrate, a child of foreign-born parents may be accustomed, during his preschool years, to regard his father as the head of the house, to whom his mother, as well as the other members of the family, are subservient. It is difficult for him when he enters school to understand and appreciate the fact that American children tend to defer to their mothers' rather than to their fathers' wishes. The child may experience a conflict of attitudes which can become intensified if he attempts in the home to follow the example of his schoolmates, thereby pitting his father against his mother.

Other cultural attitudes that may need to be changed with the widening of cultural horizons are food tastes, religious views, and attitudes toward ethnic background. Racial, national, and religious prejudices and definite political affiliation may be experienced by the child who has lived with and absorbed the attitudes of adults who possess narrow, self-satisfied attitudes toward people who differ from themselves in any of these respects. Sometimes, in spite of opportunities to appreciate the fundamental likenesses among people, an individual may carry into his adult associations with them those biased attitudes which he acquired during childhood years.

SUGGESTION AS A STIMULATOR OF ATTITUDE The developed attitudes referred to in the foregoing and many others are molded as the result of imitation and suggestion. The attitudes of his parents, teachers, playmates, and other admired individuals exercise a potent influence on a child's attitudes. Without recognizing the reasons for his attitude, he reflects the likes and dislikes, the points of view or beliefs of those with whom he is closely associated. A boy quotes what his father says as if it were his own attitude, even though he may not fully understand the import of what he is saying. A girl defends her mother's cooking or housekeeping procedures against any possible criticisms.

As the child experiences various relationships with the adults and young people in his environment, suggestions by word or gesture exert a powerful influence on his attitudes. Dorothy's parents did not deem it wise to reprimand her in public for disapproved behavior. Hence, if she did anything undesirable, one of the parents would indicate disapproval by raising the eyebrows. The child developed the habit of watching for this sign of disapproval. This attitude has persisted throughout Dorothy's adulthood. She is extremely sensitive to people's facial expression. There are times, however, when a child is in so highly emotionalized a state or so eager to follow his own pattern of behavior that his response to suggestion runs counter to the one intended. A boy or girl, for example, may have definite play likes and dislikes. So strong is his or her attitude, that any suggestions by playmates to engage in one of the disliked games is met with violent opposition and perhaps withdrawal from the group.

Stages in Attitude Development   Infants and young babies experience simple feelings of physical well-being or discomfort. During his first year, the happy, healthy child displays outgoing, possibly affectionate, behavior toward those adults who form his narrow environment, but may be relatively withdrawing with strangers. From the ages of one through four, the child shows attitudes of wanting approval and of possessiveness. He may develop an attitude of resentment toward any attention given by his parents or close relatives and friends to other children. These are the years during which a child tends to develop a kind of negative attitude. He is likely to iterate, "No, No," shake his head vigorously, or push away from any suggestion offered either in words or actions. In spite of the seeming resistance, however, he may accede in action to the suggestion which he apparently negates so violently.

During elementary school years, the child becomes more independent; he acquires definite attitudes toward himself and toward other individuals, conditions, and situations. He also is more likely to appreciate his own attitudes and those of his teachers and schoolmates. He may develop strong likes and dislikes, and he continues to seek approval of his behavior. His attitudes tend to be relatively specific. The primary school child knows that he should obey his father and mother, but he still may need to learn that he should have a similar attitude toward his teacher, as a parent substitute. George, a kindergarten child, was an energetic little boy whose parents had encouraged him to participate in much physical activity. Consequently, he continually wanted to run around the classroom. When he was admonished by the teacher to sit quietly, his answer was, "My mommy and daddy let me play a lot. I don't have to obey you." It took considerable effort on the part of both the parents and the teacher to convince George that he must develop an attitude of obeying the teacher as well as his parents. Some children learn this so well that they acquire the attitude of accepting their teachers' dicta rather than their parents'! As adolescents, they even may be inclined to give greater weight to the expressed attitudes of peer associates than they do to the opinions of their own family members.

By the time a child approaches adolescent years, he probably has developed many generalized attitudes, some desirable and others undesirable. These are not always understood by adults. They sometimes wonder how a young person who, as a child, was agreeable, cooperative, and amenable to suggestion, suddenly can develop such "queer notions." They fail to realize that the preadolescent and early adolescent years constitute a struggle for increasing independence and self-realization. A young person's developing attitudes toward himself, his associates, and environmental regulations and restrictions are no more than symptoms of this struggle. He either conforms or he does not conform to expected patterns of behavior. He may view himself as a potential adult rather than as a child. He is driven by the physical and emotional changes that are taking place within him to want to behave as an adult and to be treated as if he were one. Yet his relative immaturity causes him to become confused as he attempts to transform his growing attitudes into satisfying activity.

One preadolescent or adolescent becomes very much concerned about the ills of other people. He wants to participate in projects having to do with the amelioration of unfavorable living conditions, even beyond his physical or mental ability to do so. Another young person has the urge to engage in adult activities such as smoking, drinking, or emulating adult social activities. These are expressions of adolescent growing-up attitudes. Often the realization does not fulfill his expectation, and the young adventurer in adult living must reconstruct his attitudes toward himself and his place in society.

Because of adverse home conditions, a young person unfortunately may need to assume attitudes of responsibility for family welfare long before his maturational pattern has prepared him for their assumption. Moreover, an adolescent, in his relations with adults, can come to believe that the latter are narrow-minded and intolerant, and that he possesses a more understanding attitude toward conditions and situations, especially those in which he is involved. Incidentally, the average preadolescent's or adolescent's attitudes can be extremely prejudiced in favor of his personal needs and desires. The resulting conflicts between adults and the young person may take a heavy toll in the form of resentment or the development of antisocial attitudes by him.

Attitude and Opinion   An opinion is supposed to be the expression of a deep-seated attitude. Too often, an expressed opinion represents mere verbalization rather than a possessed attitude. A young child repeats, parrot-fashion, the opinions he hears expressed by his elders, often without understanding the meaning of what he says. An older child, adolescent, or adult may agree with the opinions of others in order to avoid arousing antagonism toward himself or hurting the feelings of others. One young person expresses approval of another's choice of clothing, for example, lest he lower the self-esteem of the other.

A developing individual may not understand the motivation that underlies his behavior. This makes it difficult to distinguish between an expressed opinion and an attitude. The pupil may seem to be interested in study and participation in school activities for their own sake, when, as a matter of fact, his attitude is one of gaining prestige among his schoolmates from his behavior. An individual may express the opinion that those who *can* should engage in projects aimed at the welfare of those who *cannot* help themselves. This is a socially approved attitude. In his daily activities, however, his behavior is motivated by an attitude of selfishness and self-interest. The child, as well as the older person, attempts to rationalize his beliefs or actual attitudes by expressing opinions that will gain the approval of his associates which would be lacking if he said what he really believed.

Uncertainty about the degree to which expressed opinion coincides with actual attitudes is characteristic of many opinion polls. The purpose of a poll usually is to determine attitudes toward issues that deal with community affairs. Individuals differ in their reactions to them in spite of the fact that some polls yield reliable data. A person may believe that he is expressing a valid opinion, but discovers that he possesses no definite attitude toward an issue and is relying on an uninformed snap judgment. It is possible for an individual to be reluctant to express his real attitude lest it be too different from the opinions of others in the situation. One of the dangers inherent in responses given to questions asked by an inquiring reporter, for example, is that relatively uninformed lay people may attempt to express their opinion concerning technical matters. In such situations, if a general concensus is accepted as the criterion for "truth," four out of five answers could be in the area of unsupported opinion; one opinion (that of the expert) would be in accordance with fact, but would not be given its correct status. For opinion polls to have value, projected questions need to be answered honestly and sincerely by persons whose attitudes are rooted in knowledge of verifiable data.

QUESTIONS AND TOPICS FOR DISCUSSION

1. List some of your adolescent interests that were latent during middle childhood years.

2. Name several of your strong interests. For how long a time have you experienced them? How did they start?

3. What may be the interest lacks of a young person who is talented in a field such as mathematics or science?

4. Are there any work activities which for you take on the nature of play? Explain.

5. How have your reading interests changed during the past five years? Explain any changes.

6. As a class project, compare the television habits of your classmates.

7. List some of the motion picture programs available in your community that have educational significance.

8. If you have made a vocational choice, when did this occur and what motivated your decision?

9. Which of your attitudes do you believe reflect the cultural influences to which you have been exposed? Be specific.

10. Illustrate the possible differences between a verbalized opinion and a felt attitude.

11. *Special Project:* Note differences of interests among your four subjects. How do you account for any observable differences? Give

special attention to their play interests. Note their reading and television interests. What kind of motion pictures do the two older children seem to enjoy? Select three areas of day-by-day activities, and try to discover the attitude of each of your subjects toward these particular situations or conditions. What do you think their attitudes toward you are?

SELECTED REFERENCES

Allport, G., *The Nature of Prejudice.* Cambridge: Addison-Wesley Publishing Company, Inc., 1954.

Clark, K. B., *Prejudice and Your Child.* Boston: Beacon Press, Inc., 1955.

Coffin, T. E., "Television's Impact on Society," *The American Psychologist,* 10: 630–641, 1955.

Foshay, Arthur, *et al., Children's Social Values.* New York: Bureau of Publications, Teachers College, Columbia University, 1954.

Goodman, M. E., *Race Awareness in Young Children.* Cambridge, Mass.: Addison-Wesley Publishing Company, Inc., 1952.

Graduate Division Xavier University, "Of Children and Television," Report of Research conducted by Xavier University, Cincinnati, Ohio, 1951.

Hildreth, Gertrude, "The Social Interests of Young Adolescents," *Child Development,* 16: 119–121, 1945.

Himmelweit, Hilde T., Opperheim, A. N., and Vance, P., *Television and the Child: An Empirical Study of the Effect of Television on the Young Child.* New York: Oxford University Press, 1958.

Itkin, W., "Relationship between Attitudes toward Parents and Parents' Attitudes toward Children," *Journal of Genetic Psychology,* 86: 339–352, 1955.

Jersild, A. T., and Tasch, R., *Children's Interests.* New York: Bureau of Publications, Teachers College, Columbia University, 1949.

Lyness, P. I., "The Place of Mass Media in the Lives of Boys and Girls," *Journal Quarterly,* 29: 43–54, 1952.

Norvell, G. W., *What Boys and Girls Like to Read.* Morristown, N. J.: Silver Burdett Company, 1958.

Pope, B., "Socio-Economic Controls in Children's Peer Culture Prestige Values," *Genetic Psychology Monographs,* 48: 157–220, 1953.

Thorpe, L. P., Meyers, C. E., and Sea, M. R., SRA Profile Folder for "What I Like to Do," An Inventory of Children's Interests. Chicago: Science Research Associates, Inc., 1954.

14

THE SELF AND PERSONALITY DEVELOPMENT

IN PREVIOUS CHAPTERS attention has been directed to the child's needs, urges, and drives, and the various ways in which he attempts to satisfy these motivations of behavior. His gradually formed habits of thinking, feeling, and doing, in light of his developing personal and social interests and attitudes, are aimed at the evolvement of the self-concept and set the pattern of his personality.

THE CONCEPT OF SELF

An adequate concept of the self is basic to an interpretation of personality. In any discussion of the self, terms such as the following are commonly used to denote the various aspects of selfhood: "self-consciousness," "self-realization," "self-preservation," "self-confidence," "self-assertion," "self-dependence," and "self-esteem."

The Beginnings of Self-Realization   The child's gaining of insight into his personal qualities is a slow, difficult process that may not be achieved adequately until adulthood, if ever. The *self* or *ego* can be interpreted as including all an individual's feelings and actions as these emerge from his needs, wants, and interests. The egotist is concerned only with the fulfillment of his own desires and interests. The term "egotist" thus interpreted applies to the behavior pattern of the young child, since to him all environmental elements are regarded as catering to his wishes.

Even as the child acquires greater social consciousness, he probably can be considered to be an egoist. He still is concerned primarily with the fulfillment of personal needs and urges, but he also is aware of the drives that motivate the behavior of others about him. He learns to accede to their wishes, recognizing to some degree, at least, their rights in relation to his own. Insofar as the child gradually acquires an understanding of human interrelationships, his growing self-awareness becomes self-realization in that he now attempts, consciously or unconsciously, to fulfill self-satisfactions within the framework of the social good.

The Freudian Concept of Self   Sigmund Freud explained the development of personality according to a self-concept mechanism that protects the *libido* or basic instinctual energy (see Chapter 15). He includes in his explanation of the self-concept three systems: the *id*, the *ego*, and the *superego*,[1] which represent three stages of the developing self-concept.

THE ID   In light of his clinical work, Freud became aware of the effect upon his patients of the unconscious elements of their mental life. Consequently, he postulated the concept of the *id* as that which "contains everything that is inherited that is present at birth, that is fixed in the constitution." [2] The *id* gives free discharge of energy and the satisfaction of bodily needs. Awareness of self emerges from the id. It is regarded as the source of instinctual energy and is sometimes referred to as the "little man" who directs one's energies.

Instinctual energy seeks many diverse outlets, thereby giving rise to conscious or unconscious struggles between differing impulses. According to Freud, all behavior represents such struggles which, for the most part, are unconscious. The sleepy child, for example, feels the need to go to bed, but he does not want to miss the activities in which he is participating with other members of the family, and a struggle ensues. Al-

[1] Freud, S., *An Outline of Psychology*. New York: W. W. Norton Company, copyright 1949.
[2] *Ibid.*, p. 14.

though the functioning of the id changes with the child's increasing maturity, it remains an impulsive, relatively unconscious and irrational behavior motivator.

THE EGO   The ego system becomes active as the child becomes increasingly aware of the effect upon his instinctual impulses of environmental influences. Anna Freud explains the *ego* as a differentiated sense of awareness that develops when a young child's needs are not met.[3]

The child becomes aware of the barriers set by the external world to his gratification of immediate impulses. The mother or the mother substitute is regarded by the child as the source of his gratifications. If or when she does not meet his needs or wants immediately, he begins to recognize an "I" and a "not I." Awareness comes of a differentiation between the self and the nonself or of the ego in a social world that is dependent for the fulfillment of needs first upon the "mother" and later upon other persons in the child's environment. This awareness represents an increasing maturity that causes the child to seek those perhaps delayed gratifications which will earn for him greater ultimate satisfaction in light of his relationships with other people about him. Freud does make the point, however, that the ego is concerned primarily with self-gratification rather than with concern about the feelings or welfare of others.

THE SUPEREGO   According to the Freudian theory, the *superego* emerges as a result of the young child's early awareness of his own body and his relationships with his parents. The superego can be said to function as the child's conscience or the moral code which he has developed for himself in light of the strict discipline he may have experienced during his early years. The superego also can be regarded as the ego-ideal or the child's understanding of what his parents and others regard as morally good.

As the child matures, he comes to understand and accept certain moral and ethical codes and sets of values common to his culture. To the extent that the maturing child or older individual recognizes the worth of behavior taboos he attempts to regulate his own behavior accordingly. This adherence to rules and regulations apart from immediate pressure from other individuals lies in the superego. Much of such self-regulation of behavior is unconscious, although consciousness of guilt may be provoked by any failure to guide one's behavior according to cultural taboos

[3] Freud, Anna, "Some Remarks on Infant Observation," in Ruth S. Eisler *et al.* (eds.), *The Psychoanalytic Study of the Child,* Vol. 8, pp. 9–19. New York: International University Press, 1953.

in which one believes. Anxiety arises when instinctual needs are so strong that it is difficult to compromise between their gratification and standards of conduct which are recognized to be desirable.

Constant conflict takes place among the id, ego, and superego or, to categorize these concepts according to an older classification, among the "body, mind, and spirit." The relationships that exist among the basic id, the more socialized ego, and the "restraining" superego constitute the elements of personality structure. According to the psychoanalytic theory, by the time a child has reached the age of six, the child's fundamental personality pattern is relatively fixed, and thereafter is subject to only slight modification.[4]

The Importance of the Self   From early childhood, an individual is concerned about the self. The baby or young child is dependent on others for his welfare; he has little confidence in himself. As he matures, his behavior is marked by a growing attitude of self-assertion. He strives to gain self-confidence in the management of his own affairs and to shift from dependence on others to dependence on self. To the extent that his strivings meet the approval of his associates, he develops satisfying self-esteem and comes to recognize himself as an individual, like, yet different from, every other individual—he has achieved the self-realization that is fundamental to the development of his personality pattern.

A study was made by Perkins[5] of the influence of four factors concerning perceptions of children's self-concepts. Included in the study were social-emotional climate, in-service training of teachers, teacher acceptance of self and others, and changes of children's self-concepts on two grade levels: the fourth and the sixth. Evidence of a child's self-concept and his ideal self was obtained by having 251 children in seven elementary schools in Maryland perform a self-sort and ideal sort three times within a six-months' period. The influences of the factors on changes in children's self-concepts are:

1. The self-concepts and ideal selves of children become increasingly significantly congruent through time.

[4] For a further discussion of the concept of self in light of personality development, see Watson, Robert I., *Psychology of the Child,* Chapter 5, New York: John Wiley and Sons, Inc., 1959; Baldwin, Alfred, *Behavior and Development in Childhood,* Chapter 22, New York: Dryden-Holt, Henry Holt and Company, 1955; Brandt, Richard M., "Self: Missing Link for Understanding Behavior," *Mental Hygiene,* pp. 24–33, January, 1957; and Anderson, Camilla M., "The Self-Image: A Theory of the Dynamics of Behavior," *Mental Hygiene,* pp. 227–244, April, 1952.

[5] Perkins, Hugh V., "Factors Influencing Change in Children's Self-Concepts," *Child Development,* 29: 203–230, 1958.

2. The self-ideal self congruencies of girls generally are significantly greater than those of boys.

3. Sixth-grade children and children whose teachers have completed child study show significantly greater self-ideal self congruency than do children, respectively, in the fourth grade and those whose teachers have never participated in this child study program.

4. There is little or no relationship between changes in children's self-ideal self congruency and (a) changes in their school achievement, and (b) changes in their acceptance by peers.[6]

Although the various aspects of the self cannot be measured exactly, they can be modified to the extent that they are affected by interactions among themselves and with other selves. During his developing years the child responds to the impact on himself of various external forces: social customs, rules and regulations, moral standards, and ethical codes (see Chapter 16). The child is sensitive to adult attitudes and tries to pattern his behavior accordingly. He is motivated to evaluate himself in light of adult standards. His felt need to pattern himself in imitation of his adult associates may or may not help his personality development, depending on the kinds of models they provide for him.

By the time the young person reaches adolescence or early adulthood, he should have acquired adequate self-dependence to be able to meet adult responsibilities. Emotion-disturbing crises, such as sudden illness or misfortune, can cause a loss of self-determining abilities, however, and result in the individual's returning to a state of dependence on others for his personal well-being. The achievement of personal strength to guide one's own destiny is an extremely significant aspect of personality development. Self-realization connotes much more than mere self-awareness. The young person who recognizes his strengths and weaknesses can be enabled by his knowledge of himself to adjust adequately to life's successes as well as encountered vicissitudes.

THE STRUCTURE OF PERSONALITY

A relatively consistent pattern of integration takes place among the child's various characteristics, as he passes through the many aspects of change that he experiences during his development from the prenatal period through childhood and adolescence to adulthood. His all-over pattern of physical, mental, and emotional qualities at any stage of matura-

[6] *Ibid.*, p. 230.

tion is regarded generally as his *personality*. Both the layman and the psychologist appreciate the relationship between an individual's personal qualities and his demonstrated degree of success in life relationships. Their recognition of the fundamental bases of personality differ, however.

Lay Attitudes toward Personality   Lay persons often use the term "personality" loosely to evaluate a child's or an adult's superficial characteristics that are liked, admired, or respected, or that are disliked, disapproved, or viewed with contempt. The layman tends to describe a person as good or bad, cheerful or grouchy, pleasant or annoying, attractive or repulsive, adjusted or maladjusted. If one's personality is found to be unattractive or nonstimulating, he often is regarded as "having no personality." Some people appear to identify personality with the person himself, as for example, in saying, "He is a stimulating personality."

Interest in achieving a socially desirable personality has been a common concern since earliest times. Leaders in successive stages of culture have recognized and attempted to explain differences among people in observable personality qualities. Amongst early peoples, various methods were employed to insure their producing children whose personality patterns would be socially acceptable. Some of these earliest methods included exposure of physically unfit children and the use of incantations and charms. Later, astrology, phrenology, and anthropometric measurements were utilized to determine the kind of personality a child might be expected to develop.

Modern advertising media place considerable emphasis on the relationship that is supposed to exist between an individual's personality and matters dealing with his appearance: care of teeth, use of deodorants, hair-do, general grooming, and style of clothing. Advertisers stress not only the effect on others of one's maintaining an attractive appearance, but also the self-bolstering results of believing that one is physically pleasing to his associates. Without minimizing the value of desirable external appearance, it is important that we recognize the superficiality of the general lay attitude toward what constitute the fundamentals of personality.

Unfortunately, group standards, individual ideals, and personal prejudices too often affect lay attitudes toward overt manifestations of personality characteristics. It also is difficult for an individual, especially a child, to evaluate his own personality objectively. The child derives his concept of "good" from the attitudes displayed by his elders toward his behavior. He is good if he obeys his parents and teachers, refrains from getting into mischief, and avoids experiencing any of those many "accidents" to which children are prone. The child is not concerned about his personality, as such, but he may be extremely sensitive to what his elders think of him as compared with their judgment about other children.

Little Ann's father constantly called to her attention various forms of misbehavior observable in other children. In each instance he admonished her not to behave in the disapproved fashion. Consequently, Ann developed the habit of watching other children and deciding whether or not she dared follow their example. She had a strong desire to earn her father's approval. Hence, unconsciously, she was accustomed to view herself in relation to other children as one who either did or did not imitate them. It was difficult for her to regard herself as an individual with personal attitudes toward desirable behavior. It was not until Ann had reached late adolescence that she was able to guide her behavior according to consciously formed standards of right and wrong, rather than in comparison with the actions of her associates.

In light of childish experiences similar to Ann's, it is important that anyone involved in working with children and young people gain as objective and clear an understanding as possible of personality. The parent, the teacher, and the religious and community leader need to learn to interpret personality—its meaning, its relation to human interactions, and the factors that condition its patterning.

Psychological Interpretation of Personality Personality is not a "certain something" or an indefinable quality that a child or older person either possesses or lacks. Yet, to define it exactly is almost an impossible task. Personality includes all aspects of development: physical, motor, mental, emotional, social, moral, and ethical. It is an abstract or theoretical generalization, connoting the qualitative nature of development. Personality is more than the sum total of its components. The personality pattern represents the interrelating and integrating of personal characteristics and the degree to which they influence one another and the individual's behavior.

According to Munn, "Personality may be defined as the most characteristic integration of an individual's structures and activities. The integration is characteristic in a dual sense. Because of its uniqueness, it *differentiates one individual from another*. It is also fairly consistent, representing the *customary integration of a given individual's structures and activities*." [7]

[7] Munn, Norman L., *The Evolution and Growth of Human Behavior,* p. 448. Boston: Houghton Mifflin Company, copyright 1955.

The term "personality" is derived from the Greek word *prosopon,* a term used to identify the mask worn by a Greek actor to signify the kind of role he was enacting. A child tends to exhibit a variety of character-istics in his relations with others. To the extent that there is unity of response he is displaying his personality. Insofar as he tends to behave differently toward his parents, his playmates, and strangers, he can be said to give evidence of differing facets of his personality. He is showing differing faces or masks. Any one of these reactions may or may not be a true indication of his inner feelings, since personality can be regarded as a complex of relatively flexible and modifiable components.

In attempting to define personality, psychologists have stressed vari-ously the physiological, biological, and adjustive aspects. It is necessary to recognize and appreciate factors in past and present cultures that exer-cise potent influences on a child's biologically inherited constitution and innate potentialities. It is only through such knowledge that one can gain an understanding of the many subtle elements that are inherent in the child's developing dynamic personality pattern. Landis says: "Personality is dynamic, a growing entity. Physiologically, it is vested with the capacity for maturation. Except as mutilated by environment, physical traits fol-low their predestined course from childhood to maturity. Psychologically, it is plastic, capable of an infinite number of modifications by external stimuli. Sociologically, it is dependent on the group to provide the pat-terns of development, for human nature is a group product." [8]

The total, dynamic developing organism in its total environment is implied in the functioning of the child's personality. The functioning whole is characterized by physique, ambitions, attitudes, hopes, purposes, ideals, intelligence, habits, knowledge, emotions, and standards of values. These significant attributes of the individual determine his social stimulus value. Beginning in early childhood, the individual, throughout his life, constantly is trying to adjust his own wants and interests to the needs and desires of others, either with benefit to himself and others (good adjust-ment), or having personally and socially harmful effects (maladjust-ment). From this point of view, personality can be interpreted as *the dynamic integration of psychophysical factors that are fundamental to an individual's adjustments as he reacts to environmental stimuli in light of inner compulsions.*

[8] By permission from *Adolescence and Youth: The Process of Maturing,* 2nd ed., p. 73, by Landis, P. H. New York: Copyright 1952 by McGraw-Hill Book Company, Inc.

THE DYNAMIC NATURE OF PERSONALITY

The fact that the child's personality is dynamic and is therefore subject to change cannot be denied. How these changes come about and to what extent inner drives can be modified in light of external factors of influence are matters that challenge the careful study of all who are concerned with child-rearing. Breckenridge and Vincent comment on this matter as follows:

> Exactly how personality develops as a product of the interaction between the inner impulses and needs of the individual and the play of his environment upon him needs much study. We do not yet know how parental influence can be made to stand against gang influence, or when it should. We do not know as much as we should about how to produce or to control aggressiveness, or how much of it is desirable at the various stages of development. We are only beginning to understand the influence of physical vigor upon personality functioning, or the effect of the various grades of intellect. We have made good beginnings in investigations into the effect of cultural or community demands upon personal and social development, and in the effect of routine demands, and of creative opportunity upon the unfolding of native capacity.[9]

Degree of Integration Although personality is an integrated unity, the degree of integration can vary in the same child from time to time, and from one child to another. A child cannot be expected always to be consistent in his behavior. Environmental conditions are always changing. Home, school, and community conditions vary as well as the child's reactions to them. (See Chapters 19 and 20.) Sometimes his horizons broaden so quickly that his relative immaturity causes him to be unprepared to understand and respond adequately to the stimuli to which he is exposed. Too often the world becomes a mass of blooming confusion for him. Behavior patterns that served him well in a narrower environment now are inadequate; his personality seems to have undergone a complete change. Mothers, recognizing the difference without realizing its reason, are wont to say, "I do not know my own child." Then they will list what to them are undesirable alterations in personality, such as irritability, quick temper, moodiness, daydreaming, and other unaccustomed reactions. The fact probably is that the child no longer knows himself. He is struggling to develop a consciousness of himself in a new world. He is experimenting with new forms of behavior; he may be trying to regain the confidence in himself he formerly had and achieve security in his new experience.

[9] Breckenridge, M. E., and Vincent, E. L., *Child Development*, 4th ed., pp. 436–437. Philadelphia: W. B. Saunders Company, copyright 1960.

The child becomes temporarily resistant or aggressive, or unduly submissive and apathetic. His personality pattern is undergoing dynamic changes. Yet certain consistencies are present. If he is not thrown into a new and different world too quickly, he usually can depend on the fact that those personality qualities that served him well in his preschool days will come to his rescue amidst what might seem to be cataclysmic conditions.

We know that even during early years, children's personalities differ. One child tends to behave in a given manner under certain conditions, and another child acts differently. Hospital nurses claim that even newborn infants give evidence of differing potentialities of personality development. Before the environment has had an opportunity to influence the infants in the nursery, one will cry continuously, another will not; one will seem to be apathetic, another will appear to be alert and energetic. Various reasons have been assigned to these differences. Hereditary factors may play their role, as may experiences during the prenatal period. Psychoanalysts stress the effect on the neonate of the birth trauma.

As children develop year by year through their first six years, various personality characteristics begin to show themselves. Quadruplets born in 1959 gave evidence of this before they were one year old. The mother of the Kajouras quadruplets observed personality differences among the four children by the time they had reached their first birthday. (See Figure 89.) For example, she noted that Anthea giggled a great deal;

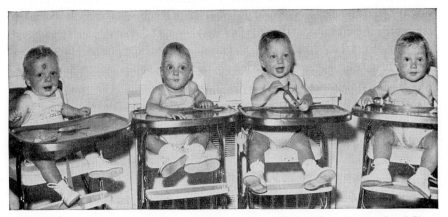

United Press International Photo

Figure 89. The Kajouras Quadruplets Celebrate Their First Birthday
(From Left—Anthea, Paul, Leon, Michael)

Paul was alert and easily stimulated to laughter; Leon was generally quiet and serious; and Michael tended to fake cries and laughter.[10] At this early age each was displaying a personality pattern peculiar to himself.

Any nursery school, kindergarten, or first-grade teacher realizes that there are as many different personalities in the room as there are children. A child early gains the reputation among his elders and playmates of being talkative or taciturn, cheerful or grouchy, aggressive or submissive, unafraid or timid. Natural tendencies, imitation of adults, and preschool experiences account for many of the personality qualities of six-year-olds. Sometimes, at this age or older, it is difficult to discover the subtle forces that are effective in molding personality patterns.

Consistency of the personality pattern is desirable in that a person's general behavior tendencies can be predicted in given situations by his associates, especially if the qualities exhibited are socially acceptable. For example, the child who habitually is prompt in the performance of designated chores, who is punctual, cheerful, and generally dependable, is a boon to a parent or a teacher. Yet, too great adherence even to desirable habits of behavior may be dangerous, insofar as an individual thereby becomes resistant to change or "goes to pieces" in a situation where his habit cannot function adequately. Grace, for example, was reared in a rigid home environment in which lack of promptness in the exercise of duty took on almost the proportions of a deadly sin. Consequently, Grace learned to pride herself on her extreme punctuality in all situations. It became almost a fetish with her. One day, however, she was delayed, by traffic conditions, in reaching her high school on time. She had an examination during her first period. Although she was only a few minutes late, she became so emotionally disturbed that her performance on the test was far below her average work. Consistency is an asset, but also needed is the ability to respond flexibly to changing conditions. Otherwise, the child may become confused, fearful, impaired in judgment, or emotionally disturbed.

Personality Traits   Although personality is generally regarded as a functioning, interrelated whole or *Gestalt,* there are specific differences in the various qualities, characteristics, or traits that comprise the whole personality pattern. For example, one child is taller than another, or more cooperative.

At one time psychologists regarded a trait as a personality dimension

[10] For more detailed information see a special article in the *World-Telegram and Sun,* New York, June 24, 1960.

that acted independently of the others. Modern psychologists hold that various traits interact with one another and thereby affect the whole personality. The tall girl wears clothes well; she takes pride in her appearance. Yet the fact that she is taller than many men may cause her to be embarrassed at a dance, for instance. This attitude can affect her personality if she envies smaller "cuddly" girls and regards herself as a social liability.

A trait can be interpreted as a dynamic quality or characteristic that does not function in isolation but combines with other traits into a unique totality of behavior motivators, and has social stimulus value. Behavior can be described in light of trait functioning. Observers are able to predict how a person can be expected to behave insofar as he tends to display certain traits habitually. We are wont to refer to our associates as generally honest or dishonest, industrious or lazy, generous or miserly, aggressive or submissive, and the like. It may be, however, as we evaluate anyone's traits we are basing our opinion on his behavior in certain situations; we do not know how he reacts in other situations. A child, for example, may seem to his teacher to be most cooperative. In the home that same child might be very demanding. Moreover, trait names describe forms of behavior reaction but do not explain the reasons for their display. Why, for instance, does a child sometimes act differently in school from his accustomed mode of behavior in the home?

Although the situation in which an individual finds himself can influence the functioning of a personality trait, certain traits tend to be deep-rooted in or basic to the personality structure. In the English language there are well-nigh 200 terms that represent personality dimensions or traits that vary in organization and relative strength. This number does not include sets of synonyms to describe human behavior. Woodworth and Marquis [11] reduced the large number of common traits into a list of twelve primary traits and their opposites, as follows:

Primary Traits	Opposites
1. Easygoing, genial, warm, generous	Inflexible, cold, timid, hostile, shy
2. Intelligent, independent, reliable	Foolish, unreflective, frivolous
3. Emotionally stable, realistic, steadfast	Neurotic, evasive, emotionally changeable

[11] Woodworth, Robert S., and Marquis, Donald G., *Psychology*, 5th ed., pp. 91–92. Copyright, 1947, by Holt, Rinehart and Winston, Inc., and reprinted with their permission.

Primary Traits	*Opposites*
4. Dominant, ascendant, self-assertive	Submissive, self-effacing
5. Placid, cheerful, sociable, talkative	Sorrowful, depressed, seclusive, agitated
6. Sensitive, tenderhearted, sympathetic	Hard-boiled, poised, frank, unemotional
7. Trained and cultured mind, esthetic	Boorish, uncultured
8. Conscientious, responsible, painstaking	Emotionally dependent, impulsive, irresponsible
9. Adventurous, carefree, kind	Inhibited, reserved, cautious, withdrawn
10. Vigorous, energetic, persistent, quick	Languid, slack, daydreaming
11. Emotionally hypersensitive, high-strung, excitable	Phlegmatic, tolerant
12. Friendly, trustful	Suspicious, hostile

Other psychologists also have attempted to reduce the number of traits into their primary form. Thurstone identifies seven primary trait factors: a pressure for activity, masculinity-femininity, impulsiveness, dominance, emotional stability, sociability, and reflectiveness.

As a child's displayed personality traits are modified by social reactions to them, or by their success or failure in satisfying his needs and interests, he tends to develop some relatively permanent and distinctive modes of behavior motivation. Furthermore, although the developing child's personality is more than a combination of many traits or characteristics, one trait may seem to dominate his behavior in such a way that other traits seem to be insignificant. A pupil, for example, may be so ambitious, so eager to excel, that this behavior motivator becomes so strong that he may disregard personal appearance and other needs, such as sleep, in his efforts to master his studies. Another pupil, motivated by the same urge, although an honest individual in money matters, may attempt to lie or cheat his way to the head of the class. Either pupil may have other admirable qualities but they sink into insignificance in light of his obsessive ambition.

Attempts to Explain Personality   Many attempts have been made to elucidate organized types of personality. We already have referred to the Freudian concept of self in the personality structure. Other writers have attempted to explain personality according to the predominance of certain trait combinations. One of the earliest attempts was that of Hippocrates (400 B.C.) who grouped personality types according to the four humors: sanguine, choleric, melancholic, and phlegmatic. This theory has been discarded, but it slightly resembles present-day acceptance of a relationship between the functioning of the endocrine glands and emotional states, and endocrine types of personality.[12]

Emphasis has been placed on physical types by Kretschmer, and Sheldon and his associates. According to Kretschmer [13] there are four physical types: *athletic, asthenic, pyknic,* and *dysplastic.* Recent studies of physique disprove his belief that there are these distinct types. Sheldon and his associates [14] photographed male college students from various angles. Anthropometric measurements derived from the photographs led to the conclusion that the three dimensions of variation are: *endomorphy* (abdominal prominence), *mesomorphy* (muscular prominence), and *ectomorphy* (fragile structure, as of bones). Comparisons between physique and personality were then organized on a seven-point scale in the form of somatotypes. This system probably provides little justification for predicting personality on the basis of physique.

A relatively popular explanation of personality is contained in Jung's theory that human beings fall into two major categories in light of their attitude toward people and situations. *Extroverts* are sociably adaptable and interested in other people; *introverts* are socially shy, sensitive, or retiring. This theory does not provide for the categorization of normal people who may display behavior that can be regarded as either extrovert or introvert. Consequently, a third term, *ambivert,* has been added to describe individuals who do not fit completely into either of the original groupings. Classification as extrovert or introvert applies more generally to the mentally ill than to relatively well-adjusted individuals.

No one of these or other theories seems adequate, in its original form, to explain personality. Each has contributed something, however. More study of children's developing personality patterns is needed to achieve a better understanding of the functioning of human characteristics.

---

[12] See Cannon, W. B., *Bodily Changes in Pain, Hunger, Fear, and Rage,* New York: Appleton-Century-Crofts, Inc., 1929; Berman, L., *The Glands Regulating Personality,* New York: The Macmillan Company, 1929; Cameron, A. T., *Recent Advances in Endocrinology,* London: Churchill, 1933.

[13] Kretschmer, E., *Physique and Character,* New York: Harcourt, Brace and Company, 1923.

[14] Sheldon, W. H., Stevens, S. S., and Tucker, W. B., *The Varieties of Human Physique,* New York: Harper and Brothers, 1940; Sheldon, W. H., *et al., Atlas of Men,* New York: Harper and Brothers, 1954.

PERSONALITY DEVELOPMENT

Since the personality pattern is so complex, it is difficult to trace its sequential development. Psychologists differ as to when a more or less patterned personality structure begins to show itself. Some writers, as we have indicated, seem to believe that personal differences begin to show themselves at birth; others claim that no definite structuring takes place until the child develops social awareness. Certain factors of influence, both within and outside the child, begin to affect him early. In addition, differences in behavior are evidenced early and seem to maintain some consistency during the developmental years.

Factors Influencing Personality Development   The child's personality is built through the constant interaction between his own potentialities and limitations and environmental experiences. Various combinations of outer influences on inner reactions result in various forms of personality integration.

INNER FACTORS OF INFLUENCE   A child's behavior is affected by his physical structure, physiological condition, and mental, emotional, and motor potentialities. His own awareness of the various aspects of his constitution and other people's attitudes toward them affect his reactions toward himself and become grounded in his personality pattern.

Physical strength or weakness, tallness or shortness, stoutness or slenderness, as well as color and curliness of hair, color and size of eyes, texture and condition of the skin—all these physical characteristics tend to affect his status among his associates. Undue emphasis on his attractiveness or derogatory comments concerning any aspect of his physical appearance are likely to influence a child's self-esteem. He tends to respond in kind to the favorable or unfavorable attitudes of others. The child who suffers a physical handicap is likely to display overaggression, irritability, timidity, or emotional instability, unless he receives wise guidance toward helping him live with his disability.

The child's degree of mental alertness or the extent of his possession of a special talent or aptitude wields considerable influence over the kind of behavior in which he will engage and its underlying motivation. The mentally superior as well as the mentally retarded child lives in a world of people of average intelligence to which either may find it difficult to adjust. The child's emotional reactions, of course, are tied in with the other phases of his developing self. The healthy, mentally able child usually is the emotionally well-adjusted child, unless he is the victim of too many

outside pressures. The physically frail or handicapped or mentally retarded youngster is prone to engage in socially undesirable behavior,
instigated by emotional instability or resentments.

ENVIRONMENTAL FACTORS OF INFLUENCE   All the persons, conditions, and situations that constitute a child's environment influence tre-
mendously his developing personality. Perhaps the most significant of
these are the home, the school, peer associates, and factors in his neighborhood or community that affect him more or less incidentally. Since,
in Chapters 19 and 20 we discuss the child's relationships in these areas
of experience, we shall consider here briefly a few other factors of influence.

The approved patterns of behavior common to a particular culture
can be significant molders of a child's personality. Differences in expected
behavior attitudes of boys and girls have their bases in cultural attitudes.
Also related to personality development are cultural ideals in matters
dealing with traits such as honesty, trustworthiness, cooperation, loyalty,
industry, and sex relations.

A child's personality is affected by the extent to which he is permitted to engage in personal interests or hobbies which themselves are
outgrowths of his personality development. Whether these be short-lived
or more enduring, the child who participates in such activities is likely
to be extroverted or outgoing, especially if he shares his activities with
other children.

A child's attitude toward himself can be influenced by the effect upon
himself and others of his name—either the first name or the combination
of first name and surname. Some parents cause embarrassment to boys
who are given the father's first name. The use of "Junior," "Little
———," "Young ———," or a diminutive of the name may endure
well into adolescence. A six-foot, nineteen-year-old, for example, winces
every time his relatives and close friends call him *Bobby*. "At least," he
said on one occasion, "they could call Dad 'Rob' and me 'Bob.' "

A child whose surname is difficult to pronounce may be made to
feel uncomfortable if playmates or teachers are unable to pronounce his
name correctly. A married graduate student insisted on continuing to
use her maiden name because, as she said, "Everybody murders my
married name, and I just can't take it." It happened in this instance that
his wife's attitude annoyed her husband to the point that it was a basic
cause of disagreement between them. He was an extremely sensitive
person who believed that the woman's rejection of the name was, in fact,
a rejection of himself.

Personality Patterning in the Young Child   Even during their neonatal period, differences in behavior are evidenced by children in the same family in characteristics such as muscle tone and energy, degree of coordination, kind and amount of activity, readiness to smile or to cry, and tolerance of physical discomfort. Some psychologists hold that these early responses indicate the "nucleus" of personality that results from the infant's sex and degree of glandular functioning and nervous plasticity. The early activity pattern tends to persist, according to some writers, but can be modified during the developing years by physiological and psychological changes. One child may display a relatively definite behavior pattern by the time he is three years old, but another child may not show similar consistency until he enters school, or later. A basic reason given for these differences is rooted in the degree to which the child has achieved security in social relationships.

The preschool child's personality is much affected by his attachment to his mother. His acceptance of his father depends in good part on the extent to which the latter shares in caring for his needs. The child may resent his father if he believes that the mother is giving him attention which the child considers to be rightfully his own. Some psychologists make much of the effect on the whole personality structure of the child's attitudes toward his parents. A child's relations with other siblings is discussed in Chapter 19. Much attention is given by some psychologists to the effect on personality of being an only child. Order of birth and the number of boys as compared with girls also are considered to be significant.

Children often exhibit behavior outside the home that differs from what they do and say in the home. Some children have better manners when they are among strangers than they display in the presence of close relatives or friends. If a child is reared strictly, he may, when he is away from his parents, exhibit antisocial behavior in which he would not engage in the home. Some preschool children seem to fit their behavior to adults' moods. They know their elders' particular interests and when it might be wise to follow adult wishes. They already are beginning to give evidence of personality flexibility.

Personality Development during Later Childhood   The elementary school child is a relatively independent, self-reliant, and happy child. Within the limits of innate potentialities, personality traits are being molded according to socially acceptable standards. The child dislikes what to him seems to be an unreasonable curbing of his interests, but he usually is quick to forgive and forget.

During this period, children still feel the need of security in the affection and approval of adults, although boys especially tend to discourage any demonstrations of affection from their elders. Girls, even in the fourth grade, are likely to want to "cuddle up" to a beloved adult. Both boys and girls, however, tend to evaluate themselves according to adult opinions of them as good or bad, quick or slow, helpful or lazy, and the like. Most children attempt to change adult-disapproved behavior to conform to adult standards.

A growing child's attitudes and behavior traits can be greatly influenced by his peer associates. This is the period of same-sex "best friend" relationships. Some of these friendships may be of short duration, especially among little girls. While they last, however, they tend to be extremely intense. As the two "pals" discuss with each other their interests, their hopes and fears, and their secret ambitions, they are laying the foundation of whatever philosophy of life that later becomes uniquely theirs.

Elementary school children participate freely and happily in unorganized group relationships. Teachers find that group projects are enjoyed by their pupils. It is true that disagreements and quarrels may occur, and one group may be disbanded and another formed. With intelligent adult guidance, however, these experiences in social living can be excellent molders of social realization. The formation of leadership qualities and attitudes of good sportsmanship can be encouraged that will serve children well in their later life.

Personality Development through Early Adolescence With the onset of puberty, the physical changes that have begun to occur seem to bring about radical changes in the young adolescent's personality. Ideals and personality traits admired before may seem to be babyish and to be held in contempt. A new set of values is emerging that is only partly understood by the young person. Hence he is confused and at loose ends. Although basic attitudes and behavior patterns that had become habituated during childhood years may persist, they take on new meanings and form.

The developing individual is experiencing new attitudes toward himself and in his relationship with others, especially members of the opposite sex. There often is a conflict between still needed security in the good opinion of adults and dependence on their care, and a growing attitude of independence. Boys and girls want to impress both their elders and their peer associates with their own growing self-appreciation. Yet they can be extremely sympathetic and helpful if their interest becomes involved with the misfortunes of others.

During this period of development, most young people are eager, within their potential limits, to discover all they can, not only about their immediate community, but also about far-flung places. They are generous in giving their opinions about all manner of things, conditions, and situations. Sometimes they honestly believe that they are expressing their own considered judgment, even though they merely are repeating something they have heard or read. Moreover, they will defend vehemently any opinion expressed by themselves which is contradicted by a schoolmate or other same-age associate. They may even enlist the services of adults to "prove a point," and become much chagrined if they discover that they are wrong. A favorite expression used by young people in a situation of this kind is, "Well, it could have been the way I thought it was!"

The young adolescent boy is likely to give evidence of desired leadership. The twelve-year-old wants to be an individualist, defying adult-evolved regulations. Yet, earlier training determines the extent to which the boy will give overt expression to his defiance. At this age the boy is likely to be daring, fearless, and skillful and active in sports. Although as a younger child he may have been willing to allow girls to join in his games, he now wants to participate in all-boys' activities. During this period, boys tend to regard same-age girls as nuisances; they can be tolerated but they must be excluded from boys' activities. As the boy approaches middle adolescence, his personal interests and attitudes change somewhat. He wants to be manly, and he follows the behavior patterns of an admired male adult—his father, a favorite teacher (often an athletic coach), or a friend of the family who takes an interest in him.

The girl's developing personality pattern differs somewhat from that of a boy. At twelve she is likely to admire and try to emulate a favorite adult's attitude and behavior. Interest in boys, although not always admitted, is characteristic of girls at this age. By the age of fifteen the girl probably has lost much of her admiration for older adults among her associates. She is attracted by glamour. She herself wants to be an unusually glamourous person. She engages in many activities; she is a successful leader in parties and other adolescent social activities.

Personality Traits Admired in Members of the Opposite Sex
Girls and boys as young as twelve to fourteen are keenly aware of personality qualities of their peers of the opposite sex. We present here the reports of eight fourteen-year-old teen-agers: four girls and four boys.

As we trace some of the personality trends of young adolescents, as well as of younger individuals, we must keep in mind that these are more or less general patterns. One cannot evaluate the personality pattern of any young person in light of more or less general trends. This is something that parents, teachers, and community leaders need to remember

Traits or qualities admired in boys by 14-year-old girls:

1. To be quite frank, the first thing I look for is looks. Then I make sure the boy is not a lemon. I like a boy who can protect me. I also like a boy who is possessive. The boy should be mature and well-mannered. I hate cry babies. I like boys who know when to kid around and when to be serious. I like a boy who does not whistle at another girl when I'm around. I like a boy to be well-groomed.

2. I like a boy who has good manners and isn't a show-off; a boy who acts his age and not like a baby; a boy who knows how to get along with people; a boy who would not leave me flat when he sees another girl; a boy who isn't a sloppy dresser, eater, etc.

3. Before I like a boy I look for many things. Above all he must have a pleasing personality. That is, he should be clean and neat, courteous, kind and considerate. He should show respect for me and he should be truthful. He should be a nice dresser. I don't actually care if he's good looking or not, but of course it helps, and he should not be too forward. He should be sensible and not silly.

4. The kind of boy I admire is a boy who is clean, neat, and respected. I would like the boy to be a little taller than I am and a little smarter. The boy must also have a good sense of humor and must stick up for me. He should have good manners, not be too shy, and have a good disposition. I also admire a boy who can tell the truth, is not dull, and knows how to dance.

Traits or qualities admired in girls by 14-year-old boys:

1. I like a girl who acts like a girl and not like a tomboy, a girl who is pretty and talks nice, and a girl who doesn't hang around with a bunch of boys or tough girls.

2. I admire a girl's appearance—whether she is neat or whether she is untidy. I would like her to be of average intelligence. I don't like girls that put on too much makeup or who giggle or pass notes around the classroom. I would not like her to look like something from a nightmare.

3. I like a girl who smiles and dresses nicely. One who is friendly and has a good sense of humor. I like a girl who likes to have fun at parties.

4. I like a girl who is kind and considerate and who thinks of someone besides herself. I like a girl who is good looking even though good looks are supposed to be only skin deep.[15]

when they are dealing with the members of any group of children or adolescents.

The personality structure of everyone reflects the impact upon it of

---

[15] Crow, Lester D., "Personality Traits Admired by Adolescents," *The Clearing House*, 29: 25, 1954.

inner compulsions and outer influences. To judge any one young person according to a fixed set of expectations and to assume that he will meet them may do him irreparable harm. It is only insofar as adults can or will attempt to establish a favorable environment in which young people's personal abilities and interests can develop, and to provide wise guidance when it is needed, that the maturing child or adolescent can realize his potentialities for acquiring a healthful and satisfying concept of self and a wholesome personality structure.

PERSONALITY EVALUATION

Various methods are employed to ascertain progress in the child's personality development. The significance of these approaches depends on their value in giving information concerning the innate and environmental factors that underlie personality formation. The dimensional aspects of personality development include interests, attitudes, physical constitution, general intelligence, specific aptitude, achievement or performance, and emotional status.

Through the administration of personality tests we are able to measure and to evaluate such qualities as cooperativeness, perseverance, honesty, sincerity, social adaptability, attitudes toward customs or beliefs, initiative, responsibility, introversion or extroversion, ascendancy or submissiveness, and emotional stability or neurotic tendencies. By applying these measuring instruments at different age levels, one also is enabled to trace certain developmental changes that may occur. Some of the more commonly used approaches to personality evaluation are: observation of behavior; use of questionnaires, rating scales, and standardized paper-and-pencil tests; use of projective techniques and the case-history method.

Using Observation   Parents and teachers have many opportunities to observe children's behavior. It is difficult, however, to divorce casual observation from subjective bias or prejudice. Adults are likely to miss important aspects of behavior unless they are trained to look for certain behavior and personality traits. Insight into the background motivation of children's behavior is increased as the adult gathers and carefully studies accumulated data about a young person.

In many teacher-education institutions, student teachers are encouraged to develop skill in observation by participating as observers in various classrooms. In order to pinpoint their observations they are given suggestions that have to do with the behavior of individual children. They are encouraged to look for such personality characteristics as the following:

1. Total behavior of children as they strive to gain attention and approval from teachers or associates
2. Tendency of the child toward mastery or submission
3. Extent of participation in classroom activities by each child
4. Study habits of each child
5. Reading practices of each child
6. Extent to which each child volunteers answers to questions
7. Manner in which each child displays interest in his work
8. The kind and number of questions asked by each child
9. The speech and language habits of each child
10. Nature of attention given to the lesson by each child
11. Nature and extent of physical handicaps
12. Nature and extent of cheating
13. The extent to which a child is a teacher's pet
14. The extent to which self-discipline has been developed
15. The child's responsiveness to punishment
16. The effect of the personality of the teacher on the developing personality pattern of the child

Various studies of children have been made by using the controlled observational approach, in which data were gathered and reported but not interpreted projectively. For example, Shirley [16] studied twenty-five babies. In her study, she subjected the children at frequent intervals during their first two years to anthropometric, physical, and psychological test situations. She scored incidental responses such as vocalization, manipulation, irritability, attention, and attempted escape. She also obtained a case history for each child. From her data, Shirley obtained information about each baby's characteristic behavior pattern, differences among the babies, and later development of traits.

Another study is that of Hartshorne and May in which children's personality was investigated in controlled situations.[17] Barker, Dembo, and Lewin studied children's behavior in free play situations where the element of frustration was introduced.[18] These and similar studies have merit

[16] Shirley, Mary M., *The First Two Years,* Vol. III, "Personality Manifestations." Minneapolis: University of Minnesota Press, 1933.
[17] Hartshorne, H., and May, M., *Studies in the Nature of Character,* Vol. I, *Studies in Deceit.* New York: The Macmillan Company, 1928.
[18] Barker, R. G., Dembo, T., and Lewin, K., "Frustration and Regression: An Experiment with Young Children." University of Iowa Studies: *Studies in Child Welfare,* 18, No. 1, 1941.

but they are limited in scope, and the judgments of the investigators may be arrived at subjectively.

Using Other Personality Evaluation Procedures Rating scales and interest inventories which represent varying degrees of validity and reliability are available to measure personality. These usually are in the form of questionnaires with questions organized in such a way that the answers can be scored by using a key. The Bell Inventory is for children and the Bernreuter Personality Inventory for adolescents and adults. These inventories can be answered by the use of *Yes, No,* or *?.* In the Bernreuter Inventory six different aspects of personality are measurable by the same answers through the application of six different scoring keys. The personality components emerging are: social dominance, introversion-extroversion, emotional maturity, emotional security, self-sufficiency, and security.

Personality also can be evaluated through the medium of projective techniques in which the individual reacts freely as he is presented with relatively unstructured situations. These responses are believed to be overt expressions of inner attitudes and ideas that are representative of his personality pattern. Important among projective techniques for personality evaluation are verbal techniques, drawing and painting, play and dramatics, the Rorschach Ink-blot Test, and other pictorial techniques such as the Thematic Apperception Test.

The young person reveals something about his personality as he completes an open-end sentence, or participates in a word-association test in which he responds with the first word that comes to mind as he is given a series of words, one at a time. The Rosenzweig Picture Association Test for assessing reaction to frustration illustrates this principle. A picture, accompanied by a statement, is presented in comic-strip fashion. The individual places his responses in the blank spaces provided for his reactions.

The personality and behavior of children also continue to be studied through one-way vision screens or through glass domes. Not only can their reactions to each other be recorded but the type of activities in which they engage also can be discovered. As a child is encouraged to give expression to his interests, creative abilities, and inner tensions through media such as finger-painting, drawing, and water-color or oil painting, his conceptual appreciation of persons and things in the environment, his imaginative powers and his emotional behavior can be studied and evaluated. Insight concerning personality structure can be gained by persons who are trained in the use of these projective techniques.

THE RORSCHACH INK-BLOT TEST   This is one of the projective techniques that is used by trained administrators to discover personality traits of children and young people. The value of its use in the study of personality was demonstrated by Ames, Learned, Métraux, and Walker [19] in a study of twenty-five boys and twenty-five girls over a period of eight years. They found that personality structure differs from age to age and between the sexes. At two years of age the average number of responses is 9.6, with the ink blot being responded to as a whole. At three years there is an increase in the amount of movement, conformity, and self-control, with responses averaging 12.9. At three and one-half years of age boys give more responses and mention sex and elimination more frequently than do girls. At the age of four and one-half the average responses are 14.2; by five and one-half they fall to 13.64; by six they are 15.78; seven, 18.32; eight, 15.86; nine, 18.58; ten, 16.30.

By the age of four and one-half a great deal of confusion and instability is shown. The general Rorschach responses show definite sensitivity that varies among children indicating strong emotionality and unpredictable behavior that is somewhat different from child to child.

The Rorschach responses of the five-and-one-half-year-old child are clear. The behavior constellations become clear-cut in contrast to those that either precede or follow directly. Not only is the behavior unpredictable at this time but the emotions also are uncontrolled. In the words of the authors:

> At this age probably more than at any other to date, the age characteristics can be determined directly from the table of determinants, without recourse to more "qualitative" considerations. There are at this age significant changes with regard to nearly every major determinant, which set off the 5½-year-old response clearly from responses characteristically given at surrounding ages.[20]

The qualitative description at the age of six is in part as follows:

> Six is not only egocentric, but extremely stubborn, domineering, unsubmissive, and generally opposed to the commands or suggestions of others. This strong oppositional tendency is borne out in the conspicuous occurrence of both S (response to white space within or adjacent to the blot) and WS (response to the whole, including the white spaces) responses in the Rorschach. S occurs here more than at any other age except 5½ years, and WS more than at any ages except 5½ and 7. This high use of oppositional responses in an extratensive setting indicates marked opposition to the environment.[21]

[19] Ames, L. B., Learned, J., Métraux, R. W., and Walker, R. N., *Child Rorschach Responses*. New York: Hoeber Company, copyright 1952.

[20] *Ibid.*, p. 191.

[21] *Ibid.*, p. 206.

During the age of seven, inwardizing tendencies show in the response; in fact, the inwardizing of unpleasant and morbid experiences reaches an all-time high. Age seven is the high point for responding to shading, and to the whole ink blot, including the white spaces, and scenes. At this age, differences between the sexes also become significant. Again we quote:

Sex differences are quite marked at this age—probably more so than at any other age in our range—with respect to many different aspects of the Rorschach response. As to number of responses, boys give many more than do girls, an average of 21.3 for boys, of only 15.2 for girls. Furthermore, girls' responses tend to be neat, concise, and generalized. The boys' records are often long and involved; their comments and explanations are complicated and rambling; and their elaborations are often confabulated.[22]

By eight the child tends to vacillate between uncertainty and accuracy. Many qualifying phrases are used in the responses. By nine, suggestions for change in the ink blot are frequently made. By the age of ten some children display great confidence in their responses; others show more than a normal degree of vacillation and uncertainty. Some confuse animals and people; others tend to emphasize two objects or persons.

The Rorschach responses given by children at each age in their development not only give their reactions to the ink blots but also reveal characteristics displayed by children during these ages. The researchers believe that personality patterns change with age and that the Rorschach test is an effective instrument for measuring the child's basic personality structure through his developing years.

CHILDREN'S APPERCEPTION TEST (CAT)   In the study of the personality of children the *Children's Apperception Test* is concerned with the analysis of apperceptive material in which the focus is on *what* rather than *how* one sees and thinks. It is used as a clinical instrument to aid in the determination of the dynamic factors that might help a child's reaction in various situations in which he has experience. Responses tend to revolve around the familiar constellations and disclose childish resentments and emotionalized attitudes.

In the Manual accompanying the test is included a description of, and typical responses to, the pictures of animals that are presented in various settings. For example, Figure 1, Chapter 2 shows a kangaroo having a bonnet on her head, carrying a bottle of milk in a basket and, in her pouch, a baby kangaroo with a balloon. A larger kangaroo off-

[22] *Ibid.,* p. 226.

spring is riding a bicycle. As a child views this picture, he is likely to give expression to feelings of sibling rivalry or of curiosity about the origin of babies. The relationship between mother and child is a factor. Concerning possible child behavior responses, we quote from the Manual: "Sometimes a child who is an older sibling will identify himself with the pouch baby, thus indicating a wish to regress in order to be nearer to the mother. On the other hand, a child who is in the reality situation of the younger one, may identify himself with the older one, thus signifying his wish for independence and mastery. The basket may give rise to themes of feeding. A theme of flight from danger may also occasionally be introduced. Our experience thus far suggests that this can be related to unconscious fear in the area of father-mother relationship, sex, pregnancy, etc." [23]

QUESTIONS AND TOPICS FOR DISCUSSION

1. Evaluate critically Freud's concepts of the id, ego, and superego.
2. What is the difference between an egoist and an egotist? Illustrate.
3. How are self-awareness and self-realization similar?
4. Can an individual have no personality? Explain.
5. Critically evaluate the statement that personality is a dynamic entity.
6. Why is complete consistency of behavior difficult, if not impossible, to attain?
7. Try to evaluate your personality. Have another person who knows you well do the same for you. What differences can be found? If you try this evaluation and your friend includes some unfavorable qualities can you "take it" without resentment? If so, what does it indicate about you?
8. Are you an extrovert, introvert, or ambivert? Justify your opinion.
9. Are stout people usually slow-moving and cheerful? Are tall, rangy people prone to be quick and given to moodiness? Justify your opinion.
10. List some apparently minor characteristics of people that annoy you. What can you do about them?
11. If possible, under your instructor's supervision, observe a class in elementary school. Note any outstanding personality traits displayed by the children, according to the list of characteristics presented in this chapter.
12. *Special Project:* Through tactful questioning, try to discover the

[23] Bellak, Leopold, and Bellak, Sonya Sorel, *Children's Apperception Test,* p. 4. New York: C. P. S. Company, copyright 1949 and 1958 by Leopold Bellak.

strength of the self-concept possessed by each of your four subjects. Compare their personality patterns. Which traits, if any, seem relatively fixed?

SELECTED REFERENCES

Abt, L. E., and Bellak, Leopold (eds.), *Projective Psychology: Clinical Approaches to the Total Personality.* New York: Grove Press, 1959.

Allport, G. W., *Becoming: Basic Considerations for a Psychology of Personality.* New Haven: Yale University Press, 1955.

Cattell, R. B., *Personality and Motivation Structure and Measurement.* Yonkers: World Book Company, 1957.

Fisher, S., and Cleveland, S. E., *Body Image and Personality.* Princeton: D. Van Nostrand Company, 1958.

Gillham, Helen L., *Helping Children Accept Themselves and Others.* New York: Bureau of Publications, Teachers College, Columbia University, 1959.

Hall, C. S., and Lindzey, G., *Theories of Personality.* New York: John Wiley and Sons, Inc., 1957.

Henry, W. E., *The Analysis of Fantasy; The Thematic Apperception Test in the Study of Personality.* New York: John Wiley and Sons, Inc., 1956.

Murphy, L. B., *Personality in Young Children,* 2 Volumes. New York: Basic Books, Inc., 1956.

Smith, Henry C., *Personality Adjustment.* New York: McGraw-Hill Book Company, Inc., 1961.

Spivack, S. S., "A Study of a Method of Appraising Self-Acceptance and Self-Rejection," *Journal of Genetic Psychology,* 88: 183–202, 1956.

Stuart, Harold C., and Prugh, Dane G. (eds.), *The Healthy Child: His Physical, Psychological, and Social Development,* pp. 220–339. Cambridge, Mass.: Harvard University Press, 1960.

Vernon, P. E., *Personality Tests and Assessments.* New York: Henry Holt and Company, 1954.

Witkin, H. O., *Personality Through Perception.* New York: Harper and Brothers, 1954.

Witner, H., and Kotinsky, R., *Personality in the Making: Fact Finding Report of Mid-Century White House Conference on Children and Youth.* New York: Harper and Brothers, 1953.

15

PSYCHOSEXUAL
DEVELOPMENT

SOME CULTURES OF the recent past regarded the child as sexually innocent until glandular changes, marking the beginning of adolescence, resulted in the display in overt behavior of the developing sex urge. Psychoanalysts and clinicians, however, have presented evidence that sexuality may begin in infancy and continue to progress through differing stages during childhood. Sigmund Freud, as a result of his treatment of maladjusted adults, became interested in tracing the course of the sexual pattern through the early years of his patients. His findings and those of his followers have influenced present concern with the psychosexual aspects of personality development.

PSYCHOANALYTIC THEORY OF SEXUALITY

According to psychoanalysts, there is continuous association between the sexual nature of the child and adult sexuality. Sexuality can be considered to be the fundamental human motive of behavior. The sexual life of the individual is viewed, moreover, as including all of his behavior;

it is not viewed in the narrow sense as referring only to sex-stimulated activity, as in the sex act.

The sexual energy of the individual from birth on, which can give him pleasure, is regarded as the *libido*. This energy is general in that pleasure can be gained from any act, but its expression is specifically sexual. Freud held that the roots of sexuality are in specific biological drives, but that sexual behavior is displayed generally in tendencies to experience emotional involvement in people or things (cathexes). When these impulses are not accepted by society, they can be sublimated in such ways that they will be socially desirable.

The libido can be satisfied in various ways as the individual passes through progressive stages of development. In Chapter 14 we referred to the *id, ego,* and *superego.* According to Freud, these expressions of the self are developed as the child's attitudes toward himself, his impulses, and his relations with others change as a result of maturation, environmental experiences, and the acceptance of cultural standards of behavior.

The child passes through the following periods of sexual development: oral, anal, phallic, latent, and genital. During early infancy the child derives libidinal satisfaction from oral activity and sucking. During the second year the libido expresses itself through anal activities, which finally give way to genital libidinal satisfactions. We now shall consider each of the stages of sexual development, including some of the problems and anxieties of the various stages as the self-concept matures from the satisfaction of id impulses through ego and superego controls. It must be remembered that although each stage will be treated separately, there may be much overlapping among the stages.

The Oral Stage   The stimulation of any of the highly sensitive erogenous zones of the body results in what can be called erotic pleasure. The first of these zones from the stimulation of which the child receives satisfaction includes the lips, tongue, mouth, and cheeks. The child enjoys sucking his mother's breast, his thumb, or other objects. The fact that during the first year of his life every small thing the baby can reach finds its way into his mouth indicates the pleasure to his libido of stimulating these erogenous zones.

Oral activity at first is relatively passive. The young infant sucks anything that comes to his mouth, but he does not seek objects to place there. This phase of oral activity is important to psychoanalysts, as it represents a tendency of the individual in later life to meet the problem of accepting gratuities patiently, being dependent on others for one's welfare, and trusting others. Some adult problems of maladjustment can be regarded as stemming from oral activity during infancy.

The more active oral period begins with the eruption of the first teeth. The pain of their eruption causes the baby to bite, thereby causing suffering to the mother and interfering with her attempts at weaning. Psychoanalysts refer to this period as the oral-sadistic period. The pain of teething causes the infant to bite; the biting gives pain to the mother; the mother takes from the infant the satisfaction of sucking the breast. Weaning is accompanied by hostility to the mother since she thereby is depriving the infant of a much needed satisfaction.

The child may have ambivalent feelings toward the mother. At one and the same time he wants to be incorporated in her and is hostile toward her. This may induce anxiety in him. Young children differ in their ability to accept this early area of deprivation. The disturbed child may indulge in constant thumb-sucking, a habit which may be repeated in later life during a period of crisis. For example, if the five- or six-year-old is jealous of a new baby in the family, he may regress to this form of infant behavior. In fact, it is possible for any individual of any age to find it extremely difficult to adjust to any deprivation. He may be motivated to respond to frustrating experiences by taking what is wanted without consideration of the rights of another person or by hostile attacks on the one blamed by him for the deprivation. It is also believed by some psychologists that poor adjustment during the oral period may give rise to the development during later life of a generally pessimistic or mistrustful attitude. Contrariwise, contentment and good adjustment during the oral period are likely to give rise to an habitual optimism.

The Anal Stage The oral stage usually has ended by the beginning of the second year. The anal stage, as a period of libidinal satisfaction, continues from about the age of eighteen months to about three years. In our culture it is associated with toilet training. The child derives pleasure from excretion. He also senses the mother's attitude toward his bowel movements. She is pleased when he excretes, bothered when he does not.

According to psychoanalytic theory, the child realizes that he is giving his mother a present when he defecates, but she flushes his gift down the toilet. He wants to retrieve it. Hence he may throw a toy into the toilet and take it out again.

The time at which an attitude of disgust toward his excretion begins depends on adult stimulation. Cleanliness, neatness, and punctuality are learned responses. The child achieves an understanding of what they mean by imitation of adult example. Moreover, the child who does not take readily to toilet training may suffer frustrations in his relationship with his mother. He may display his hostility by expulsion at the wrong time or by refusing to defecate when he is supposed to do so.

The anal period sometimes is referred to as the anal-sadistic stage because of the elements of expulsion and destruction associated with it and the hostility engendered by the mother's insistence upon the child's following her will in matters of defecation and urination. According to some writers, the child also is gaining some independence of muscular activity or the achievement of autonomy. Moreover, Freud believes that the toilet training process can give rise to the development of an "anal character" possessing the traits of orderliness, obstinacy, and stinginess.

The Phallic Stage From about the third to the sixth year the child passes through the phallic or early genital stage during which the genital zone becomes the center of libidinal satisfaction. Although fingering of the genitals and body exploration may have occurred earlier, this form of pleasure is intensified at this age period, with the boy in the penis, and the girl in the clitoris. The boy is more masculine, the girl more feminine.

Freud believed that the *Oedipus complex* develops in the boy and the *Electra complex* in the girl. To this time, the mother has been the love object of the child. As the boy grows more aware of the fact that the father is given privileges by the mother which are denied him, he becomes jealous of his father as a rival. In fact, he is hostile to all of society. He also fears castration or the loss of his penis or injury to it. This attitude can be caused in part by the fact that his parents may have threatened to do something with his penis in order to stop masturbation. Gradually, the boy loses his great involvement with his mother but may continue to be hostile to his father. Eventually, a feeling of tenderness is likely to develop toward both parents.

The shift in loyalty from the mother to the father may be more difficult for the girl than it is for the boy. The latter began with his love for the mother, which is intensified. The girl's first object of love was the mother. She becomes aware of the differences in the genital organs of the male and the female. She recognizes the fact that she has no penis and wants to have one. This is called by psychoanalysts *penis envy*. Since she also may have developed feelings of hostility toward her mother as a result of weaning and toilet training, the satisfaction of libidinal energy is achieved through shifting her love to the father—the Electra complex. She identifies with the mother as a rival for the father's affection.

During the phallic period, the superego or conscience develops. Earlier anxieties become guilt feelings. Although the child is not aware of the causes of his changed attitudes toward his parents, he has gained some consciousness, through his parents' suggestions, as to what is expected of him by society. His struggles to accede to their wishes lead to the control of behavior by internalized forces rather than by outside controls. Sexual impulses are sublimated. Watson illustrates the superego thus:

"For example, oral pleasures may be sublimated by the child in pleasure in speaking, and later he may go into politics. The child may sublimate his interests in anal matters by playing with finger paints and later by becoming a sculptor, or the child may seek knowledge of nature study, and later carry on as a biologist as a sublimation of his phallic interests." [1]

The Latency Stage Between the ages of about six to puberty, no new libidinal pleasure areas are experienced. This is referred to as the latency period, although this does not imply that there are no sexual satisfactions during these years. Masturbation and body play occur. Sexual interests may be less evident, however. Involvement with parents now takes the form of respect and affection.

The child becomes engrossed in many activities and wants to do things with individuals outside the home, especially members of peer-age and same-sex groups and other interesting persons whom he meets in the school and community. As his environmental horizons broaden, he becomes curious. His behavior is governed increasingly by the direction of his superego or conscience. He tends not to suffer from anxieties and feelings of guilt.

The Later Genital Stage The later genital stage begins in the prepubertal period, starting at the age of about ten, and is intensified during the pubertal period. The prepubertal period may be marked by a return to earlier stages of libidinal satisfaction. Oedipal desires show themselves in the form of daydreams and fantasies in which castration and penis envy play their part. The personality of the child appears to change. Aggressive behavior may be displayed; anxieties concerned with the self are experienced.

During the prepubertal period, habits of cleanliness may be disregarded or become intensified. Some writers claim that asceticism and

[1] Reprinted with permission from Watson, R. J., *Psychology of the Child*, p. 160. New York: John Wiley and Sons, Inc., copyright 1959.

intellectualization are evidenced. The young person arises early; he takes cold showers; he seems to lose interest in the companionship of his peers. Contrariwise, the child may engage with members of his peer group in philosophic discussions of religion, love and marriage, and life in general. These discussions usually have little meaning, since the child's philosophic concepts still are immature.

The physical changes that take place during the pubertal period cause the child to become extremely interested in sex and sex differences. The first menstruation of a girl can be an emotion-charged experience for her if she has not been prepared for the eventuality. Likewise, nocturnal emissions can be a worry to a boy.

In still childish ways a girl of this age attempts to attract the attention of older boys, since same-age boys are likely to show their growing sex interest by a superficial lack of interest in the other sex. The child may develop a "crush" on an older member of the same or opposite sex. These involvements usually are short-lived, however. During this period, the young person seems to dislike any overt expressions of parental affection toward him. He becomes extremely objective in his relationships with them. In his attitudes toward his parents and toward members of both sexes outside the home, he is beginning to give evidence of his gradual unconscious preparation for later heterosexual activities. Freud believed, however, that the individual may have been impressed by his experiences in one of the earlier stages of sexual development, such as the oral, the anal, the phallic, or the genital to the extent that in his adolescent or adult personality pattern he will display characteristics of that age period.

DEVELOPMENT OF SEXUAL INTERESTS

Some psychologists believe that the child's sexual interests can affect his attitudes and behavior, but are unwilling to accept the psychoanalytic theories. These psychologists contend, for example, that Freud was influenced in his thinking by the fact that he was dealing with maladjusted patients. His emphasis on the satisfaction of all the child's needs in light of constancy of the pressures associated with the functioning of libidinal energy also is questioned. Yet Freud has influenced thinking about psychosexual development. In previous chapters we discussed the gradual emergence of the significant physical and social needs of the child. Here we shall concentrate briefly on his displayed sex interests as these change with maturation and experience.

Personal and Social Significance of the Sex Drive That the sex drive plays an important role in the life of an individual cannot be denied. Especially is sexuality a significant factor in most maladjusted behavior. Sex problems need to be included in any discussion of the child's total life adjustment. Masturbation and sex play during nursery school and kindergarten age children cause much concern to parents and teachers. The demands of a culture determine to some extent at least the nature of the child's developing pattern of sex interest.

In some more permissive cultures the child, following the example of his elders, displays his sex interests freely. In our more rigid society the child's natural impulses may need to be inhibited, with the result that he may seem to be suffering thwartings and frustrations. In the average modern home, modesty is emphasized. Before he is mature enough to recognize the reasons for his parents' attitudes, the child may find that certain natural tendencies, such as viewing his parents when they are undressed, or a little boy's and little girl's going to the bathroom together are *verboten*. These denials of his freedom may cause wonderment. He may develop anxieties or guilt feelings about such matters, especially if he has attempted to engage in any sex-stimulated behavior which he has learned to be unacceptable to his parents. The child's playing with his genitals is a case in point.

The Role of the Parent The role played by each of his two parents also can affect a child's attitude toward sexual matters. If the father is the authority figure, and the mother is submissive to male dominance, the child is likely to identitfy himself or herself with the female parent and share her fear of the male. It has been found that some adults have had difficulty in achieving good marital status because of the effect upon them of the relationship that existed between their parents, and of parents with themselves. However, there may or may not be any association between sexual behavior during childhood and later heterosexual adjustment. The whole process of socialization (see Chapter 11) makes its imprint on the child's development of sex interests and his personal and social adjustment in his sex life.

Age Differences in Sex Interests The young child's needs include, as we have intimated in earlier discussions, not only provision for his physical needs but also for loving care. He needs to be secure in the affection or regard of those who surround him. This need probably exists throughout the individual's life, although the first source, the mother, may give way to other individuals. These individuals include, at first, peer-age associates, adults outside the home, and then fellow workers, friends, and other associates.

The child's concern with sex changes with age. According to Gesell and Ilg [2] the five-year-old child's interest in reproduction increases, and exhibitionism and sex play are indulged in. The seven-year-old dreams about changing sex, and the eight-year-old, especially a girl, may ask how a baby comes. By the ages of nine and ten there is awareness of sexual differences and a curiosity about the genitals of his own sex. The ten-year-old girls are concerned about breast development. Questions about sex are asked by them of their mothers and by boys of their fathers. Prepubertal physical changes are resulting in more interest in sex.[3] At age eleven, girls show definite adolescent reactions, and boys have frequent erections, tend to masturbate (although girls also may engage in this activity), and are curious about the sex life of animals. By the age of twelve, heterosexual interests begin to develop, and concern with sexual matters becomes more realistic. This attitude continues through successive years. By the fourteenth year at least half of the boys have ejaculations. Girls have individual friends, but boys tend to engage in gang activities. There appears to be less displayed interest in the opposite sex. At fourteen years, physical sensations accompany heterosexual feelings; anxieties may arise concerning the body. Boys may engage in sexual activities, including masturbation. During the fifteenth year, gang activity is popular, with little pairing off between the sexes but rather group activities including members of both sexes. By the time the young people reach their sixteenth year, girls have come to accept their sexual roles and boys may find it difficult to control their sexual interests.

The increased amounts of male or female sex hormones liberated in the blood stream stimulate the growth and development of accessory sex organs and result in the appearance of secondary sex characteristics. The changes that begin to occur at puberty include alterations in body contours, voice changes in boys, and breast development in girls. Some of the developmental changes in boys from age nine to twenty are illustrated in Figure 90. These trends result from direct physical examination of young boys. Kinsey and his co-workers obtained data from the retro-

[2] Gesell, A. L., and Ilg, F. L., *The Child from Five to Ten*. New York: Harper and Brothers, 1946.

[3] Gesell, A. L., Ilg, F. L., and Ames, J. B., *Youth: The Years from Ten to Sixteen*. New York: Harper and Brothers, 1956.

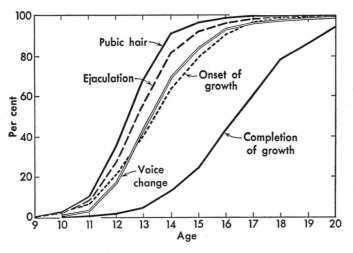

Figure 90. Physical Development in Adolescent Boys.

Courtesy of Kinsey, A. C., et al., *Sexual Behavior in the Human Male,* p. 185. Philadelphia: copyright by W. B. Saunders Company, 1948.

spective reports of older men concerning the development of pubic hair. His findings are compared with three other studies in Table 20.

The appearance of secondary sex characteristics is likely to be accompanied by differing emotional reactions among boys and girls. Most boys are embarrassed by voice changes; they may be very proud of the appearance of pubic hair. They look forward eagerly to the time when, like their fathers and other male adults, they can shave. Girls may become exceedingly aware of changes in bodily contours. Especially are they concerned about breast development. The slow developer may want to wear "falsies" to imitate the larger breasts of earlier developing girls. The girl whose breasts mature quickly may be unduly conscious of the fact that they "stick out."

The attitudes of growing boys and girls toward the physical and physiological changes that are taking place are much influenced by cultural mores in matters dealing with sexual maturation. In some sophisticated societal groups or subgroups these changes are played down. The young person is expected to continue his education and his accustomed mode of life until early adulthood or late adolescence. Sexual urges and interests are supposed to be sublimated until he is financially and socially fitted to choose a mate and accept adult responsibilities of marriage and family raising. In more primitive or simpler cultures the maturation of sex characteristics is considered to represent the onset of adulthood and the

TABLE 20

Comparisons of Data Obtained in Four Studies on Pubic Hair Development *

Age	Crampton, 1908 Per cent	Crampton, 1908 Cumulated per cent	Dimock, 1937 Per cent	Dimock, 1937 Cumulated per cent	Shonfeld, 1943 Per cent	Shonfeld, 1943 Cumulated per cent	Present study Per cent	Present study Cumulated per cent
9	...	....	...	....	...	....	0.2	0.2
10	...	....	2.0	2.0	...	....	2.0	2.2
11	7.0	7.0	15.0	17.0	12.0	12.0	7.7	9.9
12	24.0	31.0	21.0	38.0	30.0	42.0	25.5	35.4
13	28.0	59.0	22.0	60.0	25.0	67.0	33.5	68.9
14	25.0	84.0	27.0	87.0	12.0	79.0	22.8	91.7
15	11.0	95.0	11.0	98.0	19.0	98.0	5.5	97.2
16	4.0	99.0	2.0	100.0	1.0	99.0	2.0	99.2
17	1.0	100.0	...	....	1.0	100.0	0.7	99.9
18	...	....	...	....	...	....	...	99.9
19	...	....	...	....	...	....	...	99.9
20	...	....	...	....	...	....	0.1	100.0
Cases	3,835		1,406		1,475		2,511	
Mean	13.44 ± 1.51		13.08		.....		13.45 ± 0.03	
Median	....		.....		13.17		13.43	

* Kinsey, A. C., Pomeroy, W. B., and Martin, C. E., *Sexual Behavior in the Human Male*, p. 130. Philadelphia: W. B. Saunders Company, copyright 1948.

assumption of adult responsibilities for which the individual was prepared during his later childhood years.

Both parents and their children can become concerned about the attainment of normal sex development. Temporary or more permanent retardation may cause considerable anxiety. Abnormally early sexual overexcitment may arouse guilt feelings in the young person who is not yet mature enough to recognize the operation of individual differences in the sexual aspects of personality. Especially disturbing is the development of sexual characteristics and feelings to a young adolescent who has been imbued during his childhood with the attitude that "sex" is unclean or evil. Unless he receives wise guidance during his childhood, the individual may become much inhibited in responding to normal impulses.

Many parents have ambivalent feelings toward sexual development. The parent wants his child to develop a normal, active sex life, yet he does not want changes to come too soon or too rapidly. The mother, especially, does not want to lose her "baby." She resents the child's possible indifference to or overt criticism of his home or family. Both parents become worried about their child's associations with other members of both sexes and the kinds of activities in which he may be engaging when he is away from the home. The worries and anxieties of both parents and children can be reduced to a minimum if the relationship between parent and child is one of trust and confidence, and the young person has been exposed from early years to intelligently presented education concerning sex development and attitudes toward sexual matters.

EDUCATION FOR SEXUAL UNDERSTANDING

The term "sex education" has come into some disrepute because it is popularly interpreted as meaning only the giving of information about sex acts and the physical structure and function of the sex organs. The American Social Health Association prefers to use the term, "education for home and family life." Education for sexual understanding includes both physical structure and physiological function, and the development of wholesome attitudes toward one's own body and toward members of both sexes. In referring to sex education, we are including all aspects of education in this area.

Attitudes toward Sex Education   Many parents and educators

Figure 91.   A Brother of Six and a Sister of Four-and One-Half Years Enjoy Their Bath Together.

of the past viewed with distrust any attempts to prepare a child for his sexual life. It was presumed that in one or another fashion he gradually would learn all that he needed to know. The results were that (1) some children accumulated much misinformation from older boys and girls who themselves were misinformed or had acquired abnormal attitudes toward sex, or (2) some young adults entered into the marital state impulsively with little or no comprehension of their role as mate or parent.

There is a growing agreement among parents, teachers, and community leaders that children need some preparation for participation in the sex-motivated aspects of life. The question arises as to who should offer this education. The authors believe that it should begin in the home and that much of it should be continued there. Religious leaders also can share this responsibility. To what extent the school should participate in this area of education still is a matter of controversy.

In the classroom, boys and girls can be motivated by an emotionally well-adjusted teacher to develop attitudes of respect and friendliness toward members of the opposite sex. In biology classes on the secondary school level, physical structure and physiological function can be presented. Health education can stress healthful living. Literature is replete with fine examples of good home relationships which can be brought to the attention of young people. The approach of the school probably should be indirect, except as an individual child discusses his own difficulties in private with a wise counselor in whom he has confidence.

The responsibility for early sex education is being assumed by an increasing number of parents. Some mothers and fathers are hesitant, however, to engage in this activity. Their own sexual inhibitions cause them to be embarrassed; they recognize their own ineptitude in the field, and fear that they may do more harm than good; they are not yet convinced that education of this kind is needed. Some parents seem to believe that the school should take full responsibility for this phase of education, as it does (or should do, according to these parents) for all other forms of education. Other parents object to their children's receiving any teaching in this area, fearing that it will place too much emphasis on sex, especially in mixed classes, or under the guidance of a teacher who himself is not well adjusted sexually.

Regardless of who offers the instruction, it needs to be presented objectively and unemotionally. Much of it, especially attitude development, can be indirect and permeate all the relationships with the child.

Perhaps the attitude aspect is even more important than the mastery of factual material. The program of education can be well organized and presented gradually when the child is ready for it, step by step. A frank, honest approach, with no undue overemphasis, does not shock young children, make them unduly curious, or lead to experimentation and socially unacceptable behavior. The children can receive this information in their stride as they accept what they learn in other areas of knowledge.

Many good books and pamphlets are being published and are available for use by parents, teachers, religious leaders, and community leaders.[4] These materials present helpful hints on various approaches that can be used. Of course, the attitude of the person offering the instruction is extremely important. An insecure, neurotic individual probably would fail in his efforts. Answering the following questionnaire probably would have value for anyone who at present is engaged in this activity or expects to be in the future.

YOUR ATTITUDES ON SEX EDUCATION [5]

A healthy attitude toward sex is a prerequisite for providing your children with good sex education. This inventory is designed to help you take a closer look at your own attitudes. There is no "score" to be made but the "best" answers are shown below.

1. Are you fearful that a discussion of sex matters with your child will cause morbid curiosity and experimentation?   Yes   No

2. Do you believe that fathers should give sex education to the sons, mothers to the daughters?   Yes   No

3. Assuming it was expected of you, could you talk freely and objectively on matters of sex education?   Yes   No

4. Are there aspects of sex in your own growing up which still confuse or bother you?   Yes   No

5. Does the toilet training of children seem a disagreeable task to you?   Yes   No

6. Does any public expression of affection seem in poor taste or embarrassing to you?   Yes   No

7. Do you think that there can be some humor in situations involving sex?   Yes   No

8. Do you, or have you, dreaded the need for talking with children about sex?   Yes   No

---

[4] For suggestions consult American Social Health Association, 1790 Broadway, New York 19, New York.

[5] Kirkendall, Lester A., *Helping Children Understand Sex*, p. 6. Chicago: Science Research Associates, Inc., copyright 1952.

9. Do you think that proper sex education can lead to a richer, more complete life?   Yes No

10. Would you find it more difficult to talk about sex with children at one age than another?   Yes No

11. Have you been afraid to admit an interest in sex?   Yes No

12. Do you sometimes feel antagonistic toward members of the other sex in general?   Yes No

(Correct answers are: Nos. 3, 7, 9, "Yes." Nos. 1, 2, 4, 5, 6, 8, 10, 11, 12, "No.")

Age Steps Education to help the child gain an understanding of sex can begin in babyhood. The correct names of all parts of the body, including the so-called "privates," should be given whenever there is any occasion to use the terms. As soon as the child begins to ask questions, these should be answered briefly but correctly. For example, if the preschool child asks where babies come from, it may be sufficient to answer, "From inside the mother's body." Children usually are satisfied with short but what to them seem to be honest answers.

If the child persists by asking further, "How does the baby get there?" the parent can answer simply, "The father places a little seed in her body which then starts to grow and comes out as a baby." It is not intended here to present suggested answers to all of children's questions. Various adults answer children's questions differently. We wish to emphasize the fact that the parent or other adult should not engage in long explanations, much of which may be beyond the child's comprehension. Children who help their parents in the garden or who are encouraged to have pets can learn much from their experiences, especially if the parents encourage questions and answer them appropriately.

Sometimes parents believe that the best approach with a child who has learned to read is to supply him or her with one of the simple books on the subject which now are available. Getting information from a book is better than receiving no information or misinformation, but better attitudes are developed if parent and child together read and discuss the material. Children tend to bring their first questions to the mother. (See Figure 92.) This is to be expected as the mother, at least in the early years, is the chosen confidante of the child. Gradually, however, both father and mother can participate in this activity, preferably together.

As children approach adolescence it may be well for the mother to prepare her daughter for her first menstruation, and the father for his son's first ejaculation. Some parents tend to delay this preparation until the child experiences the first manifestation of changed physical status.

Figure 92. Mother Discusses Important Matters Pertaining to Sexual Development with Her Daughter and Her Friends.

Preparation, enough in advance to avoid anxiety-stimulating situations, has been found to be very helpful to the maturing young person. It also has been the experience of adults who have given time, effort, and perhaps prayerful consideration to the sex education of their child, that as the young person meets problems of sexual adjustment during the adolescent years, the boy or girl will bring these problems to the adult for help in solution.

QUESTIONS AND TOPICS FOR DISCUSSION

1. Write a short biography of Sigmund Freud.
2. Explain why you believe Freud became interested in the sexual interests of developing individuals.
3. Explain what psychoanalysts mean by the libido. What is the relationship, if any, between the libidinal theory and the hedonistic theory?
4. Trace the progress of the child's sexual life through Freud's stages of development: oral through genital.

5. What is your opinion of the Oedipus complex? The Electra complex? What are the sources of these terms?

6. How are the sexual interests of the child related to his physical growth and social development?

7. In what way does parental behavior affect the child's attitude toward sex?

8. How were you affected by the onset of puberty?

9. Why are parents concerned about the activities of their young adolescent children?

10. According to your opinion, from whom should a child receive his education about sex? Justify your answer.

11. Discuss the importance of attitudes in the sex life of an individual. Be specific.

12. Describe the kind of sex education that would be emotionally mature and objective.

13. What should a parent do if a child does not ask questions about sex?

14. Why should fathers participate in this area of education?

15. *Special Project:* From whom are your selected children receiving their sex education? What seems to be their attitude toward sex?

SELECTED REFERENCES

Baruch, Dorothy W., *New Ways in Sex Education: A Guide for Parents and Teachers.* New York: McGraw-Hill Book Company, Inc., 1959.

Crow, Lester D., and Crow, Alice, *Sex Education for the Growing Family.* Boston: The Christopher Publishing House, 1959.

de Schweinitz, K., *Growing Up,* 3rd rev. ed. New York: The Macmillan Company, 1953.

Eissler, Ruth, Freud, Anna, Hartmann, Heinz, and Kris, Marianne, *The Psychoanalytic Study of the Child,* Vol. III. New York: International Universities Press, 1958.

Freud, S., *An Outline of Psychoanalysis.* New York: W. W. Norton and Company, 1949.

Fried, Edrita, *The Ego in Love and Sexuality.* New York: Grune and Stratton, 1960.

Hall, C. S., *A Primer of Freudian Psychology.* Cleveland: The World Publishing Corporation, 1954.

Ilg, F. L., and Ames, L. B., *Child Behavior.* New York: Harper and Brothers, 1955.

Kirkendall, L. A., *Helping Children Understand Sex.* Chicago: Science Research Associates, Inc., 1952.

O'Brien, J. A., *Sex-Character Education*. New York: The Macmillan Company, 1952.

Schmidt, J. E., *Libido*. Springfield, Ill.: Charles C Thomas, 1960.

Strain, Ruth, *New Patterns of Sex Teaching,* rev. ed. New York: Appleton-Century-Crofts, Inc., 1957.

Watson, R. I., *Psychology of the Child,* Chapter 5. New York: John Wiley and Sons, Inc., 1959.

Character formation represents a gradual process of reaction in light of inner and outer attitudes and behavior motivators.

The Early Years During babyhood, behavior is impulsive and motivated for the most part by the experiencing of physical satisfactions. By the time he has reached the age of one year, however, the child has learned to respond to adult expressions of approval or disapproval of his conduct. The two-year-old has some awareness of what it means to be a "good" or a "bad" child. During the third year (sometimes earlier) the child develops a negativistic attitude. He seems to want to do what he wants to do in his own way and at his own time.

Through intelligent handling the child emerges from this period of noncooperation with a greater understanding of what is expected from him in the way of accepted behavior. At the same time he appears to have little regard for other people's rights of possession. He tends to appropriate for himself anything that interests him, especially outside the home. Some children of this age take great pride in exhibiting to others what they have taken as their own.

As the child nears the end of his third year, he evidences greater understanding of desirable and undesirable behavior and seems to exercise some degree of self-control in his relationships with adults and other children. He may even attempt to direct the behavior of a younger child. For example, Gerald, a little boy of three, was very much concerned about his two-year-old brother's welfare. If the boys were walking along the street, Gerald made it a point to walk nearer the curb, because, as he said, "Baby doesn't know what he does. He'll run out into the street and get hurt."

The three-year-old will share his toys. He recognizes some of the rights of others, although life still centers around himself and his interests. By this time he has gained some understanding of the use of money, especially pennies, as a means of buying something, but he has little or no concept of money value as such.

The Child from Three to Six During the later preschool years, the maturing youngster continues the developmental behavior patterns begun earlier. He has gained some insight into what it means to be honest, obedient, and cooperative. He tends to obey adult-made rules and regulations, even though he may not comprehend their purpose. Sometimes he resents the restrictions placed by adults on his behavior. Although he is relatively honest in matters dealing with other people's possessions, he may attempt to lie himself out of deserved punishment for wrongdoing. The extent to which he does this depends in good part on the attitude toward discipline displayed by his parents. A fearful child is likely to become proficient in the use of alibis and evasions to cover up an intentional or unintentional misdeed. Often, any expression of regret for a mischievous act is verbal rather than an outer expression of inner remorse.

The child, during this age period, usually is very loyal to his family. He likes to boast of the achievements of his father, the beauty of his mother, and the activities of older brothers or sisters. The nursery school or kindergarten child is likely to exhibit his prized possessions to his little schoolmates, sometimes offering them to special pals. He enjoys pets, but usually is more interested in watching them or playing with them than in caring for their needs.

The five- to six-year-old child is curious, he wants to know how things are made. Consequently, he is destructive in his handling of his toys, but often shows great confidence in adult ability to put them together again. Although some children are careless in the handling of their own and other people's possessions, others have been trained in habits of carefulness and may be extremely interested in keeping their toys, clothing, and other possessions in good order and condition.

Later Childhood Years   From the ages of six through twelve, children gradually develop an understanding of and willingness to control their behavior according to rules and regulations formulated for their safety and well-being. As his power of reasoning and judgment increases, the child gradually comes to recognize, on a more adult level, his responsibilities in group living. He is beginning to comprehend what may be desirable conduct in differing situations.

By the time the child nears the end of this period, he probably has achieved definite ideas of justice and honesty. He demands that other people exhibit these virtues in relation to himself. He, himself, because of his relative immaturity, may fall from grace, but he is vehement in his verbal condemnation of cheating, lying, stealing, telling improbable tales, or hurting younger children or small animals. He probably has not yet consciously developed standards of values that inhibit him from engaging in misdeeds; he still tends to control his behavior in light of possible punishment for wrongdoing. The elementary school child is likely to set up for himself various standards of behavior in light of possible satisfactions—one for the home, another for the school, and still another in his "gang." Since children of this age period are extremely interested in group activities with their peer-age associates, they also tend to draw sharp comparisons between the members of their current school or play group and outsiders, to the detriment of the latter.

In his progress toward character formation, the child gives evidence of an increasing awareness of the functions of social groups and becomes more and more influenced by group standards, even when these differ from the values exhibited by adults in his environment. Yet he seeks approval from his elders, and can recognize their reasons for their disapproval of some of his conduct. He is beginning to experience some of the conflict that later in his life may become a significant factor—that of "following the herd," yet ordering his conduct according to principles of behavior engendered in him by his parents and teachers.

Although the child may exaggerate about matters dealing with his own or his family's prestige, he is less likely to lie about his conduct, and knows when he is deviating from the truth. In fact, he is much concerned about any lying among his peer associates or adults. He also is much interested in collecting intriguing gadgets of all kinds, and usually takes good care of them. Girls, more than boys, are neat in appearance and dress-conscious. Money also has come to have real meaning for the elementary school child. He likes to be given an allowance and may do odd jobs, such as mowing lawns, running errands, or selling newspapers and magazines, to earn money to be saved or spent for desired articles— a bat, a bicycle, a story book, an article of clothing, or a gift for a relative or friend.

During this age period, the child still is inhibited from wrongdoing by fear of consequences (a characteristic that continues through adulthood), but he is gaining a greater personal appreciation of what constitutes acceptable and unacceptable behavior. He does not like to admit that he has been in the wrong, but he wants approval of his actions, and can apply concepts of right and wrong in differing situations. Usually, he is eager to live up to adult standards of social behavior. He may suffer deep remorse when he has failed to behave acceptably, and is unhappy until he receives adult forgiveness for his misdeeds.

Early Adolescent Years The young adolescent tends to exhibit those patterns of behavior that will be characteristic of him during his later adolescence and his adult life. He probably has formulated for himself certain standards of behavior which, on occasion, he will fail to follow. He is aware, however, of his shortcomings. He regrets his impulsive acts, and often tries to make amends for any damage or harm he may have caused. His growing attitudes of independence may lead him to resent an adult's restrictions on his freedom. He may experience conflicts between desired independence and still needed dependence on his elders, but he is gaining a more adult understanding of rightness and wrongness, and tends to do what is right according to his standards.

The developing adolescent is extremely sensitive to group standards and group pressures. He wants to be a well-accepted member of various groups of his choice. He often is impelled by self-consciousness in group situations, however, to act in such ways that he avoids group disapproval or censure. Hence group ideals exercise a potent effect on character formation.

The young adolescent is not mature enough to distinguish between verbally expressed standards and actual conduct among his same-age and adult associates. As a result, he may become very much confused by divergencies which he finds between what people say and what they do. His reactions in such situations are determined to a great extent by the behavior values he has achieved through his years of experience with those adults who have attempted to guide his attitudes and conduct toward the development of worthwhile self-control.

THE DEVELOPMENT OF SELF-CONTROL

Various theories have been promulgated concerning the nature of the newborn child. According to some early religious doctrines, the child was born in sin. The function of his religious training was to drive the devil out of him. Hence his rearing needed to be extremely rigid; natural urges, desires, or wants had to be subjugated so that eventually he might gain salvation. Another theory was that the child was born "good." Any "badness" that he might develop resulted from the effect of the evil about him by which he was stimulated. Consequently, he needed to be protected from such influences. At present, a newborn child is regarded as an individual with potentialities that may be good or bad in light of his experiences in the culture into which he is born and the social standards of those responsible for his rearing. He is not born with self-control or self-discipline; he acquires it gradually with the help of those who surround him.

Discipline   For a child to develop self-control or self-discipline he needs to experience discipline that is administered by sympathetic and understanding adults or that is inherent in the social situations in which he finds himself.

Meaning of Discipline To the layman the term "discipline" is synonymous with punishment. If a child behaves in a socially unacceptable manner, he needs to be disciplined or punished. Psychologically interpreted, discipline implies that the child must learn the way of life approved by his cultural group. It is essential that the child experience such disciplinary direction as will help him gear his responses in accord with his own welfare and the rights of other people.

The child needs assistance in forming habits that, as they become automatic, will serve him well in his relationships with other people and that, at the same time, will be satisfying to himself. As the child attempts to satisfy his needs and desires, he may tend to engage in socially unacceptable behavior. In such instances he must learn to substitute desirable behavior for the undesirable.

Disciplinary Approaches To some extent, discipline refers to control of a child's behavior by forces outside himself. Yet, if discipline thus interpreted is to function for the good of the child, the inner drives that activate a child's behavior must be considered. The child's fundamental needs, physical and social, should be met, but some of his desires, born of his immaturity, may have to be denied him. The form of the thwarting, rather than the denial itself, is important.

The young child cannot be expected to take responsibility for all his actions. Much of his so-called misbehavior is unintentional. Hence not only the act itself, but the reason for it requires adult understanding. The baby who has satisfied his hunger pushes his food away from him, perhaps overturning his cup. The three-year-old, motivated by curiosity, picks up and drops a parent's prized ornament, possibly breaking it. A little boy or girl takes and will not relinquish another child's toy which intrigues him. Are these acts symptomatic of deliberate naughtiness or are they signs of the child's growing awareness of his needs and urges? This is the question which the adult must answer before he attempts to deal with the situation.

Some writers use the term "surface discipline" to describe the giving of attention by a parent, teacher, or other adult to the undesirable act, without considering the basic reason for the behavior. *Constructive discipline* is employed when the adult recognizes the child's behavior as undesirable but, at the same time, understands and treats the underlying cause of the overt act. A little girl, for example, refused to eat vegetable soup. It took patient and sympathetic understanding on the part of the mother to discover the reason for her child's refusal. Unfortunately, the child had heard the soup referred to as "garbage" soup. As a result, she became nauseated by the sight of it. The mother wisely decided that the child should not be forced to eat the soup. Instead, she encouraged the little girl to help her prepare the vegetables for the soup, thereby learning through experience that clean ingredients were used and the garbage discarded. The result was that the child overcame her dislike for this particular kind of food.

Not all instances of unacceptable behavior can be treated in this way. There are times when an immediate solution must be found. The cause of the undesirable behavior may be reluctance to conform to adult standards, immaturity combined with a growing attitude of independence, or actual willfulness. Punishment is needed for intentional wrongdoing, but not for unintentional breaking of adult-made rules and regulations. Moreover, the offense needs to be punished, not the child. The child should have explained to him, in language appropriate to his stage of maturity, the reason for the application of the disciplinary measures. Although a positive approach is most effective, the very young child can learn to respond to a "No" spoken calmly, combined with a shake of the head or a frown. This approach is understood if, when the child acts in an acceptable manner, he receives a smile, a nod, and a spoken "Yes, that's good."

To the age of about three years, the child can be given approval or disapproval of his conduct by the adult's use of a few simple words, such as "fine," "good," "nice," or "bad," "hurt," "naughty." Since young children have short memories, frequent repetitions are needed. As the child matures, he can benefit from longer explanations concerning the effect of his behavior on himself or on other people.

It is possible to prevent a child's engaging in undesirable behavior by warning him of the possible consequences of an impulsive act. This admonition, however, should not be given in the form of a threat. For example, a child living on a busy street can have explained to him the danger of running out into the middle of the street in the path of traffic. This is quite different from saying to him, "Don't let me catch you running out into the middle of the street!" The latter admonition is likely to be regarded by the child as a curb on his freedom; the former is recognized as a reasonable request motivated by loving concern for his safety.

Attitude toward Discipline   The relationship that exists between an adult and a child exercises considerable influence on the latter's attitude toward disciplinary measures. If the child is secure in the affection of an older person, he is likely to recognize the value to him of having his impulsive or noncooperative behavior disapproved. Many children recognize their need for disciplining. When it is administered they may resent it momentarily, but they recover quickly from their hurt feelings and usually promise never again to fail the adult in this respect. Of course their memories are short. The same situation may arise, but if it is handled well each time it does, there is a greater possibility that self-control gradually will be built.

Reward and Punishment Whatever adults do in the way of rewarding good behavior and punishing unacceptable conduct needs to be consistent. In this way a child learns what is and is not expected of him. He thereby comes to understand that he is free to engage in some activities but needs to control many impulsive acts. To the extent that behavior is recognized by adults as good or bad at one time, and not evaluated at another, the child may become confused. Moreover, he is likely to feel frustrated when he tries to please his elders and they are seemingly unaware of his efforts. His resentment of punishment also may be greater if undesirable activities, which generally are glossed over, suddenly receive severe disapproval.

Psychologists have found that a reward such as a smile or a small gift for good behavior is more effective as a motivator of self-control than is punishment. One study of children's reactions to rewards and punishment, for example, led to the conclusion that the giving of material rewards for good behavior was more likely to be a predictor of good conduct outside the home than was punishment for noncompliance with parents' admonitions.[3] Yet, mischievousness or other forms of noncooperation and naughtiness should not be disregarded. Something needs to be done to alert the child to the seriousness of his offense. The young person should recognize the fact that the behavior, not the child, is receiving disapproval.

Whether the punishment is administered by a parent, a teacher, or another adult, his attitude should be objective and calm. He should explain the reason for his action and make certain that the child is not unduly resentful of the punishment or does not hold a grudge against the person for disapproving his behavior. In general, spanking or hitting should be avoided, although some mothers find that an occasional light tap on the legs of a child who refuses to stand up, for example, may surprise the child into doing what he is expected to do. The pain or the loss

[3] Crandall, V. J., Orleans, S., Preston, A., and Rabson, A., "The Development of Social Compliance in Young Children," *Child Development*, 29: 429–443, Sept., 1958.

of prestige caused by a spanking may serve as an immediate deterrent of a misdeed but, if this method of punishment is used constantly, the child tends to become immune to it or to develop deep resentment toward the person administering it.

Constant nagging is another ineffective behavior adjuster, especially if it is continued long after the original situations which started it could have been forgotten by the child. Putting the child into a dark closet or sending him to his room usually does little more than give him an opportunity to nurse his grievance and plan ways in which he will "get even" with the adult. One mother was accustomed to punish her little girl for misdoings by having her sit on a stool in a large closet. She found that she had to give up this method. When the mother told her daughter that she could come out of the closet, the child would insist that she liked it there and was staying. This usually caused a serious argument between the two that worsened the situation.

Forms of punishment to which children usually respond sensibly are: being sent to another part of the room where they can see the others who disapprove their behavior; making amends for any damage they have caused, such as paying for a window which was broken while playing ball in the street; being deprived of a desired treat. It is important, of course, that the child understand the relationship between his behavior and the punishment, and that he recognize the justice of the treatment which he receives. The immature child should not be expected to do the impossible in regulating his conduct, however.

Various studies that have been based on the types of child control used by parents indicate a wide variation among them. Radke [4] studied the kinds and extent of changes in approaches to the domination of children or the exercise of authority. Her subjects were forty-three children enrolled in the nursery school and kindergarten of the Institute of Child Welfare, and the parents of these children. Radke found that the most common modes of control were isolation, verbal appeals, natural results of conduct, depriving, rewards and praise, and spanking. Less often reported were ignoring, shaming, withdrawing love, and frightening.

Radke also attempted to discover, through parents' reports, how their disciplinary approaches differed from those which their own parents were accustomed to use. (See Figure 93.) The comparisons are interesting. There seemed to be greater trends among the parents than among the grandparents toward approaches that variously were democratic, lax,

[4] Radke, Marian J., *The Relation of Parental Authority to Children's Behavior and Attitudes*. Minneapolis: University of Minnesota Press, 1946.

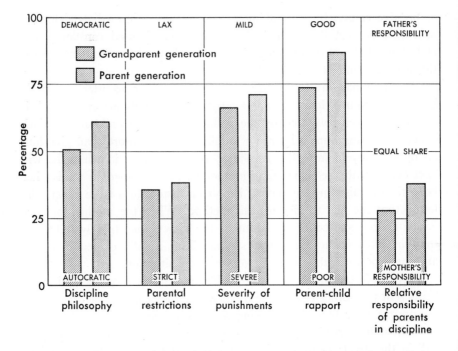

Figure 93.   Comparison of Discipline in Parent and Grandparent Generations.

From Radke, M.J., *The Relation of Parental Authority to Children's Behavior and Attitudes,* p. 38. Minneapolis: University of Minnesota Press, 1956.

mild, and good. The differences between the two generations were not so marked, however, as might be expected.

As a result of interviews with the children, Radke attempted to discover how they were affected by parental punishment. The results of this part of her study are shown in Table 21. The children also were asked by Radke what methods they used to "control" their parents. Their responses are indicated in Table 22. Differences in boys' and girls' techniques in relation to their respective parents are worthy of note. Some children, of course, utilized more than one technique with either or both parents.

Another study [5] based on reports of interviews with mother samples followed somewhat the pattern set by Radke. Making a distinction between positive and negative sanctions, Sears, Maccoby, and Levin found that many of the mothers used praise (almost 80 per cent) and tangible

[5] Sears, R. R., Maccoby, E. E., and Levin, H., *Patterns of Child Rearing.* Evanston, Ill.: copyright 1959 by Row, Peterson, and Company.

TABLE 21

Feelings of Children Resulting from Parental Punishments *

Responses to punishment	Percentage of cases
Feelings of penitence or resolutions for better behavior	14
Feelings of sadness, unhappiness, pain	63
Feeling that punishment was unjustified	7
Didn't feel better or worse	5
Don't know how they feel	11

* Radke, Marian J., *The Relation of Parental Authority to Children's Behavior and Attitudes,* p. 57. Minneapolis: University of Minnesota Press, 1946.

TABLE 22

Percentage of Children Using Various Methods of Controlling Their Parents *

Method	Used with mother		Used with father	
	Boys	Girls	Boys	Girls
Pay no attention	26	25	39	29
Cries, has tantrums	21	26	17	14
Refuses parent's request	50	26	41	19
Whines, begs, and so on	47	39	53	33

* *Ibid.,* p. 66.

awards (about 60 per cent). These were found to reinforce preceding behavior. The negative sanctions (punishment) included spanking and slapping, deprivation of privileges, withdrawal of love, and isolation. Physical punishment, from slight to severe, was used by about 80 per cent of the mothers, with only 1 per cent reporting that they did not use any such punishment. The authors of this study concluded that parental punishment does not function over a long period of time, although it might have an immediate effect. We quote: "Our evaluation of punishment is that *it is ineffectual over the long term as a technique for eliminating the kind of behavior toward which it is directed.*" [6]

Relation of Self-Control to Form of Discipline As we intimated in the foregoing, the value of punishment as a behavior control is questioned by some writers. Yet, one or another form of control is needed by growing young people to help them develop standards by which they gradually can come to exercise self-control.

Democratic versus Rigid Controls As we know, adults differ in their attitudes toward socially unacceptable behavior. Some are ex-

[6] *Ibid.,* p. 484.

tremely permissive, others are unduly autocratic or rigid. No one can be permitted complete freedom of action. Hence rules and regulations are needed to protect the common welfare. The child who is excused, because of his immaturity, from learning to follow simple rules of conduct is likely to form behavior habits that show lack of consideration for others.

Figure 94.   Parents Can "Keep an Eye" on Children's Safety without Constant "Fussing."

(From Your Child Grows Up, op. cit., p. 9.)

From early childhood on, an individual can be helped to realize his responsibility for so ordering his conduct that he does not bring hurt either to himself or to the people about him. This is a democratic approach to the achievement of self-control—a kind of two-way street. Others protect him and he must protect them.

Rigid, authoritarian discipline is the antithesis of the democratic approach. The adult judges the child's conduct according to adult standards, and demands conformity to them. Rules and regulations are established in the home or school, for example, that are to be obeyed because of adult pressure rather than in light of their reasonableness. The effect on a child of being reared in a democratic home as compared with training in a rigidly controlled home differs greatly.

According to Baldwin, the democratic home is likely to produce an active, aggressive, fearless, planful child. He has leadership qualities, may be relatively cruel, curious, and noncomforming. The child reared in a controlled home tends to be a quiet, nonresistant, well-behaved, nonaggressive child, having restricted curiosity, originality, or forcefulness.[7] It can be recognized that the completely permissive home might

[7] Baldwin, Alfred, L., "Socialization and the Parent-Child Relationship," *Child Development,* 19: 129, 1948.

produce children who could be characterized by extremes of the qualities developed in the democratic home. Certain self-regarding and self-aggressive attitudes might become so habitual that, as an adult, the individual becomes completely engrossed with himself, his needs, drives, and interests.

The child reared under rigid controls either may become a submissive, self-restrained adult or, when he is freed from parental domination, can make an about-face—becoming domineering and demanding. Delinquent behavior during the adolescent years may well be an outgrowth of experiencing either extreme permissiveness or too rigid behavior control during childhood years.

Self-Control and Democratic Discipline   Fundamental to the purpose of discipline are the goals of the society in which it is employed. In a democratic society, behavior controls need to be democratically evolved. Democratic discipline is effective and valuable to the child because it:

1. Promotes the development of his self-direction.
2. Develops his concept of self as a worthwhile person—one worthy of respect.
3. Enables him to know himself better as a unique person.
4. Utilizes the principles of freedom, justice, and equality of opportunity.
5. Encourages him in changing his understanding of situations.
6. Encourages him to see new ways of meeting his needs.
7. Makes use of judicious controls.
8. Increases his readiness for further self-direction.
9. Aims at his initiating the action rather than being forced to behave according to the dictates of others.
10. Operates in a basically consistent manner.
11. Utilizes intrinsic rewards.
12. Avoids the use of punishment as a planned deterrent.
13. Avoids the use of blame and recrimination.

Self-control is developed by guiding the child carefully through early child impulsiveness to more mature understanding of his social role. Through imitation and contagion the child comes to realize his need for social conformity. He achieves knowledge of what is expected from him not only through adult example and precept but also through age groups in play and learning activities.

The child gains control of his motivations as he develops awareness of his need to conform to external rules and regulations. He learns that he should give explicit obedience to these rules as he lives with his family in the home and with teachers and other children in the school, and participates in children's games. Although, at any age, an individual's behavior is influenced by fear of social disapproval or of punishment of his conduct, he gradually becomes motivated by his conscience or inner controls to assume his proper role in society. He gains independence in controlling his behavior but maintains some interdependence with others in adjusting his own wishes and interests in light of theirs.

The child needs many opportunities to develop self-control. He needs freedom within appropriate limits. Boys, however, usually require greater external control during their developing years than do girls. Both boys and girls should have help in finding ways in which to develop an attitude of accepting responsibilities, such as conforming to reasonable regulations, developing skill in group relationships, engaging in home chores and school study willingly, and doing a little more than minimum requirements in assigned tasks. According to Leonard, parents, teachers, and other adults lessen the possibility of good behavior and discourage the development of adequate self-control by "being impatient with children, denying them a consistent climate of love and support, expecting too much of children, over-disciplining them, lacking insight into a child's feelings and point of view, failing to accept each child as an individual, imposing unsolved personal problems on children." [8]

Leonard includes the following points as embodying a positive approach to the prevention of socially unacceptable behavior among children:

Love him with "no strings attached."
Show confidence in his abilities.
Encourage his initiative.
Enjoy his growing skills.
Give him ways to help.
Help him feel he belongs.
Give him space of his own.
Give him freedom plus responsibility.
Give him the right to choose.
Keep your personal fears out of his life.
Let him speak without fear or shame.

[8] Leonard, Charles W., *Why Children Misbehave*, p. 26. Chicago: Science Research Associates, Inc., copyright 1952.

Discipline him gently and consistently.
Give him something to believe in.[9]

Unaided, a child cannot attain satisfactory self-control. The home, the school, and other appropriate community agencies are responsible for helping the young person form habit patterns that will protect him from physical harm and the effects of his own immature impulses, prevent him from harming other people, and aid him in understanding and submitting to rules and regulations formulated for the general welfare. As the growing individual gradually comes to recognize his role as a social being with responsibilities to himself and others he is gaining in self-control or self-discipline and is strengthening his character.

QUESTIONS AND TOPICS FOR DISCUSSION

1. Distinguish between personality and character. Use examples.
2. To what extent is reputation related to character?
3. Trace the steps in character formation from preschool years through early adolescence.
4. What do you consider to be your strongest character traits? Your weakest?
5. Distinguish between discipline and self-discipline. What is the relationship between the two?
6. In your own childhood, what were your experiences with parent-applied rewards and punishment?
7. Discuss the advantages and disadvantages of corporal punishment.
8. What is a good way of handling an eight-year-old who willfully engages in a misdeed?
9. Present your interpretation of democratically applied discipline. Give examples.
10. State at least six rules or regulations that a child should be expected to obey in the home; in the school.
11. Name some of the causes of behavior difficulties of children.
12. Give examples to indicate that physiological status may cause behavior problems in children.
13. Indicate ways in which the mores of the group affect child behavior.
14. What are the dangers of too much parent domination or of too much permissiveness in relation to the development of self-discipline?
15. *Special Project:* Compare the extent to which specific character

[9] *Ibid.,* adapted from pp. 42–48.

traits are displayed by the younger and the older children. Also, cite examples of their behavior to indicate the extent to which they have developed self-discipline.

SELECTED REFERENCES

Baruch, Dorothy W., *New Ways in Discipline*. New York: McGraw-Hill Book Company, Inc., 1949.

Doty, R. S., *The Character Dimension of Camping*. New York: Association Press, 1960.

Gavian, R., *Understanding Juvenile Delinquency*. New York: Oxford Book Company, 1954.

Jones, Vernon, "Character Development," in L. Carmichael (ed.), *Manual of Child Development*, 2nd ed., pp. 781–832. New York: John Wiley and Sons, Inc., 1954.

Krug, O., and Beck, H. L., *A Guide to Better Discipline*. Chicago: Science Research Associates, Inc., 1954.

Leonard, C., *Why Children Misbehave*. Chicago: Science Research Associates, Inc., 1952.

Ligon, E. M., *Dimensions of Character*. New York: The Macmillan Company, 1956.

Moustakas, C., *The Teacher and the Child*. New York: McGraw-Hill Book Company, Inc., 1956.

Redl, Fritz, and Wineman, D., *Control from Within*. Glencoe, Ill.: Free Press, 1952.

Roback, A. A., *The Psychology of Character*, 3rd ed. Cambridge, Mass.: Sci-Art Publishers, 1952.

Sheviakov, G., and Redl, F., *Discipline for Today's Children and Youth*, rev. ed. Washington, D. C.: Association for Supervision and Curriculum Development of NEA, 1956.

I7

DEVELOPMENT OF MORAL AND RELIGIOUS VALUES

THE CULTURE INTO which a child is born adheres to certain moral standards, ethical principles, and spiritual values which are peculiarly their own. Whether during his developing years a young person remains in that culture or moves into another, he is expected to accept and abide by the standards, principles, and values which the group regards as behavior guides to preserve and improve their kind of civilization.

DEVELOPMENT OF MORAL VALUES

Viewed historically, differing cultural groups have placed varying emphases on what can be considered acceptable behavior. Each group, however, stresses the need to follow the moral code established by the group for the welfare of its people. Yet, certain aspects of morality appear to be general for many peoples in our present stage of civilization. The precepts of the Ten Commandments, for example, seem to be accepted by most national and racial groups regardless of religious affiliation. The interpretation of the moral code may vary with the group, however.

Before we trace the development of moral values in the growing child, it is necessary that we possess an understanding of what it is he must learn to accept, as well as why most individuals conform to the principles of good conduct as established by their group.

Moral Standards and Ethical Principles   Behavior conformity to the customs or standards of the moral code is important in the meaning of the term "morality." A person may not always conform to the code, however. If he does this intentionally, his behavior is regarded as *immoral*. If the person breaks the accepted code unintentionally, because of ignorance, he may hurt the general good but his conduct is recognized to be *unmoral* or *amoral*.

Ethical principles are closely related to the moral code, although they differ somewhat. Certain ideals of conduct are supposed to govern an individual's social relationships. Morality has a religious significance, while ethics and ethical standards are more closely related to cultural or social well-being. Ethics refers more directly than does morality to the philosophy of human behavior and a determination of the basic principles of right conduct.

To the extent that by moral standards and ethical principles is meant conformity to accepted group standards of behavior, they point to the attainment of a good society. What may have been permitted by a group at one time may be condemned later because the formerly accepted behavior has been found to encourage long-range ill effects. Variations in the moral code may exert tremendous effects upon a society's fundamental welfare. A few examples of past situations such as these are: socially approved child labor during the early days of industrialism, the acceptance by various national groups of religious persecution, and Negro slavery in our own country. At present, there is much concern over the "rightness" of our high divorce rate, of democratic versus totalitarian government, of the limitation of citizenship rights to certain segments of a population, and of the utilization of atomic power in warfare. People differ also in their moral attitudes toward participation in such forms of behavior as the amount of respect that should be given authority, the drinking of alcoholic beverages, smoking, engaging in premarital sex relationships, and other forms of conduct that are considered by many, but not all individuals, as militating against physical and mental health.

The Bases of Conformity   Fundamental to an individual's willingness to conform to the moral code of his culture is his desire to be accepted by the group. We stressed in Chapter 16 the value to everyone, young or old, of earning a respected place for himself in the opinion of his associates. We also discussed in Chapter 16 the inner and outer influences that work for or militate against the acquiring of a good character and the achieving of self-control. Basically, these aspects of development cannot be considered apart from the effect upon the growing young person of the moral standards to which he is exposed.

An individual's reasons for accepting and following the moral code of his group differs with the stage of maturity and the environmental factors by which he is surrounded. According to Strang, after the individual has emerged from early childhood egocentrism (thinking only of oneself), he passes through various stages of moral development. These are, not in fixed sequence:

Sociocentrism—obedience and respect for moral rules and customs.

Social awareness in the form of fear of social disapproval.

Negative reciprocity stemming from fear of disapproval or from a feeling of guilt.

Positive reciprocity stemming from a desire to maintain a good relation with one's friends.

Sense of justice.

Satisfaction in subordinating one's own interests to make others happy.[1]

People differ in their motivation toward moral behavior, of course. Some never go beyond fear of social disapproval; others may tend to sacrifice, beyond the point of favorable returns, their own needs and interests. They can become a kind of doorstep on which anyone can step without fear of reprisal. What is just and right can be interpreted in light of strong individual self-aggrandizement. Strang's list of basic reasons for engaging in accepted behavior can be substantiated at least partly by tracing the child's moral development.

STAGES IN MORAL DEVELOPMENT

From birth on, as we have noted frequently, the child's maturing potentialities are molded by the environmental influences by which he is

[1] Strang, Ruth, *An Introduction to Child Study*, 4th ed., p. 289. New York: copyright 1959 by The Macmillan Company.

surrounded. He is not born either moral or immoral. His continuing experiences with people and things in his environment help him acquire whatever moral sensitivity he gradually acquires. His personal and social choices become moral issues. Although children differ in their growing ability to comprehend moral and ethical concepts, certain patterns of development show themselves during the maturing stages.

From Birth through Five Years The newborn infant is amoral. As the young child reacts with people and things about him, he has at first no awareness or intent of breaking moral codes. He attempts to meet his needs and interests in ways that will be satisfying to his ego. Through the application by adults of more or less intelligently administered rewards and punishments, the young child gains some understanding of the difference between good and bad behavior. He may be impelled to do the right thing when he is observed, but not when he is alone.

Gradually, the child develops the beginnings of a conscience. Internalized standards, the "voice of conscience" or the superego, restrains him from wrongdoing even when he is alone. He may become overconforming, especially if he is subjected to rigid parental discipline. He may be disturbed by his own actions. A little four-year-old was playing with a suitcase while she was in a room alone. Inadvertently, she broke off the end of a strap that had become worn through use. Later, her mother put the suitcase away without noticing the damage to it. The child, who had hidden the broken end of the strap in her pocket, worried about her supposed misdeed. The situation was made more difficult for the child by the fact that her mother had not discovered that the end of the strap was missing. The little girl's conscience "hurt" her so much that, a few days later, she tearfully admitted her guilt to her mother, exhibiting the bit of leather and wanting to know if she couldn't "put it back on." Fortunately, the woman realized that her daughter had not been intentionally naughty, and assured the child that no serious damage had been done. Even at this young age, however, serious conflicts and anxieties may arise because of the child's strong desire to earn adult approbation of his behavior.

Ages Six through Twelve During elementary school years, the child may become oversensitive to approval and disapproval. Conscience continues to function, but as Allinsmith [2] puts it, some children are "other-directed," following the views of peers or of young and older leaders rather than inner standards. This can be illustrated by the in-

[2] Allinsmith, Wesley, "Conscience and Conflict: The Moral Force in Personality," *Child Development*, 28: 469–474, 1957.

fluence that the leaders of children's gangs have over the behavior of the other members. Other aspects of moral needs that, according to Allinsmith, need further study include the *perceived source* of standards, the *like or dislike* of conscience, relative *emphasis on ideals as opposed to prohibitions,* and *vigilance* or the keeping on guard at all times, and looking for any moral lapses in their own or in the behavior of others.[3] The father to whom we referred in another discussion, because he constantly admonished his little daughter to observe undesirable behavior in other children and to refrain from imitating it, was developing an attitude of extreme vigilance in the child.

Elementary school children are developing their concepts of justice. Piaget [4] studied the reactions of 167 French children between the ages of six and twelve relative to what should be done "if someone punched you." He found that the younger children were in general agreement that the misdeed should be reported to an authority person; the older children favored returning the aggressive act. Piaget also attempted to test children's attitudes toward intentional and unintentional wrongdoing. He asked children which boy they thought was bad: "(1) One boy intentionally gave wrong directions to a man, but the man did not get lost." "(2) Another boy unintentionally gave the man the wrong directions, and the man did get lost."

The seven-year-olds seemed to decide wrongdoing in light of material consequences, so they accused the second boy of naughty behavior. The nine-year-olds were more sensitive to the intentions of the two boys and condemned the behavior of the first boy.

Piaget believes that gradually moral reality becomes moral relativism. In light of his studies, he suggested that the growth of morality, in general, can be divided into three such periods as the following:

1. To about the age of seven or eight years, justice depends on adults.

2. From eight to eleven years, "equalitarian" justice prevails—the needs and rights of others are considered.

3. By the age of eleven or twelve, a regard for equity modifies equalitarian morality.

Durkin [5] checked Piaget's findings concerning children's concepts of

[3] *Ibid.,* pp. 472–474.

[4] Piaget, J., *The Moral Judgment of the Child,* New York: Harcourt, Brace and Company, 1932; Piaget, J., *The Construction of Reality in the Child,* New York: Basic Books, Inc., 1954.

[5] Durkin, Dolores, "Children's Concepts of Justice: A Comparison with the Piaget Data," *Child Development,* 30: 56–67, 1959.

justice by presenting a story situation to 101 boys and girls in grades 2, 5, and 8. The majority of the children in all three grades came from homes having average economic ratings. This was the story situation:

"(A) One day when they were out at recess, Bennett hit Van.
        What should Van do?
        Why?
"(B) What if Van hit Bennett back and gave him a push besides?
        What do you think of that?
        Why?"

The findings in this study show that:

1. Piaget's contention of a relationship existing between chronological age and justice concepts is substantiated. However, the data do not support his more specific proposal that acceptance of reciprocity as a justice-principle increases with age.

2. In no instance did acceptance of reciprocity include approval of returning aggression that was different from the aggression received. The unanimous reaction duplicates the Piaget finding that children who approve of reciprocity do not accept "a sort of arbitrary punishment whose content bears no relationship to the punishable act."

3. Older children tend to show concern for possible mitigating factors in the situation being judged. This bears out Piaget's finding concerning the emergence of "equity" with increase in age.

4. The role of intelligence in moral-judgment development remains undefined. Data concerning the relationship of intelligence and kind of justice concept are conflicting. However, findings do support the hypothesis of no relationship between intelligence and "the feeling of equity." [6]

As the older elementary child or preadolescent, more or less unconsciously, internalizes his moral values and is exposed to differing models in the form of family members, playmates and schoolmates, teachers, and other adults, the young person is motivated to assess the various concepts of morality which he encounters. Insofar as his earlier social experiences have encouraged good emotional balance, he now is ready to test differing codes and select from among them those concepts that to him have personal and social value.

The growing young person gradually develops a more flexible and mature conscience or superego. He still responds, as he probably always will, to group approval and disapproval, and he does not become a model child. Occasionally, even the best adjusted young person yields to temptation and engages in impulsive and self-centered behavior. Yet he is likely

[6] *Ibid.*, p. 66.

to recognize the way in which and the extent to which he has deviated from moral standards and ethical principles. Unless, as a result of too rigid upbringing, he has developed severe feelings of guilt or anxiety when he falls from grace, he can be expected with increasing maturity to attain good self-control and socially respected character traits.

DEVELOPMENT OF RELIGIOUS VALUES

Religion can be regarded as a way of life that motivates the religious person's thinking, acting, and feeling as he strives to uphold the social mores. Religion stresses love of God and man. It places greater emphasis on spiritual, nonmaterialistic values than on the amassing of material goods.

Value of Religion   Religious motivation finds various expressions that emphasize the development and maintenance of high moral concepts which are aimed at the furthering of the common good. The meeting of former President Dwight D. Eisenhower with Pope John XXIII gave emphasis to religious values. (See Figure 95.) Religious development helps a child acquire a feeling for moral values and a sense of personal honor, with a minimum of fear of outside behavior controls and of reliance on superstitious taboos.

Orientation to belief in God with adherence to religious principles gives dignity to human life. It motivates the individual's behavior through its high standards, beliefs, appreciations, and loyalties. The religious attitude toward life can strengthen an individual's self-respect and arouse the desire to participate in the solution of social problems that arise out of unfair competition and unjust treatment of underlings. Religion stresses spiritual values; this attitude leads to the recognition of the dignity of man and the omnipotence of the Godhead.

Influence of Religious Education   The child's receiving of religious education is interwoven with his experiences in the home and the school. Hence it cannot be claimed with certainty that the development of good character is the result solely of the religious instruction which the child receives. Results of studies indicate, however, that children who attend religious schools tend to score higher in tests of honesty and other character traits than do nonattenders.

Religious education can integrate individual and social life by providing regulating life principles. The religious person is motivated in his behavior by the standards of the religious group with which he is affiliated.

United Press International Photo

**Figure 95. Religious Values Take on Great Significance as President Dwight
D. Eisenhower Meets Pope John XXIII.**

The intelligent worshiper is able to reconstruct his conduct in light of
changing conditions. His strong faith and his interpretation of the will
of God help him maintain peace and harmony in his personal life and
good accord in his relationships with his fellows. The individual who
has profited from religious education rarely exhibits pessimism, hatred,
despair, cynicism, or other destructive life attitudes.

Intellectual evaluation and scientific truth are not at variance with
intelligent concepts of religion. Each has its place in group progress. To
the extent that constructive religious education supports good social
customs and mores, the religiously trained group opposes any practice
that undermines human dignity, such as illegal sale of narcotics, drugs,
or alcohol, or participation in prostitution, slavery, and any other destructive social activities. Through the centuries the influence of reli-

gious ideals has alerted people to worthy principles for the solution of group problems. One of the chief purposes of religious education at present is to stimulate the people to apply these principles, which are so well known, to the mitigation of social ills in particular situations.

Attendance at religious services has special value for both young and older worshipers in that, for at least relatively short periods each week, an individual can remove himself from the hustle and bustle, the problems and anxieties, of his daily life pattern. In an atmosphere of peace and quiet, he can lose himself in the contemplation of spiritual, other-world values. He can make peace with himself and his God, and then return to the world of affairs strengthened by the respite from possible worries, anxieties, and concern with materialistic matters. Whatever a young person's attitude may become in adulthood, he should not be denied the privilege of religious experiences during his developing years.

STAGES IN THE ACQUIRING OF RELIGIOUS IDEALS

The child's religious development is closely allied with the attitudes toward religious beliefs evidenced in his home and his immediate neighborhood. Even God-fearing parents find it relatively difficult to guide a child's religious experiences. In spite of their best efforts, the child may fail to achieve any but a verbal understanding of religious matters. It is only as the young person is encouraged by his parents and associates to continue to practice religion that he finally acquires a deep appreciation of spiritual values and applies them in his life activities.

The Preschool Child's Attitude toward Religion The baby is neither religious nor nonreligious. The concepts of life and death have no meaning for him. If the two-year-old eats with his family he can be taught to bow his head during the saying of grace before meals; he also can repeat a few words of a single prayer. These activities are born of example and precept; they do not originate from inner associations.

The three-to-five-year-old usually learns to enjoy repeating simple prayers. He asks God to bless a long list of persons and things, including his parents, other members of the family, favored friends, and his prized possessions. He asks God or Jesus to make him a good boy. To the child during this age period, God usually is a kind old man with a white beard who sits "up in heaven" and watches everything that the child does. This concept of God results from the child's viewing of pictures in religious books illustrated for children and from what he hears from his parents.

The young child may develop a strong feeling that a close personal relationship exists between him and God. Like his father or Santa Claus, God rewards him when he is good by granting his wishes or bestowing gifts, but punishes him when he is naughty by withholding these or causing him to have unpleasant experiences. In fact, if something unpleasant happens to some children they become very much concerned about what they may have done to displease God, and ways in which they can make amends. Unless he has to sit too long, a young child seems to like to attend Sunday school or other religious services. Some wise parents permit young children who attend services of worship to look quietly at interesting pictures in an appropriately illustrated religious story book.

The child may have been encouraged to regard God as very wise and forgiving and interested in the welfare of everyone. Although he has little conception of the meaning of death, the child can come to believe that when a person dies he goes to heaven where he will be very happy. In light of his experiences with death he may believe that only old people die. The child may recognize the fact that death is a time of sadness. Yet, although he may miss the presence of an older relative or friend who has died, he rarely experiences any personal sorrow.

The Elementary School Child's Attitude toward Religion   By the time a child has reached the age of six, his early religious concepts have become strengthened, especially if he has had continued religious training. His relationship with God has become extremely personal, and he is likely to pray fervently for many things. He attempts to control his behavior according to what God, as well as his parents, expect from him. He enjoys going to Sunday school and engaging with other children in interesting projects that have a religious purpose. He likes to sing simple little hymns. A more emotionalized attitude toward death is developing, one of the child's greatest fears being that his mother may die.

From the ages of seven through ten, the child is acquiring a more mature attitude toward religion. He becomes more curious about God and asks many questions about Him. He may be bothered by the fact that God is supposed to be all around him but yet is invisible. The child gives evidence of at least a verbal understanding of the difference between the *body* and the *soul*. The latter sometimes is confused with conscience. He also learns that when a person dies, it is the soul but not the body that goes to heaven. This often is a difficult concept for the child to understand. He may picture the soul as a ghostlike entity that rises from the dead body and floats upward as an invisible angel. To the child, death may still be regarded as associated with old age, but through experiences with the death of younger people he is coming to realize that it may be caused by accident or disease. He also has learned that only good people go to heaven when they die. This may cause a little boy or girl to try to be good and obey parents and teachers.

Maturing Attitudes toward Religion The older child or pre-adolescent becomes more understanding in his attitude toward God as a Spirit. He recognizes the fact that he cannot understand all the mysteries associated with the concept of religion. He is beginning to differentiate between spiritual and material values, although he rarely understands the spiritual except that it implies those intangibles that govern his being. The religiously educated child continues to engage in morning and evening prayers. These may become relatively routine, however, except in what the child regards as a crisis, when they become extremely fervent.

An eleven-year-old girl, for example, became very much distressed one evening by a violent quarrel between her parents. She went to her room, kneeled down, and prayed God to do something to stop the quarrel. While she was praying, a friend dropped in for a visit. To the child, this was a direct answer by God to her prayer. Her religious faith was deepened by this incident.

During this age period a child develops a more mature attitude toward death. He tends to think about it, however, only when he is faced with the death of a close relative or friend. In light of religious training, he may accept the concept that the spirit of the person is hovering about him and concerned with his welfare. Hence, by praying to the spirit of the deceased, he may experience comfort from the sorrow caused by the death.

The growing child enjoys the social stimulation of attending Sunday school. He gains pleasure from attending religious services and is much interested in reading the Bible. He may become a member of the choir or join other religious organizations. He and his young friends tend to participate in serious discussions about religious matters. The extent to which the child engages in these activities depends, of course, on his parents' involvement in religious matters and their encouragement of his following their example.

Many religious organizations encourage children to participate at the age of twelve or thirteen in a rite or ceremony at which they confirm their intention of taking personal responsibility for the religious institution in which they expect to become or remain active participants. To most boys and girls this rite signifies an important step in the assumption of adult responsibility. Hence they take it very seriously. The solemnity of the ceremony impresses them to the degree that they usually experience a deep emotional fervor.

By the time a young person reaches early adolescence he probably has discarded his early religious attitudes, especially the personalized concept of God. Since he still is too immature to accept abstract and generalized belief, he may experience inner conflict. What happens then depends in good part on the attitudes toward religion of his close relatives and friends, and his school experiences. He may drift away from his early religious practices. If he continues to remain involved with his childhood religious affiliations, he may develop a deep, abiding faith, accepting the fact that the mysteries associated with the concept of an Infinite Power cannot be comprehended fully by the finite mind. He accepts God as the basic spiritual influence on his life, and recognizes his responsibility for adhering to a moral code in his human relationships. Concerning maturity in this area, Strang says:

Attainment of religious security and maturity involves the development of values, a philosophy of life, and an orientation to the universe. Religious adjustment is related to other aspects of life, especially to human relations. The church supplies an appropriate place to worship and a quiet time in which to view one's life in relation to something greater—an ideal, a goal, or God. The social aspects of worship give a sense of belonging, of sharing a common purpose.[7]

Religious experiences during the maturing years help the young person develop worthy and lasting peace and happiness in spite of occasional misfortune. It aids him in avoiding fixations and narrow inhibitions, and in organizing a scale of values dominated by religious and spiritual sentiments. The developing individual acquires religious understanding through participation in religious activities. He can come to accept intellectually basic religious tenets and apply them to his behavior.

The devoted worshiper experiences religious belief, faith, hope, awe, and reverence. His emotional life can be purged of overconcern with what may be termed the baser emotion stimulators. There is a difference between intelligent optimism and emotional enthusiasm. The truly religious

[7] Strang, Ruth, *An Introduction to Child Study,* 4th ed., p. 508. New York: copyright 1959 by The Macmillan Company.

person has achieved a philosophy of life that is based on the belief that, in spite of untoward circumstances, the right and the good can be expected to prevail.

The following comments were made by two adolescents—a boy and a girl—about their attitude toward religion and their reasons for attending religious services. We present their statements.

The Boy: My attitude toward religion is the realization that religious beliefs are a real necessity to my life. This realization is brought forth through experiences I have had in my environment. One method of obtaining religious beliefs is by attending religious services. Once one realizes that religion is important to him, he discovers that it is achieved through attending and participating in religious services. Religion is far more than belonging to a particular group. It is a way of life. I feel that all people have a religion. Some may be difficult to recognize while others may be strict and quite apparent. Whichever the case, each person has a means of furthering, protecting, and insuring his convictions.

The Girl: My attitude toward religion is one of sincerity and simplicity. I feel one must be honest, self-giving, and sincere about religion. There are many different faiths in our world. The important thing is that people believe in a faith. However, having something to believe in and trust in seems to give courage, hope, peace of mind, and a will to live. One should be sincere in his belief.

QUESTIONS AND TOPICS FOR DISCUSSION

1. Distinguish between morality and ethics. What do the two terms have in common?
2. What is the relationship between moral and cultural values?
3. Trace the child's developing moral concept.
4. Give examples of adults' telling the child to adhere to certain ethical standards and then themselves breaking these principles.
5. Show that scientific truth and intelligent concepts of religion are not at variance.
6. Critically evaluate the statement that children should have religious experience.
7. Differentiate between materialistic and spiritual values.
8. What was your own thinking toward religion and religious services during your early teen years?
9. *Special Project:* Ask your two older subjects what they would do in the situation used by Durkin to discover children's moral concepts. Note their responses. What are the religious attitudes of your subjects? What is their concept of God? Have they had any experiences with death? If so, how have they reacted to them?

SELECTED REFERENCES

Bloom, L., "A Reappraisal of Piaget's Theory of Moral Judgment," *Journal of Genetic Psychology,* 95: 2–12, 1959.

Buckley, M. J., *Morality and the Homosexual: A Catholic Approach to a Moral Problem.* Westminster, Md.: Newman Press, 1960.

Clark, Thadeus B., *What Is Honesty?* Chicago: Science Research Associates, Inc., 1952.

Clark, Walter, *The Psychology of Religion.* New York: The Macmillan Company, 1958.

Crow, L. D., and Crow, A., *Sex Education for the Growing Family.* Boston: The Christopher Publishing House, 1959.

Ginsberg, Eli (ed.), *Golden Anniversary White House Conference on Children and Youth.* New York: Columbia University Press, 1960.

Havighurst, R. J., "Moral Character and Religious Education," *Religious Education,* 51: 163–169, 1956.

Johnson, P. E., *Psychology of Religion,* rev. ed. Nashville, Tenn.: Abingdon Press, 1959.

Kardiner, A., *Sex and Morality.* Indianapolis: The Bobbs-Merrill Company, Inc., 1954.

Montagu, A., *Helping Children Develop Moral Values.* Chicago: Science Research Associates, Inc., 1953.

Ross, M. G., *Religious Beliefs of Youth.* New York: Association Press, 1950.

18

PERSONAL
ADJUSTMENT AND
MENTAL HEALTH

INDIVIDUAL BEHAVIOR AND social attitudes do not develop in a vacuum. In his attempts to fulfill his personal and social needs, a child makes a variety of adjustments to people, circumstances, and events. Those which are favorable to him are called positive adjustments; those of little value to him or others are referred to as maladjustments. These adjustments, both mental and emotional, differ among individuals and also in the extent to which they are wholesome and constructive, or unfavorable.

ADJUSTMENT AND MALADJUSTMENT

When an individual makes sufficient change to experience success and contentment in any activity, he is believed by most laymen to have made satisfactory positive adjustment. To the psychologist, however, to adjust includes both inner and overt changes that individuals experience during their growing-up years. Adjustment is two-edged; it embodies both personal and social experiences. The child lives with himself in a society patterned by others. From early childhood he develops, within the limits of his own capacities and the existing environmental influences, those patterns of behavior that describe him as a well-adjusted individual or as one who is maladjusted.

Meaning of Adjustment and Maladjustment   The majority of individuals are motivated by the desire to complete many activities. These include being successful in school, experiencing a happy home life, marrying, rearing children, and earning success in a chosen vocation. If in these pursuits the relationship between individual wants and environmental factors predisposes toward wholesome and constructive attitudes and behavior, the individual is said to have achieved *good adjustment* to life experiences. When or if he does not achieve successful fulfillment of his desires and aspirations in his relationship with other persons or with conditions, his behavior may reflect this lack of satisfaction. He displays behavior symptoms of *maladjustment*.

In order to avoid confusion, the terms "good adjustment" and "maladjustment" are being used because adjustment may represent either constructive and satisfying behavior, or behavior that is nonsatisfying. Some psychologists prefer to describe behavior as either that which is satisfying to both the person himself and others, or that which is annoying and destructive, and interferes with the individual's meeting his social and personal obligations acceptably. We shall use *good adjustment* to emphasize the satisfying aspect, and *maladjustment* to connote the undesirable.

Areas of Life Adjustment   Each individual faces the problem of achieving maximum satisfaction in his home life, his school activities, his social living, and his work, without interfering with the satisfactions that rightly belong to others. Good adjustment in these respective activities begins in childhood and continues, step by step, throughout life.

A child's behavior tends toward the attainment of a series of more or less individually sought and socially accepted goals. His concept and evaluation of the goal itself may be realistic or they may be incomplete and faulty. His evaluation of his ability to achieve the goal may not always be correct or adequate. The developing individual constantly is attempting to make use of those forms of behavior that satisfy his impulses to achieve. Thus he changes or adjusts his behavior until he achieves the goal or until he loses interest in it. According to Burgum,[1] in his attempt

---

[1] Burgum, M., "Constructive Values Associated with Rejection," *American Journal of Orthopsychiatry*, 10: 312–326, 1940.

to achieve good adjustment, the rejected child believes that he needs to protect himself. He looks for praise, rewarding experiences, and help from others as he seeks to compensate for deprivation experienced in his home. Constructive factors in his experience may help in establishing readjustment.

Good adjustment always is made in light of some values found in the situation. These may be personal or social. Personal values usually reflect those of a group or groups. The process involved in acquiring group attitudes begins early in life and follows the pattern of family attitudes and behavior motivations associated with religious, humanitarian, political, economic, esthetic, and materialistic. Interwoven with all these value areas, and predictive of the overt behavior of the individual in the adjustment processes, are the group standards and attitudes reflected by the individuals and the situations by which the individual is surrounded.

A child constantly is stimulated by animate and inanimate factors in his environment as he struggles toward the attainment of self-expression, self-realization, and security. His inner desires, wants, and ambitions are expressed through his overt behavior. Both his inner compulsion toward expression and his overt behavior are influenced by environmental factors. If he sets for himself ego-satisfying rather than socio-satisfying goals, he may be confronted with frustration or conflict in his struggles toward good adjustment, with the result that unhappiness, discontent, resentment, or maladjustment occurs.

PROBLEMS ASSOCIATED WITH FRUSTRATION

It is difficult for even a child to experience continuing success as he engages in activities in which he is interested. He meets and grapples with opposing forces of one kind or another, including rules, codes of behavior, interests of others, unfulfilled desires, or levels of aspiration beyond immediate achievement and similar thwarting situations. Any force that interferes with desired activity becomes a psychological barrier or a frustration when or if the individual recognizes it as a threat to his self-realization. This unsatisfied need or thwarted desire is known as *frustration*. It is experienced when there is an awareness of the fact that an individual believes he is unable to satisfy a felt want.

Sources of Frustration Frustration situations appear early in the life of the child. A baby wants food or sleep; he wants to engage in kicking and cooing; he wants to be comfortable. When or if any one of these wants is not satisfied, he is being frustrated and he displays one or another form of disturbed behavior such as crying. Some of the frustrations encountered by an individual are relatively mild and can be overcome easily; others may seem so serious to the individual that he sees no way out of the difficulty.

Stresses and Strains in Frustration   Innumerable forces appear to block an impulse. Also, what sometimes appears to the onlooker to be no more than a mild source of annoyance may deeply stir the individual concerned. Emotional stresses often are produced when there is great interest in a situation or a problem. Although important at the time, some thwartings cannot be recalled ten years later. Many minor obstacles cause annoyances or stresses that do not result in actual frustration. Such experiences as stubbing one's toe, breaking one's glasses, missing the train, misplacing a key, and the like provoke stresses but may not produce frustrations, since most individuals adjust quickly to such stress-provoking stimuli. In a study of frustration and dependency made by Sears, Whiting, Nowlis, and Sears [2] of forty preschool children by means of teachers' ratings, doll play situations, fifteen-minute observations, and interviews with mothers, the investigators found that the child's dependency tendencies and aggressive drives were determined largely by the kind and amount of frustration and punishment experienced by him.

An individual is confronted by many thwarting situations and conditions which present difficult problems. In his attempt to satisfy his physical needs, an individual tends to follow the accepted customs of his culture. Increasingly, the fulfillment of his desires and urges, emanating from interpersonal relationships, becomes important to him. In his attempts to develop good adjustment, he strives for attention, seeks the approval of his peers, and struggles for success in school and in social and vocational areas.

Sometimes environmental conditions or events act as obstacles to the realization of strong interests or desires. Disease, death of a relative, storm, fire, or any other serious event may become the basis of frustration. The child may be caught in a school violation during a fire drill, or found annoying another child. He may be tempted to break the moral, ethical, or legal code. Each of these experiences can be the basis of frustration. The degree of his frustration in any situation depends upon the extent to which emotional tensions are established.

[2] Sears, R. R., Whiting, J. W. M., Nowlis, V., and Sears, P. S., "Some Child-rearing Antecedents of Aggression and Dependency in Young Children," *Genetic Psychology Monographs*, 47: 135–236, 1953.

The basic source of frustration usually lies within the individual him-self. The attitudes he develops in his daily living condition the degree of good adjustment he is likely to make. The physically handicapped child who is denied participation in activities common to those engaged in by the normal child is liable to experience discontent, resentment, and frustration. Likewise, the child who is mentally subnormal may become frustrated when brought into unfair competition with children who are mentally superior. He often attempts to imitate behavior that is socially undesirable, gets caught in the act and is punished while his more able associates seem never to be discovered in their wrongdoing. This frustrates him. He fails in competition because he cannot comprehend the factors that account for his failure and for the success of his peers.

The intellectually gifted child experiences frustration as he wrestles with problems peculiar to his superior mental status. He is alert to many situations. His keen insight and powers of discrimination often enable him to evaluate conditions, situations, and human relationships more quickly and more accurately than can his less able associates. He also is more aware of his potentialities, and his interests and desires are more numerous than those of his less able peers. His emotional development, however, does not always keep pace with his mental progress. He under-stands much of what is happening around him, but is not mature enough to realize its full value to him or to others. The gifted child may be ex-pected to perform feats beyond his age limitations. Sometimes, when he attempts to help parents or teachers, he is reprimanded for assuming responsibility without permission from his elders. If he fails in competi-tion with another gifted child, he may suffer intense feelings of frustra-tion.

Levels of Aspiration   It is through the setting and meeting of goals that individuals attain good adjustment. These goals and the extent to which they are met differ widely among individuals. Successful goal attainment depends on a background of appropriate experience, and is inspired by the fulfillment of a felt need, want, urge, or desire. The goals that children set for themselves may have temporary significance, or they may represent the completion of more remote projects or the realization of deep-seated and permanent interests and ambitions.

The demands made upon an individual and what may be expected of him by members of his family, friends, or associates exert an impact on his level of aspiration. One child may aspire to become a fireman, another a policeman; neither of them retains this aspiration very long. However, as each grows into adulthood, one may be satisfied to make only enough money to feed and to clothe himself and his family; the other may aspire to achieve something of value to himself and to society. A life goal represents a *level of aspiration*.

Great interest is being shown in attempts to raise the levels of aspiration of low-aspiration-level children. Whether these levels represent long-range ambitions or the attainment of short-term goals, they vary with individuals and culture patterns. Any attempts to raise the level of aspiration are accompanied by hazards because many children suffer frustrations that are associated with fear and worry arising from new situations. The child's level of aspiration depends on his inner motives and the degree to which he perceives the goal as contributing to his maintenance of prestige. Although the demands of others influence the levels of aspiration, an individual gains or loses self-esteem as he succeeds or fails to reach his stated goals. Thus, his level of aspiration is influenced by his estimate of the attitudes of others toward him, his attitudes toward himself, and his ability to perform.

Through experience, individuals discover the level of aspiration they reasonably may expect to attain in any given area of activity. They learn to lower or to raise the aspiration level, thus avoiding many frustrating experiences. The young person who is faced with working his way through college or not attending, shows a high aspiration level if he decides to secure a college education in spite of his financial handicap. A low aspiration level is shown by the secondary school pupil who selects the easy course which will enable him to earn a diploma even though he may not be prepared to attend college.

Frustration Tolerance The extent to which a child is able to endure frustrating experiences without becoming emotionally disorganized can be considered to be representative of his frustration tolerance. This varies with age, health, previous experience, the nature, size, and importance of the obstacle, and the motive basic to the frustration. The child experiences many of these frustrating situations and disappointments as he grows into adulthood.

The level of aspiration helps determine whether the situation is likely to cause undue overt emotional reactions or not. What causes bitter disappointment to one person may not become an emotion stimulator for another. Everyone meets failure, but some learn to accept these frustrations without great disorganization; others are easily aroused by mildly disturbing factors in the situation. The individual who is able to use his failure to rally his strength and personal resources to overcome the forces that caused the failure has *high* frustration tolerance. However, when he becomes so discouraged by failure that he is unable to use his energy and talent to try again, he gives evidence of *low* frustration tolerance.

Each individual has his own level of frustration tolerance which varies with goals and levels of aspiration. A habitual procrastinator, for example, is sincere in his intention of completing a task when expected, but failing to do so gives evidence of low frustration tolerance. Although he intends to complete it on time, he seldom leaves enough time to complete it after he decides to start the action. The individual who completes a needed task when assigned to it gives evidence of *high* frustration tolerance. The latter individual soon earns a reputation as one on whom others can depend. He completes the project by overcoming all obstacles in the form of annoyances or thwartings that may seem to impede his progress. Mental, emotional, social, and spiritual growth are strengthened as the individual meets and solves his frustrations.

PROBLEMS ASSOCIATED WITH CONFLICT

Feelings of stress, strain, and frustration are closely associated with the arousal of conflicts within the individual. Conflicts arise out of failure to adjust satisfactorily to people or things in the environment, or inability to choose between two different interests or goals. Since most conflicts result from strong feelings of frustration, they may be considered to be frustration conflicts. A conflict is closely associated with mental and emotional disturbance, and can be described as the inner state, attitude, or behavior that results from mutually exclusive or opposing tendencies, impulses, or desires. A conflict may cause a denial of a personal satisfaction or a thwarting of social ambition.

Conflict Situations The child endows each new experience with values of feeling and emotional significance. His daily experiences are affected by the feeling tones of earlier experiences. He responds more or less consistently to some motivating stimuli, but is little affected by others. Conflicts, however, arise when habitually motivating stimuli are opposed by another set of stimuli that suddenly have been introduced into the situation. Opposing desires also may set up tensions that are incompatible with a repressed, unsatisfied drive or need. Conflicts result as respective ideas, feelings, and emotions compete for an outlet in the *psyche.*

In a study by Jersild and Markey [3] concerning the conflicts among fifty-four preschool children in a nursery school (ages twenty-two to fifty months), the investigators discovered that there was more frequent conflict between two older children or between two young children than between an older and a younger child. Same-sex conflicts appeared more often than opposite-sex conflicts. The decline in frequency of conflict occurred with age, although it was irregular and inconsistent. There were more conflicts, such as aggression and verbal and personal attacks, per child in the second year of nursery school. Conflicts increased along with increase in language skill. There was a tendency of the teachers to decide an issue in favor of the child who lost many fights when he was unaided.

Some degree of personal conflict is inevitable throughout all the child's developmental stages. Antagonisms arise, even in early years, between one set of values or standards and another. In a study of emotional problems associated with 469 children in their breast-feeding, Childers and Hamil [4] found, through the use of case histories, parents' and teachers' reports and records of breast-feeding that children weaned between one and six months of age showed the greatest undesirable behavior manifestations; those who were never breast-fed were next in frequency; while the children who were breast-fed for more than eleven months had the fewest such traits.

Every growing child is likely to be faced with choosing between two or more alternatives such as making a choice between two simple objects or actions, between two paths to a goal, between two or more interesting and important goals, and between making and not making a decision. The making of successful choices leads to good adjustment; indecision or the making of poor choices often leads to maladjustment. Various conflict patterns and their serious effects on an individual's chances of making good adjustment are given by Cameron as follows:

> When we speak of *conflict,* we mean *the mutual interference of competing reactions which prevents the adequate development, continuation or consummation of ongoing motivated behavior.* The competing reactions may be conceived of (a) as overt or covert attitudes and responses, (b) as antagonistic patterns of change in muscle tension and relaxation or (c) as mere shifts in action, potentials,

[3] Jersild, A. T., and Markey, F. V., *Conflicts between Preschool Children, Child Development Monographs,* No. 21. Teachers College, Columbia University, 1935.

[4] Childers, A. T., and Hamil, B. M., "Emotional Problems in Children as Related to the Duration of Breast Feeding in Infancy," *American Journal of Orthopsychiatry,* 2: 134–142, 1932.

demonstrated or inferred. For our purposes, conflicts can be conveniently grouped as *adient-avoidant, double-adient,* and *double-avoidant* reactions.

Adient-avoidant conflicts. The typical adient-avoidant conflict consists of two incompatible reactions, arising in the same act, one of them directed toward an object, activity, or goal (adient), and the other directed away from it (avoidant). Adient-avoidant conflicts appear early in childhood when punishment or restraint prevents the adequate development, continuation, or consummation of an act, but does not terminate it. If, for example, each time a child reaches toward some object, an adult slaps his hand, restrains him or scolds him, he may develop an avoidant reaction without, however, losing his original adient one. If reaching and withdrawing tendencies are approximately equal, the child's hand may remain suspended part way to the object or execute oscillatory movements toward and away from it, until fatigue, distraction, or a rage response tips the balance. The reverse situation develops when an adult coaxes or compels a child to face something toward which the child's original reaction, still present, is one of avoidance.

However, as every mother knows, even the certainty of punishment does not always prevent an adient reaction from going on to consummation, nor will the most attractive reward always overcome a child's avoidant reaction. Both children and adults do and refuse to do many things in spite of their accurately anticipating painful retaliation. One reason for this, of special importance in behavior pathology, is that the sustained tensions of conflict can become in themselves so intolerable that they make one reckless of consequences. The normal small child may terminate his conflict in an outburst of rage or aggression against an interference or an offending object. In young and old alike, an outburst has the immediate, though unplanned, effect of reducing the tensions of conflict. But as a child grows older, this technique becomes less and less successful in getting rid of conflict, because of society's rising scale of taboos against temper tantrums with increasing biosocial maturity.

Among children and adults, prolonged adient-avoidant conflicts are prime sources of anxiety, and anxiety is a prominent constituent of many behavior disorders. Thus, sustained conflict often leads directly into anxiety disorders, anxiety attacks, and panic reactions. The anxiety of adient-avoidant conflict may under some circumstances lead instead to phobic, compulsive, or hysterical reactions. These often protect the individual from direct anxiety at the high cost of chronic neurosis, but they do not actually resolve the conflict situations. What we call *guilt* is a special case of adient-avoidant conflict. The temptation to do something forbidden is the adient tendency while the partial inhibition of that forbidden adience, derived perhaps indirectly from previous punishment or threat, is the avoidant tendency which prevents or delays the adient consummation. The adient-avoidant conflict of guilt is clearly responsible for many delusional and hallucinatory developments, such as those we shall meet in paranoid disorders, in schizophrenia, and in mania, depressions, and delirium.

Double-adient conflicts. The typical double-adient conflict consists of two incompatible reactions arising in the same act, both of which are directed toward the same object, activity, or goal (*convergent adience*), or each of which is directed toward a different object, activity or goal (*divergent adience*). In *convergent adience* there is one object, activity or goal, but two competing, incompatible attitudes are aroused toward it. In *divergent adience* there are two objects, activities or goals, and one's adient attitude supports competing responses toward both at once.

Double-adient conflicts of both kinds develop in numerous common ambivalent situations. Convergent adience is seen, for example, in the simultaneous appearance of hostile aggressive attitudes and affectionate accepting attitudes toward one's parent, one's beloved, or one's child.[5] Divergent adience appears in situations that offer a person parental reward, filial, community, or celestial reward, in exchange for abandoning something else which he dearly wants. No matter which adient reaction he begins, he will find that he cannot escape the pull of the other adient-reaction tendency.

Double-avoidant conflicts. The typical double-avoidant conflict consists of two incompatible reactions, arising in the same act, each of which is directed away from an object, activity, or goal. The man in double-avoidant conflict is like a tennis ball in play; whichever way he travels he gets hurt. This is the dilemma of the child or adult who, for example, is threatened with pain, privation, or rejection if he does not go through with a disagreeable, humiliating, or frightening situation. It also was Hamlet's dilemma and the one confronting a great many suicides. Hysterical disabilities are not uncommonly the outcome of double-avoidant conflicts. Faced with the social demand that he perform some dangerous or distasteful duty, a person may be unable to escape it without incurring social retaliation and disgrace, unless there are extenuating circumstances.[6]

The intricate pattern of human nature and the complex character of human relationships preclude the likelihood that anyone, even for a short period during his lifetime, will achieve a completely nonthwarted state of self-satisfaction. Many of a child's unpleasant experiences represent desirable elements of personality development and adjustment, but maladjustment results from those inadequately resolved conflicts that tend to recur or persist.

MENTAL HEALTH AND ADJUSTMENT

For many years the possession of good physical and mental health has been considered important. An old Chinese custom was to pay a doctor to keep one well; in Western cultures there is an attempt to avoid ill health and to seek medical aid only when curative treatment is necessary. In the field of mental health, parents and teachers are concerned

---

[5] *Adience* should not be confused with the so-called "pleasure principle." Adience refers to relative *direction*. A hostile aggression is adient in the same general sense that a loving approach is adient.

[6] Cameron, N. A., *The Psychology of Behavior Disorders,* pp. 131–134. Boston: Houghton Mifflin Company, copyright 1947.

both with prevention of mental illness and the preservation of good mental health.

No longer are temper tantrums, truancy, or other forms of delinquent behavior considered to be inner manifestations of a child's selfishness or meanness. They result in part from inexpert guidance on the part of adults. Whatever can be done to develop emotionally stable children must begin with a consideration of their potential strength as this is revealed indirectly through their heritage, and the educational and environmental influences which affect their interests, attitudes, and activities.

Meaning of Mental Health Good adjustment or normal mental functioning is a matter of degree. A person who adjusts well to environmental situations and interpersonal relations gives evidence of possessing good mental health. Although occasionally he deviates from his accustomed mode of behavior, he soon returns to normality with little or no aid from others. A severe shock or other emotion-disturbing experience may so affect an individual that he needs help to regain his normal patterns of adjustment. If for one reason or another, a person loses his ability to solve personal problems having emotional concomitants, he is considered to be mentally ill or maladjusted, and may require the services of a trained expert to provide curative measures. Specialists in this field include psychiatrists, clinical psychologists, psychiatric social workers, and physical, recreational, and occupational therapists.

The Mental Hygiene Movement Early in the twentieth century there was started a movement called the Mental Hygiene Movement (now Mental Health) which emphasized the preventive, preservative, and curative aspects of mental health. Clifford Beers authored a book, *A Mind That Found Itself,* and, with Adolph Meyer, a psychiatrist who became interested in the story of Beers' experiences in a mental hospital, founded the first state mental hygiene organization. Interest in the application of the principles of mental health spread rapidly. Shortly thereafter a National Committee of Mental Hygiene was established. Through its influence much help has been given to those who suffer maladies associated with mental illness.

In child psychology the emphasis is placed on *prevention* of maladjustment and mental disruption. The early experiences provided by parents and teachers are so vital to the good adjustment or mental health of each child that whatever knowledge can be applied in dealing with children will be reflected in their behavior and attitudes. The mental health of each child is rooted in the interaction between his inborn characteristics and the environmental forces. Just as the treatment of physical ill health is left in the hands of trained doctors, so is the treatment of mental and emotional disturbances assigned to trained professional personnel.

Positive Mental Health Approaches The attitudes and behavior displayed by parents, teachers, and others toward the fulfillment of a child's mental, emotional, or social needs affect the state of mental health exhibited by the individual. Overemphasis on one area of inherent needs with disregard for others may have disrupting effects. The young child, for example, is aggressive, demanding, and selfish. He needs guidance of his behavior, since these traits are his weapons of defense. During his early years, when he wants something he grabs it. Later he learns how to ask politely for it. When something that he wants is taken away from him he is bewildered, becomes disappointed, and cries. Thus he communicates his feelings to others. Whatever mental health principles can be applied will enable the child to overcome these limitations and develop good adjustment at the same time. The application of preventive and preservative principles of mental health by parents and teachers can exercise a continuous healthful influence on the child's personal and social adjustment.

MENTAL HEALTH APPROACHES TO ADJUSTMENT

An individual constantly is faced with making adjustments to even minor stresses and strains. A child becomes restless if his mother is delayed in attending to his needs, or becomes upset if one of his favorite toys is broken. He also may be frightened by strange noises or by reports of "bug-a-boos" in the basement. Such incidents represent stresses and strains that usually are temporary; good adjustment is made easily. Other incidents evoke behavior signs of resentment, repression, suspicion, cruelty, shyness, or bullying. These cannot be removed so easily and may show themselves in maladjustment.

The results of thwarting, frustration, or conflict cannot be overcome by the application of simple rules or panaceas. The individual himself is responsible for building self-realizing experiences, although he can be helped by parents, teachers, nurses, and other leaders. He meets maladjusting influences: by launching a direct attack, during which time he attempts to master the situation; by arriving at a compromise; or by retreating from the situation. In a direct attack he attempts to do something positive about the difficulty. In the compromise approach he tends to alleviate the stresses in the situation by utilizing face-saving devices. By retreating, he tends to run away from the problem because he feels inadequate to meet the frustrations and conflicts involved.

UTILIZATION OF SELF-ADJUSTIVE APPROACHES

In his attempt to meet maladjustive elements in his environment, a child may utilize an aggressive *fight* approach or he may give evidence of *flight* tendencies. He may attempt to compensate in one way or another for his own deficiencies, or he may try, in various ways, to circumvent the obstacles to the fulfillment of his interests or desires. In these behavior expressions he more or less unconsciously is making use of what are referred to as *self-adjustive approaches* or *mechanisms of adjustment*.

The utilization of one or more of these mechanisms can serve as a self-bolstering device to the individual. As he attempts to resolve frustration and conflict during his developing years, the child makes use of most of these techniques. Some of these approaches produce a better-adjusted, stronger personality; others tend to affect adversely an already inadequate personality. We shall explain briefly some attitudinal and behavior patterns associated with important adjustment approaches used by the child.

Aggressive Behavior   The child uses aggression in an attempt to control, remove, or destroy an obstacle, or he attempts to compensate for it in order that he may maintain his ego. If he feels inferior he may become demanding, constantly insisting on the maintenance of his "rights." He sometimes makes himself conspicuous by his desire to demonstrate his importance. Although the child is expected to repress his aggressive responses, it may be a good adjustment practice if he "blows off steam" occasionally.

Compensatory Behavior   The term "compensation" sometimes is used to describe any form of deviate behavior that aids in the alleviation of tensions caused by inability to gain satisfaction under usual or normal conditions and modes of behavior. A child uses compensation in an attempt to meet frustrating situations by overacting in the same general function in which he has a defect. For example, a cripple attempts to help others, a short girl wears high heels, a stout boy overexerts. Compensation is an attempt on the part of the individual to overcome a real or imagined defect.

In his use of compensation, a child utilizes a satisfactory form of behavior to reduce tensions that result from a recognized failure or inadequacy. A parent may attempt to compensate for his failure to enter a vocation of his choice by influencing his child to enter that field for the latter's life work. A boy who has gotten into difficulty may put forth great energy to help authorities find the culprit, and so on.

Attention-Getting Behavior   Some children take every opportunity to attract attention to themselves. This is especially characteristic of some children when they are on the defensive. They may make faces, gesticulate, walk in stiff-legged fashion, or find some other way to "show off." As they grow older, they employ more subtle tactics to attract attention to themselves. They strive for recognition because they do not want to be ignored. The attention-getting urge is especially strong during adolescence.

A few attention-getting devices of children and young adolescents include boasting of family status or personal accomplishments, displaying bad manners in social situations, engaging in hobbies, teasing and tormenting, and wearing special clothing. Sometimes a young person's desire for attention is so strong that he engages in asocial or other abnormal behavior in order to gain the approval of his peers. Delinquent behavior sometimes can be traced to the child's attempt to satisfy his urge for attention.

Introjection   A child unconsciously acquires ideas, emotional attitudes, and ideals from the people with whom he lives. As he lives with his parents and other members of his family as well as with other associates, he gradually absorbs the attitudes and ideals exhibited by them. The impact of all these forces and influences upon him is referred to as *introjection*. The child experiences his own feeling tones, but his beliefs result from the beliefs and ideals of parents, brothers and sisters, and others in his environment. He develops his own ideals and values through the interaction between himself and his home and educational influences. Since introjection tends to function indirectly, the need is great for parents and teachers to exhibit model behavior.

Identification   A child who still is "finding his way" toward successful achievement has a tendency to identify himself with a successful person or group. A boy identifies with his father, a space pilot, or a baseball player whom he admires, and proceeds to pattern his behavior accordingly. A girl identifies herself with her mother, a motion picture actress, or a favored aunt, and imitates the behavior of the model. Such identification is desirable if or when the child is helped to develop thereby a fine personality and character. This technique is used profitably by most growing boys and girls. Strong loyalties to groups are built as the individual gets a lift from the fact that he is a member of a successful group and contributes to its achievement.

Identification can be damaging to an individual if he attempts to assume the attitudes or behavior characteristics of another person to the loss of his own identity. If the child loses his individuality in the personality of his hero, he is faced with a serious maladjustment. Frustration, rather than stress alleviation, will be induced when a child attempts to pattern his behavior on that of another, especially if he lacks the necessary qualities for successful achievement in the area.

Projection A tendency to blame another person for one's own errors or shortcomings is a common practice. Most children dislike to admit their errors or their inability to perform successfully. The tendency of a child to place the blame on another person for errors made by himself, or to fail to admit his own shortcomings is known as *projection*. It seems that in the adjusting process it is easier to blame others than to accept the blame for mistakes made. The child blames his team-mates for the loss of a game; the pupil in school traces his lack of success to the teacher; the adolescent blames the group for rejecting him as a member, and so on. Care must be taken that a child does not develop habits of blaming others for personal errors, otherwise he may develop deep-seated resentments or become a chronic fault-finder.

Sometimes the tension is reduced by excusing one's acts by reporting that "John is just as bad as I," or "If I hadn't done it someone else would have." The child caught in the act attempts to advance the idea that he was not so bad as the one who did not get caught. The boy apprehended in the act of throwing a wad believes that he should not have been punished since he had not thrown as many as did his classmates, and so on. Many individuals apprehended in performing antisocial acts believe that they were less offensive than others. The breaking of windows, swearing, cheating, and lying by associates are more serious offenses than are the acts of the child who is reprimanded. These attempts to temper unsatisfactory consequences of one's own bad behavior represent undesirable projection.

Rationalization *(Self-Deception)* Rationalization is a form of self-deception employed by a child when he attempts to explain something he has done that he knows is undesirable or foolish. He attempts to bolster his ego by explaining his behavior in such a way that he avoids criticism. The making of excuses or giving unrealistic reasons for behavior that one knows is undesirable or foolish is known as *rationalization*. The individual attempts to conceal the real reason for his behavior. With confidence, he gives plausible explanations rather than honest reasons for his acts. Thus he hopes to save face and maintain his self-esteem.

It is not always easy for a child to admit to himself and to others the reasons for his acts. He tends to manufacture ways of protecting himself from punishment which he suffered in the past when he made similar mistakes. The child often uses rationalization to ease the punishment for himself. The expectations of parents and others and his level of aspiration determine in part the nature and extent to which he uses rationalization. As the standards of conduct are raised, there may be an increase in the use of self-deception, especially if the individual feels inadequate in achieving those standards. The sour-grapes approach is accepted but, if rationalization is indulged in consistently as a means of self-justification for undesirable behavior, resentment on the part of others is directed toward the individual who indulges in this form of self-deception.

Sublimation   Sublimation represents substitute activity in children. A child may have a strong urge to engage in a particular form of activity, but the desired activity is interfered with because of personal inefficiency or social standards. He then may attempt to engage in substitute activity which to him seems to be both satisfying and achievable. The child, for example, wants to take a toy train apart; his mother does not want him to do this and gives him an erector set which he may dismantle. Soon he learns to utilize another project for that in which he is not supposed to engage.

The purpose of sublimation sometimes is to express less desirable forms of behavior in other more socially acceptable forms. For example, one may redirect the sex urge away from immediate forms of expression toward higher, more socially acceptable, forms of behavior. Thus the primitive emotional reactions are directed toward socially approved goals.

Egocentrism   The child develops egocentric behavior as a result of the amount of praise he receives, whether or not it is merited. A child needs approval of behavior; praise for work well done can be an excellent emotion stimulator. During his early days he held the center of attention; as he grows older he tends to use many egocentric approaches to continue to hold the center of the stage. Temper tantrums, for example, are attempted. There comes a time, however, when the child needs to become less egocentric and more interested in the activities and interests of other people. Egocentric traits that are highly developed in childhood may be very frustrating when the young person discovers that other children are unwilling to give him the attention he craves. He needs guidance toward the experiencing of interests that are centered in others.

Daydreaming Daydreaming represents the imaginary satisfaction that is not attained in real experience. It serves a useful purpose in solving problems that defy solution in reality for the individual at his stage of development. Imagination is often used as a means of escape when an individual is confronted by a perplexing problem. It is easy to move from the factual world, where problems are solved in terms of reality, into an imaginary world where successes are readily and easily achievable. (See Chapter 12.)

If a child is stimulated by examples of other persons who have won approval for their behavior and if he is helped to achieve his aim, he learns to direct his thinking and behavior into desirable channels. Too often, however, the exploits of heroes who are far removed in ability or opportunity from the child who is being motivated by such tales stimulate unachievable dreams. A nursery-school child can use his imaginative powers realistically by preparing a birthday card for his mother, thereby achieving acceptable outcomes.

Daydreaming permits the imagination to make use of ideas that afford immediate satisfactions. They need not be harmful to the child. Because of the many associations of ideas, it is impossible to hold in focus one thought for an extended length of time. Consequently, differing ideas and images emerge. Thus do many individuals find the materials for the solution of problems. The individual, however, should not indulge in these mental wanderings to the extent that he is unable to focus on the problem at hand.

The healthy child is not likely to be harmed by his daydreams if he is given opportunity for successful achievement within the limits of his abilities. His real world at first consists of fairies, goblins, brave princes, and beautiful princesses. He should be helped to move away from this world of fantasy and imagination. He gradually can be inducted into the real world of adults through experiences with people and with children's literature. Long before he is old enough to participate in adult activities, he can be stimulated by success stories of others. It is common for an adolescent, for example, to let his mind drift into thoughts of things he hopes to do. Daydreams of this kind can serve as incentives toward self-improvement and self-realization; those associated with wish fulfillment are likely to lead to disaster. Daydreaming or fantasy is not likely to be undesirable if a balance between good adjustment and imagined satisfactions is maintained.

Sympathy Many forms of self-adjustive behavior give evidence of attention-getting. The child exhibits these striving-for-sympathy traits in numerous ways. He likes the assistance he receives from his parents or others who care for him. The child who fails when he is denied sought-for help often seeks sympathy from others. He may tell them how hard he has worked, how unfair his parents are, how his teacher favors other children, and the like. He often attempts to satisfy his feelings by playing on the sympathy of his friends.

Withdrawal Behavior When a child retreats from a participation in certain life experiences, he exhibits withdrawal behavior. Most children are timid in at least some life situations, especially those for which they are not prepared. Included in withdrawal behavior are shyness, negativism, and regression. The withdrawing attitude is a maladjustment only when social effectiveness is disrupted.

shyness The shy and timid child seldom disturbs others. Hence his maladjustment often goes unnoticed by parents and teachers. Shyness is not a general characteristic. A child may be shy in one situation and courageous in another. He may be shy in the classroom with his classmates, but courageous and confident on the playing field. When a child is shy in most situations, his personality needs bolstering. The timid and withdrawing child is liked by his teachers because he creates no annoyance in the classroom. However, if he is not given social experiences, he is likely to retreat more and more into himself until later he may need psychiatric help.

The shy child experiences great fear, but hesitates to share his problem with anyone: parent, teacher, or even peer associate. He usually has a strong desire to participate in the activities of others, but, because of shyness, builds up tensions and frustrations which keep him from doing so. The child who has been overprotected or disciplined too rigidly by his parents may develop attitudes of retreat from doing things with others. With increasing age, the conflict tensions are likely to become more severe unless the teacher and the parent, working together, help him develop a feeling of belongingness as he participates in group activities.

negativism Negativism is a common adjustment mechanism in which the child deliberately refuses to recognize the real situation, and displays behavior that is rebellious against the suggestions of authority. It represents a stage in the child's development during which he replies with a "No," even though he complies with the request. This is a behavior manifestation of the three- and four-year-old and is likely to pass shortly. There is danger in the negative response only if it continues beyond early childhood years and if it is accompanied by temper tantrums.

Negativism usually is not deep-seated and does not persist unless parents and teachers stimulate the child adversely. Often, if he is asked to perform tasks that are beyond his ability to complete successfully, he may refuse to attempt them but gives no real reason for his attitude. He protects his ego lest his deficiencies be discovered. His behavior, in these situations, is based on fear.

REGRESSION   The utilization, at a later stage of development, of behavior patterns that brought satisfaction to a child at an earlier age is known as *regression*. A four-year-old child often exhibits helpless tendencies when his mother gives too much attention to his baby brother or sister. He may insist on being helped in eating, dressing, and getting his toys, even though before the arrival of the baby he was able to perform most of these acts creditably.

The child may derive satisfaction from shifting the responsibility of making decisions from himself to his mother or other person. He is strengthened in acquiring attitudes of decision-making if he receives special training in his early childhood. Assuming responsibility is not inherited, it must be learned through experience promoted by wise guidance of those in authority. If he is well-trained in the ability to make his own decisions, the child is less likely to fall back on his earlier levels of response when he is thrown on his own resources. Earlier habit patterns are resorted to only when a child faces a difficult situation fraught with possible frustration. It is no surprise that an individual coddled at home soon develops a case of "homesickness" when he goes away from home for the first time to camp, to boarding school, to college, or to the army.

Neurotic Behavior   In his attempt to escape frustration or conflict an individual may display symptoms of mental illness or of physical disability. This is called neurotic behavior. If the individual is confronted with important issues for which he sees no solutions, mental conflicts may arise. Neurotic symptoms once fixed are not easily changed. They are symbolic and take the form of *phobias, obsessions, and compulsions.*

PHOBIAS   A phobia represents an unusual fear for which there is no sound basis or reason. It is difficult for most individuals who have experienced phobias to explain the cause of them or to describe clearly their own emotional behavior in relation to them. They are symbolic and associated with unpleasant experiences. (See Chapter 10.)

OBSESSIONS   An obsession refers to ideas that are unreasonable, yet tend to persist. Even though they are recognized as illogical or unreasonable, they tend to persist or recur and interfere with clear thinking. Obsessions take many forms and may relate to an individual's atttitude toward himself and to forces that will affect him. He may develop a fixed belief that something bad is going to happen or that his friends are planning to poison or kill him in some way. This fixation persists in spite of evidence to the contrary.

COMPULSIONS   A compulsion can be considered to be a tendency to perform acts that are recognized by others to be irrational. Behavior that is continued by the individual because of his strong desire to engage in it without good reason is referred to as *compulsive behavior*. This urge is so strong and so persistent that emotional tension is relieved only if and when the act is performed. Examples of compulsive acts of children include touching or counting objects; stepping on or over cracks in the sidewalk; throwing a stone at a target; imitating elders; carrying a special token or coin, a rabbit's foot, and the like. Sometimes, superstition acts as a stimulus for compulsive behavior. Some compulsions lead to activities that are harmful, personally and socially. The compulsion to set fires (*pyromania*) and the urge to steal (*kleptomania*) are examples of unwholesome compulsions.

ADJUSTMENT PROBLEMS OF THE PHYSICALLY HANDICAPPED CHILD

Adjustment problems of physically handicapped children are the concern of both the individuals themselves and the members of the society in which they are found. The child with a handicap should be helped to understand that he differs from other children and the nature and extent of this difference. Other children, in turn, should be helped to understand the handicapped individual. Each should be aided in appreciating the psychological and physical bases of these differences and be assisted to develop attitudes that will be personally helpful in their relationships with each other. We discuss briefly some of the adjustment factors involved as the handicapped individual lives with himself and others. The types of handicaps we shall discuss include the delicate individual, the cripple, the child with defective vision, the child with hearing defects, and the child with defective speech.

The Delicate Individual The child who is sickly and helpless from infancy usually is coddled so much that he becomes "spoiled." If the condition continues, those who care for his needs usually add to his spoiling. Thus he gains the sympathetic attention of those elders who wait on him. Soon he has developed an attitude of dependence on others, and capitalizes on it as much as possible. Wise parents orient him toward thinking that, although he is deserving of special consideration, attention also needs to be given to others of his age. If this is accomplished before the child starts to school, he will find it easier to relate to his schoolmates; those personal attitudes that should be established can be given a chance to develop. Too often the siblings in a home fail to understand that it does not always mean parental favoritism when parents give the delicate child a preference in such things as special toys, a place to play, and so on. Disharmony in a home can be avoided if parents bring the special problem to the attention of all members of the family.

Both at home and at school, the delicate child should be given an opportunity to perform tasks that are within the limits of his strength. He should not be pampered but encouraged to achieve success in as many activities as possible. Teachers should be informed concerning the nature of the weakness so that proper activity programs can be provided. At best, the adjustive problems of the delicate child in school are great. They may be even greater for him than for children with other more obvious handicaps. Good liaison between the school and the home is always helpful to a delicate child.

Many delicate children get a poor start in school. Because of their irregular attendance they are forced to miss many stimulating school experiences. Too often they are passive observers of many strenuous activities of their schoolmates in which they secretly would like to participate. They sometimes lack the energy to complete the work in which they are interested. The children need good food, medical care, adequate equipment, home cooperation, and an intelligent attitude toward healthful living which are basic to the growth and adjustment of the delicate child.

The Cripple Like the delicate individual, the child who has been crippled from birth has need for special care at home; as he receives it, he may learn to lean upon others for sympathetic attention. During his infancy and early childhood, his parents can help him acquire a proper attitude toward his infirmity, if he is to develop other-centered interests. Parents can plan his experiences in such a way as to help the crippled child develop wholesome attitudes toward his handicap as well as toward himself and others. His handicap should not be the center of special attention or discussion.

Parents and teachers need to realize that a crippled child has hopes and ambitions similar to those of other children. Often he wants to do much more than can safely be left to him. He develops a restlessness as he grows into later childhood and into adolescence. Sometimes he develops a negativistic attitude because he is denied participation in many activities pursued by normal children. He needs to be given activities in association with his classmates that will enable him to experience success. These experiences will give him consideration for others and enable him to develop attitudes that will make it possible for him to become a good home and school citizen. As these children are educated in classes with normal children, they develop social interests and amenities. Modern transportation and building facilities make it possible for the cripple to be transported to regular classrooms where he can mingle with children of his own age.

The Child with Defective Vision The child with extremely defective vision has many difficult adjustments to make. If blindness or near blindness occurs at birth or in infancy, he is unable to understand his limitations of experience. With an increase in maturity he comes to have an awareness of his limitations; he may develop attitudes that are understandable but difficult to change. The child with extremely defective vision may retreat into himself, and may be left to himself by those parents who lack the needed ability or the time to devote to his special needs. He usually is shy, and prefers to be with his mother or alone. When companions are available, he prefers to limit his friendship to one or two individuals who reciprocate his friendship. As he grows into adolescence, this best friend often is one who also has defective vision.

The child with defective vision may become impatient at school, partly because he believes that he imposes on the time of his peers. As a result, he develops withdrawal tendencies, and engages in activities which he can do alone. He needs social experiences with those who are sighted. Young children seem to make excellent progress in special schools for the blind or near-blind. Here they receive training in personal, educational, and vocational adjustment. They come to realize that even those who have defective vision also can, with proper training, serve as teachers. Helen Keller, whose hearing as well as sight was destroyed before she was two years old, is an example of a severely handicapped individual who succeeded. The fine attitudes she has displayed through the years have taught others with physical handicaps the value of persistence in over-coming a handicap.

The Child with Defective Hearing The child who cannot hear receives little stimulation in the home, and usually has trouble with his speech and language. This fact aggravates his problem. When training is given in the development of language, a deaf individual makes progress and can begin to relate to those of normal hearing. Since the totally deaf child cannot hear the voices of others, he strives to imitate the speech patterns of a speaker after studying the movements of his throat, lips, and tongue in attempted speech. The struggle to overcome these limitations is rewarding, but requires much patience of parents and teachers. As the deaf and the normal are educated together, the former are saved from becoming a group apart.

The problems faced by the hard-of-hearing are somewhat different from those of the completely deaf but are significant to the afflicted and to those with whom they associate. Unfortunately, many children are un-willing to admit that they cannot hear well. They prefer to fail in school or to be considered less able mentally than reveal the fact that they have difficulty in hearing. Hearing loss now is usually discovered through yearly examinations and through vigilant teacher observation and check-up. The deaf child is suspicious of what is being said. He sees that comments, laughter, and gestures are engaged in by others and imagines that deroga-tory remarks are directed at him. Fortunately, modern hearing aids can correct most hearing difficulties of hard-of-hearing individuals.

The Child with Defective Speech Some children have poor speech as a result of imitation of inadequate speech; others have defective speech because of defective dentition or of improper use of the tongue. The kind and nature of the defect must be evaluated in light of the total effect on the child. The home influence sets the speech pattern. The child's imitation of the speech that he hears in the home fixes his speech patterns. Whatever careless, inaccurate, or slovenly speech he acquires usually is the result of these early experiences. Once these speech patterns are formed, the establishment of new and different patterns is not easy. Parents, not realizing that speech maturation often is delayed, become alarmed because the child is slow in talking. However, if a child uses odd speech he should be helped, not ridiculed, in overcoming the difficulty. The mother, for instance, should not attempt to use baby talk when speaking to a young child. It may be the speech of the baby, but the infant understands the adult speech much better than his own crude attempts to express himself.

Speech defects caused by irregular or badly formed teeth, by improper use of the tongue, or by throat or nose difficulties can be remedied if the child is given medical and dental care. Speech difficulties, such as stammering and stuttering, seem to accompany disturbed emotional states, although exact causes are not fully known. Nevertheless, parents can do much to help the child so afflicted to overcome his difficulty by reducing or eliminating the emotional disturbance that causes the stuttering. For example, a child who stutters in the classroom often does not exhibit that speech defect on the playground. (See Chapter 6.)

The attitudes of others become important to the child who has a speech difficulty. He needs a lift during these trying experiences. He must be motivated to want to correct any speech errors. More than routine drill is necessary to improve speech difficulties. He needs to be encouraged to want to improve until finally he develops the confidence that he can do it. Although drill and special exercises are required for improvement, the speech handicap should never be overemphasized.

SEVERE MENTAL AND EMOTIONAL DISORDERS

The extent to which and the nature of the adjustments made vary widely among individuals even in the same family. The child, for example, who is physically strong and active and mentally alert may respond to restrictions on his behavior with open rebellion; his brother who is weaker, less active, and possessing lower mental ability may exhibit passive, withdrawing behavior and tend to retreat from anxiety-producing stimuli or situations. Through the use of adjustment mechanisms, each child, either by his own efforts or with proper guidance, usually can recondition his behavior and become a well-adjusted person.

Emotional Disturbances among Children   Some preschool children display symptoms of emotional disturbance. Strong tensions caused by inherent weakness and improper rearing may result in the development of habit disorders, such as abnormal attitudes toward food taking, sleep, and elimination. The child may become a nail-biter or thumb-sucker; eating may cause him to vomit. He may sleep fitfully or have bad dreams. He may suffer from diarrhea or constipation, or enuresis (bed-wetting). These difficulties usually can be overcome early with the aid of a good pediatrician who seeks and treats the underlying cause which, in many cases, is the effect on the child of a neurotic mother. Hence both the child and the mother may need the care of a psychotherapist, especially if the symptoms persist beyond the early childhood years.

Neurotic Tendencies Normal children, as we have noted in earlier discussions, tend occasionally to show signs of disturbed emotional states, but these usually pass with increase in maturation. Among some children, however, disordered behavior tends to persist. The child may have speech problems; he becomes unduly destructive; he is oversensitive, excessively timid and dependent; he engages consistently in temper tantrums; he suffers from severe phobias. His apparent timidity actually may be the inhibition of aggressiveness. Clinicians have found that these behavior signs may be the result of inner conflicts.

The child, for one reason or another, suffers from anxieties to which normal expression is not or cannot be given. The condition is latent, but many rituals are engaged in that give indication of the disturbed state. Obsessive thoughts run through his head; he has certain compulsions, such as counting steps as he goes up and downstairs, sometimes in units of two's and three's, or walking in the snow rather than on the sidewalk. If the causes of the anxious state are discovered, the child may be able to make a more realistic adjustment to his pattern of living. Otherwise, the situation may be worsened and a psychopathological condition may emerge.

Psychopathological Difficulties Among psychopathological disturbances can be included psychosomatic disorders and the psychoses. According to Maslow and Mittelmann,[7] some of the psychosomatic reactions displayed in childhood are allergies (having an emotional base), fever and headache, gastrointestinal pain, and ulcerative colitis. Maternal rejection can be associated with the display of these psychosomatic symptoms. Here, again, intensive study of the causes of the difficulty and psychotherapy are needed.

Psychoses are severe disturbances that affect much of the behavior of the child. The roots of a psychosis usually can be found in conflict between strong urges and ambitions of the individual. These desires and wants sometimes extend far back into early childhood. They are the predisposing conditions that lead to the development of abnormal symptoms when the individual is subjected to emotional shock or other disturbing stimuli. The continuance of faulty habits or responses to life situations

[7] Maslow, A. H., and Mittelmann, B., *Principles of Abnormal Psychology: the Dynamics of Pychic Illness,* rev. ed., pp. 349–353. New York: Harper and Brothers, 1951.

long after these habits should have been replaced by more socially acceptable ways of behavior also may cause the disturbance. These causes and whatever may have been inherited in the way of predisposing factors combine in a display of disordered behavior.

Unhealthy tendencies can be intensified by exposure to unfavorable environmental conditions. A child of emotionally unstable parents, reared in a conflict-ridden, emotion-disrupting home, for example, is a victim of disaster-encouraging forces both within himself and in his surroundings. Some disorders have an organic base.[8]

Fortunately, very few children develop a psychotic state. Some tension-filled adolescents become a prey to schizophrenia, although a few children as young as two years of age give evidence of schizophrenic symptoms. In responses to test situations, schizophrenic children display confused thinking and flightiness.[9] Other symptoms are withdrawal into fantasy, speech deviations and poor communication or language skills, apathy, abnormal interpersonal relationships, delusions of persecution, and general nonuniformity of development. Children vary with age in their display of schizophrenic symptoms.

Organic disturbances of the nervous system also may result in the development of psychiatric syndromes. Head injury, for instance, may result in impaired mental functioning. Chorea can be caused by rheumatic fever. Encephalitis, sometimes referred to as sleeping sickness, is an inflammation of the brain, especially of the brain stem, and can be caused by measles, scarlet fever, severe burns, or vaccination.

Treatment of Emotional Disturbances As we said earlier in the chapter, the pediatrician can be extremely helpful in assisting parents to prevent the onset of emotional disturbances in a child. As he treats both mother and child, he is alert to conditions that may be unfavorable to the child's best development and adjustment. Child guidance clinics can give indirect psychological care in cases of mild functional disorder. These include attempts to change or modify the child's environment. More severe forms may need treatment, usually referred to as psychotherapy. A much used technique of psychotherapy with children is play therapy. The child is given opportunities to work out his tensions, aggressions, and anxieties as he participates in free play activities, either alone or in the company of a small balanced group of other disturbed children. The

[8] See Anderson, C. M., "Organic Factors Predisposing to Schizophrenia," *Nervous Child*, 10: 38–42, 1954.

[9] See Des Lauriers, A., and Halpern, F., "Psychological Tests in Childhood Schizophrenia," *American Journal of Orthopsychiatry*, 17: 57–67, 1947.

therapist carefully watches the children's reactions, but keeps himself in the background, offering suggestions only when possible danger to a child is indicated.

Emotional difficulties that seem to have an organic base are treated by the administration of drugs, special diets, operations, and the like, in addition to psychotherapy. Severe cases of emotional disturbance (schizophrenia, for example), especially among older children, may need to be treated in a mental hospital. In most instances, parents, no matter how cooperative they are, need guidance in dealing with the disturbed child.

QUESTIONS AND TOPICS FOR DISCUSSION

1. Differentiate between the well-adjusted and maladjusted individual. Give specific examples.
2. Give examples of frustrations which you have experienced. Why did they arise and how did you resolve them?
3. List some of the frustrations that a child may experience in school; at home.
4. Discuss the relationship between mental and emotional factors in frustration.
5. Give examples of frustration tolerance in a child; in an adolescent; in an adult.
6. Recall several conflicts of interests you experienced during your developing years. How serious did they seem at the time of their occurrence? How important do they appear in retrospect?
7. Present an original example for each of the following types of conflict: adient-avoidant, double-adient, double-avoidant.
8. Which of the self-adjustive approaches presented in this chapter have you employed to meet frustrating situations? Select one and describe its functioning.
9. Formulate a general principle of treatment that can apply to all physically handicapped children and help them achieve good mental health.
10. If possible, visit the children's ward of a hospital for the mentally ill. Study the reactions of a few of the children. Try to obtain their case histories and compare cause-and-effect relationships.
11. Describe the behavior of a child or an older person who has a tendency toward regression.
12. Explain why any obsessions or compulsions acquired in childhood are difficult to overcome later.
13. Identify some of the adjustment problems that arise in the parent-child situation; in the teacher-child situation. Suggest ways of dealing with them.

14. *Special Project:* Try to discover, through tactful questioning, the level of aspiration of each of your four subjects. What differences do you find? If any one of your subjects is experiencing a conflict at present, what can you do to help him resolve it? Evaluate the degree of mental health possessed by each of your subjects. Note any utilization of mechanisms of adjustment.

SELECTED REFERENCES

Baker, Harry J., *Introduction to Exceptional Children,* 3rd ed. New York: The Macmillan Company, 1959.

Baldwin, H., and Baldwin, R. M., *Management of Behavior Disorders in Children.* Philadelphia: W. B. Saunders Company, 1960.

Berkowitz, Pearl H., and Rothman, E. P., *The Disturbed Child: Recognition and Psychoeducational Therapy in the Classroom.* New York: New York University Press, 1960.

Crow, Lester D., and Crow, Alice, *Readings in Child and Adolescent Psychology.* New York: Longmans, Green and Company, Inc., 1961.

Escalona, Sibylle, *Understanding Hostility in Children.* Chicago: Science Research Associates, Inc., 1954.

Jourand, Sidney M., *Personal Adjustment.* New York: The Macmillan Company, 1958.

Miller, Daniel R., and Swanson, Guy E., *Inner Conflict and Defense.* New York: Henry Holt and Company, 1960.

Moustakas, Clark E., *Psychotherapy with Children.* New York: Harper and Brothers, 1960.

Opler, M. K. (ed.), *Culture and Mental Health: Cross-Cultural Studies.* New York: The Macmillan Company, 1959.

Sarason, S. B., *et al., Anxiety in Elementary School Children: A Report of Research.* New York: John Wiley and Sons, Inc., 1960.

Smith, Henry C., *Personality Adjustment.* New York: McGraw-Hill Book Company, Inc., 1961.

Spoerl, Dorothy T. (ed.), *Tensions Our Children Live with: Stories for Discussion.* Boston: Beacon Press, 1959.

Thorpe, L. P., *The Psychology of Mental Health,* 2nd ed. New York: The Ronald Press Company, 1960.

19

THE CHILD
IN THE HOME

THE CHILD RIGHTLY can expect that his physical and psychological needs will be met in the home. He needs parental care that protects him from bodily harm. He also requires the kind of rearing that will ensure for him the developing of personally and socially adequate attitudes and behavior. In the home he should experience modes of living that will prepare him to assume an active role in managing his own affairs and in providing for the needs of others. Here he gains his first knowledge of the world and the people in it. He receives, he shares, he makes decisions, and he learns how to behave. Under the guidance of his parents he develops the ability first to live with his family, and later to function as a member of a school or other social group. The kind of home in which the child receives his early training will determine in good part the kind of individual he will become.

THE ATMOSPHERE IN THE HOME

A home should be a place in which the child not only can participate in activities but also can relax and recuperate his energy. Whatever can be done by parents and other members of the family to achieve such an atmosphere for him will be valuable as a tension reducer.

Nature of the Home A favorable home is one in which there is good emotional balance. Both parents are present and willing and able to adjust well to each other and to the child. Every member of the family recognizes his rightful relationship to every other member. The family is a strong, well-knit social unit that holds a respected position in the community.

Unfortunately, not all homes offer an atmosphere in which the developing child can thrive. Absence of one parent, lack of consideration of one mate for the other, constant bickering and nagging, sibling rivalry, too strict discipline or too permissive an attitude on the part of parents, or any other unfavorable condition that may exist in the home can deny the child his rightful social heritage. The socio-economic status of the home also is a significant factor in child-rearing.

Wallace [1] investigated "home tone" and adjustment in a study covering a period of four years. The subjects were 248 children who were referred to a traveling child guidance clinic. Sixty-three per cent of these children were from harmonious homes (homes that displayed a good atmosphere), and 37 per cent were from unharmonious homes. The study yielded the following results: 81 per cent of the children who came from harmonious homes and 71 per cent who came from unharmonious homes made good adjustment. Included in the study were also 161 children for whom adjustment only (not home tone) was considered. Of the total number of cases (409), 308 were followed up. The results of the follow-up are given in Table 23.

TABLE 23

Kinds of Adjustments Expressed in Percentages of 308 Children *

Kinds of adjustment	Per cent of cases
Excellent	26
Good	46
Fair	7
Unchanged	13
Worse	3
Institutionalized children	5

* *Ibid.*, compiled from data in the study.

A study by Bruch [2] deals with obesity in childhood and personality

[1] Wallace, R., "A Study between Emotional Tone of the Home and Adjustment Status in Cases Referred to a Traveling Child Guidance Clinic," *Journal of Juvenile Research*, 19: 205–220, 1935.

[2] Bruch, H., "Obesity in Childhood and Personality Adjustment," *American Journal of Orthopsychiatry*, 11: 467–474, 1941.

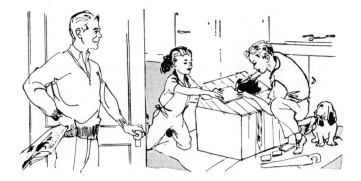

Figure 96.   Children's Welfare, Not the Parents' Comfort, Comes First.

(From Your Child Grows Up, op. cit., p. 31)

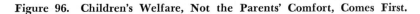

development. Two hundred children, from 25 to 150 per cent overweight, were studied. These were accelerated in their physical and mental development but retarded emotionally and socially. In fact, 40 per cent of the children over six years of age were still suffering from enuresis. Significant characteristics of these children include excessive food intake and low motor activity.

The stimulating factors in the conditions of these children included a lack of provision in the home for meeting the fundamental needs of a child, a weak father, and a dominating mother. Some mothers, who in their own childhood had experienced hunger and poverty, compensated for their former lacks partly by emphasizing food unduly. The obese children tended to derive their greatest satisfaction from eating, and used it to protect themselves from threats to their egos by their great size.

From the findings of these and similar studies it can be concluded that a good home atmosphere is provocative of ease of child adjustment. Yet, some children can be helped by agencies outside the home to improve their attitudes and behavior. Of course, home cooperation is extremely valuable in any attempted rehabilitation of a child who, for one or another reason, has failed to make an acceptable adjustment to personal and social requirements. Often, however, re-education is needed by parents and other family members as much as by the child, if not more so.

The Good Home   The ideal home environment provides an atmosphere in which all its members can develop their best potentialities, and the needs of all are met constructively and with a minimum of emotional imbalance. As a group, the family members recognize the fact that they have certain common goals which they all strive to achieve within their limits of responsibility. No one child in the family becomes the center of attention, neither is any child neglected in favor of others. An attitude of justice and cooperation, instilled by the parents, permeates all of the family's activities. It must be admitted that with our present emphasis on individualism, it is difficult to achieve the ideal in home relationships. We now shall consider some of the factors that militate for or against the achieving of family accord.

THE SOCIO-ECONOMIC STATUS OF THE HOME

Sociologists categorize socio-economic status as upper, middle, and lower class. Results of studies dealing with economic status seem to yield positive correlations, for example, between the financial situation in the home and the kind of opportunities provided for child development, regardless of the methods used for evaluating them.[3]

Since economic status is only one of the variables responsible for a child's personal and social development, the sole cause for acceptable or undesirable rearing cannot be associated with the economic classification of the family, even though the child may be affected unfavorably by poor or insufficient food, inadequate or unsanitary living conditions, low standards of living, limited educational opportunities, or frequent changes of home as the father migrates from place to place in search of employment. At the same time, the kind of home in which a child is reared may be closely associated with the kind of parents he possesses.

Although a parent, through no fault of his own, may be unable to provide the necessities of life for his family, it is generally agreed that economic status depends in part on an individual's degree of potential ability to earn success in occupational endeavors. The child of the unsuccessful bread-winner may well inherit those characteristics which have functioned in the adult's life pattern.

The Underprivileged Home   Many problem children come from so-called lower status homes. This situation often is caused by differences in the standards of living and behavior considered acceptable by the lower class but disapproved by upper and middle class families. Poverty alone is not the chief factor in the child's development of socially unacceptable behavior. True, the child of poor parents may be denied the luxuries enjoyed by economically more favored children. Yet, if the parents maintain a clean, neat home, in which the child's fundamental requirements

---

[3] See Finch, F. H., and Haehn, A. J., "Measuring Socio-Economic or Cultural Status: A Comparison of Methods," *Journal of Social Psychology,* 33: 51–67, 1951.

are met, and his psychological needs are fulfilled by loving and understanding even though financially underprivileged parents, the young
person may be more fortunate in his parents than is one who is economically more secure but whose parents are less mindful of their responsibilities to their child.

Studies conducted by Davis and Havighurst [4] have yielded some definite differences between child-rearing in middle class and lower class
families. They found, for example, that lower class babies are more
often breast-fed than the others. Children of middle class homes take
more frequent daytime naps and come home earlier from the movies
and other activities outside the home than do lower class children. The
latter children also are freer to play outside the home and are expected
to assume fewer home responsibilities than middle class children.

The Effect of Mobility   Most parents follow the accepted custom of their social class in matters of child-rearing. There tends to be
greater regimentation in lower socio-economic homes, and more modern
attitudes toward discipline in higher class areas. In the latter homes there
is more reasoning with the child and explanation of what is meant by
good behavior. More punishment for unacceptable behavior is found in
less privileged homes.

Since there is considerable flexibility in American society, it is possible
for a family to move from a lower class status to a higher one. It has
been found that when this occurs, parents tend to accept the standards
of their new group and apply them in child training. Thus it may happen
that the younger children of a family are expected to follow a regimen
quite different from that to which their older brothers or sisters were
exposed. This may result in the acquiring of very different behavior patterns between the two groups, sometimes becoming the cause of considerable family friction. Sibling rivalry may stem from other causes, however, and will be discussed later.

The Home and the School   A significant class difference is parental support of the school. Stendler [5] studied attitude differences among
parents of children in the first grade of elementary school. She gave attention to differences in five areas: preschool attendance, parental aspirations for the child, preparation for school, parental criticism of the school,
and parental reception of the report card. The number of families dis-

[4] Davis, A., and Havighurst, R. J., "Social Class and Color Differences in Child-
Rearing," in Kluckhohn, C., and Murray, H. A. (ed.), *Personality in Nature, Society
and Culture*. New York: Alfred Knopf, Inc., 1953.

[5] Stendler, Celia B., "Social Class Differences in Parental Attitude toward School
at Grade 1 Level," *Child Development*, 22: 37–46, 1950.

tributed among five social class groups included nine upper, fifty-one upper-middle, sixty-one lower-middle, seventy-six upper-lower, and fifteen lower-lower.

The study was conducted in a midwestern community. The method employed was to hold two interviews with each of the mothers—one just before the child entered the first grade (median age of the children at this time being 6.3 years), the other about two months after entrance and after the first report cards had been distributed. The results of the study are summarized here.

PRESCHOOL ATTENDANCE The public schools of this community did not include preschool facilities. Hence five-year-olds could attend fee-paying private schools, a tuition-free University School, or a fee-paying kindergarten operated by the Parent Teachers Associations in public school buildings. Preschool attendance is shown in Table 24.

TABLE 24

The Child's Chances of Attending Preschool *

Social class	Per cent attending preschool	Number of children
Upper	100	9
Upper-middle	98	50
Lower-middle	73	44
Upper-lower	31	24
Lower-lower	14	2

* *Ibid.,* p. 40.

It can be seen that the percentage of children attending preschool declined with social class. The reasons given for sending children to the preschool included social improvement, preparation for the first grade, and the fact that others send their children. Some parents who did not send their children to preschool, although they could afford it, felt that their brothers and sisters at home would meet their needs or that "they will get enough of school after they start in the first grade."

PARENTAL ASPIRATIONS FOR THE CHILD The responses to the question relative to the school level the child might attain, yielded the results that are shown in Table 25. These figures represent parental aspirations for the six-year-old. Although they follow a to-be-expected pattern, changes in attitude can be experienced by these parents as their children approach adolescence and display varying degrees of success in school attainment.

PREPARATION FOR SCHOOL When parents were asked what they

TABLE 25

School Level That Mothers Expect Child to Attain *

Expect child to go	(cases)	Upper (9) %	Upper-middle (51) %	Lower-middle (61) %	Upper-lower (76) %	Lower-lower (15) %
"As far as he can"		12	4	6	16	50
Through high school		0	2	8	18	50
Beyond high school		_ 0	4	10	24	0
Through college		87	89	76	41	0

* *Ibid.*, p. 41.

TABLE 26

Items Taught Children at Home before Attending School *

Important items	(cases)	Upper (9) %	Upper-middle (51) %	Lower-middle (61) %	Upper-lower (76) %	Lower-lower (15) %
Alphabet		66	38	23	24	16
Nursery rhymes		100	95	92	85	66
Write or print name		100	95	84	66	66
Count		83	95	100	88	100
Read		66	22	16	14	16

* *Ibid.*, p. 42.

did to prepare their children for school entrance their answers fell into the patterns shown in Table 26.

As can be observed, most parents taught children to count. Other areas show a declining interest with decreasing social status in teaching preschool children. Stendler noted that many mothers reported that they had refrained from teaching the alphabet or encouraging the child to read because they had been requested by the school not to do so.

CRITICISMS OF THE SCHOOL MADE BY PARENTS   At the second interview two questions were asked mothers in this area: "Are there some rules and regulations of which you do not approve?" and "What do you say to the child when he criticizes the school?" Since the children had been in school so short a time, there were only seventeen mothers of the total number who showed some dissatisfaction with the school. These were scattered through the various social levels.

It has been the experience of these writers that parental support or nonsupport of the child is related closely to a parent's school expectation or aspiration for his child. Upper class parents often offer constructive criticisms to school people, although in light of an emotionalized attitude toward their own child's opportunities for school success, they may accuse the school of lack of appreciation of the young person's superior abilities. Lower class parents usually have great respect for education. Although they may do little or nothing to help the child succeed in his school work, they will defend the teacher against childish criticism. Here again, of course, one finds the occasional emotional parent who accuses the school of favoritism in light of social class status of the children.

PARENT REACTION TO REPORT CARDS   Responses to the question, "What did you say to him about the report?" were classified according to the data in Table 27. (In one of the schools teacher-parent conferences were substituted for report cards. Not all parents attended these conferences.)

TABLE 27

Responses of Mothers to Question about Report Card *

Response	(cases)	Upper (9) %	Upper-middle (51) %	Lower-middle (61) %	Upper-lower (76) %	Lower-lower (15) %
Liked report card without reservations		16	64	51	56	46
Accepted report card with reservations		50	35	40	36	30
Disappointed in report card		33	0	8	6	0
Report not obtained by parent		0	0	0	1	23

* Ibid., p. 44.

It will be seen that in the upper class group was the greatest percentage of parents who had reservations about the report card or were disappointed in it. Lower class parents were the only ones refusing to come for the interviews. Stendler concludes her summarization of the results with this comment:

If we accept the five areas analyzed as revealing pertinent data, it may be said that some social class differences in four of the areas do exist with regard to parental belief in and support of the school at Grade I level. What meaning these differences have for the child and how they may affect his school behavior need to be explored.[6]

THE BROKEN HOME

The home that is broken by divorce, the death or absence of one parent, or the mother's working outside the home has a significant in-

[6] Ibid., p. 46.

fluence on the life of a child. In a good home, father and mother share in the rearing of the children. Unfortunately, approximately every four-teenth child is reared in a fatherless home.

The Death of a Parent The death of either parent places a double responsibility on the child who has lost a parent. Not only does the child who has lost a parent through death need to make an adjust-ment to a home in which the remaining parent must become both father and mother, but the bereaved mate may suffer many tensions as the result of the changed home status. The remaining parent may variously tend to overprotect or overindulge the child, neglect or resent the child, or attempt to replace the lost mate by the child, thereby developing a strong emotional tie between the two. Widows are likely to stress the emotional relation; widowers may attempt, often ineffectually, to be both a mother and father to the child; under pressure of his own loss and his occupational responsibilities he may neglect the child or children, or expect a young person, especially the oldest but still immature girl of the family, to take over the management of household affairs. In any case, family unity is broken. It is only when the remaining parent can handle the situation intelligently and with a minimum of emotional imbalance that children can achieve a healthful adjustment in a home broken by the death of a parent.

Divorce or Separation A home broken by divorce or separation of parents is likely to be conducive of much emotional disturbance and conflict in a child. The actual separation of parents is bad for the child. The disturbed atmosphere in the home preceding the separation may be devastating. Other things being equal, the average child wants to respect and look up to both parents. When the child is exposed to constant bicker-ing, nagging, recriminations, and name-calling between parents, he ex-periences a conflict of loyalties that can be most distressing. He even may be called upon to take sides in marital arguments. He is not yet mature enough to judge the rightness or wrongness of either side, but it is equally difficult for him to remain emotionally neutral. He often suffers as much as do the parents in situations of this kind. Unfortunately, a parent who is giving way to emotional tantrums in relations with the mate rarely is in a position to recognize the harm that is being done to the child.

If or when a separation occurs, there may seem to be relative peace in the home. The child or children must of course adjust to a one-parent family. How effective the change is in maintaining a calmer atmosphere depends on the remaining parent. Mothers often become so embittered by their marital experiences that they "take out" their emotionalism on the children, who usually stay with the mother. She may transfer her involvement with her erstwhile mate to the child, smothering her off-spring with what she may term love but which really is an outlet for her emotionalism. If a child commits a misdeed, she may make unjust comparisons between the child's conduct and that of the father.

Especially difficult for the child of divorced or separated parents is a stipulated policy that he spend some time each month or year with the parent who has left the home. An arrangement of this kind can cause each parent to vie with the other in "buying" the child's affection and loyalty. The child is overindulged by either or both parents. Sometimes the child learns to play one parent against the other. It is especially dis-tressing for the child who still loves his absent parent to give a full ac-counting to the other of everything that happened when he visited the former. A mother may catechize a child on his return home from such a visit concerning every detail of the stay, expecting the child to be un-favorably critical of the absent parent's behavior, living conditions, and new wife if he has remarried. Some children in these circumstances de-velop an astonishing ability to color their reports according to the mother's wishes, without displaying disloyalty to the father.

The Absent Mother The present high rate of employment of mothers outside the home, though not resulting in a broken home in the sense that one parent is definitely separated from the family, may intro-duce certain factors that give the child a feeling of insecurity and help-lessness. Especially is this the case if both the child's parents leave the house before he starts for school or if he comes home in the afternoon to a vacant house or apartment.

Some career women employ a housekeeper who cares for the child's physical needs and who may be able to build a friendly mother-substitute relationship with him. During her time in the home, however, the working mother needs to offer the child the warmth, affection, and displayed interest in his activities which every child seeks from his parents. If this relationship exists between the mother and the child, the latter may be as proud of his mother's achievements outside the home as he is of his father's. Moreover, when there are siblings in the family, older children often take pride in assuming household responsibilities during the mother's absence. If these are not carried to an extreme, much excellent experience in the meeting of family problems can be gained.

According to a study by Roumann,[7] the youngest child in the family of a working mother tends to substitute fantasy for real life achievement

[7] Roumann, Jack, "School-Children's Problems as Related to Parental Factors," *Understanding the Child*, 24: 50–55, 1955.

and to lack a cordial relationship with people. He also found that in homes where there is no adult male, the child is likely to lack a sense of motivation or standards and a feeling of personal worth. Adjustment to step-parents is another difficult task for most children, less so for a younger child than for an older one. The latter can be expected to lack a sense of personal freedom, and to experience emotional tensions.

The Institutionalized Child The attitudes of an institutionalized child present evidence to show how the close relationships that exist between parents or foster parents and himself are lacking in an institution, even though the home itself may fall short of the ideal. Goldfarb [8] studied the reactions of fifteen children aged about twelve years, who had been reared in institutions for the first three years of life, and fifteen others who had lived in foster homes during the same age period. He found that the institutionalized children were less well adjusted. Among other lacks there were absence of normal inhibitory tendencies, "emotional imperviousness, and social regression."

Various factors militate against an institutionalized child's making a good social adjustment. He lacks the feeling of security that comes from the sense of belongingness experienced by the child in the home. The attendants are kind in the treatment of their charges; yet child care becomes a routine matter, often wanting in any close contacts between the worker and individual children. Young babies need more than adequate physical care. Goldfarb,[9] in another study, found, for example, that infants placed in an institution during the first six months differed from those institutionalized at a later age. The former gave evidence, even after they had been placed in foster homes, of lacks in independence, security, and feeling for others.

It is generally agreed that young children suffer from being institutionalized except for a brief period. Moreover, less harm seems to be done to children if their earlier experiences are in a home situation and before they are institutionalized, which should not be, if at all, until after the age of two years.

ORDINAL POSITION OF A CHILD IN THE FAMILY

Much has been written about the effect on a child of his birth order in a family. To be an "only" child, the oldest, or the youngest, for exam-

[8] Goldfarb, W., "Psychological Privation in Infancy and Subsequent Adjustment," *American Journal of Orthopsychiatry*, 15: 247–255, 1945.

[9] Goldfarb, W., "Effects of Psychological Deprivation in Infancy and Subsequent Stimulation," *American Journal of Psychiatry*, 102: 18–33, 1945.

ple, is supposed to carry with it certain particular results in personality development.

Birth Order   According to some writers, the oldest child is more adult-oriented than younger children. Because of his relationship with his parents, he may be less or more confident than the others. He may be more serious. If there is an age span of more than five years between the oldest and other children, this child, especially a girl, can share in the care of the younger ones, becoming at times a kind of mother substitute. The second child may tend to be more peer-oriented, friendly and less serious. The youngest child supposedly is indulged more than the others, and given greater freedom of action than the older siblings. Some youngest children report, however, that the oldest children serve as mentors of their behavior and may be more strict than the parents in their attitudes concerning what the young person may or may not do. To be an only girl among boys or an only boy among girls probably has some effect on the child, but this relationship differs with families.

Goodenough and Leahy [10] studied 322 clinic children from ages two to nineteen and 293 kindergarten children, of ages five and one-half years to six. They found among clinic children that the oldest children most often engaged in misconduct, but that middle children displayed characteristics such as stealing and social offenses, fear, worry, and general negativistic qualities. No special traits were noticeable in youngest children.

The kindergarten children were distributed as follows: 22 per cent were the oldest in the family, 20 per cent were in the middle, 42 per cent were youngest, and 16 per cent were only children. Among other characteristics, oldest children lacked leadership, were low in self-confidence, and were introverted. Middle children were gregarious, desired affection, and were suggestible. Youngest children had no special characteristics. Only children were more self-confident and aggressive, wanted affection, and were likely to be excitable, moody, gregarious, and distractable.

Lasko [11] investigated parental relations with first and second children by studying the reactions of mothers to forty pairs of first and second children matched for age at the time of the study. The Fels Parent Rating Scale (explained later in the chapter) was used. According to the findings of the study, mothers tended to protect and be more solicitous of the second child, giving it more warmth and less control than were

[10] Goodenough, F., and Leahy, A. M., "The Effects of Certain Family Relationships upon the Development of Personality," *Pedagogical Seminary and Journal of Genetic Psychology,* 34: 45–71, 1927.

[11] Lasko, J. K., "Parent Behavior toward First and Second Children," *Genetic Psychological Monographs,* 49: 97–137, 1954.

given the older child. Differences in treatment were most evident at the preschool level. First children who were displaced by siblings at the age of three years seemed to mind it more than the four-year-olds. Children born relatively close together shared parental care more than when there was a wide disparity in age. The birth of a third child seemed to cause the mother to treat the second child somewhat as she had acted toward the first child after the birth of the second child.

The Only Child Opinions differ about what it means to be an only child. Since parents tend to concentrate much of their attention on the child, he may be reared strictly or overindulged. If the financial situation of the family permits—and often it does since the only child usually is the product of an upper class home—he receives many advantages. His health is well cared for, and he receives as many educational advantages as he can profit by.

Some studies seem to find definite differences among children in light of position in the family or being an only child. Present opinion, however, is that although no two siblings have exactly the same relationship with parents, the order of birth usually is not the determining factor. Rather is parental attitude toward children associated with the whole complex of family relationships. Perhaps, too, the fact that many family units now are more loosely knit than formerly may be a factor of influence on the treatment accorded by parents to any one child—whether there are siblings or whether he is an only child.

PARENT-CHILD RELATIONS

Although all that we have said in the foregoing is associated, from a broad viewpoint, with the relationships that exist between parent and child, we now shall consider the effect on the child of some of the specific attitudes that parents display toward their children. We have referred in previous discussions to the overindulgent parent, the restrictive parent, and the overprotective or the dominating mother. When the child leaves the home for participation in outside groups, he brings with him the traits or characteristics that have been fostered during his early years as a result of parental attitudes and behavior toward him regardless of home status or position in the family.

The Mother and the Baby The mother's attitude during babyhood years can have relatively serious effects on the child's developing behavior. Unintelligent attitudes of the mother toward feeding, weaning, and toilet training, for instance, may lead to such behavior in the child as anorexia (refusal to eat), enuresis or bed-wetting (assigned by some writers to lack of love or separation from the mother), thumb-sucking, or temper tantrums. As the mother becomes increasingly worried by such displays, she may become less able to handle the situation. There probably is no ideal pattern, however, of mother-child relationships. Too many subtle factors of influence are inherent in the nature and previous experiences of the parent, the inherited potentialities of the child, and the conditions prevailing in the home to make the establishment of definite rules of maternal conduct feasible or even possible.

Parental Attitudes According to Nimkoff,[12] ideal parent-child relationships include: stimulating the child to put forth effort, having similar interests, conducting activities together, and motivating self-reliance. Further, Stout and Langdon,[13] as a result of the study of the home life of 158 well-adjusted children, concluded that the basis of the good adjustment of these children could be found in the attitudes of the parents toward their children and to the basic family unity growing out of them.

Another study of parental attitudes toward children was conducted by Bishop.[14] She investigated the reactions of thirty-four mothers and their children, seventeen boys and seventeen girls who ranged in age from three years and four months to five years and seven months. According to Bishop's findings, positive correlations indicated that the children reflected directly in their own behavior the mother's use of directing-interfering-criticism, strong stimulation, and suggesting types of control, and also the tendency toward nonacceptance of stimulation. Bishop said:

Correlations ranging from +.43 to +.63 between categories of mother behavior indicated that the mothers who tended to remain out of contact with the child also tended to be more highly specific in their control and more unwilling to accept stimulation when interaction was in progress.[15]

Evaluation of Attitudes Various instruments have been devised to study the effects on children of their parents' attitudes toward them. The Samuel S. Fels Research Institute of Antioch College, Ohio, devel-

---

[12] Nimkoff, M. F., *The Child*, pp. 167–171. Philadelphia: J. B. Lippincott Company, 1934.

[13] Stout, J. W., and Langdon, Grace, "A Study of the Home Life of Well-Adjusted Children," *Journal of Educational Sociology*, 23: 442–460, 1950.

[14] Bishop, Barbara M., "Mother-Child Interaction and the Social Behavior of Children," *Psychological Monographs*, 65: No. 325, 1951.

[15] *Ibid.*, p. 33.

Wide World Photo

Figure 97.   Children Enjoy a Picnic with Their Parents.

oped one which describes contrasts in parents' behavior, such as stimu-
lative-inactive, emotional-rational, approving-deprecating, and socialized-
individualized.[16] Utilizing these rating scales, the Fels Research Institute
engaged in a longitudinal study of the relationship between parents'
behavior and children's development.[17] The rating scales are divided into
eight areas, with subdivisions in each. The main areas are:

1. Home atmosphere
2. Contact of child and mother
3. The control and influence of parent on child
4. Babying and protectiveness
5. Criticism and evaluation of the child
6. Readiness of explanations

[16] Champney, Horace, "The Variables of Parent Behavior," *Journal of Abnormal
and Social Psychology,* 36: 525–542, 1941.
[17] Baldwin, A. L., Kalhorn, J., and Breese, F. H., "Patterns of Parent Behavior,"
Psychological Monographs, 58: No. 268, 1–75, 1945.

7. Emotional relationships
8. Miscellaneous: understanding, emotionalism, affectiveness, rapport [18]

The home visitors who gather the data on parental attitudes used these scales on their two visits a year to the home of each child studied. At the time of the report of this study the number of children attached to the clinic was 158, the oldest being 14 and the youngest still prenatal. For the purpose of this report, the fifth round ratings of 125 children were used.

As a result of statistical treatment of the data gathered, three major syndromes emerged: Democracy in the Home, Acceptance of Child, and Indulgence. The attitudes of parents and their effects on children were analyzed according to the following types of parental behavior: acceptant, casual, and rejectant.[19] Many combinations of patterns were found, namely, acceptant-indulgent, casual-indulgent, democratic-indulgent, casual-autocratic, intellectual-democratic, and so on.

Without going into the many details of the study, we shall present some of the findings. We quote:

The *democratic* parents seem to surround the child with an atmosphere of freedom, emotional rapport and intellectual stimulation. . . .

The *indulgent* home, unless it is highly intellectual, is not stimulating. . . . On the other hand, the indulgent home, at least during the preschool years, is a warm friendly place with emphasis on the social virtues. . . . The actively and repressively rejected children are marked throughout their development by a highly emotional noncomformist attitude. . . . The children whose rejection is less active and more nonchalant are generally milder in their symptoms. . . . Children from *casual-indulgent* homes are asocial. They are, on the whole, conforming and unemotional.[20]

The authors of the study interpret their results in these words:

In summary, we have found that the children, selected on the basis of parental behavior, do show consistent uniformities. For some of the groups, the *democratic,* the *indulgent,* and the *actively rejected,* the patterns are clear-cut; for the others, they are only suggestive. The existence of these patterns lends further support to the syndrome analysis of parent behavior and leads us to believe that the method is empirically fruitful.[21]

[18] Adapted from authors *ibid.,* pp. 7–8.
[19] *Ibid.,* Chapters II, III, IV and V.
[20] *Ibid.,* 69–70.
[21] *Ibid.,* p. 70.

The Fels Institute study confirms the findings of many other studies as well as the more or less casual observation of persons, such as teachers and religious leaders, who constantly are dealing with parents and their children. There is need for further study in cultural influences and parent-child relationships. Yet it is probably safe to conclude that intelligent parents in a democratic home accept the child for what he is, are warm and understanding, and utilize constructive disciplinary measures that will produce children who can make good adjustments both in their home and in out-of-home relationships. Overindulgence or overprotectiveness and complete or partial rejection by the parents of a child are likely to hamper him in his social adjustment. For example, Foster [22] found that jealousy in children can be associated with homes in which there is an emphasis on physical punishment. The amount of attention received from parents and parental and sibling teasing also were factors. The jealous child seems to be limited in his social contacts in play, and tends to be selfish and pugnacious and suffer from sleep disturbances and emotional tensions. It would seem, from all evidence available, that parental attitude is a much more significant factor in child development than are the physical conditions of the home or its socio-economic status.

The Father's Role in the Family   Viewed popularly, the father's role in the home is that of the breadwinner whose relation with his children is that of enjoying them for short periods when they are good, and punishing them when they are naughty. In most homes of the past, caring for and rearing the children were the mother's job. There probably always have been weak or insecure mothers who, when a child committed a misdeed, threatened the child with punishment administered to him by the father when the latter returned home from work. Situations of this kind are unfortunate. The tired male parent does not enjoy punishing a child who has been recalcitrant during his absence; the child suffers anxiety while he is waiting for the threatened punishment. Moreover, mothers who themselves cannot handle cases of misconduct usually lose the respect of their children.

Modern parents are tending to show a more cooperative attitude in their relations with their children. Both fathers and mothers back up the dicta of the mate in matters dealing with child training. It is true that some girls and boys continue to play one parent against the other in their attempts to receive approval of a desired behavior action, such as participating in a peer group party, going to the movies, watching a

---

[22] Foster, S., "A Study of the Personality Make-Up and Social Setting of Fifty Jealous Children," *Mental Hygiene,* 11: 53–57, 1927.

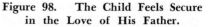

Figure 98.   The Child Feels Secure
in the Love of His Father.

particular television program, obtaining a particular toy or other gadget, refraining from eating certain foods, and all the other day-by-day interests that mean so much to the growing young person. Instances of one parent overriding the decisions of the other are decreasing, however, as more parents are learning the value of consistency in the treatment of the child. Parents also are attempting more than formerly to engage in a minimum of disagreements about the child, especially in the child's presence.

Observation and investigations appear to indicate that in homes in which the father plays an active role in child training, boys tend to identify with the father and girls with the mother. A father is likely to be tempted to indulge a daughter who resembles the mother, especially if a good marital adjustment exists between the mates. A father, however, may be overambitious for his son. If the father enjoys his own occupational work, he is likely to encourage the boy to enter the same field. Contrariwise, if the father is not happy in his work, he may insist that the boy prepare for a kind of occupation, often a profession, in which the boy will gain more social prestige than is experienced by the father. In either case, the parent may attempt to pressure the boy into the father-selected vocation, regardless of the boy's interests or abilities. Parental efforts in these directions may cause the developing boy considerable anxiety and discouragement. If he accedes to the father's wishes, he may be unhappy in his life work, but be afraid to change to a field nearer to his own desires and potentialities; if he resists parental pressure, he may enjoy the work that he himself selected, but carry a feeling of guilt because of his noncompliance with his father's ambitions.

Although fathers, as well as mothers, encounter difficulties in determining just how they should play their role of wise parenthood, they are assuming an increasing amount of responsibility for their children's wel-

Figure 99. Children Appreciate the Attention Given to Them by Their Fathers.

Wide World Photos

fare. Although the father may remain in the background, especially during the child's early years, he plays a supportive role, often becoming the final authority in major decision-making situations. The mother may be the parent in whom the child confides and with whom the child may have the greater rapport, but the father can be the bulwark of strength on whom both mother and children lean.

Ruth Tasch [23] conducted a study of the kinds of activity in which fathers engage with and for their children. According to Tasch, "This investigation was designed to obtain information concerning the role of the urban American father in the family as revealed by the report he gives of his activities, satisfactions, and problems, and the attitudes and opinions he expresses regarding his concept of the paternal role." [24] The study included 85 fathers having a total of 160 children, 80 boys and 80 girls, between the ages of birth and seventeen and over. The families lived in New York City, and were diversified according to nationality, occupation, and religious affiliation.

The reported activities of the fathers were distributed according to thirteen major categories. These categories and the number of fathers engaging in each are given in Table 28.

TABLE 28

Activities of Fathers According to Major Categories *

Major category †	Number of fathers
Routine daily care and safety	80
Development of motor abilities, acquiring skills	74
Development of intellectual abilities and interests	74
Going to places of recreation	68
Development of social standards, conduct and control	63
Emotional development	35
Moral and spiritual development	33
Maintaining family unity	32
Assignment of chores, work, allowance	31
Development of artistic interests	26
Development of personal characteristics	26
Radio, movies, comics	21
Giving material objects, presents	20

* Adapted from *ibid.*, p. 323. Materials in Tables 28 to 31 are used by permission of *Journal of Experimental Education*.

† The complete list of activities and description of categories is available on microfilm, University of Michigan, publication No. 2358.

[23] Tasch, Ruth, "The Role of the Father in the Family," *Journal of Experimental Education,* 20: 319–361, 1952.

[24] *Ibid.*, p. 319, by permission of *Journal of Experimental Education*.

TABLE 29

Distribution among Major Categories of Total Present Reported Activities *

Category Number	Brief description of major category	Percent of activities per age group Age in years				
		0–4 (N = 489)	5–8 (N = 455)	9–12 (N = 389)	13–16 (N = 117)	17+ (N = 53)
1	Going to place of recreation	10.8	8.6	8.5	7.7	11.3
2	Radio, movies, comics	0	3.3	4.6	10.3	11.3
3	Giving material objects, presents	1.4	2.4	1.5	0	1.9
4	Maintaining family unity	3.9	3.7	2.8	4.3	11.3
5	Development of motor abilities, acquisition of skills, interests	15.9	11.9	13.6	19.6	9.4
6	Routine daily care and safety	35.4	18.0	10.3	6.0	5.7
7	Assignment of chores, work, allowance	0.4	6.6	11.6	11.1	13.2
8	Development of intellectual abilities and interests	13.1	20.4	21.8	13.7	11.3
9	Development of artistic interests	1.6	2.8	1.5	3.4	0
10	Development of social standards, conduct and control	8.8	12.5	14.4	20.5	5.7
11	Development of personality traits	2.2	3.3	2.6	0.8	3.8
12	Emotional development	3.9	3.1	2.3	0.8	5.7
13	Moral and spiritual deveopment	2.4	3.3	4.4	1.7	9.4

* Ibid., p. 326.

The fathers explained the approaches they used in these areas of activity. For example, they attempted to develop a sense of responsibility by trying to strengthen the child's feeling of family responsibility and kinship through assignment of various kinds of chores and by attempting to develop a sense of moral and spiritual responsibility.

In Table 29 are reported the distribution of major activities according to per cent of activities for each age group, and in Table 30 the activities according to sex of child. A study of these tables indicates the extent of paternal cooperation in child-rearing. Tasch explains in detail the implications of the material contained in these and other summaries of data, such as related activities of children, instructional activities, methods of discipline, paternal satisfactions, and problems and relationships of activities and concepts of the parental role. It is interesting to note that the fathers differed in their conception of how they played their own role and the advice they would give to future fathers. These are presented in Table 31.

TABLE 30

Fathers' Reported Activities as Related to the Sex of the Child *

Category Number	Brief description of major category	Percent of children Boys N = 80	Girls N = 80
5	Development of motor abilities, acquisition of skills, interests	72.5	52.5
8	Development of intellectual abilities and interests	71.2	66.2
10	Development of social standards, conduct, and control	61.2	57.5
1	Going to places of recreation	58.7	67.5
6	Routine daily care and safety	52.5	71.2
7	Assignment of chores, work, allowance	33.7	32.5
2	Radio, movies, comics	31.2	22.5
4	Maintaining a family unity	28.7	33.7
13	Moral and spiritual development	26.2	27.5
12	Emotional development	21.2	31.2
11	Development of personality characteristics	20.0	21.2
3	Giving material objects, presents	13.7	17.5
9	Development of artistic interests	13.7	15.0

* Ibid., p. 328.

TABLE 31

Relative Rank of Categories Relating to the Concept of the Paternal Role *

Category	Present concept	Advice to future fathers
Economic provider	1	2
Guide and teacher	2	3
Contributor to species	3	8.5
Authority	4.5	7
Person supplying protection, stability, emotional security	4.5	12
Companion	6.5	5
Child-rearing	6.5	1
Maintainer of family unity	8	6
Parenthood as "restraint"	9.5	4
Example of masculinity	9.5	12
Parent-child reciprocity	11	10
Personal characteristics and habits	12	8.5
Disciplinarian	13	12

* Adapted from ibid., p. 347.

As one of her conclusions, Tasch states, "The fathers of the present investigation show, on the conceptual level, some measure of recognition of the several functions which are implicit in their reported activities. In other words, what they do with and for their children has some correspondence to what they think a father should be." [25] This is an interesting study. Its findings are limited somewhat by the fact that all the subjects came from one large urban area. Follow-up studies of activities of fathers in other parts of the country and in various sized communities would be much worthwhile.

QUESTIONS AND TOPICS FOR DISCUSSION

1. Critically evaluate the statement that the kind of home in which the child is reared will determine in good part the kind of individual he will become.
2. How do you react, in light of your experiences, to Stendler's findings?
3. If you know a child who is the product of a broken home, what are his reactions to the situation?
4. Note the ordinal position in the family of yourself and your classmates. Do you find any special characteristics that can be accounted for by position in the family? What are they, if any?
5. Do you know any "only" children? What is your evaluation of their personality pattern?
6. Consult the Fels Institute Research Study of parent-child relationships. From the data presented, differentiate among the kinds of children produced by democratic, indulgent, and rejectant parents, respectively.
7. Why is parent attitude toward a child more important than other home factors in child-rearing? Illustrate.
8. What do you think the father's role in the family should be? Substantiate your judgment by specific examples.
9. *Special Project:* What are the home conditions, place in family, and other pertinent conditions of each of your subjects? Are attendant circumstances, in your opinion, conducive of differences among them? Note any specific instances of differences.

SELECTED REFERENCES

Ackerman, N. W., "The Principle of Shared Responsibility of Child Rearing," *International Journal of Social Psychology*, 2: 280–291, 1957.

Bachmeister, R. W., *Your Children's Manners*. Chicago: Science Research Associates, Inc., 1952.

Bell, R. O., "Attitude Studies of Parent-Child Relations," *Child Development*, 29: 324–338, 1958.

[25] *Ibid.*, p. 358, by permission of *Journal of Experimental Education.*

Bernett, Eleanor R., *America's Children: An Analysis of Economic and Social Factors Affecting the Nation's Children*. New York: John Wiley and Sons, Inc., 1958.

Block, J., "Personality Characteristics Associated with Fathers' Attitudes toward Child Rearing," *Child Development*, 26: 41–48, 1955.

Ginsberg, Eli (ed.), *Golden Anniversary White House Conference on Children and Youth*. New York: Columbia University Press, 1960.

Glick, P. C., *American Families*. New York: John Wiley and Sons, Inc., 1957.

Hess, R. D., and Handel, Gerald, *Family Worlds: A Psychological Approach to Family Life*. Chicago: University of Chicago Press, 1959.

Hymes, J. L., Jr., *Effective Home-School Relations*. Englewood Cliffs, N. J.: Prentice-Hall, Inc., 1953.

Liebman, Samuel (ed.), *Emotional Forces in the Family*. Philadelphia: J. B. Lippincott Company, 1959.

Sears, R. R., Maccoby, E. E., and Levin, H., *Patterns of Child Rearing*. Evanston, Ill.: Row, Peterson and Company, 1957.

Sorokin, P. A., *Social and Cultural Mobility*, rev. ed. Glencoe, Ill.: Free Press, 1959.

Stott, D. H., *Unsettled Children and Their Families*. New York: Philosophical Library, 1956.

20

THE CHILD
IN THE SCHOOL
AND THE COMMUNITY

THROUGHOUT THIS BOOK we have directed the reader's attention to the various environmental forces that affect the child during his growing years. In this concluding chapter we are summarizing the major influences in the school and community that can encourage or discourage good development. We may iterate points that have been discussed previously, but our purpose is to emphasize those points that have major significance in the life of the child. It must be remembered that not all children react in the same fashion to stimulating factors; individual children respond differently to differing situations.

THE CHILD IN THE SCHOOL

When the young child enters school for the first time, whether it be nursery school, kindergarten, or the first grade of the elementary school, he brings with him those attitudes and patterns of behavior that he has developed in the home during his preschool years. He is leaving a relatively sheltered environment in which most things were done for him and comes into a new situation in which gradually he must learn to achieve for himself the satisfactions which are so important.

During the school day and week the new school entrant is expected to engage in a schedule of activities that may differ greatly from his home program. He must adjust to new adults in the form of teachers, and may be overwhelmed by the large group of children which surrounds him. He is stimulated to adopt one or another attitude toward "going to school" according to the kind and amount of preparation for the event given him by his parents, and the influence on him of his older brothers and sisters or neighbors' children who already are attending school. The first day at school can be a joyful event for a child or it can constitute a serious emotional crisis.

Nursery School and Kindergarten Experiences   Parents differ in their attitudes toward sending the young child to a preschool. Some mothers and fathers believe that their child is still too young and immature to leave the home and its sheltering environment. A mother who is tied emotionally to the young child cannot tolerate the thought of his becoming dependent on anyone else for the meeting of his needs. Other parents recognize the fact that their child probably can benefit from greater opportunities for socialization with peer-age children. Educators are not agreed as to whether the nursery school child, for example, is better prepared for entrance into the kindergarten or first grade than is the child who comes directly from the home. Some claim that the great freedom permitted in nursery school may interfere later with the child's ability to conform to a more formalized schedule of activity. Others hold that in the nursery school and then in the kindergarten, the child learns to adapt his behavior to that of other children and to an adult other than his mother, so that by the time he enters the first grade he has some feeling for social responsibility.

Attendance at nursery school offers advantages to a child. It gives trained workers with children an opportunity to help the youngster, at an early age, make any improvements in his general behavior that are needed as a result of unwise rearing in the home. As can be expected, there are great differences among children of nursery school age. The unfavorable as well as the favorable factors of influence treated in the previous discussion of the home leave their marks on the child. Nursery school teachers soon discover that children of well-adjusted parents have fewer difficulties in matters dealing with health, work, relatives, and making friends than do less fortunate children. Attendance at nursery school can increase even a "problem" child's sense of security.

It is important that nursery school teachers know something about the homes of their children. According to Baldwin [1] the home environment exercises a potent effect on nursery school children. Children who are raised democratically tend to be active and extraverted; they may be hostile as well as friendly; they rate high in originality, constructiveness, and intellectual curiosity; they usually are popular with other children. Children having indulgent parents display characteristics that are opposite to those of democratically reared children. Indulged children also lack skill in motor activities.

Crying in nursery school can be associated with poor methods in home training. Boys seem to cry because of conflicts with adults and frustrations by objects in the environment; girls tend to cry because of a real or imagined injury to their person. Children tend to cry in sympathy with one another, but the longer a nursery school child cries the less sympathy the other children give him. Laughter is contagious. The younger children laugh in situations which involve the motion of self. They then laugh at make-believe, socially understandable situations, and those in which there is some humor.

During the first few days in nursery school, especially among very young children, there are frequent displays of tears, anxieties, dreamy watching, and rejections. Gradually the children relax; temporary groups are formed; curiosity about the equipment in the room is displayed. A temporary group may manipulate together one set of materials for a short time, and then break up to form another group and become interested in other equipment, such as blocks, toys, doll houses, slides, and the like. A few children may prefer, for a relatively long time, to do things alone. They will engage in easel painting, for example, or they will appropriate a toy and refuse to share it with others. Tendencies developed in the home show themselves. Usually, the extraverted children in the group are able to bring the shy, withdrawing child into their activities.

In a good nursery school the teachers guide the children's activities indirectly through suggestions; they do not attempt to direct what a child should do, unless he is likely to hurt himself or another child, or interferes with the freedom of others. Each child is watched carefully, however. He is encouraged to give expression to his innate abilities; any phys-

1 Baldwin, A. L., "The Effect of Home Environment on Nursery School Children," *Child Development*, 20: 49–61, 1949.

ical or emotional difficulties are noted and provision for their care made possible.

As the child participates with the other children in singing simple songs and dancing to music, eating snacks, taking brief naps, playing, removing or hanging up his wraps and putting them on, washing his hands before he eats, and engaging in other intriguing activities, he is gaining in social awareness and social poise. Although, in a good home, a child receives training in acceptable manners and thoughtfulness for others, there is value in his developing these skills in the company of his peers. He achieves attitudes of cooperation which will benefit him in his later school and social life.

Mothers, too, can profit from their children's attendance at nursery school. The children are away from the home usually for a morning or an afternoon, rarely for the whole day, unless the school is organized to care for the children of working mothers. Much as a mother may love her child, she needs a respite from caring for his wants. During this time she can attend to household duties without tension. Moreover, nursery schools invite (sometimes require) mothers periodically to spend a session at the school and observe the behavior of their children without interfering with the routines.

Usually the nursery school teachers hold group and individual conferences with the parents in which, in a friendly manner, the general or the special problems of the children are discussed. A mother can learn much about child-rearing from such meetings with a trained person. Through these conferences, the teacher also can learn about the idiosyncrasies of individual children and be helped thereby in meeting some of the behavior problems that may arise.

Regular School Experiences Whether or not the child has had preschool experiences, entrance into the elementary school may be accompanied by the need to make an adequate adjustment to his new mode of life. Progressively, he meets teachers who, no matter how understanding they may be, are individuals in their own right. The child must adapt his behavior to meet their wishes. He is brought into daily contact with children who are like him in that usually they are in his age group. They may differ from him, however, in degree of mental ability, in emotional maturity, and in social status.

Modes of conduct which are sanctioned in the home may be inadequate in the larger school group. The content of what he learns may stimulate or bore him. He may not receive the amount and kind of attention from the school group to which he was accustomed at home,

Figure 100.   Ready for School in the United States and in Japan.

or he may find that he has become an individual among individuals and that his ego is being satisfied in a way that he did not experience in crowded home conditions. The child in his school relationships is becoming a social being in a social world as he participates in small or larger group projects—athletics, dramatics, musicals, etc. (See Figure 101.)

In light of his home training, the school child is able to make a continuing good adjustment to his school experiences or encounters many problems. School people are becoming increasingly aware of the learning needs of individual children on all school levels. They are attempting to adapt curricular offerings, insofar as this is possible in large group situations, to learning needs and interests. They are providing opportunities for social and recreational experiences, and are attempting to motivate the improvement of emotional reactions of the child whenever change in displayed behavior seems needed.

In their attempts to educate the whole child, school people are recognizing the importance of working closely with parents. Guidance counselors and teachers invite parents to meet them at school for individual or group conferences in which the aims of the school and the progress of the children are discussed. In some schools, if the parents cannot or will not come to the schools, home visitors are provided to go to the parents and encourage their aid in the solution of any adjustment problems their children may have. In an increasing number of communities, the schools are assuming considerable responsibility for the continued development, according to socially accepted standards, of all their pupils.

United Press International Photo

Figure 101. A Violin Concert Given by 1,500 Japanese Children.

Provisions for the Mentally Exceptional Child   Generally, before the present century, the main purpose of the elementary school was to teach children the rudiments of education, usually referred to as the three R's. If a child failed to master the fundamentals, the chief reason assigned for his lack of success was his unwillingness to learn. We now realize that children differ in their ability to profit from educational offerings. Consequently, creditable progress has been made in modifying learning materials for mentally retarded children. Special courses of study have been devised that include the minimum essentials of elementary kinds of learning. Emphasis is placed on the emotional and social aspects of living. The slow or retarded child is encouraged to find a place for himself, in light of his mental limitations, in the home, the field of work, and social living.

To the recent present, the mentally superior child has been allowed, in great part, to fend for himself, at least on the elementary level. As a result, many bright children became bored as they were forced to watch their less able classmates struggle with learning materials that to them were easy to master. As a relief from boredom, some bright children engaged in mischievous acts; others daydreamed; some became aggressive; many failed to exert their best efforts.

Various approaches have been utilized to stimulate these children to exercise their superior abilities. Skipping a grade, once popular, has been found to leave gaps in the learning process. Some schools place them in special classes where, in the company of their mental peers, they can receive the mental challenge which they so much need, and complete their school work in less time than is required by mentally average pupils. In many school systems, superior elementary school children are kept in regular classes but are offered an enriched program. They are encouraged to go beyond the study requirements of the other children by engaging in special research. They also may be motivated to help less able pupils during school periods. Many of these able young people can become active leaders of their class group.

In addition, some elementary schools are beginning to engage in special programs, such as the identification of the gifted and higher horizons. The first of these relatively new programs is organized for use in the early grades. Its purpose is to discover, as soon as possible, who the mentally superior children are, so that special provision can be made for them. The higher horizons program is intended to offer children, especially those who come from economically less favored homes, an opportunity to learn about the many advantages provided by the community for their benefit, educationally and socially.

Furthermore, as schools attempt to meet the educational needs of exceptional children, they keep in close contact with the parents of these children. Thereby, parents are helped to assume a more realistic attitude toward their child's exceptionality. Left to themselves, these parents may fail to give the child the kind of treatment he needs. Parents of a slow or retarded child are likely either to overprotect him or to reject him; they may be so bothered by the child's inability to function as more normal children do that they attempt to keep him away from others or make invidious comparisons between him and other siblings or neighbors' children. It is difficult for a child handled in either of these ways by his parents to achieve an adequate self-concept.

Contrariwise, unwise parents of a bright child tend to overplay his special talents. They may expect him to perform for supposedly very much impressed friends and neighbors, thus often causing the child much embarrassment. Perhaps they contrast the ability of their child with that of other children, to the detriment of the latter who may come to dislike or resent the child who is held up to them as a model of all virtues. Some parents, eager to give their superior child every possible educational advantage, compel him to continue his learning after regular school sessions by sending him to take special lessons in dancing, music, dramatic arts, a foreign language, or the like. The overstimulated child has no time left to play with other children or engage in activities that give him some recognition of his being a normal child among other normal children. To the extent that school people can help change the attitudes of such parents, they are doing much to encourage the good social adjustment of exceptional children.

Teacher-Pupil Relations   Much as a school can do through its organizational pattern to assist the child in his learning experiences, the fundamental factor of influence on the school child is the relationship which he develops with his teachers. To the young child the teacher is a mother substitute, to the older child the teacher can be a respected and admired adult whose behavior the child tends to imitate. It is important, therefore, that the teacher possess those characteristics that can serve as effective and worthwhile models for the child.

Teacher-education institutions are becoming more selective in their acceptance of applicants for teacher-education programs. They realize that mastery of subject matter and the acquisition by the student of good teaching techniques is the responsibility of teacher-trainers. They also know that the would-be teacher should possess such basic personality qualities as sincerity, interest in other people (especially children), the ability and willingness to learn to understand them and work with them on their own level, a high idealism combined with a comprehension of realistic situations, and other outgoing characteristics. Unless the teacher exhibits such traits in his relationships with children, he becomes a hearer of lessons, not a stimulating and effective teacher.

Children are sensitive to teachers' attitudes. Since most teachers belong to the middle socio-economic class, it is easier for them to understand and work with children of their own group than with children from homes that represent other social or cultural values. Children are quick to recognize problems that the teacher experiences in dealing with them. They may be cruel in their reactions to such a teacher—defying him or poking fun at his attempts to win their loyalty and cooperation.

Many teachers who are thoroughly interested in their work find it difficult to solve problems of teacher-pupil relationships when there is a clash between group standards of what constitutes desirable behavior. A teacher, for example, found a junior high school girl smoking outside the building after school hours. When the teacher reprimanded the girl for her behavior, the girl's answer was, "I don't smoke in school. This is public land. My mother smokes and I smoke with her. You're too fussy." What answer can a teacher give to a child who draws this fine distinction between parental and teacher standards?

In general, children are responsive to the teacher's suggestions. They tend to pattern their behavior in light of teacher expectations. Trager and Yarrow [2] conducted an experiment on the effect of teacher attitudes on their pupils. Two groups were studied. In one group of first and second year children, the teacher attempted to create an atmosphere of intergroup understanding. No such attempt was made in the sessions held with a control group. Changes in the attitudes of the first group toward children of differing cultures were found that did not hold for the second group. One of the most serious problems of the teacher is to learn how to bring about desirable changes in those pupils' attitudes which are closely tied to the customary but socially unacceptable attitudes developed in the home.

The atmosphere in a classroom usually reflects the teacher's attitude. In the classroom of a teacher who uses dominating techniques, such as ruling by commands, threats, and insistence on conformity, the children tend to become rigid and inflexible. A more democratic teacher, however, motivates his pupils to consider the rights of others and to be more flexible in their general behavior.[3] Fortunately, children are malleable. If they have one experience with a dominating teacher, for example, and then pass on to the classroom of a democratic teacher, interested in the integrative process, the young people's attitudes and behavior patterns change to conform to the new classroom atmosphere.

Because of the disruptive effects of autocratic management of a teacher, however, one of the prime responsibilities of a teacher-education

[2] Trager, H. G., and Yarrow, M. R., *They Learn What They Live: Prejudices in Young Children.* New York: Harper and Brothers, 1952.

[3] See Anderson, H. H., Anderson, G. L., "Effects of Teachers' Dominative and Integrative Contacts on Children's Classroom Behavior," *Applied Psychological Monographs,* 8: 88–122, 1946.

program is to demonstrate, by precept and example, the value of the teacher's maintaining an atmosphere within socially acceptable standards of behavior in the classroom. This does not mean that a *laissez faire* policy, in which anything goes, should prevail in the classroom. Children respect the teacher who is "strict" if his disciplining is fair and just and emphasizes the behavior of the child, rather than the child himself.

The teacher's function is to help the child make adjustments from feelings of failure to satisfactions gained in personal achievement, from dependence on others to self-reliance. The child probably will experience some feelings of more or less severe failure in his school achievement. The teacher needs to help the child face reality to an extent that may not occur in the home. If the child recognizes the fact that the teacher has faith in his ability to succeed (provided he is not forced beyond his power to perform), he is likely to use a failure as a stepping-stone to the putting forth of greater effort to overcome a learning weakness. Children soon learn whether a teacher is able and willing to explain any points in a learning area that may not be understood by them.

There usually are a few children in a class who ask many questions. Sometimes this is done to waste time. It may result from the pupils' lack of attention during the time in which the points of the lesson were discussed; it can be a cover-up for inadequately prepared home assignments. However, most children are honest in their desire to have further teacher help in understanding. Children lose respect for the teacher who seems unable to carry a point beyond what is contained in a textbook, who ignores questions or hedges in answering them. It is difficult for a teacher to meet every learning need of every pupil in a large class, but children appreciate his endeavors in their behalf.

In general, children like teachers who know their subject matter, and present it in an interesting and challenging manner. They admire the teacher who is just in his treatment of all pupils. A teacher who "plays favorites" is resented by the nonfavored pupils, and causes embarrassment to those who for no apparent reason become his pets. Children want their teacher to be interested in them as individuals, to be willing to listen sympathetically to accounts of their joys and disappointments. Children also appreciate the teacher to whom they can bring their problems, confident that they will receive needed help. Moreover, a child's relations with the peer group often reflect his relationships with the teacher.

Parent-child relations often can be improved, as parents and teachers work closely together, sharing in the activities of Teacher-Parent Associations and meeting for individual conferences. The modern teacher or other school-faculty member does not limit his relationships with parents to the reporting of childish misdeeds in the school or failure in learning achievement. Parents are encouraged to bring their problems of child-rearing to the school personnel and to talk over with them their plans and hopes for the child. Of course, a parent's attitude toward the school and its teachers exerts a tremendous influence upon the child. Hence the closer the cooperation between the school and the home, the more likely will children be to make a good school adjustment. The teacher who can stimulate a cooperative attitude in both the child and the parent is an extremely important factor in the child's likelihood of continuing good personal and social adjustment. Concerning parent-child coopera-tion, Sister Mary Amatora, in introducing the Teacher-Pupil Relation-ships issue to which various writers contributed articles, says:

"A parent's words and a teacher's words build images for children—images of themselves and their future. The writers hope that, more and more, these adults build with their attitudes not a static snapshot of a child, but moving pictures in 3-D which help children become curious, alive and eager for the future with its jobs, its friendships, its satisfaction in doing things with and for others." [4]

THE CHILD IN THE COMMUNITY

The physical and cultural conditions of a community include all the environmental factors that exert a great influence over the developing child. The term "community," interpreted broadly, comprises all the elements of group situations and conditions to which the child is exposed. Viewed thus, the community includes the child's home and school experi-ences. In our present discussion we are directing our attention to those factors outside the home and the school that have a bearing on the child's maturing personality pattern.

The very young child generally is affected only indirectly by the social factors that lie outside the home. The elementary school child finds him-self becoming increasingly involved in the many facets of both his immediate neighborhood and the larger community.

Improved Methods of Communication and Transportation The number of one-way media of communication is increasing steadily.

[4] Sister Mary Amatora, O.S.F., "Teacher-Pupil Relationships: Introduction." Reprinted from the September 1954 issue of *Education,* p. 12, by permission of the Bobbs-Merrill Company, Inc., Indianapolis, Indiana.

The child's growing awareness of differing inanimate objects, conditions, and people is encouraged by his experiences with radio and television, motion pictures, comics, and advertising posters and billboards. To the extent that he is exposed to worthwhile materials, his horizons constantly are broadening. Two-way communication with people removed from the child also is made possible through his use of the telephone, which, in this modern era, is taking the place of much written communication.

In school and in many homes children are motivated to keep abreast of important happenings in the world. Listening to newscasters and reading the daily newspapers or specially prepared news sheets for use by younger readers, as well as discussions with adults, help children gain some understanding of what it means to be a member of a small home community or of a state, national, or world community. They may not always be mature enough, of course, to comprehend all that they hear or read. Yet, if the materials to which they are exposed are well selected by intelligent adults, young people can build for themselves a solid foundation upon which more mature points of view later can be erected.

Increase in family possession of automobiles, good highways, growing popularity of air travel, and shortened work days and work months are providing opportunities for most children to become acquainted with and learn about communities that may be some distance from the home environment. Group visits to museums, industrial plants, and other places of educational interest are sponsored by school people. As the child is prepared beforehand for what he can observe on the visit, and then, after the visit, discusses his observations with his teacher and classmates, he is receiving training in evaluating community facilities. For example, a fourth-grade teacher in New York City took her class on a trip to visit Freedomland two days after it opened in June, 1960. Their experiences in viewing interesting aspects of the history and geography of their country in an exciting setting did much to enliven their study of American history and geography. They felt that they were a part of the progressive steps in their country's development. They thrilled to the pony express, the Chicago fire, and the other events about which they had read but now seemed to be experiencing in person.

Community Facilities for Recreation and Socialization At one time, especially in rural areas and even on quiet urban streets, the child's playground was the great outdoors. In rural communities he could climb trees and jump fences; he could run, jump, and skip. However, unless his family was large or farms were not too distant from one another,

Wide World Photo

Figure 102. Children on the Playground in Munich, Germany.

he might lack playmates. His playtime might be restricted also by the amount of time which he needed to devote to the household chores. Today, in crowded urban areas, there may be no lack of playmates but also no place to socialize with them except in dangerous streets or small overcrowded homes.

Community leaders in all areas of our country—rural, suburban, and urban—are providing facilities for children to meet, play, and socialize. Although sufficient space for these activities is difficult to find in crowded city neighborhoods, good beginnings have been made. The school buildings and grounds are made available during the late afternoons and evenings for quiet games, sports, and other social activities. Community centers are established in which children and older young people can enjoy recreational activities with a minimum of adult supervision but much helpful guidance of activities. Many of the large housing projects furnish playgrounds or recreational facilities for the children of tenants, where the children receive supervision of their activities from trained adults.

Formation of Social Groups Young people are sociable. They want to be with and do things with their peers. We have discussed peer groups and gangs in Chapter 11. Unless opportunities for participating in wholesome group activities are provided, children and older young people are likely to form their own gangs and, for lack of something better to do, engage in asocial activities. It is not easy for energy-filled individuals to stand around at street corners in a city and just talk. They need to plan and execute projects that offer a challenge to their ingenuity. They need a place to meet and a program in the planning of which they have had a share.

An increasing number of our young citizens are finding outlets for their energy and imagination by participating in the activities of national groups, such as the Boy Scouts and Girl Scouts, Boys' and Girls' Clubs of America, 4-H Clubs, and Future Farmers of America. Adolescents also can enjoy social and recreational privileges by being members of Young Men's and Young Women's Christian and Hebrew Associations. In well-organized, fully equipped, and indirectly supervised groups such as these, young people have an opportunity to supplement the socializing activities which they carry on in the home and the school.

Religious Organizations In Chapter 17 we discussed the functions of religious education. Here we shall consider briefly the place of a religious organization as a community agency, the purpose of which, in addition to offering spiritual help, is to provide socializing and recreational opportunities for young people. Most religious groups establish clubs for their young people, thereby giving their younger members an opportunity to meet for social purposes, although many of these groups also engage in religious activities of one kind or another. Some conduct daily Bible schools during the summer in which religious instruction is supplemented by recreational projects. Some religious groups maintain community centers which are available for their members to carry out projects of interest to them.

During the school year some religious organizations hold mid-week sessions for religious instruction, usually after regular school hours. In some communities these are held during school hours and children whose parents wish them to attend are excused from school to attend the weekly class in religion. There is considerable controversy among people about the wisdom of this plan, however. Some religious groups send their children for daily religious instruction after the regular school session. In general, religious organizations are recognizing their responsibilities for providing adequate facilities for the social and religious growth of children.

Summer Camps Summer camps for boys and girls of all ages, ranging from two through adolescence, have been flourishing for many years. These have been sponsored by schools, newspapers, Rotary Clubs or other similar clubs, and community chests. They can be found in all states, and range from free camps for the underprivileged to average cost and expensive private camps. In these camps are found social and sports activities of all kinds. Some camps are removed from the home environment and operate on a twenty-four-hour-a-day basis; others are local and available for daytime play and recreation only.

Summer camps which assume full responsibility for the health and welfare of the child for a specific length of time, such as six, eight, or ten weeks, contribute much to the social and health development of the child. The benefits to the child often are greater than those derived from the sunshine, good meals, regular hours of sleep, and wholesome outdoor play with peer-age children. The camper is afforded opportunities to develop personal and social skills through swimming, horseback riding, engaging in various sports, participating in dramatic performances, and other challenging activities.

United Press International Photo

Figure 103. Demonstrating Artificial Respiration in a Summer Camp.

Camp life gives the child experiences in social living with other children. Under the guidance of counselors, the individual receives intelligent supervision in his play, during his meals, and in his "bunk." He learns to respond to an authority other than that of his parents. This living with people other than members of his family promotes consideration for others and establishes self-control. Many camps regulate the number of times that parents may visit, thereby promoting the child's independent behavior and weaning him from dependence upon his parents. The counselor treats the child objectively and helps him develop respect for the rights of others. These children enjoy the opportunity of experiencing the give-and-take required for good social living. They get great satisfaction not only from participating in the activities offered in the camp program but in doing them under the trained leadership of the camp counselor. They learn to like the counselor, the other children, the activities, and the total camp experience. At the end of the season they usually are eager to return the next year.

Day camps or recreational centers are found in cities and offer camp and recreational opportunities to children who are unable to spend six to ten weeks away from home. They are supervised by competent leaders, who plan a careful schedule of activities for the time the children attend. Some of the activities are creative and educational; others are purely recreational. Informal approaches or almost complete freedom in play is found in some day camps. Here the scheduling of activities and supervision of behavior is kept to a minimum. The home functions more closely with the activities of day camps than with those of the summer camps. The day camps and recreational centers, or play schools, serve a useful purpose to the parents, to the children who attend, and sometimes to the young people selected as the leaders of the children. It gives young men or women who plan to teach a more or less unstructured situation in which to learn how to work with children.

Community Improvement We conclude this discussion with a brief consideration of the community's responsibility for the general welfare of all children as well as of their elders. Throughout the book we have stressed the importance of providing for the growing child a wholesome, healthful environment in which he can develop his latent potentialities to the fullest. The provision of facilities for recreation and socialization is valuable; essential to the welfare of the child is his opportunity to be reared in a community that offers the best that can be obtained for complete living.

In some communities, both rural and urban, there still exist unsanitary and unhealthful living conditions. Those of us who live in large urban areas are aware of some of the bad living conditions, but take it for granted that rural areas do not have this blot. Slum clearance probably is needed in all parts of our country, except, perhaps, in small suburban towns. This, together with the erection of modern low-cost housing, is a must for every community.

Continually increasing emphasis is being placed on the value to an individual of having and maintaining good physical and mental health. Barring accidents and contagions, the physical health pattern of an individual is established during the early years. Recognizing this fact, more and more communities are providing health centers for the care of mothers and their children. At these centers mothers not only are cared for physically, but also receive instruction concerning pregnancy and the early rearing of children.

Schools have the services of a nurse and a physician. The health centers provide home nurses; more hospitals for the physically and mentally ill are being constructed and are better equipped. Physicians and nurses are becoming more aware of the fact that they are not only treating the illness, but the whole person. This is especially true in the treatment of children who can become disturbed emotionally during an illness unless the attending physician and nurse are gentle and understanding.

In Chapter 18 was discussed the mental health of children. The community can do much to prevent the development of unnecessary tensions and anxieties in the child by providing opportunities for fathers to engage in satisfying and constructive work activities, by improving housing conditions, by helping to educate young people for healthful marriage and parenthood, by providing more schools and more and better prepared teachers for the children, and by safeguarding children, insofar as this is possible, from community factors of conflict and disorder. This may seem to be an ideal that is impossible of achievement. Yet many communities already have made an excellent beginning in realizing these goals.

QUESTIONS AND TOPICS FOR DISCUSSION

1. List some of the attitudes and behavior patterns the child may have developed during preschool years.
2. Name five probable differences between a child's home experiences and school experiences.
3. What are some of the advantages of sending a child to nursery school? Some of the disadvantages?

4. How much should a nursery school teacher know about the home conditions of her pupils? How can these needed data be obtained?

5. If possible, observe the behavior of children in a nursery school or kindergarten class. Report some differences you found in the behavior of the children.

6. What are the values to mothers of observing their children in the classroom? In what ways can parent-teacher conferences help parents and teachers? Be specific.

7. Name and describe at least three conflict situations a child may experience in school. What can be done to help him resolve these problems?

8. What are some of the adjustments to be made in the home and in the school by the mentally superior child and the slow child?

9. Give specific ways in which the regular school curriculum can be enriched for the bright child; modified for the slow child.

10. Name what to you are the five most important characteristics of a teacher. Why have you selected these?

11. Recall two teachers whom you admired and two whom you disliked in elementary school or the early grades of the secondary school. What characteristics of these teachers affected your attitude toward them?

12. What influence outside your home and school aroused you most during your childhood days? If you belonged to any community groups, of what value were they to you?

13. Which do you think is better for a child: to spend a vacation away from home with his parents, or to attend a summer camp? Justify your answer.

14. Evaluate your community in light of attempts at improvement.

15. *Special Project:* Review your notes on your four selected children. How well have you come to know them? What changes, if any, would you suggest in their home and school experiences? How objective have you been in your study of them? Of what value has this project been?

SELECTED REFERENCES

Abraham, W., *Common Sense about Gifted Children*. New York: Harper and Brothers, 1958.

Bonney, M. E., and Nicholson, E. L., "Comparative School Adjustments of Elementary School Children with and without Preschool Training," *Child Development*, 29: 125–133, 1958.

Bühler, C., Richardson, S., and Bradshaw, F., *Childhood Problems and the Teacher*. New York: Henry Holt and Company, 1952.

Hutt, M. L., and Gibby, R. G., *The Mentally Retarded Child*. Boston: Allyn and Bacon, Inc., 1958.

Langford, Louise M., *Guidance of the Young Child*. New York: John Wiley and Sons, Inc., 1960.

Leeds, C. H., "Teacher Behavior Liked and Disliked by Pupils," *Education,* 75: 29–37, 1954.

Mitchell, L. S. (ed.), *Know Your Children in School*. New York: The Macmillan Company, 1954.

Moore, Eleanora H., *Fives At School: Teaching in the Kindergarten*. New York: G. P. Putnam's Sons, 1959.

Moustakas, C. E., *The Teacher and the Child*. New York: McGraw-Hill Book Company, Inc., 1956.

Read, K. H., *The Nursery School: A Human Relations Laboratory,* 3rd ed. Philadelphia: W. B. Saunders Company, 1960.

Rosenzweig, Louis E., and Long, Julia, *Understanding and Teaching the Dependent Retarded Child*. Darien, Conn.: The Educational Publishing Corp., 1960.

Ruben, Margaret, *Parent Guidance in the Nursery School*. New York: International Universities Press, 1960.

Witty, Paul, *Helping the Gifted Child*. Chicago: Science Research Associates, Inc., 1952.

RECOMMENDED

MOTION PICTURE FILMS

THE FILMS LISTED here can be used to supplement the material of the text. In general, each film applies to a particular area of discussion, yet may apply equally well to other areas. For most effective use, the instructor should preview each film before class showing in order that best results can be achieved in the classroom showing.

All films included in the list are 16mm. For each film are given the initials of the producer, the running time in minutes, and the chapter or chapters of this text to which it relates. The addresses of the producers and publishers are given at the end of the list.

Administration of Projective Tests (PSU, 19). Includes several tests but not the Rorschach (Chaps. 2, 14).

Angry Boy (IFB, 32). A ten-year-old boy strikes out blindly at life to relieve the turmoil of his emotions that result from hostility toward his parents (Chaps. 10, 18).

Child At Play (TC, 18). Shows undirected play of a three-year-old (Chaps. 9, 13).

Child Care and Development (M-H, 17). Depicts the habits of daily care that insure a healthy, happy child (Chap. 19).

Child Development (EBF, 11). A series of ten films produced at the Yale University Clinic of Child Development.
Baby's Day at Forty-eight Weeks (Chap. 4)
Baby's Day at Twelve Weeks (Chap. 4)
Behavior Patterns at One Year (Chap. 4)
Early Social Behavior (Chap. 11)
From Creeping to Crawling (Chap. 5)

Growth of Infant Behavior: Early Stages; Later Stages (Chaps. 3, 4)
Posture and Growth (Chap. 5)
Learning and Growth (Chap. 8)

Children Are Creative (IFB, 33). Shows motivation, creative work, and evaluation of finished product in an elementary art class (Chap. 9).

Children's Emotions (M-H, 22). The major emotions of childhood—fear, anger, jealousy, curiosity, and joy—are described, and methods of dealing with them are explained (Chap. 10).

Children's Fantasies (M-H, 21). Shows reasons for child fantasies, how they develop and how they affect children (Chap. 9).

Children Growing Up with Others (UWF, 30). Shows the development of self-reliance in children in their group relations (Chap. 11).

Children Learn by Experience (UWF, 40). Shows that children learn many things through play and imagination (Chaps. 9, 13).

Children's Play (M-H, 20). Presents examples of play behavior of one to eight-year-olds (Chaps. 9, 13).

Development of Locomotion (UC, 10). Shows developmental sequence from ages six to fifteen months, with examples of various methods of locomotion (Chap. 5).

Development of Self-reliance (C, 10). Shows how self-reliance is essential to all successful endeavor (Chap. 14).

Discovering Individual Differences (M-H, 25). Shows how the teacher learns to understand her children and how she adapts her teaching to meet individual needs (Chap. 20).

Early Social Behavior (EBF, 11). Presents Dr. Arnold Gesell's study of the behavior of children in various social situations (Chap. 11).

Emergence of Personality (EBF, 30). Indicates ways in which differences in personality, including the impact of heredity and environment, can be explained (Chap. 14).

Endocrine System, The (EBF, 11). Shows nature and function of endocrines; animated diagrams (Chaps. 4, 10).

Experimental Studies in Social Climates of Groups (IFB, 30). Presents a comparison of the effects upon boys' behavior of various forms of group organization (Chap. 11).

Farewell to Childhood (IFB, 20). Describes teen-ager, full of the emotions typical of adolescence, who longs for independence and the privileges of adulthood (Chap. 10).

Fears of Children (IFB, 32). Dramatizes some of the emotional problems of a normal five-year-old boy (Chap. 10).

From Sociable Six to Noisy Nines (NFB, 22). Gives interests, activities, and personality characteristics during these ages (Chaps. 4, 11, 14).

From Ten to Twelve (NFB, 22). Gives interests, activities and personality of children during these ages (Chaps. 4, 11, 14).

Frustrating Fours and Fascinating Fives (NFB, 22). Shows how fours and fives learn to control their bodies and develop their minds and personalities (Chaps. 4, 9, 14).

Good Speech for Gary (M-H, 22). Explains some common speech defects in young children, showing ways of remedying these defects (Chap. 6).

Growth: A Study of Johnny and Jimmy (IFB, 43). Presents the developmental pattern of twins, with emphasis upon a comparison of their behavior to the age of eight years (Chap. 5).

Growth of Adaptive Behavior (EBF, 15). Presents Dr. Gesell's study of the finer motor coordinations during a child's first five years (Chap. 5).

Growth of Motor Behavior (EBF, 15). Traces the development of motor control from birth to age five (Chap. 5).

He Acts His Age (M-H, 14). Examines the play habits of children from one to fifteen years of age and presents some characteristics of each age group (Chaps. 9, 13).

Head of the House (UWF, 40). Describes the emotional problems of a young boy who resents parental authority, especially his father's, and how the family is helped to develop better understanding (Chap. 19).

Heredity and Environment (M-H, 10). Shows the meanings of heredity and environment and their relationships (Chap. 3).

Heredity and Prenatal Development (M-H, 21). Describes the fertilization of the ovum by the sperm cell at conception and traces the development of the fetus until delivery (Chap. 3).

Human Growth (BT, 19). Traces human growth and development of the organism from mating through pregnancy and birth (Chap. 3).

Human Reproduction (M-H, 20). Presents facts concerning the human reproductive system and the process of normal human birth (Chap. 3).

Individual Differences (M-H, 23). Shows how a boy who is shy and a slow learner adjusts to a school situation with the guidance of the teacher (Chap. 20).

It's A Small World (BIS, 38). Gives routines and activities in a London Day Nursery (Chap. 20).

Large Muscle Motor Skills (EBF, 15). Shows running, balancing, hitting, pushing, etc., that are characteristic of children (Chap. 5).

Life Begins (EFB, 60). Gives Dr. Gesell's work at Yale University. Infant development from birth to eighteen months (Chap. 4).

Life with Baby (M-H, 18). Presents Dr. Gesell's study of children's mental and physical growth (Chaps. 4, 8).

Life with Junior (M-H, 18). Depicts the happenings of an average day in the life of a school-age child (Chaps. 19, 20).

Meeting Emotional Needs of Childhood (NYU, 33). Concerns the development in the child of sensitivity to and responsibility for adult community living (Chap. 10).

Motivating the Class (M-H, 19). A student-teacher learns that motivation is essential to good teaching (Chap. 12).

Personality Development: Series: Four films (EBF, each 11).
Answering the Child's Why (Chap. 14)
Baby Meets His Parents (Chaps. 14, 19)
Helping the Child to Accept the Do's (Chap. 14)
Helping the Child to Face the Don'ts (Chap. 14)

Physical Aspects of Puberty (M-H, 19). Gives physiological growth processes for a boy and a girl. Gives some problems of late-maturing boy, early-maturing girl (Chaps. 4, 15).

Preface To a Life (UWF, 29). Portrays the influence parents have on a child's developing personality, from birth to adulthood (Chap. 1).

Principles of Development (M-H, 16). Outlines the fundamentals of growth and change from early infancy, revealing that development follows a pattern that is continuous, orderly, and predictable (Chaps. 3, 4).

Problem Children (PSU, 20). Shows the effects of home and school relationships upon the personality of two children (Chaps. 18, 19, 20).

Shyness (M-H, 23). Shows three shy children and how one is helped to become an active member of the group (Chaps. 11, 18).

Sibling Rivalries and Parents (M-H, 11). Depicts sibling conflicts. The role of the parent in causing and handling them (Chaps. 18, 19).

Social Development (M-H, 16). Presents an analysis of social behavior at different age levels and the reasons underlying the changes in behavior patterns as the child develops (Chap. 11).

Studies of Normal Personality Development (NYU). (Each for Chap. 14.) Each produced by the Department of Child Study at Vassar College.
Balloons: Aggression and Destructive Games (20 minutes)
Finger Painting (22 minutes) (Also Chap. 2)
Frustration Play Techniques (35 minutes)
A Long Time to Grow: Part 1: Two- and Three-year-olds in Nursery School (35 minutes)
A Long Time to Grow: Part 2: Four- and Five-year-olds in School (35 minutes)
Pay Attention (30 minutes)
Preschool Incidents: Part 1: When Should Grown-ups Help? (13 minutes) (Also Chap. 19)
Preschool Incidents: Part 3: When Should Grown-ups Stop Fights? (15 minutes) (Also Chap. 19)

Terrible Twos and Trusting Threes (M-H, 20). Presents a close examination of the growing years between two and four (Chap. 4).

Testing the IQ (IFB, 18). Shows the administration of the revised Stanford-Binet test and the calculation of the IQ (Chaps. 2, 9).

Understanding Children's Play (NYU, 10). Designed to understand and help children through observation of their use of toys and play materials (Chaps. 9, 13).

Why Tommy Won't Eat (NFB, 16). Suggests that the basis of feeding habits is laid in early infancy. Weaning, introduction of solid foods, self-feeding, and other methods of feeding are shown (Chaps. 15, 19).

Your Child's Sleep (BIS, 23). Gives some good suggestions for helping children relax and accept sleep (Chap. 19).

PRODUCERS AND SUPPLIERS OF FILM

BIS   British Information Service, 30 Rockefeller Plaza, New York 20, N. Y.

BT   E. C. Brown Trust, 220 S. W. Adler St., Portland 4, Oregon.

C   Coronet Instructional Films, 65 E. South Water St., Chicago 1, Ill.

EBF   Encyclopaedia Britannica Films, Inc., 1150 Wilmette Ave., Wilmette, Ill.

IFB   International Film Bureau, 57 E. Jackson Blvd., Chicago 4, Ill.

KB   Knowledge Builders, 625 Madison Ave., New York 22, N. Y.

M-H   McGraw-Hill Book Co., Text Film Department, 330 West 42nd St., New York 36, N. Y.

NFB   National Film Board of Canada, 630 Fifth Ave., New York 19, N. Y.

NYU   New York University Film Library, 26 Washington Place, New York 3, N. Y.

PSU   Pennsylvania State University, Audio-Visual Aids Library, State College, Pa.

UC   University of California, Berkeley, California.

UWF   United World Films, 1445 Park Ave., New York 29, N. Y.

WU   University of Wisconsin, Bureau of Visual Instruction, University Extension Division, 1312 W. Johnson St., Madison 6, Wis.

NAME INDEX

SUBJECT INDEX